SIMPSON'S dBASE TIPS AND TRICKS

⊙ALAN SIMPSON

SIMPSON'S dBASE®
TIPS AND TRICKS

⊙ SAN FRANCISCO • PARIS • DÜSSELDORF • LONDON

Cover art by Thomas Ingalls + Associates
Book design by Ingrid Owen

dBASE II, dBASE III, and dBASE III PLUS are trademarks of Ashton-Tate.
IBM Personal Computer and IBM AT are registered trademarks of International Business
Machines Corporation.
Microsoft Word is a trademark of Microsoft Corporation.
WordStar and MailMerge are registered trademarks of MicroPro International.

SYBEX is a registered trademark of SYBEX, Inc.

SYBEX is not affiliated with any manufacturer.

Every effort has been made to supply complete and accurate information. However,
SYBEX assumes no responsibility for its use, nor for any infringements of patents or
other rights of third parties which would result.

Copyright©1987 SYBEX Inc., 2021 Challenger Drive #100, Alameda, CA 94501. World
rights reserved. No part of this publication may be stored in a retrieval system, transmit-
ted, or reproduced in any way, including but not limited to photocopy, photograph, mag-
netic or other record, without the prior agreement and written permission of the publisher.

Library of Congress Card Number: 87-60230
ISBN 0-89588-383-x
Manufactured in the United States of America
10 9 8 7 6 5 4 3 2

⊙To Susita Maria

Acknowledgments

Like all books, this one was a team effort, and many people whose names do not appear on the cover deserve credit. Primarily, credit is due the many people at SYBEX who contributed to this book, including Fran Grimble, editor; Joel Kroman, technical reviewer; David Clark and Olivia Shinomoto, word processors; George Lukas and Brenda Walker, typesetters; Suzy Anger and Jon Strickland, proofreaders; and Jim Compton, advisor in the early stages of the project. Credit is also due to the indexer, Elizabeth Molony.

Many thanks to Bill and Cynthia Gladstone, my literary agents and in-laws, for keeping my writing career alive and well.

And of course, many thanks to my wife Susan, who keeps me alive and well through many writing projects.

Table of Contents

Appendices

A ⊙ Summary of Procedures   356

B ⊙ dBASE III PLUS Compilers   370

C ⊙ dBASE III PLUS Vocabulary   394

Introduction

I wrote this book because there is currently no other dBASE III PLUS book on the market that provides a collection of practical dBASE III PLUS routines. The routines in this book can be applied to common business applications, and together they form a library of useful solutions to many business problems. I use these same routines regularly in my work as a dBASE consultant. By creating and saving the command files and procedures that are discussed in this book, I've been able to cut my own program development time down considerably because I can access tried-and-true procedures that do not require rewrites or debugging.

This library also serves to extend dBASE III PLUS beyond its off-the-shelf capabilities. For example, dBASE III PLUS itself has no built-in functions that perform financial calculations or statistical analyses, but the procedures in this book allow you to add these capabilities to dBASE III PLUS, and access each one with a single command.

⊙WHO SHOULD READ THIS BOOK

The procedures and techniques presented here are "ready-to-run," and few will require modification. However, most are explained in technical detail for those who wish to learn advanced programming techniques or who want to modify and enhance the procedures. The book is not intended for the dBASE novice. (My book *Understanding dBASE III PLUS,* also published by SYBEX, is useful as a primer for a beginner.)

Unlike my previous dBASE books, this book is intended to be more of a reference than a tutorial. An intermediate dBASE III PLUS user might find some of the programming techniques presented here a bit advanced, but technical knowledge is not a necessary prerequisite for putting the routines to work. If you find a command that is not familiar to you, take a moment to look it up in your dBASE III PLUS manual for a better understanding of how a particular routine works. Another of my books, *Advanced Techniques in dBASE III PLUS* (SYBEX) includes a general tutorial on dBASE III PLUS programming, and is also useful if you need additional information.

⊙THE STRUCTURE OF THIS BOOK

The book begins with some basic instruction for creating dBASE III PLUS command files and procedure files. While you might already know this information, it might be worth the time to review the basic techniques and commands presented in these chapters.

Chapters 3 through 9 present procedures that solve problems commonly encountered in business programming: managing financial data, performing statistical analyses, plotting data on bar graphs, and more.

Chapters 10 and 11 provide two very useful aids for programmers. The first, a debugging aid, puts proper indentations into command files, and warns the programmer of any missing ENDDO, ENDIF, and ENDCASE commands. The second aid, a program generator, can automatically develop an entire custom system for any single database in a matter of minutes, and is a great help to those who develop custom systems on a regular basis.

Appendix A is a quick-reference guide to all the procedures in the book, and Appendix B is a glossary of the dBASE III PLUS commands and functions. Appendix C is a guide to dBASE III PLUS vocabulary.

⊙GETTING STARTED

THE DOT PROMPT

Since you're a dBASE programmer (which I assume because you are reading this book), we'll dispense with the dBASE III PLUS Assistant and work directly from the dot prompt instead. While the Assistant is fine for building and managing a database, it offers little aid to the programmer. Besides that, things just move along at a quicker pace when you're working from the dot prompt, and we need to cover lots of material here.

To leave the Assistant menu and get to the dot prompt, press the Escape key while the Assistant menu is displayed. Optionally, to make dBASE III PLUS start up at the dot prompt without the Assistant menu, remove the line below from the Config.DB file on dBASE III PLUS System Disk #1 (or your hard disk):

COMMAND = ASSIST

If you want to remove the status bar from the bottom of the screen, you can remove the command

STATUS = ON

from the Config.DB file as well. You can use any word processor or text editor, including the dBASE MODIFY COMMAND editor, to remove these lines.

THE CONFIG.SYS FILE

Chances are that you may have gotten away without using a Config.SYS file on your boot-up disk for a long time. But in this book, we'll develop more advanced applications that will eventually generate the error message

Too many files are open

if you don't have the proper Config.SYS file on your boot-up disk.

You can quickly see the contents of the Config.SYS file using the DOS TYPE command. Log onto the disk you usually boot your computer from. (This may be the root directory on your hard disk, or the DOS disk you insert before turning on your computer. It is usually *not* one of the dBASE III PLUS disks.) At the DOS A> or C> prompt, enter the command:

TYPE Config.SYS

and press Return. If you do not see a configuration such as

FILES = 20
BUFFERS = 15

then you need to create a Config.SYS file. You can use any word processor (with a nondocument mode), the dBASE MODIFY COMMAND editor, or just the DOS COPY command. To use the COPY command, leave the boot-up disk in place and type the command

COPY CON Config.SYS

at the DOS A> or C> prompt. Press Return. Type in the lines

FILES = 20
BUFFERS = 15

pressing Return once after each line. Next press the F6 key (or Ctrl-Z, whichever displays the ^Z on the screen), and press Return. When the DOS A> or C> prompt reappears, you're done. To verify, enter the command

TYPE Config.SYS

at the A> or C> prompt once again. You should see the FILES and BUFFERS commands in the file exactly as you typed them in. Next time you boot up your computer, DOS will read the Config.SYS file and set aside enough memory to hold 20 files and 15 buffers open simultaneously. Which in turn means you can have lots of dBASE database and command files open simultaneously without seeing the *Too many files are open* error message.

⊙HOW TO BUY THE PROGRAMS IN THIS BOOK

If you wish to purchase copies of the command files and procedure files in this book, send a check or money order for $40.00 to:

SMS Software
P.O. Box 2802
La Jolla, CA 92038-2802

(California residents please add six percent sales tax.) Make the check payable to SMS Software and be sure to specify that you want the programs from Alan Simpson's *dBASE Tips and Tricks* book. The programs are currently available on a 5¼-inch, double-sided, double-density, PC-DOS version 2.1 disk format only. There is an order form on the last page of this book.

1

PROGRAMMING
IN dBASE III PLUS

In this chapter we'll discuss the basic commands and skills used for programming in dBASE III PLUS. If you already know how to program in
dBASE II or III, you might want just to skim this chapter. However, if you've
never written a dBASE program in your life, do read on.

A dBASE III PLUS program, or *command file,* is simply a series of
dBASE III PLUS commands stored in a file. The dBASE III PLUS MODIFY
COMMAND editor allows you to create and edit command files. The
dBASE DO command allows you to run them. Let's take a look at a simple
example.

⊙CREATING COMMAND FILES

dBASE III PLUS has a built-in text editor for creating command files. To
use the text editor, type

MODIFY COMMAND

and the name of the file you want to create or edit. For our first example,
we'll create a command file called Test.PRG. If you're using a floppy-disk
system, you might first want to use the SET DEFAULT TO B command
before creating the command file so that your file is stored on the disk in
drive B. Then, next to the dot prompt, type in the command

MODIFY COMMAND Test

and press the Return key. The screen will clear, and the message *Edit:
Test.PRG* will appear at the top of the screen. Also at the top of the screen,
you'll see a summary of control-key commands used to move the cursor
and manipulate the command file. Pressing the F1 key turns this help
screen on and off. Now type the simple two-line command file shown
below:

CLEAR
? "Testing . . . Testing . . . 1-2-3."

(The ? command means print or display.) Press the Return key after typing
each line. If you make a mistake, use the arrow keys on the numeric keypad to move the cursor around and make changes. (If you get numbers
rather than cursor movement as you press the arrow keys, press the Num

Lock key above the keypad.) Use the Backspace or Del key to delete unwanted characters.

When you've typed in both lines of the command file, enter a ^W or ^End to save it. (The ^ symbol stands for hold down the Control key, so ^W means Control while pressing W.) dBASE will briefly display a message stating that it is saving the command file.

dBASE will also automatically add the extension .PRG to the file name; hence the Test program will actually be stored on disk with the file name Test.PRG.

Now, to run the command file, type in the command

DO Test

and press the Return key. (Note: All dBASE commands are entered by typing in the command and then pressing the Return key. Hence, to avoid repetition, I won't keep reminding you to press Return.) The screen clears and displays your message followed by the dot prompt.

Testing . . . Testing . . . 1-2-3.

.

Notice that dBASE executed both lines in the command file. First, it cleared the screen (CLEAR), then it printed the message *Testing. . . Testing . . . 1-2-3.*.

Now, suppose you want to change something in a program. You can just use MODIFY COMMAND again to make the changes. From the dot prompt, type

MODIFY COMMAND Test

and dBASE displays the command file on the screen, with the cursor under the first letter of the first line, as shown below:

<u>C</u>LEAR
? "Testing . . . Testing . . . 1-2-3."

You can use the arrow keys on the numeric keypad, or the control-key commands summarized in Table 1.1, to move the cursor around and make changes.

Practice moving the cursor around by pressing the down-arrow key (↓) or ^X once to move the cursor down to the second line of the command file. Then press the right-arrow (→) or ^D seven times to move the cursor to

Key		Function
↑	or ^E	Moves cursor up one line
↓	or ^X	Moves cursor down one line
←	or ^S	Moves cursor left one character
→	or ^D	Moves cursor right one character
Del	or ^G	Deletes character over cursor
Ins	or ^V	Toggles insert mode on/off
End	or ^F	Moves cursor right one word
Home	or ^A	Moves cursor left one word
^N		Inserts a blank line at cursor position
^T		Erases one word to the right of the cursor
^Y		Deletes the entire line over cursor
^End	or ^W	Saves command file
Esc	or ^Q	Returns to the dot prompt without saving edited command file

Table 1.1: Screen control commands for MODIFY COMMAND

the "i" in the word Testing. Press the Del key or ^G three times, so the letters "ing" disappear, and the command file now looks like this:

```
CLEAR
? "Test _ . . Testing . . . 1-2-3."
```

The Del key or ^G deleted the letters to the right of the cursor.

Now, press Del or ^G ten times. The command file now looks like this:

```
CLEAR
? "Test _ . . 1-2-3."
```

Now let's try out the insert mode. Press → three times to move the cursor under the 1 in 1-2-3. Type the numbers

4-5-6

Notice that the new numbers overwrite the existing numbers, so now the command file looks like this:

```
CLEAR
? "Test . . . 4-5-6."
```

Now press ← five times to move the cursor back to the number 4. Then press ^V or the Ins key to turn on the insert mode. Notice that the word *Ins* appears at the top of the screen. Now, type the numbers

```
1-2-3-
```

With the insert mode on, the new numbers are inserted into the line, as below:

```
CLEAR
? "Test . . . 1-2-3-4-5-6."
```

The Ins key acts as a *toggle*. Press it once to switch from insert to over-write mode; the next press switches it back again.

Now that you are done editing your command file, save it by typing ^End or ^W. dBASE will again display a message about saving the command file.

To run the edited command file, once again enter the command

```
DO Test
```

at the dot prompt. You'll see the screen display:

```
Test. . . 1-2-3-4-5-6.
```

If this is the first time you've ever used a word processor or text editor, you might want to take some time now experimenting with the control keys listed in Table 1.1. Just enter the command

```
MODIFY COMMAND Test
```

to call up the Test.PRG command file again, and practice making changes. You can use ^W or ^End to save your changes to the command file, or ^Q to abandon your edits, so no changes are saved.

The command file we've just created is not terribly powerful, but if you've never written a command file in your life, it's a good idea to start out simple. In later chapters, we'll be writing far more powerful programs.

The MODIFY COMMAND editor provides a quick and easy way to create and edit command files. However, MODIFY COMMAND has one disadvantage: it cannot handle files with more than 5,000 characters. (Worse yet, it tends to just lose all characters beyond about the 5,000th character.)

As an alternative to using the built-in MODIFY COMMAND editor to create and edit command files, you can use any word processor or text editor that supports a "nondocument" or "unformatted" mode. For example, the WordStar word processor allows you to create and edit nondocument files by selecting N (for nondocument mode) from the "no-file" menu before you name the file to create or edit. Microsoft Word lets you save files in the U (for Unformatted) mode, which is suitable for command files.

When using an external word processor, be sure to add the extension .PRG to all your command file names. For example, rather than simply naming a program MyProg, you must specifically assign the name MyProg.PRG. The MODIFY COMMAND editor assumes the .PRG extension, but none of the external processors will.

Unless you have at least 380K of RAM, you'll have to quit dBASE to get back to the DOS prompt. Then you must load your word processor, edit your command file, exit the word processor, and load up dBASE again to test your changes. If you have more than 380K of RAM, and can fit your external word processor on the same disk as dBASE, then you can use the dBASE RUN (or !) command to run your word processor without exiting dBASE. For example, to run WordStar, you can enter the command below right next to the dot prompt:

    RUN WS

When you are done editing your command file and exit WordStar, you'll be returned immediately to the dot prompt with all databases still open; just as though you'd never left dBASE!

Another technique for accessing external word processors directly from dBASE is to use the TEDIT command in your Config.DB file. (Config.DB was discussed in the introduction.) For example, if you place the command

    TEDIT = WS.COM

in your Config.DB file, dBASE will "know" that the text editor you wish to use is WordStar. From this point on, any time you enter the command MODIFY COMMAND at the dot prompt, dBASE will automatically run the WordStar program (assuming WordStar is available on the same disk and directory as dBASE).

Choosing whether to use the MODIFY COMMAND editor is entirely up to you. Full-blown word processors certainly offer more power and more space to program in than the MODIFY COMMAND editor. But if MODIFY COMMAND is suitable for your needs, and you don't care to learn to use an entire word processor, you might be best off staying with MODIFY COMMAND.

Chapter 7 contains additional information on using the MODIFY COM-MAND editor and external word processors.

⊙INTERACTING WITH THE USER

Often, a program needs some general information while it is running to make decisions about what tasks to perform. For example, a program that prints an inventory report might ask the user if the report should be displayed on the screen or the printer. Several dBASE III PLUS commands present a question to the user, wait for a response, and store that answer in a database field or in a specific type of memory variable. These user-interface commands are listed on the next page, along with the way each one stores user responses.

Command	Where Response Is Stored
ACCEPT	Character memory variable
INPUT	Numeric memory variable
WAIT	Single-character memory variable
@, SAY, GET	Existing database field or memory variable, using existing data type

Accept

The ACCEPT command presents a question to the user, waits for a response followed by a press on the Return key, and stores the user's response in a character-type memory variable. For example, the command

ACCEPT "Send report to printer? (Y/N) " TO YesNo

displays the message *Send report to printer? (Y/N)* on the screen, and waits for an answer of any length, followed by a carriage return. The user's answer is stored in a character memory variable named YesNo in this example.

Input

The INPUT command displays a prompt on the screen, like the ACCEPT command, but usually stores the entered data as numeric and is therefore preferable when the question being asked involves numeric data. For example, the command

INPUT "Enter your age " TO Age

presents the prompt *Enter your age* and stores the user's answer in a numeric memory variable named Age. (INPUT stores data as character type if the entered response is enclosed in quotation marks.) Be careful not to use the INPUT command to get date information from the user. For example, the command

INPUT "Enter today's date " TO T_Date

will display the prompt and will accept information in date format (that is, 03/31/85). However, the INPUT command will actually store the entered date as 0.00113852, which is the quotient of 3 divided by 31 divided by 85!

Wait

The WAIT command presents a prompt and waits for a single keystroke without a carriage return. It differs from the ACCEPT command in that ACCEPT always waits for a carriage return after the keystroke. If the WAIT command is used without a prompt or a memory variable specified, as below:

WAIT

dBASE presents the message

Press any key to continue. . .

and waits for any key to be pressed. The keystroke is not stored. If a prompt and memory variable are included, as below:

WAIT "Send data to printer? (Y/N) " TO YesNo

the program displays the message *Send data to printer? (Y/N)* and waits for a single key to be pressed. The keystroke is stored in the memory variable YesNo (in this example) as character data. The WAIT command *always* stores data as character data. If you want to use the WAIT command to ask for a number, as you might do when asking for a menu choice, use the VAL function to convert the character data to numeric as below:

```
WAIT "Enter your choice (1-5) " TO Choice
STORE VAL(Choice) TO Choice
```

The WAIT command accepts a single character, and the VAL function converts it to numeric data.

Read

The READ command can be used to get field or memory variable data. It is always used in conjunction with the @, SAY, and GET commands. Unlike the ACCEPT, INPUT, and WAIT commands, the READ command works only with field names or memory variable names that already exist. For example, to use the READ command to get information for a menu choice, and store that information in a memory variable named Choice, you must first create the Choice memory variable as shown below:

```
STORE 0 TO Choice
@ 9,5 SAY "Enter choice " GET Choice
READ
```

These commands will first create a numeric memory variable named Choice (STORE 0 TO Choice). Then, the prompt *Enter choice* will be displayed on row 9, column 5 of the screen (@ 9,5 SAY "Enter choice "). A highlighted box for entering Choice will be displayed on the screen (GET Choice). Then the program will wait for an answer to the prompt and store that answer in the variable Choice (READ).

If you would like to try out some of the commands listed above, you can enter and run the command file shown in Figure 1.1. From the dot prompt, enter the command

```
MODIFY COMMAND ITest
```

Then enter the command file exactly as it appears in the figure and save it with a ^W or ^End. From the dot prompt enter the command

```
DO ITest
```

Answer each prompt as it appears on the screen. When you're done, the command file will show you what you've entered. The DISPLAY MEMORY command shows the currently active memory variables on the screen. (The memory variables are erased the moment the dot prompt reappears. We'll discuss techniques for saving them later in the chapter.)

dBASE III PLUS also offers two *functions* for accepting keystrokes from the keyboard: INKEY() and READKEY(). These are used in more advanced screen displays and can determine exactly which key the user pressed, including arrow keys and control-key combinations.

In later chapters we'll get much more practice with the user-interface commands and functions. For now, however, let's discuss commands that are used to control the flow in a program.

⊙LOOPING WITH DO WHILE. . .ENDDO

One of the most widely used commands in a command file is the DO WHILE loop. A loop tells dBASE to repeat a series of commands as long as some condition exists. The DO WHILE command marks the start of the loop, and the ENDDO command marks the end of the loop. Let's look at an example.

```
********************************************* ITest.PRG
*-------- Program to test the user-interface commands.
CLEAR
ACCEPT "Enter anything, then press RETURN: " TO ATest
?
INPUT "Enter a number, then press RETURN: " TO ITest
?
WAIT "Press any key to continue (no RETURN): " TO WTest

*------ READ command needs predefined variable.
*------ Here, 12 spaces are preassigned to RTest.
RTest = SPACE(12)
@ 7,5 SAY "Enter your name " GET RTest
READ

*------ Print results.
? "For ACCEPT, you entered :",ATest
? "For INPUT, you entered  :",ITest
? "For WAIT, you entered   :",WTest
? "For @, SAY, GET, READ, you entered : ",RTest
?

DISPLAY MEMORY
```

Figure 1.1:　Program to test user-interface commands

From the dot prompt, type the command

MODIFY COMMAND Count

to create a command file called Count.PRG. When the dBASE text editor appears, type in the command file exactly as in Figure 1.2.

```
**************************************** Count.PRG
*-------------- Test the DO WHILE...ENDDO Commands.
CLEAR
SET TALK OFF

*--- Start Counter at 1.
Counter = 1
*--- Repeat loop until Counter reaches 20.
DO WHILE Counter <= 20
   ? Counter
   Counter = Counter + 1
ENDDO (counter <=20)

? "All Done"
```

Figure 1.2:   The Count.PRG command file

Let's discuss what each line in the program does. First, the CLEAR command clears the screen. Then, SET TALK OFF keeps extraneous dBASE messages from appearing on the screen as the program is running. Then, Counter = 1 creates a memory variable named Counter that contains the number 1.

The next line, DO WHILE Counter < = 20, tells dBASE to start a loop that will repeat as long as Counter is either less than, or equal to, 20. The next line, ? Counter, prints the current value of the memory variable Counter each time through the loop. The next line, Counter = Counter + 1, adds 1 to the current value of the Counter memory variable each time through. The ENDDO command marks the end of the DO WHILE loop. (Every DO WHILE command in a program *must* have an ENDDO command associated with it.) The last line, ? "All Done", prints the message *All Done* on the screen when the counter has reached 20 and the program exits the loop.

Save the command file with a ^W or ^End, and run it by typing

DO Count

The command file clears the screen, prints the value of Counter, and adds 1 to Counter, as long as Counter is less than or equal to 20. Then, it prints the message *All Done,* so the screen looks like this:

```
1
2
3
4
5
6
7
8
9
10
11
12
13
14
15
16
17
18
19
20
All Done
```

If you use MODIFY COMMAND to change the program so that the loop repeats as long as Counter is less than or equal to 100, and so that the successive values of Counter are printed on the same line (using ?? rather than ?, as in Figure 1.3), dBASE would count to 100, as below:

```
 1    2    3    4    5    6    7
 8    9   10   11   12   13   14
15   16   17   18   19   20   21
22   23   24   25   26   27   28
29   30   31   32   33   34   35
36   37   38   39   40   41   42
43   44   45   46   47   48   49
50   51   52   53   54   55   56
57   58   59   60   61   62   63
64   65   66   67   68   69   70
71   72   73   74   75   76   77
78   79   80   81   82   83   84
85   86   87   88   89   90   91
92   93   94   95   96   97   98
99  100
All Done
```

```
*************************************** Count.PRG
*-------------- Test the DO WHILE...ENDDO Command.
CLEAR
SET TALK OFF

*------- Start counter at 1
Counter = 1
*------- Repeat loop until Counter reaches 100.
DO WHILE Counter <= 100
   ?? Counter
   Counter = Counter + 1
ENDDO

? "All Done"
```

Figure 1.3:   The modified Count.PRG command file

One of the most common uses for the DO WHILE command is to step through each record in a database and perform some task on each record. The command DO WHILE .NOT. EOF( ) is usually used for this type of loop. In English, the command translates to DO as long as the last record in the database *EOF( )* has not been encountered. We'll see many instances of this command in later chapters.

⊙MAKING DECISIONS WITH IF. . .ELSE. . .ENDIF

A command file can also make decisions about what to do next based upon whether a certain condition has been met. The dBASE III IF. . .ELSE. . . ENDIF commands can be used to make decisions. Let's look at an example.

From the dot prompt, create a new command file called IFTest.PRG by typing in the command

   MODIFY COMMAND IFTest

When the dBASE text editor appears, type in the command file shown in Figure 1.4.

Let's look at each line in the command file. The first command below the comments, CLEAR, simply clears the screen. The next line presents the prompt *Turn on printer? (Y/N)* on the screen, and waits for the user to type in an answer and a carriage return. Whatever the user types is stored in a memory variable named YesNo.

The next line checks to see if the uppercase equivalent of the user's answer is a capital Y (IF UPPER(YesNo) = "Y"). If so, dBASE performs all the

```
******************************** IFTest.PRG
*-------------- Test the IF...ELSE...ENDIF commands.
CLEAR
*-------------------------- Ask about the printer.
ACCEPT "Turn on printer? (Y/N) " TO YesNo

*------ Decide what to do based upon answer (YesNo).
IF UPPER(YesNo)="Y"
   SET PRINT ON
   ? "You chose the printer"
   EJECT
   SET PRINT OFF
ELSE
   CLEAR
   ? "You chose the screen."
ENDIF
```

Figure 1.4:   The IF Test.PRG command file

lines between the IF and the ELSE commands. If the user's answer is not a Y, dBASE skips all lines between the IF and ELSE, and processes the lines between the ELSE and ENDIF commands instead.

To try the command file, save it with the usual ^W or ^End. Then type in the command

   DO IFTest

The screen will clear and the message *Turn on printer? (Y/N)* will appear on the screen. If you type in a Y, followed by a carriage return, the program will turn on the printer (SET PRINT ON), write the message *You chose the printer* on paper, eject the page from the printer (EJECT), and turn the printer off (SET PRINT OFF). If you type in any letter other than a Y, the program will clear the screen (CLEAR), then present the message *You chose the screen.* In either case, the program will return to the dot prompt when done.

The last line of the command file, ENDIF, marks the end of the commands to be included within the IF. . .ELSE decision. Every IF statement in a command file *must* have an ENDIF command associated with it. The ELSE statement is optional. For example, if you just want the program to turn on the printer when the user enters Yes to a prompt but does not wish to specify an action when something else occurs, you could use an IF. . . ENDIF clause as in Figure 1.5.

An abbreviated form of the IF command is the IIF function, which can be used inside a command line, or even in a column definition in a report format or label format. The basic syntax for IIF is

IIF(*This Is True, Do This, Otherwise Do This*)

For example, the IIF command below prints the words *Less Than* if a memory variable named X is less than 10. Otherwise, the command line prints the words *Greater Than:*

? IIF (X < 10, "Less Than","Greater Than")

The IF command clause below performs exactly the same task:

```
IF X < 10
   ? "Less Than"
ELSE
   ? "Greater Than"
ENDIF
```

Notice that the big difference is that with the IIF function the ? (print) command begins the line, and the IIF function determines how to finish the command line. The IF command requires two separate ? commands to achieve the same goal.

Generally speaking, the IIF function is used where one condition leads to a single "either/or" result. The IF. . .THEN. . .ELSE commands can perform any number of steps based upon the result of a condition. We'll see many practical examples of the IIF function in later chapters.

```
****************** IFtest program without ELSE clause.
CLEAR
WAIT "Turn on printer? (Y/N)" TO YesNo

IF UPPER(YesNo)="Y"
   SET PRINT ON
ENDIF

? "Hello Hello Hello"
SET PRINT OFF
```

Figure 1.5: A program with an IF. . .ENDIF clause

IF. . .ELSE. . .ENDIF clauses and the IIF function are useful for handling responses to simple either/or or yes/no decisions in a command file. Sometimes, a program needs to decide what to do based upon several alternatives. The DO CASE. . .ENDCASE commands are used for these types of decisions.

⊙MAKING DECISIONS WITH DO CASE. . .ENDCASE

A DO CASE. . .ENDCASE clause tells a program what to do depending on which of several mutually exclusive possibilities occurs. A simple example is shown in Figure 1.6. If you want to try it out, type MODIFY COMMAND CaseTest to create the command file.

The first command of the program, CLEAR, simply clears the screen. The next command, INPUT, presents the message *Enter a number from 1 to 4* on the screen, and waits for a response and a carriage return. The typed-in response is stored as a number in a memory variable named X. The next line marks the beginning of the DO CASE clause. Beneath this, the two lines

```
CASE X  =  1
? "You entered one."
```

tell dBASE to print the message *You entered one* if the user's answer is a 1 (X = 1). The next CASE statement, CASE X = 2, prints the message *You entered two* if a 2 is typed in, and so forth for CASE X = 3 and CASE X = 4. The optional OTHERWISE command is used to cover all other possibilities. For example, if you run this command file and type in the number 37 in response to the prompt, the program will display the message: *I said from one to four!*.

```
********************************* CaseTest.PRG
*-------------- Test the DO CASE...ENDCASE Commands.
CLEAR
INPUT "Enter a number from 1 to 4 " TO X

DO CASE

   CASE X = 1
        ? "You entered one."

   CASE X = 2
        ? "You entered two."

   CASE X = 3
        ? "You entered three."

   CASE X = 4
        ? "You entered four"

   OTHERWISE
        ? "I said from one to four!"

ENDCASE
```

Figure 1.6: The CaseTest.PRG command file

The ENDCASE statement *must* be used to mark the end of a DO CASE clause in a program (beneath the last CASE or OTHERWISE commands). The OTHERWISE command is entirely optional.

The DO CASE command is most commonly found in *menu* programs, where the program displays a list of options to the user, waits for a response, and decides what to do next based on that response. We'll see plenty of applications of the DO CASE. . .ENDCASE clause in the chapters that follow.

⊙STRUCTURED PROGRAMMING

You've probably noticed that all the program examples above used indentations. These are not necessary from a technical standpoint. They are used instead to make the program more readable from a human standpoint and therefore easier to edit and debug. Take, for instance, the simple IF Test.PRG program. Without indentations, it looks like this:

```
CLEAR
ACCEPT "Turn on printer? (Y/N) " TO YesNo
IF UPPER(YesNo) = "Y"
SET PRINT ON
? "You chose the printer"
EJECT
SET PRINT OFF
ELSE
CLEAR
? "You chose the screen."
ENDIF
```

It's not too easy to see what decisions are being made in the program, because everything is lined up on the left margin. However, indenting the lines within the IF, ELSE, and ENDIF options makes it quite easy to see what decisions are being made, as below:

```
CLEAR
ACCEPT "Turn on printer? (Y/N) " TO YesNo
IF UPPER(YesNo) = "Y"
    SET PRINT ON
    ? "You chose the printer"
    EJECT
    SET PRINT OFF
```

```
ELSE
   CLEAR
   ? "You chose the screen."
ENDIF
```

Indenting commands within DO WHILE, IF, and DO CASE clauses is one of the techniques used in *structured programming* to make programs easier to work with. The concept of structured programming was popularized in the early 1970s to speed up and simplify the design and development of large custom software systems.

The basic goal of structured programming is to create programs that are *self-documenting.* In less technical terms, the goal is to create a program that is easy for you, the programmer, to read, and therefore easier to debug or modify in the future. Programs are easier to read if they follow some basic structural techniques. When programming in dBASE III PLUS, the following rules of thumb can help make your programs easier to read and work with:

- Use highly visible programmer comments to make it easier to locate parts of the program that perform a specific task.

- Indent program lines within loops and decision-making routines, so you can see the beginning and end points of these routines while working with the program.

- Try to use commands in a self-descriptive, rather than mysterious, way.

These rules can be best demonstrated by comparing two programs: one that does not use structured programming techniques, and one that does. Both programs perform *exactly* the same job; they present a main menu for a hypothetical library-management system, ask the user for a choice from the menu, and perform the task that the user requests.

Figure 1.7 presents a main menu program that does not follow structured programming rules of thumb.

There are several problems with this program. First of all, while there are some programmer comments (lines preceded by an asterisk), they are not highly visible. You need to skim through many lines of dBASE code to find the comment that reads * EXIT.

Secondly, there are no indentations in the command file. It's very difficult to figure out what is going on in this command file, and the list of seemingly disconnected ENDIF commands near the bottom of the command file is particularly confusing. If for some reason this program "crashed," it would not be too easy to dig around and find out why.

```
* MAIN menu
USE B:Library
DO WHILE .T.
CLEAR
@ 1,20 SAY "Library Management System"
@ 3,25 SAY "1. Add New Records"
@ 4,25 SAY "2. Print Reports"
@ 5,25 SAY "3. Edit Data"
@ 6,25 SAY "4. Exit"
STORE 0 TO Choice
@ 8,20 SAY "Enter choice (1-4) " GET Choice
READ
* BRANCH ACCORDINGLY
IF Choice=1
APPEND
ELSE
IF Choice=2
REPORT FORM LIBRARY
ELSE
IF Choice=3
EDIT
ELSE
* EXIT
IF Choice=4
RETURN
ENDIF
ENDIF
ENDIF
ENDIF
ENDDO
```

Figure 1.7:   An unstructured main menu program

Thirdly, there are some commands that are not very self-descriptive. The third line from the top reads

DO WHILE .T.

In the dBASE language, .T. means true. In fact, .T. is *always* true. Therefore, this line suggests that the loop will run forever. However, when you dig deep into the lines below, you'll find that the loop will not truly run forever. When the user selects option 4, dBASE performs a RETURN command which, in a sense, "jumps out" of the loop back to the dot prompt. At the bottom of the command file is the ENDDO command. There are no comments associated with it. If this were a larger program with many DO WHILE commands, it would be difficult to determine which DO WHILE this ENDDO belonged to. The same is true for the many ENDIF commands.

The program shown in Figure 1.8 performs exactly the same task as the previous program, but is written using the rules of thumb for structured programming.

```
******************************************* LIBRARY.PRG.
*------------------------- Library system Main Menu.
USE B:Library
STORE 0 TO Choice

DO WHILE Choice # 4
    CLEAR
    @ 1,20 SAY "Library Management System"
    @ 3,25 SAY "1. Add New Records"
    @ 4,25 SAY "2. Print Reports"
    @ 5,25 SAY "3. Edit Data"
    @ 6,25 SAY "4. Exit"
    @ 8,20 SAY "Enter choice (1-4) " GET Choice
    READ

    *----------- Perform according to user's request.
    DO CASE

        CASE Choice = 1
            APPEND

        CASE Choice = 2
            REPORT FORM B:Library

        CASE Choice = 3
            EDIT

    ENDCASE

ENDDO (while choice # 4)

*------------------------- When choice = 4, exit.
RETURN
```

Figure 1.8:   A structured main menu program

This command file is much easier to read than the first. To begin with, the lines of dashes in front of all the programmer's comments make them visible at a glance. Also, at the top of the program, the name of the program and a brief description of what it does is listed.

In addition, all the lines within the DO WHILE. . .ENDDO loop are indented at least three spaces. It is very easy to find the beginning and end points of the DO WHILE loop simply by running your finger down the left margin of the program until you encounter the ENDDO command.

The program also uses the DO CASE. . .ENDCASE commands to decide which task to perform based upon the user's request. This eliminates the need for the confusing ENDIF commands in the first program, making the program much easier to read. The commands within the DO CASE. . . ENDCASE lines are also evenly indented, which makes the entire DO CASE. . .ENDCASE clause stand out.

Finally, some of the commands in and of themselves are more descriptive than the commands in the first program. The command

DO WHILE Choice # 4

immediately informs us that this loop is not going to repeat itself forever. It will stop when the memory variable Choice equals 4 (the # symbol means "does not equal"). We need not "dig around" in the program to find the mysterious end to this seemingly infinite loop. In addition, the ENDDO command at the bottom of the program is followed by a comment that states

(while choice # 4)

This simple comment matches up with the DO WHILE command that is associated with this ENDDO, and makes the program easier to read and work with at a later date. In the dBASE language, anything that you type to the right of an ENDDO or ENDIF command is assumed to be a programmer comment (it does not affect how the program runs). Therefore you can do yourself a big favor by putting in reminders about which particular DO WHILE or IF each ENDDO or ENDIF command belongs to, at least where there would otherwise be confusion.

While all this may seem excessive for one small program, keep in mind that most systems are made up of many small programs, and they all add up. Also, not all programs are this small. Highly visible, descriptive comments can make spotting specific routines in large programs much easier, and therefore make programs much easier to debug or modify later.

⊙DEBUGGING TECHNIQUES

Murphy's Law dictates that few programs run right the first time. A program can "crash" because of a simple error like a misspelled command or field name. These errors are very common, and are quickly found by dBASE when you run the program. Other common errors, which are not always so easy to find, are missing or misplaced ENDDO, ENDIF, or END-CASE commands. Less common, though tougher errors, are *logical errors,* where the program runs without "crashing," but doesn't quite do the task it was meant to do. dBASE III PLUS provides many *debugging tools* that can be used to help find many types of errors and correct them, thereby making the overall programming task a bit easier.

When dBASE encounters a blatant error in a program, it displays the name of the program with the error in it, and the message

Cancel, Ignore, or Suspend ? (C, I, or S)

These three options have the following effects:

Cancel   The Cancel option terminates the program and returns to the dot prompt. Any private memory variables (those created within the command file(s)) are erased.

Suspend   The Suspend option temporarily terminates the command file and returns to the dot prompt displaying the message *Do suspended.* Private variables are not erased. The command file can be resumed at any time by entering the command RESUME at the dot prompt.

Ignore   The Ignore option ignores the error and attempts to continue processing at the next line in the command file.

(You can also interrupt the execution of a command file to bring up the Cancel, Ignore, and Suspend options by pressing the Escape key while the command file is running. You need not wait for an error to occur.)

For the rest of this chapter we'll discuss techniques that you can use to help isolate and correct the error.

DISPLAY COMMANDS

The various DISPLAY commands allow you to view the status of memory variables, open files, active index files, and other useful items of information that may be the cause of the error. If you Suspend the program (but not Cancel or Ignore it), you can enter the command

DISPLAY MEMORY

or

LIST MEMORY

at the dot prompt to see the names, contents, and data types of all active memory variables. If the error message *Variable not found* accompanied your program error, you may have misspelled a variable name, or attempted to use a nonexistent memory variable. Check for the existence and correct spelling of the variable name. If necessary, RESUME the command file, then press Escape to terminate it, and use MODIFY COMMAND to edit the command file so it creates the appropriate memory variable. (The *Variable not found* message can also be caused by attempting to access a field in an unopened database. DISPLAY STATUS and DISPLAY STRUCTURE will help determine that.)

DISPLAY MEMORY might also help uncover a data type mismatch error. For example, the line

IF Today = '12/31/86'

will generate a data type mismatch if the Today variable is the Date data type (because "12/31/86" is character data). Check the data types of variables using DISPLAY MEMORY and make corrections if necessary. (DISPLAY STRUCTURE will show the data types of fields in the active database.)

To get a hard copy of the memory variables, you can use the command

DISPLAY MEMORY TO PRINT

The TO PRINT option also works with DISPLAY STRUCTURE and DISPLAY STATUS, which is discussed below.

The DISPLAY STATUS command displays the names of all databases in use, as well as the names and contents of all active index files, as shown below:

Select area:1, Database in use: B:master.dbf Alias:Master
Master index file: B:master.ndx key:CODE

Currently selected database:
Select area:2, Database in use: B:sales.dbf Alias:SALES
Master index file: B:sales.ndx key:CODE

The DISPLAY STATUS display shows that the currently selected database, in select area 2, is B:Sales.DBF. It has no name (alias), other than the name SALES in uppercase. The active index file associated with it is B:Sales.NDX, and it is an index of the (key) field CODE. The DISPLAY STATUS command will also show the status of all dBASE SET parameters (e.g., SET TALK, SET SAFETY), function key assignments, the left-margin setting for the printer, the print destination, the default disk drive, the file search path, and the current work area.

Use these DISPLAY commands when an error occurs to check on the current status of dBASE and to look for clues as to what went wrong. Perhaps you've simply misspelled a field or variable name, or attempted to use a nonexistent field or variable. Perhaps the wrong database or wrong index file is in use. The DISPLAY commands will help you find out.

HISTORY Commands

At any time in your work with dBASE III PLUS, you can enter the command

DISPLAY HISTORY

to view the last 20 commands you've entered at the dot prompt. These 20 commands will not include lines from a command file, unless you perform certain steps first.

First of all, at the dot prompt, you can use the SET HISTORY command to determine how many lines will be recorded. When recording from a program, you may want to increase the default value of 20 to perhaps 50 or more, as in the command below:

SET HISTORY TO 50

Next, before you run your program, enter the command

SET DOHISTORY ON

This command ensures that command file lines are recorded in the history file.

When a program error occurs, you can suspend operation, and from the dot prompt enter the command

DISPLAY HISTORY

or

LIST HISTORY

to view the last 50 commands. (DISPLAY pauses the screen every 22 lines, LIST does not. You can use the TO PRINT option with either command.)

The SET DOHISTORY ON command will slow down a program's performance dramatically. Therefore, when not debugging, be sure to enter the command

SET DOHISTORY OFF

at the dot prompt.

OTHER DEBUGGING COMMANDS

Close and Clear

If a command file with several files open at once "crashes," the files will most likely still be open when you attempt to run the command file again. If you get the error message *File already open* when rerunning a command file, use the CLEAR ALL or CLOSE DATABASES command when the dot prompt reappears. This will allow you to test the program from "neutral ground."

Set Talk On

The command SET TALK OFF is often used in command files to keep dBASE's extraneous feedback messages from appearing on the screen while the program is running. If you are having a problem getting a program to run correctly, just remove the SET TALK OFF command from the program, or put an asterisk in front of it to make dBASE ignore it. Then, from the dot prompt, type the command SET TALK ON before you run the command file. Watch the various messages that appear on the screen for clues as to what might be amiss.

Set Echo On

The SET ECHO ON command allows you to see each line in a command file as the program is running. To see the entire program echoed, just type the command SET ECHO ON from the dot prompt before typing the DO command that runs the program. If you know that an error is somewhere in a small part of the program, you can put the SET ECHO ON command right in the command file to start echoing at a particular spot. The SET ECHO OFF command terminates echoing.

Set Step On

If the SET ECHO ON command presents commands too quickly to be read, use the SET STEP ON command to slow things down. With both the

ECHO and STEP commands set on, dBASE displays each line of the command file as it is being processed, but pauses after each line and displays
the message

Type any key to step — ESC to cancel

You can press any key to watch the next line being processed, or press the
Escape (Esc) key to stop the program and return to the dot prompt.

The STEP option slows a program down enough for you to follow all the
steps, thereby watching the logic of the program unfold as dBASE executes each command. This is a good technique for finding those logical
errors where a program runs without "crashing," but doesn't do quite what
you had in mind. If the STEP option doesn't solve the problem, you can
break out the heavy artillery with the DEBUG command.

Set Debug On

The SET DEBUG ON command sends all echoed statements to the
printer. (With DEBUG, it's best to use SET ECHO ON, and SET STEP OFF.)
When you use the SET DEBUG ON command at the dot prompt, dBASE
sends every line in the command file to the printer as it is being executed.
That way, you can use the printed copy of the echoed lines to follow
through each step in the command file at a leisurely pace.

CONNECTING THE CLAUSES

Perhaps the best overall debugging technique is to make a hard copy of
the command file, and then connect all the IF, DO CASE, and DO WHILE
commands with their ENDIF, ENDCASE, and ENDDO commands. As an
instructor, I find that a large percentage of the most mysterious program
errors are caused by missing or misplaced ENDDO, ENDIF, and ENDCASE
commands. These are most easily detected in a hard copy of the program.
You can use the dBASE TYPE command with the TO PRINT option to create a hard copy of a command file. For example, the command below,
typed at the dBASE dot prompt, creates a hard copy of a program named
Test.PRG.

TYPE Test.PRG TO PRINT

Once you get the printed copy, use a pen or pencil to draw arrows connect-
ing all the DO WHILE, IF, and DO CASE statements to their respective
ENDDO, ENDIF, and ENDCASE commands, as in Figure 1.9.

```
**************************************** Imenu.PRG
************* Main menu for the inventory system.
SET TALK OFF

***************** Set up loop for main menu loop.
STORE " " TO IChoice
DO WHILE IChoice # "4"
   CLEAR
   TEXT
                   Inventory System Main Menu

               1. Master Inventory
               2. Record Sales
               3. Record New Stock

               4. Exit
   ENDTEXT
   ******************** Get response from user.
   @ 10,18 SAY "Enter choice " GET IChoice PICTURE "9"
   READ

   DO CASE

       CASE IChoice = "1"
            DO Mmenu

       CASE IChoice = "2"
            DO Smenu

       CASE IChoice = "3"
            DO Nmenu

   ENDCASE

ENDDO (while ichoice # 4)
QUIT
```

Figure 1.9:   Sample program with arrows drawn

Once you have the arrows drawn, check to make sure that there are no unmatched DO CASE, ENDCASE, DO WHILE, ENDDO, IF, or ENDIF commands. Also watch out for lines that cross over one another; these might indicate a logic problem. Figure 1.10 shows a sample program with crossed-over arrows that are likely to cause problems. (Note: The Debug.PRG command file in Chapter 10 rewrites command files so that the indentations are correct, and indicates any missing ENDDO, ENDIF, or ENDCASE commands.)

THE MOST COMMON PROGRAMMING ERRORS

There are six very common programming errors: data type mismatches, illegal function arguments, misspelled command and field/variable names, records out of range, logical errors, and too many open files.

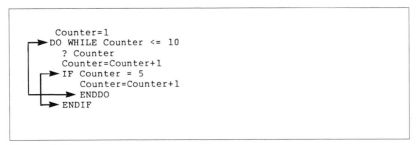

Figure 1.10:   Arrows showing crossover that might indicate a logical error

Data Type Mismatches

A data type mismatch occurs if you try to treat character data as numeric, or date data as character. For example

    LIST FOR DATE = "01/01/85"

If the DATE field is the date data type, dBASE will respond with the message *Data type mismatch,* because 01/01/85 is character data. In this example, DATE must be converted to character data so that the types match as shown below.

    LIST FOR DTOC(DATE) = "01/01/85"

A data type mismatch error often occurs when two different data types are being compared or combined. Use the PUBLIC, DISPLAY MEMORY, and DISPLAY STRUCTURE commands to check the types of the data being compared.

Illegal Function Arguments

An illegal function argument occurs if you try to use a function with the wrong type of data. For example, if memory variable X is a numeric data type, and you attempt to perform a command such as

    ? UPPER(X)

an error will occur, because the UPPER command is used to convert only character data to uppercase. dBASE will display the message *Illegal function argument,* because the argument (X) is numeric, and the UPPER command requires character data. Several dBASE functions and their "legal" argument data types are summarized in Table 1.2.

Numeric	Character	Date	None
ABS(n)	ASC(c)	CDOW(d)	BOF( )
CHR(n)	AT(c,c)	CMONTH(d)	COL( )
EXP(n)	CTOD(c)	DOW( )	DATE( )
FIELD(n)	FILE(c)	DTOC(d)	DBF( )
FKLABEL(n)	GETENV(c)	MONTH(d)	DELETED( )
INT(n)	ISALPHA(c)	YEAR(d)	DISKSPACE( )
LOG(n)	ISLOWER(c)		EOF( )
MAX(n,n)	ISUPPER(c)		ERROR( )
MIN(n,n)	LEFT(c,n)		FKMAX( )
MOD(n,n)	LEN(c)		FOUND( )
NDX(n)	LOWER(c)		INKEY( )
ROUND(n,n)	LTRIM(c)		ISCOLOR( )
SPACE(n)	REPLICATE(c,n)		LUPDATE( )
SQRT(n)	RIGHT(c,n)		MESSAGE( )
STR(n,n,n)	RTRIM(c)		OS( )
	STUFF(c,n,n,c)		PROW( )
	SUBSTR(c,n,n)		READKEY( )
	TRIM(c)		RECCOUNT( )
	TYPE(c)		RECSIZE( )
	UPPER(c)		ROW( )
	VAL(c)		TIME( )
			VERSION

Table 1.2: Functions and argument types

Misspelled Commands and Field/Variable Names

If a program contains a misspelled command, dBASE responds with the
message *Unrecognized command verb.* You'll need to correct the spelling or
syntax of the command with MODIFY COMMAND. If you attempt to use a

memory variable or field name that does not exist, dBASE displays the message *Variable not found*. Use the PUBLIC and DISPLAY MEMORY commands to check the memory variables. Use the DISPLAY STATUS and DISPLAY STRUCTURE commands to see what files are in use and what fields are available.

Records Out of Range

The record out of range error appears when you attempt to go to a nonexistent record (for example, GOTO 99 on a database with only 98 records). This error also occurs if you attempt to use a corrupted index file. Use the INDEX ON or REINDEX command to reconstruct the index file.

Logical Errors

As noted earlier, a logical error is one that, rather than making a program crash, makes a program do something other than what it was written to do. Logical errors are often caused by missing or misplaced ENDDO, ENDIF, or ENDCASE commands. Make a hard copy of the program and connect all DO WHILE, IF, and DO CASE commands with their respective ENDDO, ENDIF, and ENDCASE commands. In some cases, logical errors are caused by simply putting the right command in the wrong place (for example, a command inside an IF. . .ENDIF clause that belongs outside the clause). Use the ECHO, STEP, and DEBUG options to watch the flow of the program.

Too Many Open Files

The *Too many files are open* message is usually caused by a missing Config.SYS file on the boot-up disk. See the *Getting Started* manual that came with your dBASE III PLUS package, or the introduction of this book, for instructions on setting up a Config.SYS file for your computer.

In this chapter we've discussed some basic commands and techniques used in creating, structuring, editing, running, and debugging dBASE III PLUS command files. The programs presented throughout the book contain many practical examples of these basic commands and techniques. All of the programs have been fully tested and debugged. However, if you type a program in, there's a chance that you will make some errors, perhaps simple typographical errors or omissions. Remember to use the various debugging aids to help you locate and solve any problems that might arise.

In the next chapter, we'll discuss a special type of command file known as a "procedure file," and the commands used in conjunction with procedure files.

dBASE III PLUS
PROCEDURE FILES

2

In this chapter we'll discuss a special type of command file known as a *procedure file.* A procedure file is actually a command file that contains smaller command files. With the use of *parameter passing,* procedure files allow you to develop custom routines that can be accessed from the dot prompt or from other command files. These custom routines, which are the focus of this book, allow you to extend dBASE III PLUS beyond its off-the-shelf capabilities.

⊙CREATING A PROCEDURE FILE

Creating a procedure file is just like creating a command file. You simply use the MODIFY COMMAND editor or an external word processor. Assign any file name you like and the .PRG extension usually used with command files. Each procedure within the procedure file begins with the PROCE-DURE command, is followed by the name of the procedure, and ends with the RETURN command, which returns control to the dot prompt or calling program.

If parameters are to be passed to and from a procedure, the PARAM-ETERS command, which lists the names of the parameters being passed, must be used. The PARAMETERS command must be the second command in the procedure, immediately beneath the PROCEDURE command. A simple example will best explain procedures and parameters.

The area of a rectangle is calculated by multiplying the length by the width. That is, *area = length × width.* Let's create a procedure file to calculate the area of any rectangle.

From the dBASE dot prompt, create a command file named TestProc-.PRG by entering the command

MODIFY COMMAND TestProc

Type in the program title and CalcArea procedure, exactly as shown in Figure 2.1.

Notice that the name of the procedure is CalcArea, and that three parameters are assigned: Length, Width, and Area. Area is calculated by multiplying length times width (Area = Length * Width). The procedure ends with the RETURN command.

Once you've entered the procedure file as shown in Figure 2.1, save it with a ^W or ^End as usual. Now let's discuss techniques for accessing the procedure, as well as passing parameters.

```
******************************* TestProc.PRG
*---------------------- Sample procedure file.
PROCEDURE CalcArea
PARAMETERS Length,Width,Area
  Area = Length * Width
RETURN
```

Figure 2.1:   The CalcArea procedure in the TestProc procedure file

⊙USING THE PROCEDURE FILE

A procedure file needs to be opened before any of the procedures within it can be accessed. To do so, enter the SET PROCEDURE TO command with the name of the file.

SET PROCEDURE TO TestProc

From this point on, the procedure in the TestProc file is stored in RAM memory, and can be quickly accessed from the dot prompt or any command file.

⊙PASSING PARAMETERS

To pass data to and from a procedure, use the WITH and DO commands. WITH indicates the parameters to be passed, and DO runs the named procedure. Each parameter in the WITH part of the DO command must be separated by a comma. When several parameters are used in a procedure, both the sending DO . . . WITH command and the receiving PARAMETERS command must have exactly the same number and type of parameters. Therefore, three parameters need to be sent to the CalcArea procedure.

There are several ways to pass information to and from the procedure. First, of course, the procedure file must be opened with the SET PROCE-DURE command. Then, variables can be passed from memory variables, as in the steps below:

```
X = 5
Y = 10
Z = 0
DO CalcArea WITH X,Y,Z
```

If you now print the value of Z, you get the results of the calculation, as below:

```
? Z
   50
```

Notice that the names of the variables need not match the names used in the PARAMETERS command. The *order* of the variables, however, must match the order of the parameters.

The "sending" variables can have the same name as the receiving variables, as shown below. (With the TALK parameter on—the default—you'll see the results of the calculation immediately. However, if you've set TALK off, you need to use the ? command to display the results.)

```
Length = 20
Width = 25
Area = 0
DO CalcArea WITH Length,Width,Area
? Area
   500
```

If you attempt to pass variables that do not exist, dBASE generates the following error message:

```
Do CalcArea with J,K,L
Variable not found
              ?
Do Area with J,K,L
```

Constants may also be passed to the procedure. However, any data sent back from the procedure to the dot prompt or calling program needs to be stored in an existing memory variable. In this example, the procedure calculates and returns the area, so first you need to create a memory variable named Area, and then pass both the numbers and the area variable, as below:

```
Area = 0
DO CalcArea WITH 30,20,Area
```

To see the results, print the current value of the Area variable, as below:

```
? Area
   600
```

Calculations may be sent to the procedure too, as shown below:

```
Area = 0
DO CalcArea WITH (27^(1/3)), (5*5), Area
? Area
    75.00
```

Most importantly, you must *always* send exactly the same number of parameters as are listed in the PARAMETERS statement. In the example below, only two variables were sent, so dBASE responded with an error message, wondering where the third parameter was.

```
L = 100
W = 277
DO CalcArea WITH L,W
Wrong number of parameters
              ?
PARAMETERS Length, Width, Area
```

If you forget to specify any parameters, as in the command below:

```
DO CalcArea
```

you'll get the very cryptic error message shown below:

```
*** Unrecognized command verb
Called from—C:TestProc.prg
Cancel, Ignore, or Suspend? (C,I, or S)
```

Press C to terminate the command file and try again, this time remembering to specify the parameters after the WITH command.

⊙MODIFYING A PROCEDURE FILE

Additional procedures can easily be added to a procedure file with the MODIFY COMMAND editor. Let's add another procedure to the TestProc procedure file to test this out. Before you can change a procedure file, however, you need to close it. Type

```
CLOSE PROCEDURE
```

from the dot prompt. (If you forget to close a procedure file before editing it, dBASE will display the message *File is already open.* Just enter the CLOSE PROCEDURE command and try again.) Now, to add a new procedure to the TestProc file, enter

MODIFY COMMAND TestProc

Add the following procedure to the bottom of the procedure file (below the RETURN command), so the whole file now looks like Figure 2.2.

```
* -------------- Center procedure centers any string.
PROCEDURE Center
PARAMETERS Title,RM
   Pad = SPACE((RM − LEN(Title))/2)
   CTitle = Pad + Title
RETURN
```

```
******************************* TestProc.PRG
*---------------------- Sample procedure file.
PROCEDURE CalcArea
PARAMETERS Length,Width,Area
  Area = Length * Width
RETURN

*-------------- Center procedure centers any string.
PROCEDURE Center
PARAMETERS Title,RM
  Pad = SPACE((RM-LEN(Title))/2)
  CTitle = Pad + Title
RETURN
```

Figure 2.2:   TestProc procedure file with new Center procedure

Note that the name of the procedure is Center. It uses two parameters: Title (a title to be centered on the screen or printer), and RM (the right margin used to calculate the center). It operates by creating a variable named Pad, which is used to pad the title with leading blanks so that it will be centered. The width of the Pad variable is determined by creating a string of spaces calculated by dividing the difference of the right margin minus the length of the title by two. Then, the spaces stored in Pad and the original title are stored in a variable named CTitle.

Once you've entered the new procedure, save the command file with the usual ^W or ^End. From the dot prompt, type

SET PROCEDURE TO TestProc

once again, because we closed the procedure file earlier to edit it.

⊙PUBLIC MEMORY VARIABLES

Many procedures will not work properly unless you use the PUBLIC command. Note that in the Center procedure, two parameters are passed, Title and RM. However, the final centered title is stored in another variable named CTitle. Let's first see a problem that can occur with the Center procedure, so we can appreciate the solution. From the dot prompt, enter

SET TALK OFF

so dBASE does not display any extraneous messages. Then, enter

DO Center WITH "Sample Title",80

This command tells dBASE to do the Center procedure, using the title "Sample Title", and a right margin of 80. When the dot prompt reappears, type

? CTitle

to view the centered title. You'll notice that you get an error message, indicating that there is no variable named CTitle. That's because dBASE automatically erases all *local* variables when a RETURN is issued from a command file or procedure. Variables created from the dot prompt are *global* (not local to any particular command file or procedure), and are therefore not automatically erased. To keep the CTitle variable from being erased, you need to declare it as public with the following command:

PUBLIC CTitle

Now the CTitle variable will always be available. Once again, type

DO Center WITH "Sample Title",80

When the dot prompt reappears, enter

? Ctitle

to see the title centered on the screen, as below:

Sample Title

Making your memory variables public is a good way to make variables readily accessible throughout all levels of a system of programs. In the procedure files we develop in the following chapters, we'll use public memory variables to make the procedures more accessible, thereby making it easier to integrate these procedures into your own custom software systems.

Incidentally, you might also have noticed that the title that was passed to the Center variable was enclosed in quotation marks. As with all forms of data storage, character data passed as parameters must be enclosed in quotation marks (numeric data and variable names, however, are never enclosed in quotation marks). Hence, if the title to be centered is already stored in a variable, you need not use quotation marks. For example, the commands below store a sample title in a variable named RepTitle, pass this title as a variable to the Center procedure, and print the centered title.

```
RepTitle = "This is a sample title"
DO Center WITH RepTitle,80
? CTitle
```

The right margin (RM) can also be stored and passed as a variable. For example, the commands below assign a sample title to a variable named SamTitle, and a right margin of 128 to a variable named Right. Then, the Center procedure is called to center the SamTitle with the appropriate margin.

```
SamTitle = "Balance Sheet for First Quarter, 1985"
Right = 128
DO Center WITH SamTitle,Right
? CTitle
```

The commands above have exactly the same effect as the commands below:

```
DO Center WITH "Balance sheet for First Quarter, 1985", 128
? CTitle
```

Of course, a right margin of 128 will not center the title on the screen, but is useful for centering a title on wide paper in the printer.

⊙LIMITATIONS

There are a few limitations to keep in mind when creating and working with procedure files. First, a single procedure file can contain a maximum of 32 procedures. Procedure names can contain a maximum of eight characters, no spaces or punctuation (other than the underline), and must begin with a letter.

Only one procedure file can be open at any given time. Therefore, if you have a procedure file open, opening a new procedure file will close the existing open procedure file. To see if a procedure file is currently open at any given time, enter the command DISPLAY STATUS from the dot prompt. If a procedure file is open, its name will be displayed along with the other information displayed by this command.

The MODIFY COMMAND editor can handle a maximum of about 5,000 characters in any command file or procedure file. Therefore, if you are planning to create a very large procedure file it is best to use an external word processor or text editor such as WordStar or Edix.

In the next chapter, we'll develop some practical procedures for calculating and displaying financial data. These will also give us a chance to get more practice with public variables and parameters.

FINANCIAL
CALCULATIONS

3

dBASE III PLUS has a number of mathematical functions, such as square roots and logarithms, that manage numeric data. But for many financial applications, a dBASE user needs specific functions for calculating financial data. In this chapter, we'll develop procedures that add to dBASE III PLUS the ability to calculate payment on a loan, future value of an investment, present value of an annuity, compound annual growth rate, and logarithm base 10 (used in some financial calculations). We'll also develop some sample programs to test the procedures.

⊙THE FINPROCS PROCEDURE FILE

The procedures we develop in this chapter are all contained within a procedure file named FinProcs.PRG (for Financial Procedures). I'll assume that you are using the MODIFY COMMAND editor, though of course you can use whatever editor you wish. The entire FinProcs.PRG procedure file is shown in Figure 3.1. However, we'll develop and discuss each procedure individually throughout the chapter.

Before typing in the file, be sure that the TestProc procedure from the previous chapter is closed by entering the CLOSE PROCEDURE command at the dot prompt. Then use the command

    MODIFY COMMAND FinProcs

to begin entering the procedure file. Type in some opening comments, as shown below:

    * FinProcs.PRG
    *---------- Procedures for calculating financial data.

    *-- Make the variables FV, PV, Pmt, Cagr,
    *-- and Log10 public in the calling program.

Now we'll start adding some procedures to the file.

⊙CALCULATING PAYMENT ON A LOAN

The formula for calculating the payment on a loan is

    Payment = Principal * Interest / (1–1/(1 + Interest) ^ Term)

```
***************************************   FinProcs.PRG
*---------- Procedures for calculating financial data.

*--- Make the variables FV, PV, Pmt, Cagr
*--- and Log10 public in the calling program.

*--------- Pmt procedure calculates payment on a loan.
PROCEDURE Pmt
PARAMETERS Principal, Interest, Term
     Pmt= Principal * Interest/(1-1/(1+Interest)^Term)
RETURN

*--------------- FV procedure calculates future value.
PROCEDURE FV
PARAMETERS Payment,Interest,Term
   FV= Payment * ((1+Interest)^Term-1)/Interest
RETURN

* PV procedure calculates present value of an annuity.
PROCEDURE PV
PARAMETERS Payment, Interest, Term
     PV= Payment * (1-1/(1+Interest)^Term)/Interest
RETURN

*--Log10 calculates the base 10 logarithm of a number.
PROCEDURE Log10
PARAMETERS Number
  NatLog = LOG(Number)
  IF NatLog >= 0
     Con=(NatLog * .43429448)-INT(NatLog*.43429448)
     LRound= ROUND(Con,6)
     Log10= (INT(NatLog*.43429448)+LRound)
  ELSE
     Con=((NatLog*.43429448)-INT(NatLog*.43429448))*-1
     LRound= ROUND(Con,6)
     Log10= (INT(NatLog*.43429448)-LRound)
  ENDIF (natlog >=0)
RETURN

*------Cagr calculates the compund annual growth rate.
*------Uses Log10 procedure for log base 10.
PROCEDURE Cagr
PARAMETERS Present, Future, Years
  *--- Get log of present and future values.
  DO Log10 WITH Present
  PLog = Log10
  DO Log10 WITH Future
  FLog = Log10
  *--- Calculate CAGR.
  Cagr = (10^((FLog-PLog)/Years))-1
RETURN
```

Figure 3.1:   The complete FinProcs.PRG procedure file

where Principal is the amount of the loan, Interest is the per-period interest rate, and Term is the number of regular payments. To add a procedure that calculates payments, add the following lines to the FinProcs procedure file:

```
*-------- Pmt procedure calculates payment on a loan.
PROCEDURE Pmt
PARAMETERS Principal, Interest, Term
   Pmt = Principal * Interest/(1-1/(1 + Interest)^Term)
RETURN
```

Notice that three parameters are passed to the procedure: Principal, Interest, and Term. Based upon these, the procedure calculates the payment, and stores the result in a variable named Pmt.

To test the procedure, save the file by entering the usual ^W or ^End command. From the dot prompt, first enter the SET TALK OFF command to keep any extraneous messages from appearing. Next, make the Pmt variable public by typing

```
PUBLIC Pmt
```

to simplify passing the Pmt variable back to the dot prompt. Then, to open the procedure file, type

```
SET PROCEDURE TO FinProcs
```

And to use the Pmt procedure, type

```
DO Pmt WITH Principal, Interest, Term
```

where Principal is the amount borrowed, Interest is the per-period interest rate, and Term is the number of payments to be made. So, to determine the payment on a loan of $5,000 with an interest rate of .00833 per month (10% per year) for a period of 12 months, enter the command

```
DO Pmt WITH 5000,.00833,12
```

The results of the calculation are stored in the Pmt memory variable. To see the results, type

```
? Pmt
```

dBASE displays the monthly payment, as below:

439.57013

(which translates to $439.57 per month).

If all you know is the annual percentage rate you don't need to calculate the monthly interest yourself. Just divide the annual interest rate by 12 in the WITH part of the DO command. Similarly, if the term is the number of monthly payments in 20 years, you can multiply 20 by 12 in the WITH part to calculate the number of months automatically. For example, to calculate the payment on a loan of $168,000.00 at an annual interest rate of 9.375% for a 20-year term, type

DO Pmt WITH 168000,.09375/12,20*12

To see the results, type

? Pmt

and dBASE displays the result:

1552.29264

Later in this chapter, we'll develop a program to display a loan amortization schedule using the Pmt procedure. Let's now develop a procedure to calculate the future value of an investment.

⊙CALCULATING FUTURE VALUE

The formula for calculating the future value of an investment is

Future Value = Payment * ((1 + Interest) ^Periods−1)/Interest

To add a procedure to the FinProcs procedure file, first enter the CLOSE PROCEDURE command and then type

MODIFY COMMAND FinProcs

to edit the procedure file. Move the cursor to the bottom of the procedure file (below the RETURN command), and type in the procedure shown below:

```
*-------------- FV procedure calculates future value.
PROCEDURE FV
PARAMETERS Payment,Interest,Term
   FV = Payment * ((1 + Interest)^Term-1)/Interest
RETURN
```

Save the modified procedure file using the usual ^W or ^End keys.
The general syntax to use when figuring the future value is

DO FV WITH *Payment, Interest, Term*

where Payment is the amount deposited, Interest is the per-period interest rate, and Term is the number of regular deposits. The result is stored in the public memory variable FV. To test the procedure, first declare the FV variable as public, then open the procedure file, using the commands below:

```
PUBLIC FV
SET PROCEDURE TO FinProcs
```

Now, suppose you wish to calculate the future value of an investment of $200.00 per month at 12% interest per year for 20 years. Again, the annual interest needs to be divided by 12 for the proper per-period interest rate, and the years multiplied by 12 for the correct number of terms. Enter the command

DO FV WITH 200,.12/12,20*12

To see the results, type

? FV

You'll see that at the end of the 20 years you will have accumulated

197851.07

dollars.
    To see the future value of regular deposits of $2,000 per year at 10% per year for 30 years, enter the command

DO FV WITH 2000,.10,30

Type

? FV

to see the amount accumulated at the end of the period, which is $328,988.05. Note that for annual deposits, you need not divide by 12 to convert to monthly data.

⊙CALCULATING PRESENT VALUE

Suppose you can afford to pay $1,000 per month on a mortgage. Given that the current interest is 12% per year and you are willing to finance the house for 30 years, how much can you afford to borrow? You can figure it out by using a formula that calculates the present value of equal, regular payments on a loan. It is shown below:

Present Value = Payment * (1–1/(1 + Interest) ^Term)/Interest

To add the appropriate procedure to the FinProcs procedure file, first enter the CLOSE PROCEDURE command at the dot prompt. Then, type

MODIFY COMMAND FinProcs

Move the cursor to the bottom of the procedure file, and add the procedure shown below:

```
* PV procedure calculates present value of an annuity.
PROCEDURE PV
PARAMETERS Payment, Interest, Term
   PV = Payment * (1–1/(1 + Interest) ^Term)/Interest
RETURN
```

Save the command file. From the dot prompt, enter the following commands:

```
PUBLIC PV
SET PROCEDURE TO FinProcs
```

The general syntax for the Present Value procedure is

DO PV WITH *Payment, Interest, Term*

where Payment is the amount of each payment made, Interest is the per-period interest rate, and Term is the number of equal payments made. The result is stored in the public memory variable PV. To find out how much you can afford to borrow enter the following command:

DO PV WITH 1000,.12/12,30*12

To see the results, type

? PV

and dBASE displays the answer:

97218.33

indicating that you can borrow $97,218.33 for your new house.

⊙CALCULATING COMPOUND ANNUAL GROWTH RATE

The compound annual growth rate calculates the interest rate you'll need to reach a financial goal, given a starting sum of money, a goal, and a term. The formula for calculating compound annual growth rate is

CAGR = (10^((Log(Future)–Log(Present))/Years))–1

Unfortunately, the logarithms used are base 10, rather than the natural logarithm given by the dBASE LOG function. So, we'll just have to create a procedure to calculate the log base 10.

To add the Compound Annual Growth Rate procedure to the FinProcs procedure, first close the procedure file, then call up the FinProcs procedure file with the MODIFY COMMAND editor. Move the cursor to the bottom of the procedure file, and type in the procedure for calculating log base 10 as shown below:

```
*--Log10 calculates the base 10 logarithm of a number.
PROCEDURE Log10
```

```
PARAMETERS Number
   NatLog = LOG(Number)
   IF NatLog >= 0
      Con =(NatLog * .43429448)-INT(NatLog*.43429448)
      LRound = ROUND(Con,6)
      Log10 = (INT(NatLog*.43429448) + LRound)
   ELSE
      Con = ((NatLog*.43429448)-INT(NatLog*.43429448))*-1
      LRound = ROUND(Con,6)
      Log10 = (INT(NatLog*.43429448)-LRound)
   ENDIF (natlog >=0)
RETURN
```

The log base 10 is calculated by multiplying the natural logarithm by .43429448, taking into account several rounding steps necessary for maximum accuracy.

Next, type in the Cagr procedure, beneath the Log10 procedure as shown below.

```
*------Cagr calculates the compound annual growth rate.
*------Uses Log10 procedure for log base 10.
PROCEDURE Cagr
PARAMETERS Present, Future, Years
   *-- Get log of present and future values.
   DO Log10 WITH Present
   PLog = Log10
   DO Log10 WITH Future
   FLog = Log10
   *-- Calculate CAGR.
   Cagr = (10^((FLog-PLog)/Years))-1
RETURN
```

The compound annual growth rate is calculated by taking the log of the present and future values involved (PLog and FLog) and using these values in the appropriate formula.

Save the procedure file in the usual fashion. From the dot prompt, make both the Log10 and Cagr variables public with the PUBLIC command. Then, once again, open the procedure file by typing

SET PROCEDURE TO FinProcs

The general syntax for accessing the Cagr procedure is

DO CAGR WITH *Present Value, Future Value, Years*

where Present Value is the amount you wish to invest, Future Value is the amount you wish to have at the end of the period, and Years is the number of years that you are willing to invest the money. The answer is stored in the public memory variable Cagr.

Suppose that you want to invest $5,000, and want it to double in ten years. What interest rate would you need to meet this goal? Using the Cagr procedure, enter the command

```
DO Cagr WITH 5000,10000,10
```

Type

```
? Cagr
```

to see the result, which happens to be 7%, or

```
0.07
```

(The DISPLAY MEMORY command will show you the result carried to eight decimal places of accuracy.)

What if you wanted to triple your money in those ten years? Just change to future value from 10000 to 15000, as shown below:

```
DO Cagr WITH 5000,15000,10
```

The result will be

```
0.12
```

or 12% interest.

Incidentally, you can use the Log10 procedure as an independent procedure. The syntax is

```
DO Log10 WITH Number
```

where Number is the number you wish to calculate. The result is stored in a memory variable named Log10. For example, to compute the log base 10 of 128, type

```
DO Log10 WITH 128
```

Then type

```
? Log10
```

to see the result, which is

2.1072100000

⊙CALCULATING A VARIABLE-RATE LOAN

For the remainder of this chapter, we'll develop a couple of standard command files that access the FinProcs procedure. This will allow you to learn ways to use the procedures in programs of your own.

Begin by entering the CLOSE PROCEDURE command to close the Fin-Procs procedure. Then type

RELEASE ALL

to clear out all the memory variables. Now you are back to the dBASE dot prompt. There are no procedure files open, and no public memory variables declared. (Use the DISPLAY MEMORY command to view active memory variables if you wish.)

Now suppose you want to write a program to display the payments on a loan with a varying interest rate. Obviously, the Pmt procedure will come in handy with this program. We'll develop a program named VRate that asks for the principal, term, lowest and highest interest rates, and step value for the rate. Figure 3.2 shows the opening screen for the VRate command file with data filled in for a $168,000 loan, an initial interest rate of 9.375%, a maximum interest rate of 14.375%, and increments of 1/2%.

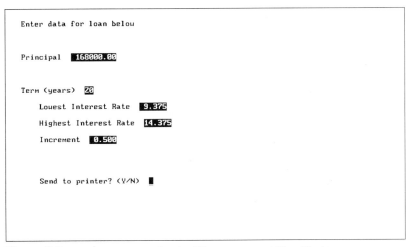

Figure 3.2: Opening screen for the VRate command file with data

After filling in the data, the screen asks if the results should be displayed on the printer. The user answers Yes or No (by typing in Y or N), and then the program displays the results as in Figure 3.3.

```
Loan Payment based on Varying Interest Rate

Principal      168000.00
Term           20 years

   Rate        Payment
  ------       -------
  9.375        1552.29
  9.875        1607.35
 10.375        1663.20
 10.875        1719.81
 11.375        1777.15
 11.875        1835.21
 12.375        1893.93
 12.875        1953.31
 13.375        2013.30
 13.875        2073.88
 14.375        2135.03
```

Figure 3.3:   Report displayed by the VRate command file

To create the VRate.PRG command file, type

MODIFY COMMAND VRate

at the dot prompt. Type in some opening comments, as shown below:

*** VRate.PRG
* Display payments on loan with varying interest rates.

To keep extraneous dBASE messages from appearing, you'll need to include the SET TALK OFF command. Then, since the VRate command file will use the Payment procedure, the command file should declare the Pmt variable as public, and open the FinProcs procedure file as below:

SET TALK OFF
PUBLIC Pmt
SET PROCEDURE TO FinProcs

Next, the VRate command file needs to ask the user for information concerning the loan. The variables Principal, Term, Lowest, Highest, and Increment are initialized, and a variable named ToPrint is created that contains a blank:

```
*--------------- Get data for calculations.
Principal = 0.00
Term = 0
STORE 0.000 TO Lowest, Highest, Increment
ToPrint = " "
```

Next, the command file clears the screen, and asks the user to fill in loan data using a series of @, SAY, GET, and PICTURE commands, along with the READ command.

```
CLEAR
@ 1,1 SAY "Enter data for loan below "
@ 5,1 SAY "Principal " ;
   GET Principal PICTURE "9999999.99"
@ 9,1 SAY "Term (years) " GET Term PICTURE "99"
@ 11,5 SAY "Lowest Interest Rate " ;
   GET Lowest PICTURE "99.999"
@ 13,5 SAY "Highest Interest Rate " ;
   GET Highest PICTURE "99.999"
@ 15,5 SAY "Increment " ;
   GET Increment PICTURE "99.999"
@ 20,5 SAY "Send to printer? (Y/N) " ;
   GET ToPrint PICTURE "!"
READ
```

The PICTURE templates with the number 9 in them limit the user's entry to numeric data. The "!" template converts any alphabetic data to uppercase.

If the user requests that the report be printed, the command file sets the printer on:

```
*--------------- Set printer on if requested.
IF ToPrint = "Y"
   SET PRINT ON
ENDIF (ToPrint)
```

Now the command file calculates and prints the data. First, a variable named Counter is initialized with the lowest interest rate for the loan. The

CLEAR command clears the screen, then the command file prints the report heading:

```
*--------------- Start processing.
Counter = Lowest
CLEAR
? "Loan Payment based on Varying Interest Rate"
?
? "Principal ",Principal
? "Term ",Term," years"
?
? " Rate Payment"
? " ----- -------"
?
```

Next, a DO WHILE loop is set up that continues processing as long as the Counter variable is less than or equal to the highest interest rate. Within the loop, the command file prints the current interest rate (Counter), calculates the payment using the current interest rate (DO Pmt. . .), prints the payment amount on the same line as the interest rate with a fixed width of 14 characters and two decimal places, (?? STR(Pmt,14,2)), and increments the Counter variable by the amount specified by the Increment variable.

```
*-- Calculate and print rows.
DO WHILE Counter < = Highest
    ? STR(Counter,7,3)
    DO Pmt WITH Principal,Counter/1200,Term*12
    ?? STR(Pmt,14,2)
    Counter = Counter + Increment
ENDDO (counter < = highest)
```

When the report is done, the following lines set off the printer and close the procedure file.

```
SET PRINT OFF
CLOSE PROCEDURE
```

Figure 3.4 shows the entire VRate.PRG command file.

Save the command file with the usual ^W or ^End command. To test the command file, enter the command

```
DO VRate
```

```
*********************************************** VRate.PRG
* Display payments on loan with varying interest rates.
SET TALK OFF
Public Pmt
SET PROCEDURE TO FinProcs

*---------------- Get data for calculations.
Principal = 0.00
Term = 0
STORE 0.000 TO Lowest, Highest, Increment
ToPrint = " "
CLEAR
@ 1,1 SAY "Enter data for loan below "
@ 5,1 SAY "Principal " ;
      GET Principal PICTURE "9999999.99"
@ 9,1 SAY "Term (years) " GET Term PICTURE "99"
@ 11,5 SAY "Lowest Interest Rate " ;
      GET Lowest PICTURE "99.999"
@ 13,5 SAY "Highest Interest Rate " ;
      GET Highest PICTURE "99.999"
@ 15,5 SAY "Increment " ;
      GET Increment PICTURE "99.999"
@ 20,5 SAY "Send to printer? (Y/N) " ;
      GET ToPrint PICTURE "!"
READ

*---------------- Set printer on, if requested.
IF ToPrint = "Y"
   SET PRINT ON
ENDIF (toprint)
*---------------- Start processing.
Counter = Lowest
CLEAR
? "Loan Payment based on Varying Interest Rate"
?
? "Principal  ",Principal
? "Term       ",Term," years"
?
? "    Rate       Payment"
? "    -----       -------"
?
*--- Calculate and print rows.
DO WHILE Counter <= Highest
        ? STR(Counter,7,3)
        DO Pmt WITH Principal,Counter/1200,Term*12
        ?? STR(Pmt,14,2)
        Counter = Counter + Increment
ENDDO (counter <= highest)

SET PRINT OFF
CLOSE PROCEDURE
```

Figure 3.4:   The VRate.PRG command file

at the dot prompt. When the screen asks for loan data, fill in the data as requested. You need not convert the annual percentage rate to monthly, because the command file itself does that. (The interest rate is divided by 1200 in the DO Pmt. . . command.) Hence, if the lowest interest rate is 9.375% per year, enter the rate as 9.375. To increment by 1/2%, enter the Increment as 0.50. Once all the prompts are filled in, the command file displays the report.

⊙CALCULATING LOAN AMORTIZATION

The loan amortization command file we'll develop next uses several procedures from the FinProcs.PRG procedure file. When run, it displays a screen asking for basic loan information. Figure 3.5 shows a sample of the screen filled out with information on a $20,000 loan at a 10% annual interest rate for a 20-year term.

After filling in the basic loan information, the program displays the amortization report shown in Figure 3.6.

Create the command file by typing

MODIFY COMMAND Amort

at the dot prompt. The command file begins with some opening comments, the SET TALK OFF command, and by declaring public the variables used in the program. Then the command file opens the FinProcs procedure file:

```
* * * * * * * * * * * * * * * * * * * * * * * * * * * * * * * * * * * * * * * * * Amort.PRG
* Amortize a loan given principal, interest, term.
SET TALK OFF
PUBLIC Pmt, PV
SET PROCEDURE TO FinProcs
```

Next, the basic loan data are initialized in memory variables, as well as a variable named ToPrint that later determines whether or not to print the results:

```
* - - - - - - - - Get data for calculations.
Principal = 0.00
Interest = 0.000
Term = 0
ToPrint = " "
```

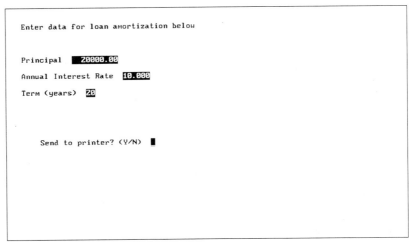

```
Enter data for loan amortization below


Principal      20000.00

Annual Interest Rate  10.000

Term (years)  20




        Send to printer? (Y/N)  ▮
```

Figure 3.5: Loan amortization screen with sample data filled in

```
Loan Amortization Report

Principal        20,000.00
Interest            10.00 % APR
Term                20.00 Years

Monthly Payment:      $193.00
Annual Payback :    $2,316.00
Total Payback  :   $46,320.00
```

Year	Beginning Balance	Ending Balance	Interest Paid	Principal Paid	Accumulated Principal
1	$20,000.00	$19,668.61	$1,984.61	$331.39	$331.39
2	$19,668.61	$19,303.02	$1,950.41	$365.59	$696.98
3	$19,303.02	$18,899.14	$1,912.12	$403.88	$1,100.86
4	$18,899.14	$18,452.97	$1,869.83	$446.17	$1,547.03
5	$18,452.97	$17,960.09	$1,823.12	$492.88	$2,039.91
6	$17,960.09	$17,415.59	$1,771.50	$544.50	$2,584.41
7	$17,415.59	$16,814.07	$1,714.48	$601.52	$3,185.93
8	$16,814.07	$16,149.57	$1,651.50	$664.50	$3,850.43
9	$16,149.57	$15,415.49	$1,581.92	$734.08	$4,584.51
10	$15,415.49	$14,604.53	$1,505.04	$810.96	$5,395.47
11	$14,604.53	$13,708.67	$1,420.14	$895.86	$6,291.33
12	$13,708.67	$12,718.99	$1,326.32	$989.68	$7,281.01
13	$12,718.99	$11,625.68	$1,222.69	$1,093.31	$8,374.32
14	$11,625.68	$10,417.88	$1,108.20	$1,207.80	$9,582.12
15	$10,417.88	$9,083.62	$981.74	$1,334.26	$10,916.38
16	$9,083.62	$7,609.63	$842.01	$1,473.99	$12,390.37
17	$7,609.63	$5,981.31	$687.68	$1,628.32	$14,018.69
18	$5,981.31	$4,182.47	$517.16	$1,798.84	$15,817.53
19	$4,182.47	$2,195.28	$328.81	$1,987.19	$17,804.72
20	$2,195.28	$0.00	$120.72	$2,195.28	$20,000.00

Figure 3.6: Loan amortization report

A *transformation string* consisting of the characters *###,###,###.##* is stored in a memory variable named DolFormat.

DolFormat = "###,###,###.##"

This character string will later be used with the dBASE III PLUS TRANS-FORM function to display numbers in punctuated format with two decimal places (e.g., 123,456.78 instead of 123456.7812).

Next the command file clears the screen and asks for basic loan data using the @, SAY, GET, PICTURE, and READ commands:

```
CLEAR
@ 1, 1 SAY "Enter data for loan amortization below "
@ 5, 1 SAY "Principal " ;
   GET Principal PICTURE "9999999.99"
@ 7, 1 SAY "Annual Interest Rate " ;
   GET Interest PICTURE "99.999"
@ 9, 1 SAY "Term (years) " GET Term PICTURE "99"
@ 15,5 SAY "Send to printer? (Y/N) " ;
   GET ToPrint PICTURE "!"
READ
```

If the user requested that the results be displayed on the printer (in the GET ToPrint command above), the command file sets the printer on:

```
* – – – – – – – Set printer on if requested.
IF ToPrint = "Y"
   SET PRINT ON
ENDIF (toprint)
```

The command file now begins printing the results. Note the use of the TRANSFORM function with the DolFormat transformation string to display the principal in punctuated format:

```
* – – – – – Print heading information.
CLEAR
? "Loan Amortization Report"
?
? "Principal ",TRANSFORM(Principal,DolFormat)
? "Interest ",Interest,"% APR"
? "Term      ",Term,"Years"
?
```

The next line calculates the monthly payment on the loan using the Pmt procedure. Note that the interest is divided by 1200 to determine the monthly percentage rate. The term is multiplied by 12 to determine the number of months. The resulting payment is displayed using the DolFormat format:

```
* -- Calculate and display payment.
DO Pmt WITH Principal,Interest/1200,Term*12
? "Monthly Payment:",TRANSFORM(Pmt,DolFormat)
```

The annual payment is calculated by multiplying the monthly payment by 12, and the result is displayed using the DolFormat format:

```
* -- Calculate and display annual payback.
? "Annual Payback :",TRANSFORM(Pmt*12,DolFormat)
```

The total payback on the loan is calculated and displayed by multiplying the monthly payment by the full term (years * 12):

```
* -- Calculate and display total payback.
? "Total Payback :",TRANS(Pmt*(12*Term),DolFormat)
?
```

The command file then prints the heading for the amortization schedule:

```
? "      Beginning Ending   Interest  Principal Accumulated"
? "Year  Balance   Balance  Paid      Paid      Principal"
?
```

Next, a DO WHILE loop begins counting at 1, and repeats as long as the Counter variable is less than or equal to the term of the loan. The Counter variable counts the number of loops, and the Accu_Prin variable keeps track of the accumulated principal:

```
* - - - Calculate and print each row.
Counter = 1
Accu_Prin = 0
DO WHILE Counter < = Term
```

Within the loop, the command file prints the year (as a character string with two digits), and the starting principal for the year using the DolFormat transformation string and the TRANSFORM function (abbreviated to TRANS here):

```
* – – – – – – – – – Print year.
? STR(Counter,2)
* – – – – Print beginning balance.
?? TRANS(Principal,DolFormat)
```

The ending balance for the year is determined by calculating the present value (using the PV procedure) on the loan after subtracting the current year from the term of the loan:

```
* – – – – – – Print ending balance.
DO PV WITH Pmt,Interest/1200,12*(Term-Counter)
?? TRANS(PV,DolFormat)
```

The interest paid for the year is calculated and displayed by subtracting the difference between the current principal and present value from the total paid for the year:

```
* – – – – – – Print interest paid.
?? TRANS((Pmt*12) – (Principal – PV),DolFormat)
```

The principal paid for the year is calculated and displayed by subtracting the interest paid for the year from the total paid for the year:

```
* – – – – – – Print principal paid.
?? TRANS((Pmt*12) – ((Pmt*12) – (Principal – PV)),DolFormat)
```

The principal paid for the current year is added to the accumulated principal (Accu_Prin variable), and displayed in the DolFormat format:

```
* – – – – – – Accumulated principal.
Accu_Prin = Accu_Prin + (Pmt*12) – ((Pmt*12) – (Principal – PV))
?? TRANS(Accu_Prin,DolFormat)
```

At this point the command file has amortized one year of the loan. Before repeating the loop, the remaining principal is recalculated to reflect the starting balance for the next year. (This starting balance is identical to the present value calculated for the current year, so the Principal variable is simply assigned the value of the PV variable.) The Counter variable is incremented by 1 (for the next year), and an ENDDO command closes the DO WHILE loop:

```
* - - - - - - - - Adjust principal.
  Principal = PV
  Counter = Counter + 1
ENDDO (counter < = term)
```

When the program is completely finished, the paper in the printer is ejected and the printer is set back off (assuming the report was printed). Then the command file closes the procedure file and returns to the dot prompt:

```
* - - Done with program.
IF ToPrint = "Y"
   EJECT
   SET PRINT OFF
ENDIF (toprint)

CLOSE PROCEDURE
```

Figure 3.7 shows the entire Amort.PRG command file.

Once you've keyed in the entire command file, save it in the usual fashion. From the dot prompt, enter the DO Amort command to try out the program. Fill in the basic data on the screen. You need not make any adjustments to the interest rate or term. For example, if the interest rate is 12% per year, just fill in the Interest part of the screen with the number 12 (or 12.000). The term should be entered as years (e.g., enter 30 for a 30-year loan).

It is very interesting to vary the interest rate and the term for a particular loan to see the profound effect on the total payback on the loan. With the Amort program, you merely need to plug a few figures into the opening screen, and dBASE does all the rest of the calculations.

⊙ GENERAL TECHNIQUES FOR USING FINANCIAL PROCEDURES

In the small sample programs we developed above, we only made public those variables necessary for use in the program. However, for full access to all the financial procedures, you should declare the FV, PV, Pmt, Cagr,

```
***************************************** Amort.PRG
* Amortize a loan given principal, interest, term.
SET TALK OFF
PUBLIC Pmt, PV
SET PROCEDURE TO FinProcs

*---------------- Get data for calculations.
Principal = 0.00
Interest  = 0.000
Term = 0
ToPrint = " "
DolFormat = "###,###,###.##"
CLEAR
@ 1, 1 SAY "Enter data for loan amortization below "
@ 5, 1 SAY "Principal " ;
       GET Principal PICTURE "9999999.99"
@ 7, 1 SAY "Annual Interest Rate " ;
       GET Interest PICTURE "99.999"
@ 9, 1 SAY "Term (years) " GET Term PICTURE "99"
@ 15,5 SAY "Send to printer? (Y/N) " ;
       GET ToPrint PICTURE "!"
READ

*-------------- Set printer on if requested.
IF ToPrint = "Y"
   SET PRINT ON
ENDIF (toprint)

*---------- Print heading information.
CLEAR
? "Loan Amortization Report"
?
? "Principal  ",TRANSFORM(Principal,DolFormat)
? "Interest   ",Interest,"% APR"
? "Term       ",Term,"Years"
?

*--- Calculate and display payment.
DO Pmt WITH Principal,Interest/1200,Term*12
? "Monthly Payment:",TRANSFORM(Pmt,DolFormat)

*--- Calculate and display annual payback.
? "Annual Payback :",TRANSFORM(Pmt*12,DolFormat)

*--- Calculate and display total payback.
? "Total Payback  :",TRANS(Pmt*(12*Term),DolFormat)
?
? "      Beginning    Ending    Interest   Principal   Accumulated"
? "Year  Balance      Balance   Paid       Paid        Principal"
?

*------- Calculate and print each row.
Counter = 1
Accu_Prin = 0

DO WHILE Counter <= Term
   *--------------------- Print year.
   ? STR(Counter,2)
```

Figure 3.7: The Amort.PRG command file

```
      *--------- Print beginning balance.
      ?? TRANS(Principal,DolFormat)

      *----------- Print ending balance.
      DO PV WITH Pmt,Interest/1200,12*(Term-Counter)
      ?? TRANS(PV,DolFormat)

      *------------ Print interest paid.
      ?? TRANS((Pmt*12)-(Principal-PV),DolFormat)

      *----------- Print principal paid.
      ?? TRANS((Pmt*12)-((Pmt*12)-(Principal-PV)),DolFormat)

      *------------ Accumulated principal.
      Accu_Prin = Accu_Prin + (Pmt*12)-((Pmt*12)-(Principal-PV))
      ?? TRANS(Accu_Prin,DolFormat)

      *---------------- Adjust principal.
      Principal = PV
      Counter = Counter + 1
   ENDDO (counter <= term)

   *----- Done with program.
   IF ToPrint = "Y"
      EJECT
      SET PRINT OFF
   ENDIF

   CLOSE PROCEDURE
```

Figure 3.7:   The Amort.PRG command file (continued)

and Log10 variables public before entering the SET PROCEDURE command, as shown below:

```
PUBLIC FV, PV, Pmt, Cagr, Log10
SET PROCEDURE TO FinProcs
```

Just in case you forget which variables to make public, the FinProcs.PRG
procedure file lists them in the comments at the top of the program.

```
*-- Make the variables FV, PV, Pmt, Cagr,
*-- and Log10 PUBLIC in the calling program.
```

Forgetting to open a procedure file altogether leads to an error message.
For example, the command below attempts to use the payment procedure
without first opening the FinProcs procedure file. Note that dBASE
responds that the file is not found.

```
DO Pmt WITH 150000,.12/12,30*12
```

File does not exist
    ?
DO Pmt WITH 150000,.12/12,30*12

(Since no procedure file was open, dBASE attempted to find a program named Pmt.PRG, which does not exist, hence the error message.)

If you open a procedure file, but forget to make the appropriate variable public, a different error occurs. In the example below, the FinProcs procedure is open, but the Pmt variable was not declared public. Hence, the procedure runs and the dot prompt reappears, but an error occurs when you attempt to print the result:

```
SET PROCEDURE TO FinProcs
DO Pmt WITH 150000,.12/12,30*12
? Pmt
```

Variable not found
    ?
? Pmt

The Pmt variable was not found because it was eliminated by the RETURN command at the bottom of the procedure. This problem is rectified by declaring the Pmt variable as public, and entering the DO Pmt WITH. . . command again.

In this chapter we've developed some handy procedures for calculating financial data. In the next chapter we'll develop some procedures for calculating statistics from a database.

STATISTICAL PROCEDURES

4

dBASE III PLUS includes the useful SUM, TOTAL, and AVERAGE commands for totaling and averaging numeric fields in a database. In this chapter we'll add some handy statistical procedures for finding the highest value, lowest value, standard deviation, and variance of fields in a database. The dBASE SET UNIQUE command displays all the distinct items that occur in a database, but does not tell you how many times each item occurs. We'll develop a frequency distribution procedure in this chapter to display this information. Finally, we'll also develop a procedure to determine the Pearson Product-Moment Correlation coefficient of two series of numbers.

To test some of the procedures as we develop them, we'll use a sample database, named Sales.DBF, that has the following structure:

```
Structure for database    : C:Sales.DBF
Number of data records : 16
        Field    Field name    Type          Width      Dec
          1      PARTNO        Character        5
          2      PARTNAME      Character       15
          3      QTY           Numeric          5
          4      U_PRICE       Numeric         12         2
          5      DATE          Date             8
        ** Total **                            46
```

Figure 4.1 shows some sample data entered into the Sales database.

Of course, you can use any database with any structure that you wish; the Sales database is for demonstration only. However, if you are following along on line, you might want to create this Sales database and add some data to it using the usual dBASE CREATE and APPEND commands.

⊙THE STATPROC.PRG PROCEDURE FILE

To analyze this data we'll create a new procedure file called StatProc-.PRG. Be sure that the FinProcs procedure file is closed by entering the CLOSE PROCEDURE command at the dot prompt. Figure 4.2 shows the entire StatProc.PRG procedure file.

If you are following along on line, use your word processor or the MODIFY COMMAND editor to enter the opening comments listed below:

```
* * * * * * * * * * * * * * * * * * * * * * * * * * * * * * * * * * * * * * StatProc.PRG
*----- Procedures for calculating database statistics.
```

RECORD#	PARTNO	PARTNAME	QTY	U_PRICE	DATE
1	A-123	Microprocessor	100	55.55	01/01/86
2	B-222	Laser Engine	2	1234.56	01/01/86
3	C-333	Color Terminal	5	400.00	01/01/86
4	D-444	Hard Disk	25	500.00	01/02/86
5	E-555	Disk Controller	50	200.00	01/15/86
6	F-666	Graphics Board	3	249.00	01/15/86
7	G-777	Modem	10	249.00	01/15/86
8	H-888	SemiDisk	50	695.00	01/15/86
9	A-123	Microprocessor	200	55.55	01/31/86
10	B-222	Laser Engine	4	1234.56	01/31/86
11	A-123	Microprocessor	10	55.00	01/31/86
12	E-555	Disk Controller	50	200.00	02/01/86
13	E-555	Disk Controller	100	180.00	02/01/86
14	F-666	Graphics Board	6	249.00	02/01/86
15	A-123	Microprocessor	20	55.00	02/15/86
16	H-888	SemiDisk	100	695.00	02/15/86

Figure 4.1: Sample database used with the statistical procedures

```
*-- The following variables should be declared
*-- public in the calling program:
*-- Max, Min, Var, StD, Pearson.
```

We'll develop and discuss each procedure independently in the sections that follow.

⊙HIGHEST VALUE IN A FIELD

The Max procedure finds and displays the highest value in a field, for all records or only certain records. For example, Max can calculate the highest sales quantity in the Sales database, the highest sales quantity for the month of February, or the highest sales total in dollars for part number A-123.

To add the Max procedure to the StatProc procedure file, move the cursor

```
**********************************  StatProc.PRG
*----- Procedures for calculating database statistics.

*-- The following variables should be declared
*-- public in the calling program:
*-- Max, Min, Var, StD, Fact, Pearson.

*------- Max procedure finds largest value in a field.
PROCEDURE Max
PARAMETERS FieldName
   GO TOP
   IF EOF()
      ? "No records match filter criteria!"
   ENDIF (eof)
   Max = -999999999999
   *-------- Find highest value.
   DO WHILE .NOT. EOF()
      IF &FieldName > Max
         Max = &FieldName
      ENDIF (&fieldname)
      SKIP
   ENDDO
RETURN

*-- Min procedure finds the smallest value in a field.
PROCEDURE Min
PARAMETERS FieldName
   GO TOP
   IF EOF()
      ? "No records match filter criteria!"
   ENDIF (eof)
   Min = 999999999999
   DO WHILE .NOT. EOF()
      IF &FieldName < Min
         Min = &FieldName
      ENDIF (&fieldname)
      SKIP
   ENDDO
RETURN

*----------------- Var procedure finds the variance.
PROCEDURE Var
PARAMETERS FieldName
   GO TOP
   IF EOF()
      ? "No records match filter criteria!"
   ENDIF (eof)
   COUNT TO N
   SUM(&FieldName),(&FieldName^2) TO TOT,TOTSq
   Correction = TOT^2/N
   Var = (TOTSq-Correction)/(n-1)
RETURN

*------- StD procedure finds the standard deviation.
PROCEDURE StD
PARAMETERS FieldName
   GO TOP
   IF EOF()
      ? "No records match filter criteria!"
```

Figure 4.2:   The StatProc.PRG procedure file

```
      ENDIF (eof)
      COUNT TO N
      SUM(&FieldName),(&FieldName^2) TO TOT,TOTSq
      Correction = TOT^2/N
      Variance = (TOTSq-Correction)/(n-1)
      StD = SQRT(Variance)
RETURN

* FreqDist procedure displays frequency distribution.
PROCEDURE FreqDist
PARAMETERS FieldName
  *- Print title
  ?
  ?   "Frequency distribution for &FieldName"
  ?
  *- Index on appropriate field.
  INDEX ON &FieldName TO TEMP
  *- Calculate and display distribution.
  GO TOP
  DO WHILE .NOT. EOF()
      Lookup = &FieldName
      COUNT WHILE &FieldName = Lookup TO FreQty
      ? LookUp,FreQty
  ENDDO (not eof)
CLOSE INDEX
ERASE Temp.NDX
RETURN

************** Pearson Product-Moment Correlation
PROCEDURE Pearson
PARAMETERS X,Y
  GO TOP
  *-- Get N.
  COUNT TO N
  *-- Sum the products and squares.
  SUM (&X * &Y),(&X ^2),&X,(&Y ^ 2),&Y TO ;
      SumProd,TotSqX,TotX,TotSqY,TotY
  SumProdXN = SumProd * N
  TotSqXxN = TotSqX * N
  TotXSq = TotX ^ 2
  TotSqYxN = TotSqY * N
  TotYSq = TotY ^ 2
  TotYxTotX = TotX * TotY
  *-- Get numerator.
  RNum = SumProdXN - TotYxTotX
  *-- Subtract squares.
  DifSqX = TotSqXxN - TotXSq
  DifSqY = TotSqYxN - TotYSq
  *-- Multiply differences.
  DifDif = DifSqX * DifSqY
  DifRoot = SQRT(DifDif)
  *-- Calculate Pearson R.
  Pearson = RNum/DifRoot
  RETURN
```

Figure 4.2:   The StatProc.PRG procedure file (continued)

to below the opening comments in the procedure file, and type in the procedure as shown below (see Figure 4.1 if you are not sure of the placement):

```
*------- Max procedure finds largest value in a field.
PROCEDURE Max
PARAMETERS FieldName
   GO TOP
   IF EOF()
      ? "No records match filter criteria!"
   ENDIF (eof)
   Max = -999999999999
   *-------- Find highest value.
   DO WHILE .NOT. EOF()
      IF &FieldName > Max
         Max = &FieldName
      ENDIF (&fieldname)
      SKIP
   ENDDO
RETURN
```

Let's discuss briefly how the procedure works. The name of the field in which you want to determine is passed to the procedure in the parameter FieldName. First, the procedure moves to the top of the database in use (GO TOP), then it tests to see if the end of the file has already been encountered. (This would occur if a filtering condition, which we'll discuss later, excluded every record in the database from the calculations.) If the end of the file is encountered immediately, the procedure displays the message:

No records match filter criteria!

Next, the Max variable is set to a very small number, −999999999999. Then a DO WHILE loop passes through each record in the database. Each time it encounters a record with a field value greater than Max, it assigns that value to the variable Max. By the time each record in the database has been checked, the Max variable contains the largest number encountered in the field of interest.

To test the Max procedure using the Sales database, save the StatProc procedure file using the usual ^W or ^End keys. Then open the database of interest, declare Max as a public variable, and open the StatProc procedure file, using the commands shown below:

```
USE Sales
PUBLIC Max
SET PROCEDURE TO StatProc
```

To perform the analysis on the entire database, just DO the Max procedure with the name of the field of interest in quotation marks. For example, to find the highest value in the Qty field, enter the command

    DO Max WITH "Qty"

To see the results, enter the command

    ? Max

and dBASE displays 200, the highest value in the Qty field.
    To see the highest value in the U_Price field, enter the command

    DO Max WITH "U_Price"

To see the results, enter the command

    ? Max

and dBASE displays 1234.56.
    To see the largest sales transaction in the entire database, do the Max procedure with the product of quantity times the unit price, as shown in the command below:

    DO Max WITH "Qty * U_Price"

To see the results, enter the usual command

    ? Max

and dBASE displays 69500.00.
    You can use the CREATE QUERY or MODIFY QUERY commands to pre-filter the database. For example, suppose you wish to see the largest sales transaction for only those records with part number B-222. First, enter the command

    MODIFY QUERY Sales

Fill in the query form as in Figure 4.3. Highlight the Exit option on the top menu, and select Save.
    To determine the largest sales transaction, enter the command

    DO Max WITH "Qty * U_Price"

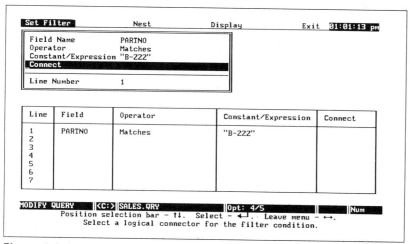

Figure 4.3: Query for part number B-222

and dBASE will then display the result, 4938.24.

Note that the filter condition remains in effect until you specifically remove it. For example, if you now enter the command

LIST

you'll see only the two records with part number B-222. To remove the filtering condition (and thereby once again have access to all the records in the database), enter the command

SET FILTER TO

at the dot prompt. (Also, if you USE a new database, or the same database again, the filtering condition is removed automatically.) If you enter the LIST command after removing the filter condition, all the records are displayed once again (and the Max procedure acts upon all the records in the database as well).

You can reinstate a previous filter condition created through a query form without using MODIFY QUERY or CREATE QUERY. Instead, use the SET FILTER TO FILE command with the name of the query form. In this example, the command to enter would be

SET FILTER TO FILE Sales

because we originally created the query form with the command MODIFY QUERY Sales. (dBASE adds the extension .QRY, so the file is actually stored on disk under the file name Sales.QRY.)

If you are not certain about the current status of a filtering condition, enter the DISPLAY STATUS command. If there is indeed an active filter condition, dBASE displays it as below:

```
Currently Selected Database:
Select area: 1, Database in Use: C:Sales.DBF Alias: SALES

Filter: PARTNO = "B-222"
```

⊙LOWEST VALUE IN A FIELD

The Min procedure works in exactly the same fashion as the Max procedure, but finds the smallest value in a field and stores its results in the public memory variable Min. To add this procedure to the StatProc procedure file, enter the CLOSE PROCEDURE command and use MODIFY COMMAND to edit the procedure file. Move the cursor to the bottom of the procedure file and enter the procedure as shown below:

```
*-- Min procedure finds the smallest value in a field.
PROCEDURE Min
PARAMETERS FieldName
   GO TOP
   IF EOF( )
      ? "No records match filter criteria!"
   ENDIF (eof)
   Min = 999999999999
   DO WHILE .NOT. EOF( )
      IF &FieldName < Min
         Min = &FieldName
      ENDIF (&fieldname)
      SKIP
   ENDDO (eof)
RETURN
```

The logic for the Min procedure is identical to that for the Max procedure, except that Min is initialized as a very high number, 999999999999, and is replaced by smaller numbers as the procedure runs.

After entering the Min procedure into the procedure file, save the file, declare the Min variable public, open the StatProc procedure file, and open the database you wish to analyze, as in the commands below:

```
PUBLIC Min
SET PROCEDURE TO StatProc
USE Sales
```

The syntax for the Min procedure is identical to that for the Max procedure. To ensure that all the database records are available for the calculation, enter the command

```
SET FILTER TO
```

To find the smallest quantity in the Qty field, enter the command

```
DO Min WITH "Qty"
```

To see the results, enter the command

```
? Min
```

which displays 2. To see the smallest sales transaction, enter the command

```
DO Min WITH "Qty * U_Price"
```

and then the command ? Min to see the result, 550.00.

As with the Max procedure (and virtually all procedures in this book), you can use the MODIFY QUERY, CREATE QUERY, or SET FILTER commands to specify records used in the calculations.

⊙VARIANCE AND STANDARD DEVIATION

Variance and standard deviation are often used to measure how tightly or loosely the values in a range are clustered together. The formula for calculating variance is shown in Figure 4.4. The standard deviation is simply the square root of the variance, as shown in the formula in Figure 4.5.

These measures are useful for a number of business decisions. For example, suppose a company wants to market a product to customers between the ages of 30 and 35 and they are trying to decide whether to

$$\text{Variance} = \frac{\Sigma X^2 - \dfrac{(\Sigma X)^2}{N}}{N - 1}$$

where

ΣX = the sum of the squared score values
$(\Sigma X)^2$ = the square of the sum of all the scores
N = the number of items used in the computation

Figure 4.4: Formula for calculating variance

$$\text{Standard Deviation} = \frac{X^2 - \dfrac{(\Sigma X)^2}{N}}{N - 1}$$

where

ΣX = the sum of the squared score values
$(\Sigma X)^2$ = the square of the sum of all the scores
N = the number of items used in the computation

Figure 4.5: Formula for calculating standard deviation

buy advertising time on a soap opera or a news channel. To do so, they ask 40 different viewers which channel they watch and record their ages in the appropriate columns.

News	Soap Opera
20	30
60	20
10	35
10	30
45	30
55	35

	News	Soap Opera
	5	35
	15	35
	60	30
	70	20
	10	25
	55	30
	21	40
	5	20
	15	40
	5	30
	36	36
	63	36
	75	37
	10	40
Average	32	32
Variance	633.14	41.48
Standard Deviation	25.16	6.44

The sample of viewers' ages for the two groups reveals that the average viewer age of both shows is 32. However, the variance and standard deviation results are very different for the two shows. Generally speaking, about two-thirds of a group will fall within one standard deviation of the mean (or average) for the group. Hence, two-thirds of the news viewers are between the ages of 7 and 57, a large spread, whereas about two-thirds of the soap opera viewers fall between the ages of 26 and 38, a much tighter group, and a better target audience for the product.

The Var and StD procedures are virtually identical, except that StD takes the square root of the variance (calculated as Var), and returns this value as StD, the standard deviation. You may want to use only the standard deviation procedure, since this is the one most commonly used to measure clusters. However, I've included the Var procedure because those who use statistics more frequently may wish to isolate the variance for other statistical formulas.

As usual, if you wish to add these procedures to the StatProc procedure file, first close the procedure file, then use the MODIFY COMMAND editor to add them to the procedure file. The procedures are shown below:

```
*----------------- Var procedure finds the variance.
PROCEDURE Var
```

```
PARAMETERS FieldName
  GO TOP
  IF EOF( )
    ? "No records match filter criteria!"
  ENDIF (eof)
  COUNT TO N
  SUM(&FieldName),(&FieldName^2) TO TOT,TOTSq
  Correction = TOT^2/N
  Var = (TOTSq-Correction)/(N−1)
RETURN


*------- StD procedure finds the standard deviation.
PROCEDURE StD
PARAMETERS FieldName
  GO TOP
  IF EOF( )
    ? "No records match filter criteria!"
  ENDIF (eof)
  COUNT TO N
  SUM(&FieldName),(&FieldName^2) TO TOT,TOTSq
  Correction = TOT^2/N
  Variance = (TOTSq-Correction)/(N−1)
  StD = SQRT(Variance)
RETURN
```

Each procedure begins with the usual PROCEDURE and PARAMETERS command and like the Max and Min procedures, each includes a parameter for FieldName. As with the Min and Max procedures, an error message is displayed if no records match any filter criterion. If there are matching records, the number of items is counted and stored in a variable named N. Then, the field in question, and the same field squared, are added together and stored in variables named Tot and TotSq. A correction factor is calculated by squaring the total and dividing by N. The variance is computed by subtracting the correction from the sum of squares, and dividing by N−1. In the standard deviation procedure, the square root of the variance is calculated.

Once you've keyed in the procedures, save the procedure file, declare the public variables, and open the StatProc procedure file. If necessary, open the database of interest (in this example, we'll use the same Sales database).

The syntax and techniques for using the Var and StD procedures are the same as those for the Max and Min procedures. Be sure to declare the Var and StD variables public, and open the procedure file using the commands below:

```
PUBLIC Var,StD
SET PROCEDURE TO StatProc
```

To test the procedures on the Sales database with all records available, you can enter the commands

```
USE Sales
SET FILTER TO
```

To calculate the variance in the Qty field, enter the command

```
DO Var WITH "Qty"
```

To see the results, enter the command

```
? Var
```

and dBASE displays 3003.40. To calculate the standard deviation for the Qty field, enter the commands

```
DO StD WITH "Qty"
? StD
```

and dBASE displays 54.80 (as does entering the command ? SQRT(Var)).

To use the previous filtering condition set forth in the Sales.QRY file, enter the command

```
SET FILTER TO FILE Sales
```

To calculate the variance of the total sales for records that match the filtering criterion in Sales.QRY, enter the command

```
DO Var WITH "Qty * U_Price"
```

and then the command

```
? Var
```

to see the result, -18289660.72.

⊙FREQUENCY DISTRIBUTION

The frequency distribution procedure lists all the distinct items in a field, and the number of occurrences of each. For example, if you are interested in knowing how many individuals fall within each zip code category in a large mailing list database, the frequency distribution procedure can figure it out and list the information on the screen or printer for you.

Frequency Distribution for Zip_Code

90001	100
90002	50
90003	125
90004	4561
90007	255
90008	11
.	
.	
.	
99999	543

You can add the frequency distribution procedure to the StatProc procedure file in the usual fashion. The procedure, named FreqDist, is shown below:

```
* FreqDist procedure displays frequency distribution.
PROCEDURE FreqDist
PARAMETERS FieldName
   *- Print title
   ?
   ? "Frequency Distribution for &FieldName"
   ?
   *- Index on appropriate field.
   INDEX ON &FieldName TO TEMP
   *- Calculate and display distribution.
   GO TOP
   DO WHILE .NOT. EOF()
      Lookup = &FieldName
      COUNT WHILE &FieldName = Lookup TO FreQty
      ? LookUp,FreQty
   ENDDO (not eof)
   CLOSE INDEX
   ERASE TEMP.NDX
RETURN
```

Let's discuss how this procedure works. A single parameter is passed to the procedure: the field name used for calculating the distribution. A title for the report is printed, then the file is indexed on the selected field, to an index file named Temp.NDX.

Next, a DO WHILE loop continues processing until the end of the file is encountered. The variable called Lookup is assigned the current value of the field being analyzed. Next, the COUNT WHILE command counts how many records match the field of interest. The result of the counting is stored in the variable FreQty, and the current value of the field (Lookup) and the quantity (FreQty) are displayed. At the end of the COUNT WHILE command, the record pointer is one record below the last record in the previous COUNT, so the loop is repeated and records for the next item are counted. When the procedure is finished, the CLOSE INDEX and ERASE commands delete the temporary index file, and the RETURN command returns control to the dot prompt or calling program.

The frequency distribution procedure requires no public variables because it displays its results rather than returning a value. Therefore, once you've entered the FreqDist procedure into the procedure file and saved it, you need only open the database and procedure file, as shown in the commands below:

```
SET PROCEDURE TO StatProc
USE Sales
```

To see a frequency distribution of part numbers in the Sales database, type

```
DO FreqDist WITH "PartNo"
```

and the procedure displays the following results:

Frequency Distribution for PartNo

A-123	4
B-222	2
C-333	1
D-444	1
E-555	3
F-666	2
G-777	1
H-888	2

For a hard copy of the frequency distribution, just set the printer on before entering the DO WITH command, as in the example below:

```
SET PRINT ON
DO FreqDist WITH "Date"
SET PRINT OFF
```

⊙PEARSON PRODUCT-MOMENT CORRELATION COEFFICIENT

The Pearson Product-Moment Correlation Coefficient (r) is used to determine whether there is a relationship between two sets of numbers. For example, suppose a company creating a new cola performs a taste test and wants to know whether there is a significant relationship between age and taste score (or rating). The scores and ages are listed below:

Age	Score
38	2.1
54	2.9
43	3.0
45	2.3
50	2.6
61	3.7
57	3.2
25	1.3
36	1.8
39	2.5
48	3.4
46	2.6
44	2.4
39	2.5
48	3.3

Is there a significant relationship between age and score (or rating) in these data? The Pearson r test will indicate this relationship. If the r value is 0, there is no relationship. If the r value is $+1.00$, then there is a perfect relationship (as Age increases, Score also increases evenly). An r of -1.00 indicates a perfect negative relationship (as Age increases, Score decreases evenly). Any values in between indicate the strength or weakness of the relationship. The formula for the Pearson Product-Moment Correlation Coefficient is displayed in Figure 4.6.

$$r = \frac{N \, \Sigma \, XY - (\Sigma \, X)(\Sigma \, Y)}{[N \, \Sigma \, X^2 - (\Sigma \, X)^2 \,][N \, \Sigma \, Y^2 - (\Sigma \, Y)^2 \,]}$$

where

     N = number of items used in the calculation

    Σ XY = sum of the products of the paired items

     Σ X = sum of the items on one variable

     Σ Y = sum of the items on the other variable

    Σ X^2 = sum of the squared items on the X variable

    Σ Y^2 = sum of the squared scores on the Y variable

Figure 4.6:   Formula for calculating the Pearson Product-Moment Correlation Coefficient

To add the Pearson procedure to the StatProc procedure file, close the procedure file and call up the MODIFY COMMAND editor. Move the cursor to the bottom of the procedure file, and type in the procedure shown below:

```
* * * * * * * * * * * * * * Pearson Product-Moment Correlation
PROCEDURE Pearson
PARAMETERS X,Y
   GO TOP
   * - Get N.
   COUNT TO N
   * - Sum the products and squares.
   SUM (&X * &Y),(&X ^2),&X,(&Y ^ 2),&Y TO ;
      SumProd,TotSqX,TotX,TotSqY,TotY
   SumProdXN = SumProd * N
   TotSqXxN = TotSqX * N
   TotXSq = TotX ^ 2
   TotSqYxN = TotSqY * N
   TotYSq = TotY ^ 2
   TotYxTotX = TotX * TotY
   * - Get numerator.
   RNum = SumProdXN - TotYxTotX
   * - Subtract squares.
   DifSqX = TotSqXxN - TotXsq
```

```
        DifSqY = TotSqYxN − TotYSq
        * − Multiply differences.
        DifDif = DifSqX * DifSqY
        DifRoot = SQRT(DifDif)
        * − Calculate Pearson R.
        Pearson = RNum/DifRoot
RETURN
```

Save the procedure file in the usual fashion after adding the new procedure. To fully test the procedure, use the CREATE command to create a database with the name AgeTest.DBF and the structure shown below:

```
Structure for database : C:agetest.dbf
     Field    Field name    Type        Width    Dec
       1      AGE           Numeric       2
       2      SCORE         Numeric       4        1
   ** Total **                            7
```

Then, add the following data to the database using the APPEND command:

Record#	AGE	SCORE
1	38	2.1
2	54	2.9
3	43	3.0
4	45	2.3
5	50	2.6
6	61	3.7
7	57	3.2
8	25	1.3
9	36	1.8
10	39	2.5
11	48	3.4
12	46	2.6
13	44	2.4
14	39	2.5
15	48	3.3

To use the Pearson procedure, you need to make the Pearson variable public, open the procedure file, and open the AgeTest database:

```
PUBLIC Pearson
SET PROCEDURE TO StatProc
USE AgeTest
```

The general syntax for the Pearson procedure is

    DO Pearson WITH *"Column X", "Column Y"*

where Column X and Column Y are the names of the fields in the database containing the pairs of numbers you want to analyze. For this example, type

    DO Pearson WITH "Age","Score"

The results of the calculation are stored in the Pearson variable. To see the results, enter the command

    ? Pearson

and dBASE displays

    0.8672

indicating that there is indeed a positive relationship between age and score. (Note: There are several tests of how "significant" a given Pearson r result is, and programmers who need more stringent statistical data are advised to consult a book on statistics with the appropriate formulas and tables.)

⊙SAMPLE PROGRAM

Figure 4.7 shows a program that performs some statistical analyses on the Sales.DBF database shown above. The program begins with some opening comments and basic SET commands, then makes public the statistical variable names used in the program, as shown below:

```
* * * * * * * * * * * * * * * * * * * * * * * * * * * * * * * * * * * * TestStat.PRG
* − − − − − Test some statistical procedures using the
* − − − − − Sales.DBF database.
SET TALK OFF
SET SAFE OFF

* − − −- Declare appropriate variables as public.
PUBLIC Max, Min, Var
```

The command file then opens the StatProc.PRG procedure file:

```
* — — —- Open the procedure file.
SET PROCEDURE TO StatProc
```

The program clears the screen, then opens the Sales.DBF database:

```
CLEAR
USE Sales
```

Next, the command file asks the user if he or she wants to perform the analysis on all the records in the database, or just to query the database to perform the analysis only on selected records:

```
* — — — — Ask about (A)ll or (Q)uery.
QorA = SPACE(1)
@ 10,10 SAY "(A)ll records or (Q)uery [A or Q] ";
    GET QorA PICTURE "!"
READ
```

If the user selects Query (by typing in the letter Q), the command file displays a query form named TestStat.QRY:

```
* — — — — Display query form, if requested.
IF QorA = "Q"
    MODIFY QUERY TestStat
ENDIF (QorA)
```

When the user is done filling in the query form, the command file clears the screen, then calculates and displays the highest value, lowest value, and variance of the product of the quantity (Qty) times the unit price (U_Price) fields:

```
CLEAR

* — —- Calculate highest value.
DO Max WITH "Qty * U_Price"
? "Highest Value: ",Max

* — —- Calculate lowest value.
DO Min WITH "Qty * U_Price"
? "Lowest Value: ",Min
```

```
* – –- Calculate variance.
DO Var WITH "Qty * U_Price"
? "Variance:    ",Var
```

```
****************************************** TestStat.PRG
*---------- Test some statistical procedures using the
*---------- Sales.DBF database.
SET TALK OFF
SET SAFE OFF

*------- Declare appropriate variables as public.
PUBLIC Max, Min, Var

*------- Open the procedure file.
SET PROCEDURE TO StatProc

CLEAR
USE Sales

*-------- Ask about (A)ll or (Q)uery.
QorA = SPACE(1)
@ 10,10 SAY "(A)ll records or (Q)uery [A or Q] ";
  GET QorA PICTURE "!"
READ

*-------- Display query form, if requested.
IF QorA = "Q"
   MODIFY QUERY TestStat
ENDIF (QorA)

CLEAR

*----- Calculate highest value.
DO Max WITH "Qty * U_Price"
? "Highest Value:   ",Max

*----- Calculate lowest value.
DO Min WITH "Qty * U_Price"
? "Lowest Value:   ",Min

*----- Calculate variance.
DO Var WITH "Qty * U_Price"
? "Variance:        ",Var

*------------ Release filter condition.
SET FILTER TO

*------------ Do frequency distribution.
DO FreqDist WITH "PartNo"

*----- Done with program.
CLOSE DATABASES
CLOSE PROCEDURE
```

Figure 4.7: The TestStat.PRG command file

Before continuing, the command file removes the filter condition created by the query form:

```
* — — — — — Release filter condition.
SET FILTER TO
```

Then the command file displays the frequency distribution of part numbers (the PartNo field) for the Sales database:

```
* — — — — — Do frequency distribution.
DO FreqDist WITH "PartNo"
```

When done, the program closes the database and the procedure file, then returns to the dot prompt:

```
* — —- Done with program.
CLOSE DATABASES
CLOSE PROCEDURE
```

Figure 4.8 shows a sample query form filled out to calculate statistics on records with part number A-123 only. Figure 4.9 shows the results of the calculations on the screen after running the TestStat.PRG command file, and filling in the query form.

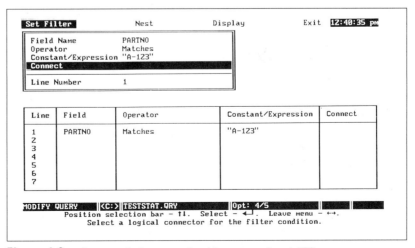

Figure 4.8: Query to isolate records with part number A-123

```
Highest Value:        11110.00
Lowest Value:           550.00
Variance:          -27614438.50

Frequency distribution for PartNo

A-123        4
B-222        2
C-333        1
D-444        1
E-555        3
F-666        2
G-777        1
H-888        2




  . _
```

Figure 4.9:   Statistics on part number A-123 in Sales.DBF

⊙GENERAL TECHNIQUES FOR USING STATISTICAL PROCEDURES

Keep in mind that the statistical procedures work only on numeric fields. Of course, you can also perform statistics on calculations of numeric fields, as in the example above where we used the product of the quantity and unit price fields ("Qty*U_Price") for the analysis. As with the financial procedures, you can use MODIFY QUERY to filter the database before performing calculations.

dBASE III PLUS GRAPHICS

5

Even though dBASE III PLUS is hardly a full-blown graphics package, there is a great deal you can do to control and enhance screen displays. In this chapter, we'll develop programs and procedures that help manage screen displays. We'll also develop a program that is capable of displaying dBASE data in bar-graph form on both the screen and printer.

⊙VIEWING THE ASCII TABLE

To gain full control over the graphics characters on your particular screen and printer, you need an ASCII table that contains the numerical codes for all 256 characters that most screens and dot-matrix printers can display. The first program we'll develop in this chapter, named ASCII.PRG, creates such a table. We will not put this program in a procedure file, because it is not the type of program that you are likely to use often. However, like any command file, ASCII.PRG can easily be placed inside a procedure file.

The entire ASCII.PRG command file is shown in Figure 5.1. Let's briefly discuss how it works.

The program begins with the usual opening comments, and the SET TALK OFF and CLEAR commands, and then it initializes the variables Row and Counter:

```
* * * * * * * * * * * * * * * * * * * * * * * * * * * * * * * * * * * * * * * * ASCII.PRG
*--------------------- Display ASCII characters.
SET TALK OFF
CLEAR
Row = 1
Counter = 0
```

Next, a DO WHILE loop is set up to repeat 256 times (since there are 256 ASCII characters). Within this loop, the variable Col is set to 0:

```
*--- Set up loop for 256 characters.
DO WHILE Counter < 256
   Col = 0
```

An inner loop is then set up for printing characters across a single row on the screen or printer. Within this loop, an @ SAY command prints the value of the Counter variable, as well as the ASCII character associated with the number stored in Counter (CHR(Counter)). The Col (column) variable is incremented by 6 so that the cursor skips to the next column each

```
********************************** ASCII.PRG
*------------------- Display ASCII characters.
SET TALK OFF
CLEAR
Row = 1
Counter = 0
*--- Set up loop for 256 characters.
DO WHILE Counter < 256
   Col = 0
   *--- Set up loop for individual rows.
   DO WHILE Col <= 72 .AND. Counter < 256
      @ Row,Col SAY STR(Counter,3)+" "+CHR(Counter)
      Col = Col + 6
      Counter = Counter + 1
   ENDDO (col and counter)
   Row = Row + 1
ENDDO (counter < 256)
RETURN
```

Figure 5.1:   The ASCII.PRG command file

time through the loop, and the Counter variable is incremented by 1 to go
to the next ASCII character:

```
* –- Set up loop for individual rows.
DO WHILE Col < 72 .AND. Counter < 256
   @ Row,Col SAY STR(Counter,3 + " " + CHR(Counter)
   Col = Col + 6
   Counter = Counter + 1
ENDDO (col and counter)
```

At the end of this DO WHILE loop, the command file prepares to print the
next row of data by adding 1 to the Row variable and closing the outermost loop. When the Counter variable has reached 256, the outermost loop
is finished and the program is done:

```
   Row = Row + 1
ENDDO (counter < 256)
RETURN
```

To run the ASCII program, just enter the DO ASCII command at the
dBASE dot prompt. To see the ASCII characters used by your printer, enter
the following commands:

```
SET DEVICE TO PRINT
DO ASCII
SET DEVICE TO SCREEN
```

The SET DEVICE TO PRINT command channels the @ SAY commands to the printer. Be forewarned that ASCII codes 12 and 140 will probably cause the printer to eject a page, so the printer version of the table might be spread out a bit. Also, some of the codes might set your printer off line. If that occurs, just press the on-line button on your printer to continue printing.

Figure 5.2 shows a part of the ASCII table on the screen, generated by ASCII.PRG. Be sure to try out the ASCII program on your own screen and printer, because the graphics characters in the range of 0–31 and 128–256 might vary with different screens and printers.

```
  0       1 ☺   2 ☻   3 ♥   4 ♦   5 ♣   6 ♠   7 •   8 ◘   9 ○  10 ◙  11 ♂  12 ♀
 13 ♪    14 ♫  15 ☼  16 ►  17 ◄  18 ↕  19 ‼  20 ¶  21 §  22 ▬  23 ↨  24 ↑  25 ↓
 26 →    27 ←  28 ∟  29 ↔  30 ▲  31 ▼  32    33 !  34 "  35 #  36 $  37 %  38 &
 39 '    40 (  41 )  42 *  43 +  44 ,  45 -  46 .  47 /  48 0  49 1  50 2  51 3
 52 4    53 5  54 6  55 7  56 8  57 9  58 :  59 ;  60 <  61 =  62 >  63 ?  64 @
 65 A    66 B  67 C  68 D  69 E  70 F  71 G  72 H  73 I  74 J  75 K  76 L  77 M
 78 N    79 O  80 P  81 Q  82 R  83 S  84 T  85 U  86 V  87 W  88 X  89 Y  90 Z
 91 [    92 \  93 ]  94 ^  95 _  96 `  97 a  98 b  99 c 100 d 101 e 102 f 103 g
104 h   105 i 106 j 107 k 108 l 109 m 110 n 111 o 112 p 113 q 114 r 115 s 116 t
117 u   118 v 119 w 120 x 121 y 122 z 123 { 124 ¦ 125 } 126 ~ 127 ⌂ 128 Ç 129 ü
130 é   131 â 132 ä 133 à 134 å 135 ç 136 ê 137 ë 138 è 139 ï 140 î 141 ì 142 Ä
143 Å   144 É 145 æ 146 Æ 147 ô 148 ö 149 ò 150 û 151 ù 152 ÿ 153 Ö 154 Ü 155 ¢
156 £   157 ¥ 158 ₧ 159 ƒ 160 á 161 í 162 ó 163 ú 164 ñ 165 Ñ 166 ª 167 º 168 ¿
169 ⌐   170 ¬ 171 ½ 172 ¼ 173 ¡ 174 « 175 » 176 ░ 177 ▒ 178 ▓ 179 │ 180 ┤ 181 ╡
182 ╢   183 ╖ 184 ╕ 185 ╣ 186 ║ 187 ╗ 188 ╝ 189 ╜ 190 ╛ 191 ┐ 192 └ 193 ┴ 194 ┬
195 ├   196 ─ 197 ┼ 198 ╞ 199 ╟ 200 ╚ 201 ╔ 202 ╩ 203 ╦ 204 ╠ 205 ═ 206 ╬ 207 ╧
208 ╨   209 ╤ 210 ╥ 211 ╙ 212 ╘ 213 ╒ 214 ╓ 215 ╫ 216 ╪ 217 ┘ 218 ┌ 219 █ 220 ▄
221 ▌   222 ▐ 223 ▀ 224 α 225 ß 226 Γ 227 π 228 Σ 229 σ 230 µ 231 τ 232 Φ 233 Θ
234 Ω   235 δ 236 ∞ 237 φ 238 ε 239 ∩ 240 ≡ 241 ± 242 ≥ 243 ≤ 244 ⌠ 245 ⌡ 246 ÷
247 ≈   248 ° 249 ∙ 250 · 251 √ 252 ⁿ 253 ² 254 ■ 255

. _
```

Figure 5.2: ASCII table displayed on the screen

If you wish to use a particular character on your screen or printer, just use the dBASE CHR function with the appropriate number in parentheses. For example, if your ASCII table shows ASCII character 2 as a happy face, type

```
? CHR(2)
```

to display the happy face. We'll discuss other techniques for displaying ASCII graphics characters throughout the chapter.

⊙VIEWING COLORS

For those of you with color monitors or monochrome monitors with special attributes, the Color.PRG command file developed next allows you to view codes that can be used with the SET COLOR command to control screen displays. Table 5.1 shows the letters used with the SET COLOR command and color monitors. (Yellow, though not on the table, is GR+, or "high-intensity brown.")

Table 5.2 shows the special attributes used on most monochrome displays. You may need to experiment a bit to find the codes for your particular screen. Check your monitor manual for codes if necessary.

The Color.PRG command file that visually displays the effects of the various codes is shown in Figure 5.3. This program uses the same basic looping technique as the ASCII program. However, three separate routines are used: one to show the basic codes, one to show the high-intensity effect of adding a plus sign (+) to the "foreground" code, and a third to demonstrate the blinking effect of the asterisk (*) code. Figure 5.4 shows roughly the output (in black and white, of course) of the Color.PRG command file.

Color	Letter Code
Black	N
Blue	B
Green	G
Cyan	BG
Red	R
Magenta	BR
Yellow	GR
White	W

Adding a plus sign (+) creates high intensity
Adding an asterisk (*) produces blinking

Table 5.1: Codes used on color monitors

Attribute	Letter Code
Underline	U
Reverse	I

Adding an asterisk (*) produces blinking

Table 5.2: Codes used on monochrome monitors

```
****************************************** COLOR.PRG
*----- Display colors & blinking for color screen.
CLEAR
SET TALK OFF

*---------- Set letters for dBASE III PLUS colors.
X0 = "N"      && Black
X1 = "B"      && Blue
X2 = "G"      && Green
X3 = "BG"     && Cyan
X4 = "R"      && Red
X5 = "RB"     && Magenta
X6 = "GR"     && Brown
X7 = "W"      && White

*-------------------- Display standard foreground.
OutLoop = 0
DO WHILE OutLoop <= 7
   InLoop = 0
   DO WHILE InLoop <= 7
      Letters = "X"+STR(OutLoop,1)
      BGround = "X"+Str(InLoop,1)
      JJ = &Letters + "/" + &BGround
      SET COLOR TO &JJ
      ?? "  "+JJ+ "  "
      InLoop = InLoop + 1
   ENDDO
   OutLoop = OutLoop + 1
ENDDO

*--------------- Display enhanced foreground (+).
OutLoop = 0
DO WHILE OutLoop <= 7
   InLoop = 0
   DO WHILE InLoop <= 7
      Letters = "X"+STR(OutLoop,1)
      BGround = "X"+Str(InLoop,1)
      JJ = &Letters + "+/" + &BGround
      SET COLOR TO &JJ
      ?? "  "+JJ+ "  "
      InLoop = InLoop + 1
   ENDDO
   OutLoop = OutLoop + 1
ENDDO

*--------------- Display blinking foreground (*).
OutLoop = 0
DO WHILE OutLoop <= 7
   InLoop = 0
   DO WHILE InLoop <= 7
      Letters = "X"+STR(OutLoop,1)
      BGround = "X"+Str(InLoop,1)
      JJ = &Letters + "*/" + &BGround
      SET COLOR TO &JJ
      ?? "  "+JJ+ "  "
      InLoop = InLoop + 1
   ENDDO
   OutLoop = OutLoop + 1
ENDDO
```

Figure 5.3:   The Color.PRG command file

```
*------ Pause before ending program.
SET COLOR TO GR+/B,N/BG,G
WAIT "Press any key when done viewing..."
```

Figure 5.3: The Color.PRG command file (continued)

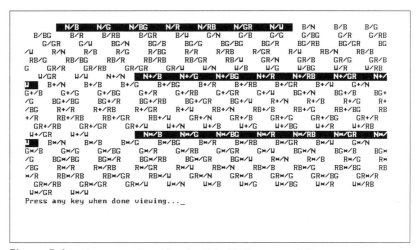

Figure 5.4: Screen produced by the Color.PRG command file

After entering and saving the command file, just enter the DO Color command to view the codes and the colors or attributes assigned to each. These codes are used with the SET COLOR command in dBASE to control screen displays.

The basic syntax for the SET COLOR command is

SET COLOR TO *Regular Screen Codes, Reverse Codes, Border*

where Regular Screen Codes are foreground/background codes for normal displays, Reverse Codes are foreground/background codes for enhanced displays (such as data being entered through APPEND or EDIT), and Border is the screen border.

For example, suppose you want your color screen to display bright yellow letters on a blue background (GR + /B), bright cyan letters on a red background for reverse characters (BG + /R), and a cyan border (BG). To set up such a display, you would enter the following command:

SET COLOR TO GR + /B, BG + /R, BG

(The Color.PRG command file ends by setting up just such a color scheme.)

To automatically install this color scheme each time you run dBASE III PLUS, enter the command

COLOR = GR + /B,BG + /R,BG

into your Config.DB file.

We'll see a couple of other tricks for using the SET COLOR command later in this chapter.

One interesting feature the Color.PRG command file uses is an *array*. The array consists of eight *elements* (numbered, or "indexed," 0 to 7), each element representing one color code (e.g., N, B, G, BG, and so forth). The variables that these color codes are stored in are *subscripted*. That is, B is stored in X1 (pronounced "X sub one"), and RB is stored in X5 ("X sub five"). The words following the && signs are merely programmer comments (like lines that start with the asterisk sign). The part of the program that sets up the array of color codes is shown below:

```
* – – – – –   Set letters for dBASE III PLUS colors.
X0 = "N"    && Black
X1 = "B"    && Blue
X2 = "G"    && Green
X3 = "BG"   && Cyan
X4 = "R"    && Red
X5 = "RB"   && Magenta
X6 = "GR"   && Brown
X7 = "W"    && White
```

Within the command file, DO WHILE loops increment the numeric variables named OutLoop and InLoop. These numeric variables are then converted to character strings using the STR function, and linked to the X variable name, which is then used in the SET COLOR command. Hence, when the value of the OutLoop variable is 2, and the value of the InLoop variable is 4, the command line

Letters = "X" + STR(OutLoop,1)

stores the string X2 in a variable named Letters. Then the command line

BGround = "X" + Str(InLoop,1)

stores the characters X4 in the variable named BGround.

The next line uses macro substitution to fill in the appropriate color codes. Since dBASE always converts macros to their stored values before processing a line, the line

JJ = &Letters + "/" + &BGround

becomes

JJ = X1 + "/" + X4

On the second pass through the line, dBASE assumes that X1 and X4 are variable names, and uses the contents of those variables in calculating the expression. Hence, the result of the expression is that the variable JJ now contains the contents of variable X1, followed by a slash, followed by the contents of variable X4. Or in other words, the variable JJ contains

B/R

The next line in the command file

SET COLOR TO &JJ

uses the variable JJ as a macro, and hence dBASE first converts the line to

SET COLOR TO B/R

then dBASE executes the line, changing the screen color to blue letters on a red background.

By using an array of color codes in this program, we were able to access each of the codes with a DO WHILE loop and numbers. Obviously, you can't have a command such as

DO WHILE Counter >= "B" .AND. Counter <= "W"

to access each color code from a loop. However, by storing the color codes in subscripted variables (X0 through X7), you can access the color codes as though they were numbers. We'll see additional uses of arrays in the BarGraph procedure file later in this chapter, and elsewhere throughout the book.

⊙A GRAPHICS PROCEDURE FILE

In this section we'll develop a procedure file made up of procedures to aid in developing fancy screen displays. This procedure file is called Graphics.PRG and is shown in its entirety in Figure 5.5. Create it with the MODIFY COMMAND editor, as we did with all the others in previous chapters. We'll discuss each procedure individually below and develop a couple of programs to test them out.

SPECIAL CODES AND SPECIAL SYMBOLS

The first procedure in the Graphics.PRG file is named KeySigns. Its job is to assign names to public variables that can be used to display special characters, such as arrow keys, and special effects, such as blinking and reverse video. The KeySigns procedure and the opening lines for the Graphics.PRG procedure file are shown below:

```
* * * * * * * * * * * * * * * * * * * * * * * * * * * * * * * * * * * * * * * Graphics.PRG
*---------- Procedures to aid in screen displays.

*-------- Set up symbols and colors in variables.
PROCEDURE KeySigns
    PUBLIC Ret, Left, Right, Up, Down, Bullet, ;
    Solid, Degrees, Reverse, Blink, Standard
    Ret = CHR(17) + CHR(196) + CHR(217)
    Left = CHR(27)
    Right = CHR(26)
    Up = CHR(24)
    Down = CHR(25)
    Bullet = CHR(249)
    Solid = CHR(219)
    Degrees = CHR(248)
    * – – Set Color macros
    Standard = "GR + /B,W + /R,BG"
    Reverse = "B/G"
    Blink = "G/R + */B"
RETURN
```

Note that the procedure begins by declaring the variables Ret, Left, Right, Up, Down, Bullet, Solid, Degrees, Reverse, Blink, and Standard as public. Then, it assigns special ASCII characters to these variables. For example, the ASCII code for a left-arrow character is assigned to the variable Left. (Note: These codes may vary; use the ASCII.PRG program to look up codes for your particular screen.)

```
*********************************** Graphics.PRG
*---------- Procedures to aid in screen displays.

*-------- Set up symbols and colors in variables.
PROCEDURE KeySigns
  PUBLIC Ret, Left, Right, Up, Down, Bullet, ;
  Solid, Degrees, Reverse, Blink, Standard
  Ret = CHR(17)+CHR(196)+CHR(217)
  Left = CHR(27)
  Right = CHR(26)
  Up = CHR(24)
  Down = CHR(25)
  Bullet = CHR(249)
  Solid = CHR(219)
  Degrees = CHR(248)
  *---- Set Color macros.
  Standard = "GR+/B,W+/R,BG"
  Reverse = "B/G"
  Blink = "GR+*/B"
RETURN

*---------------- Draw a bar of ASCII characters.
PROCEDURE Bar
PARAMETERS Char,Number
  Row = ROW()
  Col = COL()
  Target = COL()+Number
  DO WHILE Col <= Target .AND. Col < 80
     @ Row,Col SAY CHR(Char)
     Col=Col+1
  ENDDO
RETURN

*------------- Draw a column of ASCII characters.
PROCEDURE Column
PARAMETERS Char,Number
  Row = ROW()
  Col = COL()
  Target = Row() + Number
  DO WHILE Row <= Target .AND. Row < 24
     @ Row,Col SAY CHR(Char)
     Row=Row+1
  ENDDO
RETURN

*---------- Center procedure centers any string.
PROCEDURE Center
PARAMETERS Title,RM
  Pad = SPACE((RM/2)-(LEN(TRIM(Title))/2))
  ? Pad + TRIM(Title)
RETURN
```

Figure 5.5: The Graphics.PRG procedure file

In addition, the variables Standard, Reverse, and Blink are assigned codes to be used in conjunction with the SET COLOR command.

Before we test this procedure, let's discuss the other procedures in the procedure file.

DRAWING BARS AND COLUMNS

The Bar and Column procedures, shown below, are useful for drawing boxes built from special characters on the screen:

```
*--------------- Draw a bar of ASCII characters.
PROCEDURE Bar
PARAMETERS Char,Number
   Row = ROW( )
   Col = COL( )
   Target = COL( )+Number
   DO WHILE Col < = Target .AND. Col < 80
      @ Row,Col SAY CHR(Char)
      Col = Col + 1
   ENDDO
RETURN

*------------- Draw a column of ASCII characters.
PROCEDURE Column
PARAMETERS Char,Number
   Row = ROW( )
   Col = COL( )
   Target = Row( ) + Number
   DO WHILE Row < = Target .AND. Row < 24
      @ Row,Col SAY CHR(Char)
      Row = Row + 1
   ENDDO
RETURN
```

Each procedure uses two parameters, with the following syntax:

DO *Procedure* WITH *ASCII Code, Length*

For example, if you want to draw a (horizontal) bar of solid characters (ASCII code 219) 60 characters long, enter the following command:

DO Bar WITH 219,60

To print a column of happy faces (ASCII character 2) that is 20 rows long, enter the command

```
DO Column WITH 2,20
```

The bar or column will be drawn starting at the current cursor position. Therefore the commands

```
@10,2
DO Column WITH 2,20
```

begin drawing the column at row 10, column 2. We'll test these out momentarily. Let's now take a look at the last procedure in the file, used to center text on the screen.

AUTOMATIC CENTERING

The Center procedure automatically centers a string of characters on the screen or printer. Unlike the Center procedure we developed earlier, this one immediately displays the centered string rather than returning it as a public variable. The Center procedure is shown below:

```
*----------- Center procedure centers any string.
PROCEDURE Center
PARAMETERS Title,RM
   Pad = SPACE((RM/2) – (LEN(TRIM(Title))/2))
   ? Pad + TRIM(Title)
RETURN
```

The procedure expects two parameters, Title (the string to be centered), and RM (right margin). For example, to center the words "Hello There" on an 80-column screen, type

```
DO Center WITH "Hello There",80
```

⊙USING THE GRAPHICS PROCEDURES

Once you've created the entire Graphics.PRG procedure file, save it in the usual fashion. To open the procedure file, simply type

```
SET PROCEDURE TO Graphics
```

at the dot prompt. Then, as usual, type

SET TALK OFF

to keep the extraneous messages away.
    To test the KeySigns procedure, type

DO KeySigns

You won't see anything happen before the dot prompt reappears. However,
if you type

DISPLAY MEMORY

to view memory variables, you'll see that you have some new variables to
work with. You can use the ? command to display most of these. For
example, to see a left-arrow, type

? Left

You can use the symbols as macros embedded in other character strings.
For example, try entering the commands below to see the Ret (Return)
symbol displayed:

CLEAR
@ 12,5 SAY "This symbol: &Ret is the Return key"

The symbols used for Standard, Blinking, and Reverse must always be
used as macros with the SET COLOR command. For example, try entering
the following commands:

SET COLOR TO &Blink
SET COLOR TO &Reverse
SET COLOR TO &Standard

THE KEYEXAMP.PRG FILE

    KeyExamp.PRG, shown in Figure 5.6, demonstrates the use of these pro-
cedures from within a command file.
    The command file begins with the usual opening comments, the SET
TALK command, and a command that opens the Graphics procedure file.

```
******************************** KeyExamp.PRG
*-------------- Demonstrate use of graphics procedures.
SET TALK OFF
SET PROCEDURE TO Graphics
DO KeySigns

SET COLOR TO &Standard
CLEAR
*---- Show Ret and arrow keys.
? "Arrow keys: &Up  &Down  &Left  &Right "
?
ACCEPT "Press &Ret to continue..." TO Nothing

*----- Draw bar across screen.
@ 10,0
DO BAR WITH 219,79

*-------------- Show blinking.
@ 12,35
SET COLOR TO &Blink
@ 12,35 SAY "Blinking"
SET COLOR TO &Standard

*-------------- Show reverse.
@ 14,35
SET COLOR TO &Reverse
@ 14,35 SAY " Reverse"
SET COLOR TO &Standard

*--------------- Center string with bullet and degrees.
@ 19,0
DO Center WITH ;
Bullet+" Your temperature is 98.6&Degrees Fahrenheit",80
@ 23,0

CLOSE PROCEDURE
RETURN
```

Figure 5.6: The KeyExamp.PRG command file

The DO KeySigns command runs the KeySigns procedure and sets up the variables to display special characters and SET COLOR codes. These opening lines are shown below:

```
******************************************* KeyExamp.PRG
*-------------- Demonstrate use of graphics procedures.
SET TALK OFF
SET PROCEDURE TO Graphics
DO KeySigns
```

The first routine sets the screen color, defined as Standard in the Key-Signs procedure file, and clears the screen:

```
SET COLOR TO &Standard
CLEAR
```

The next lines demonstrate the use of the Left, Right, Up, Down, and Ret variables. Note that the Ret variable is embedded within an ACCEPT string:

```
*---- Show Ret and arrow keys.
? "Arrow keys: &Up &Down &Left &Right"
?
ACCEPT "Press &Ret to continue. . ." TO Nothing
```

The next command draws a solid bar (ASCII character 219) across the tenth line on the screen (79 characters), using the Bar procedure:

```
*----- Draw bar across screen.
@ 10,0
DO BAR WITH 219,79
```

The next routine moves the cursor to row 12, column 35, and sets blinking on. The word *Blinking* is displayed at row 12, column 35 (and should be blinking on most screens), then the color is set back to Standard, so that the words after *Blinking* do not blink.

```
*-------------- Show blinking.
@ 12,35
SET COLOR TO &Blink
@ 12,35 SAY "Blinking"
SET COLOR TO &Standard
```

The next routine shows the use of the reverse-video mode, using a procedure identical to that used for blinking:

```
*-------------- Show reverse.
@ 14,35
SET COLOR TO &Reverse
@ 14,35 SAY " Reverse"
SET COLOR TO &Standard
```

The last routine moves the cursor to row 19, and centers a sentence that begins with the bullet character and contains the degrees symbol. The sentence is centered on an 80-column-wide screen:

```
*--------------- Center string with bullet and degrees.
@ 19,0
DO Center WITH ;
Bullet + " Your temperature is 98.6&Degrees Fahrenheit",80
@ 23,0

CLOSE PROCEDURE
RETURN
```

Figure 5.7 shows the output from the KeyExamp command file. Again, the specific ASCII codes used for special symbols may be different on your screen.

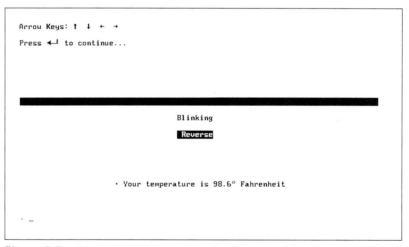

Figure 5.7:   Display from the KeyExamp.PRG command file

⊙ BOXES AND LINES

The Bar and Column procedures in the Graphics.PRG procedure file are somewhat slow, and can be replaced with the dBASE @...TO... command if all you want are single- or double-line boxes or lines. The basic syntax for these commands is

@ *Start Row,Start Column* TO *End Row,End Column*

followed by the word DOUBLE for double lines. For example, if you enter the command

@ 5,10 TO 19,70

directly at the dot prompt, dBASE will quickly draw a single-line box from row 5, column 10 to row 19, column 70. If you enter the command

@ 5,10 TO 19,70 DOUBLE

at the dot prompt, dBASE will draw a double-line box in the same area.

The @...TO commands can be used to draw lines and boxes on custom screen displays (.FMT files). They can also be used in command files to create a *splash screen* for a custom application. (A splash screen is any screen containing fancy graphics that appears when a software product is first run.) Figure 5.8 shows a sample program, named Splash.PRG, that displays such a splash screen.

The first routine in the program, shown below, checks to see if the program is being run on a color monitor (using the dBASE III PLUS IS-COLOR() function), and if so, sets up the screen for yellow letters on a blue background (GR + /B), black letters on cyan for reverse video, and a red border:

```
* – – – Set colors, if color screen in use.
IF ISCOLOR()
   SET COLOR TO GR + /B,N/BG,R
ENDIF (is color)
CLEAR
```

The next routine initializes the starting row and column positions for the first box to be drawn:

```
* – – – Initialize row and column positions.
Top = 1
Left = 1
Bottom = 23
Right = 79
```

The next routine uses a DO WHILE loop to draw a series of double-line boxes, one inside the other. By incrementally increasing the row number from the top and the column number from the left, and simultaneously

```
******************************* SPLASH.PRG
SET TALK OFF

*------ Set colors, if color screen in use.
IF ISCOLOR()
   SET COLOR TO GR+/B,N/BG,R
ENDIF (is color)
CLEAR

*------ Initialize row and column positions.
Top = 1
Left = 1
Bottom = 23
Right = 79

*----------- Draw double-line boxes inward.
DO WHILE Top < 12
   @ Top,Left TO Bottom,Right DOUBLE
   Top = Top + 1
   Bottom = Bottom - 1
   Left = Left + 2
   Right = Right - 2
ENDDO (top < 12)

*---------- Reset row and column positions.
Top = 11
Left = 21
Bottom = 13
Right = 59

*------ Reset colors, if color screen in use.
IF ISCOLOR()
   SET COLOR TO GR+/R,N/BG,B
ENDIF (is color)

*---------- Draw single-line boxes outward.
DO WHILE Top > 0
   @ Top,Left TO Bottom,Right
   Top = Top - 1
   Bottom = Bottom + 1
   Left = Left - 2
   Right = Right + 2
ENDDO (top > 0)

* Display centered message in reverse video.
Msg = "SPLASHY SCREEN FOR A SOFTWARE PACKAGE"
@ 12,22 GET Msg
CLEAR GETS

*- Perform a meaningless loop to take up time.
Counter = 1
DO WHILE Counter < 200
```

Figure 5.8:   The Splash.PRG command file

message in reverse video in the center of the boxes. The CLEAR GETS command then disconnects the displayed Msg message from READ access:

```
* — — — — — Draw double-line boxes inward.
DO WHILE Top < 12
   @ Top,Left TO Bottom,Right DOUBLE
   Top = Top + 1
   Bottom = Bottom − 1
   Left = Left + 2
   Right = Right − 2
ENDDO (top < 12)
```

Next, the program resets the column and row positions to start drawing a series of boxes from the inside out:

```
* — — — — — Reset row and column positions.
Top = 11
Left = 21
Bottom = 13
Right = 59
```

The next routine sets the screen colors to yellow on red with black letters on a cyan background for reverse video, and a blue border, assuming that a color monitor is in use:

```
* — — — Reset colors, if color screen in use.
IF ISCOLOR()
   SET COLOR TO GR + /R,N/BG,B
ENDIF (is color)
```

The second DO WHILE loop, shown below, draws a series of increasingly larger single-line boxes by decrementing the top-row and left-column numbers, and incrementing the bottom-row and right-column numbers:

```
* — — — — — Draw single-line boxes outward.
DO WHILE Top > 0
   @ Top,Left TO Bottom,Right
   Top = Top − 1
   Bottom = Bottom + 1
   Left = Left − 2
   Right = Right + 2
ENDDO (top > 0)
```

The routine below stores the text *SPLASHY SCREEN FOR A SOFTWARE PACKAGE* in a variable named Msg. A GET command displays this sage in reverse video in the center of the boxes. The CLEAR GETS command then disconnects the displayed Msg message from READ access:

```
* Display centered message in reverse video.
Msg = "SPLASHY SCREEN FOR A SOFTWARE PACKAGE"
@ 12,22 GET Msg
CLEAR GETS
```

The final routine in the command file counts to 200 simply to take up time. (For a longer pause, use a number greater than 200, and vice versa for a shorter pause.) In an actual application, you'll probably want to put a DO command and the name of the main menu program beneath this DO WHILE loop:

```
*- Perform a meaningless loop to take up time.
Counter = 1
DO WHILE Counter < 200
Counter = Counter + 1
ENDDO

* –- At this point, programmer can
* –- branch to main menu.
```

Figure 5.9 shows the splash screen after the second set of boxes has been drawn, and the message displayed in the center. To fully appreciate the activity of the program, however, you should key it in and run it.

Figure 5.9: The splash screen drawn by the Splash.PRG command file

⊙A BAR GRAPH ROUTINE

The next program we'll develop in this chapter displays data on a bar graph. The program can comfortably display up to about 12 columns of data on an 80-column-wide screen, though there is a higher limit to the number of columns that can be displayed on a printer with wide paper or in compressed-print mode.

To use the bar-graph routine, you must first assign data to memory variables for plotting. These data can be calculated directly from data in a database, as we'll see in a later example. Number values to be plotted must be stored in variables named Col1, Col2, Col3, and so on. Titles at the bottom of each bar must be assigned as character data to variables named Title1, Title2, Title3, and so on. The commands below show an example:

```
Col1 = 20
Title1 = "1985"
Col2 = 55
Title2 = "1986"
Col3 = 67.54
Title3 = "1987"
Col4 = 100
Title4 = "1988"
```

Once these variables are assigned values, you can call the bar-graph routine using the following general syntax:

DO BarGraph WITH *Graph Title, Number of Columns,;*
    Column Width, Lowest Y-Axis Value,;
    Highest Y-Axis Value

For example, the command below places the title "Sample Graph" over the bar graph and plots 4 columns, each 15 characters wide, with 0 as the lowest y-axis value, and 100 as the highest y-axis value:

DO BarGraph WITH "Sample Graph",4,15,0,100

If you want to assign colors to the bar graph, just use the SET COLOR command before the DO BarGraph command. For example, the lines below set the screen colors to white characters on a red background with a blue border, if a color monitor is in use, before drawing the bar graph:

```
IF ISCOLOR()
    SET COLOR TO W+/R,N/BG,B
ENDIF (is a color monitor)
```

DO BarGraph WITH "Sample Graph",4,15,0,100

Figure 5.10 shows the entire bar-graph procedure. Since it is a fairly large procedure, I have not included it with the procedures in Graphics-.PRG. (If you are using the dBASE MODIFY COMMAND editor, the Bar-Graph procedure will not fit in with the other procedures. If you are using some other text editor, however, you can combine the bar-graph procedure with others.)

If you just want to use the BarGraph procedure, and are not terribly concerned about all the technical details of how it works, you can key it in (or purchase it and all the other programs in this book using the coupon on the last page), and skip to the section "Plotting the Bar Graph" in this chapter. If you are curious about the internal workings of the BarGraph procedure, do read on.

The parameters that are passed directly to BarGraph.PRG are listed below:

Title	Graph title, centered over the graph
No_Col	Number of columns to display in the graph
Col_Width	Width of each bar in the graph
Lr	Lowest value on y-axis
Hr	Highest value on y-axis

These are listed in the PARAMETERS statement in the procedure, as shown below:

PARAMETERS Title,No_Col,Col_Width,Lr,Hr

The next lines in the procedure set the TALK off, turn off the status bar at the bottom of the screen, clear the screen, then display the message *Working...*:

```
SET TALK OFF
SET STATUS OFF
CLEAR
? "Working..."
```

To understand the rest of the procedure, you must remember that numeric data to be plotted are stored in variables named Col1, Col2, Col3, and so forth. Titles to be displayed at the bottom of the screen are stored in the variables Title1, Title2, Title3, and so on, before the procedure is run. As discussed earlier in this chapter, this sets up the data in an array of subscripted variables, which in turn allows the procedure to manipulate each item independently with each pass through a DO WHILE loop.

The first loop in the BarGraph program creates a variable named BLine (for Bottom Line), which consists of all the titles for the bottom line of the graph (Title1, Title2, and so forth). To ensure proper spacing, each title is either trimmed or padded to the width of each bar. The routine begins by setting the variable Counter (used in the DO WHILE loop) to 1, and by setting a variable named TWidth (for Title Width) equal to the width of each column (Col_Width) minus 2. Two spaces are subtracted from the actual column width to put space between the titles. Then the BLine variable is initialized as six blank spaces. (The blank spaces are to the left of the y-axis line on the printed graph):

```
* – – – – – – – – – Pad titles and create bottom line.
Counter = 1
TWidth = Col_Width – 2
BLine = SPACE(6)
```

Next, a DO WHILE loop repeats for as many times as there are columns (bars) in the graph, using the No_Col parameter to determine the number of loops to perform:

```
DO WHILE Counter < = No_Col
```

The first line within the DO WHILE loop stores the string equivalent of the Counter variable, with any leading blanks trimmed off, in a variable named Sub, as shown below:

```
Sub = LTRIM(STR(Counter,2))
```

The Sub variable is then used as a subscript in the Title variable name. (Hence, the first pass through the loop operates on Title1, the second pass operates on Title2, and so forth.) Each title is first trimmed to the number of characters specified in the TWidth variable, using the expression

```
SUBSTR(Title&Sub, 1, TWidth)
```

and then padded, if necessary, with enough blanks to make it the length specified in the TWidth variable:

```
+ SPACE(TWidth – LEN(Title&Sub))
```

The title is then the proper width, and is hence added to the BLine variable followed by two spaces, using the expression

BLine = BLine + Title&Sub + SPACE(2)

The Counter variable is incremented by 1 to format the next title and add it to the BLine variable:

```
    Title&Sub = SUBSTR(Title&Sub,1,TWidth) + ;
    SPACE(TWidth – LEN(Title&Sub))
    BLine = BLine + Title&Sub + SPACE(2)
    Counter = Counter + 1
ENDDO (counter)
```

The next line in the command file (split into two lines to fit in the book) pads the graph Title so that it will be centered when printed. It calculates the number of spaces to pad the front of the title using the same calculation used with a manual typewriter. However, five additional spaces are allotted in the left column because the y-axis is offset from the left of the screen about five spaces:

```
* – – – – – – Pad title for centering.
Title = SPACE((((Col_Width*No_Col) + 5)/2) – ;
    (LEN(TRIM(Title))/2)) + Title
```

Next the procedure begins drawing the graph on the screen. First, it assigns graphics characters to the variables XChar (character used to draw the x-axis), YChar (character used for the y-axis) and Bar (character used to draw bars). The graphics characters assigned below are good for the IBM Color Display monitor. You may need to experiment a little to find the proper graphics characters for your screen (use the ASCII.PRG command file discussed earlier in this chapter to view all your monitor's graphics characters):

```
* * * * * * * * * * * * * * * * * * * * * * * * * * * * * * * * * * * * * * * * * * * * * * * * * * * * *
* Display graph on screen                                        *
* * * * * * * * * * * * * * * * * * * * * * * * * * * * * * * * * * * * * * * * * * * * * * * * * * * * *

* – – – – Assign graphics characters for screen.
XChar = CHR(196)
YChar = CHR(179)
BChar = CHR(219)
```

```
******************************** BarGraph.PRG
* Procedure to plot data on bar graph.  Data to be
* plotted must be assigned in calling program using
* variable names Col1, Col2, Col3....ColN.  X-axis
* titles must also be assigned using variable names
* Title1, Title2, Title3...TitleN.
*-------------------------------------------------
* Passed parameters are:
* Title     : Title to appear at top of graph
* No_Col    : Number of columns in graph
* Col_Width : Width of each bar in graph
* Lr        : Lowest x-axis value
* Hr        : Highest x-axis value

PARAMETERS Title,No_Col,Col_Width,Lr,Hr
SET TALK OFF
SET STATUS OFF
CLEAR
? "Working..."

*------------------ Pad titles and create bottom line.
Counter=1
TWidth=Col_Width-2
BLine=SPACE(6)
DO WHILE Counter <= No_Col
   Sub=LTRIM(STR(Counter,2))
   Title&Sub=SUBSTR(Title&Sub,1,TWidth)+;
    SPACE(TWidth-LEN(Title&Sub))
   BLine=BLine+Title&Sub+SPACE(2)
   Counter=Counter+1
ENDDO (counter)

*------------ Pad title for centering.
Title=SPACE((((Col_Width*No_Col)+5)/2)- ;
     (LEN(TRIM(Title))/2))+Title

      *******************************************
      *           Display graph on screen       *
      *******************************************

*--------- Assign graphics characters for screen.
XChar=CHR(196)
YChar=CHR(179)
BChar=CHR(219)

*-- Create y-axis, x-axis, and bar for screen graph.
Line=SPACE(1)+YChar
XLine="  "+REPLICATE(XChar,No_Col*Col_Width)
Bar=" "+REPLICATE(BChar,Col_Width-1)

*------------------ Draw graph background.
CLEAR
@ 0,0 SAY Title

*------------------ Draw y-axis.
?
BCount=0
Cntr=1
```

Figure 5.10:   The BarGraph.PRG command file

```
    DO WHILE Cntr<21
       Left=SPACE(5)
       IF (((Cntr-1)/4=INT((Cntr-1)/4)).OR.Cntr=1).AND.Cntr<20
           Left=STR(Hr-((BCount/5)*Hr),5)
           BCount=BCount+1
       ENDIF (cntr-1)
       ? Left+Line
       Cntr=Cntr+1
    ENDDO (while <21 lines printed)

    *--- Draw x-axis and bottom line.
    ? STR(Lr,5)+XLine
    ? '  '+BLine

    *------- Set up outer loop for drawing bars (OLoop).
    ColPos=7
    Div=(Hr-Lr)/10
    OLoop=1
    DO WHILE OLoop <= No_Col
       VName='Col'+LTRIM(STR(OLoop,2))
       @ 21,ColPos SAY ' '
       Col=2* &VName/Div
       Row=21
       *-------------- Draw bars on screen.
       DO WHILE Col > 0
           @ Row,ColPos SAY Bar
           Row=Row-1
           Col=Col-1
       ENDDO (while Col > 0)
       ColPos=ColPos+Col_Width
       OLoop=OLoop+1
    ENDDO  (OLoop)

    *--------------- Ask about printed copy of graph.
    @ 23,0 SAY " "
    WAIT "Press any key..."
    CLEAR
    WAIT 'Send graph to printer? (Y/N) ' TO YN

        **********************************************
        *   Display graph on printer, if requested   *
        **********************************************

    *- If printed graph not requested, exit.
    IF UPPER(YN) # 'Y'
       RETURN
    ENDIF (upper yn)

    CLEAR
    ? "Working..."
    *------------------ Set up printer graphics characters.
    XChar=CHR(45)
    YChar=CHR(124)
    BChar=CHR(35)

    *------- Create x-axis, bar, and blanks for printed graph.
    XLine=REPLICATE(XChar,(No_Col*Col_Width)-1)
    Bar=REPLICATE(BChar,Col_Width-1)
    Blanks=SPACE(Col_Width-1)
```

Figure 5.10:   The BarGraph.PRG command file (continued)

```
*------- Center title on printer graph.
CLEAR
SET PRINT ON
? Title
?
*--------- Start graph loops.
LCount=1
CCount=1
BCount=0
*--------- Build printed graph line (GLine).
DO WHILE LCount<21
   GLine = SPACE(5)+YChar
   IF (((LCount-1)/4=INT((LCount-1)/4)).OR.LCount=1).AND.LCount<20
         GLine=STR(Hr-((BCount/5)*Hr),5)+YChar
         BCount=BCount+1
   ENDIF (lcount)
   DO WHILE CCount<=No_Col
      VName='Col'+LTRIM(STR(CCount,2))
      GLine = IIF(LCount>20-(2*(&VName/Div)),GLine+Bar,GLine+Blanks)+' '
      CCount=CCount+1
   ENDDO (for ccount)
   *------- Print graph line (GLine) and proceed through loop.
   ? GLine
   CCount=1
   LCount=LCount+1
ENDDO   (lcount)

*------------- Print bottom titles and x-axis.
? STR(Lr,5)+" "+XLine
? ' '+BLine
EJECT
SET PRINT OFF
RETURN
```

Figure 5.10:   The BarGraph.PRG command file (continued)

The next lines create some new variables used in the graph. The variable Line is a space followed by the YChar graphics character, and is used to draw the y-axis line down the left side of the graph. The variable XLine contains the XChar graphics character replicated for the width of the graph, calculated by multiplying the number of columns by the width of each column (No_Col * Col_Width). XLine is the x-axis line on the graph. The Bar variable consists of a space followed by the BChar graphics character replicated for the width of each column minus one (Col_Width − 1):

```
* – Create y-axis, x-axis, and bar for screen graph.
Line = SPACE(1) + YChar
XLine = " " + REPLICATE(XChar,No_Col*Col_Width)
Bar = " " + REPLICATE(BChar,Col_Width − 1)
```

Now the procedure clears the screen and displays the graph title, which has already been padded for centering:

```
* – – – – – – – – – Draw graph background.
CLEAR
@ 0,0 SAY Title
* – – – – – – – – – Draw y-axis.
```

Next, a DO WHILE loop draws the y-axis down the left side of the graph. The variable named Cntr is incremented by 1 with each pass through the loop. Since the graph uses 20 lines on the screen, the loop repeats 20 times. In most passes, the y-axis line is simply preceded by five spaces. However, numbers to the left of the y-axis are displayed on every fourth line, and the first (top) line. The expression

IF (((Cntr – 1)/4 = INT((Cntr – 1)/4)).OR.Cntr = 1).AND.Cntr<20

is used within the DO WHILE loop to determine when the Cntr counter variable is 1, is evenly divisible by 4, and is still less than 20.

The y-axis is drawn from the top of the graph downward. Therefore, the first number displayed beside the y-axis is the highest value in the graph (passed as the parameter Hr). Each number beneath Hr, to be displayed to the left of the y-axis, is calculated with the expression

Hr – ((BCount/5)*Hr)

where BCount is incremented by 1 each time another number is displayed next to the y-axis. The routine in BarGraph.PRG that draws the y-axis down the left side of the graph is shown below:

```
?
BCount = 0
Cntr = 1
DO WHILE Cntr<21
   Left = SPACE(5)
   IF (((Cntr – 1)/4 = INT((Cntr – 1)/4)).OR.Cntr = 1).AND.Cntr<20
      Left = STR(Hr – ((BCount/5)*Hr),5)
      BCount = BCount + 1
   ENDIF (cntr – 1)
   ? Left + Line
   Cntr = Cntr + 1
ENDDO (while <21 lines printed)
```

The x-axis for the graph is drawn with the lowest value for the y-axis (passed as the parameter Lr) to the left of it. Bottom titles for the graph, now stored in the variable named BLine, are displayed below the x-axis:

```
* - Draw x-axis and bottom line.
? STR(Lr,5) + XLine
? ' ' + BLine
```

Now comes the tricky part. Given the space taken up by numbers and the y-axis at the left of the screen, the first bar will be drawn at column 7. The variable ColPos keeps track of the actual column position of each bar to be drawn, and is hence initialized to 7.

A divisor is then set up that will help calculate the distance that a bar needs to be "pulled up" from the bottom of the screen. This value is stored in the variable named Div, and is calculated with the expression

$$(Hr - Lr)/10$$

where Hr is the highest y-axis value, and Lr the lowest y-axis value. Two nested loops then draw the actual bars. The outermost nested loop is controlled with the variable OLoop. The outer loop is repeated once for each bar to be drawn.

Within the outer loop, the variable VName stores the name of the variable being operated upon at the moment, either Col1, Col2, Col3, or one of the other ColN values to be plotted. The VName variable gets its value from the expression

```
VName = 'Col' + LTRIM(STR(OLoop,2))
```

The command

```
@ 21,ColPos SAY ' '
```

positions the cursor at row 21 to start drawing the bar.

Then the variable Col stores the row number that the bar must reach up to, which is calculated with the expression

```
Col = 2 * &Vname/Div.
```

(&VName is a macro, and hence will be converted to Col1, Col2, Col3, or whatever, depending on the pass through the loop.) The row number for the cursor is set to 21 to start drawing the bar.

Everything that has been said in the last three paragraphs is summarized in the routine from the BarGraph procedure shown below:

```
*  − − −  Set up outer loop for drawing bars (OLoop).
ColPos = 7
Div = (Hr − Lr)/10
OLoop = 1
DO WHILE OLoop < = No_Col
   VName = 'Col' + LTRIM(STR(OLoop,2))
   @ 21,ColPos SAY ' '
   Col = 2* &VName/Div
   Row = 21
```

Now that the procedure knows how many rows a particular column must extend upward (as calculated and stored in the Col variable), a simple DO WHILE loop repeats as many times as is necessary, each time drawing the Bar characters on the next row up, as shown in the routine below:

```
*  − − − − − − −  Draw bars on screen.
DO WHILE Col > 0
   @ Row,ColPos SAY Bar
   Row = Row − 1
   Col = Col − 1
ENDDO (while Col > 0)
```

When the single column (bar) is drawn, the command file increments the column position (ColPos) by the width of each column to prepare for drawing the next bar. The OLoop variable, which controls the outer loop, is also incremented by 1, and the ENDDO command marks the bottom of the outer loop, and repeats the outer and inner loops to draw the next bar:

```
   ColPos = ColPos + Col_Width
   OLoop = OLoop + 1
ENDDO (OLoop)
```

When the outer loop has run its course, the screen graph is drawn. The procedure only needs to position the cursor and pause for the user to press any key to continue, as shown below:

```
*  − − − − − − − −  Ask about printed copy of graph.
@ 23,0 SAY " "
WAIT "Press any key..."
CLEAR
WAIT 'Send graph to printer? (Y/N) ' TO YN
```

Now comes the task of printing the graph on the printer, if the user requested a printed copy. The IF clause below returns control to the calling program if the user does not request a printed copy of the graph:

```
* * * * * * * * * * * * * * * * * * * * * * * * * * * * * * * * * * * * * *
* Display graph on printer, if requested          *
* * * * * * * * * * * * * * * * * * * * * * * * * * * * * * * * * * * * *

*- If printed graph not requested, exit.
IF UPPER(YN) # 'Y'
    RETURN
ENDIF (upper yn)
```

The next routine sets up graphics characters for the printed copy of the graph, again using the variable names XChar, YChar, BChar. I've used somewhat neutral characters below, because every printer will use different graphics characters. You may need to experiment to find the best characters for your printer, and again the ASCII.PRG command file presented at the beginning of this chapter can help you select the best ones:

```
* – – – – – – – – – Set up printer graphics characters.
XChar = CHR(45)
YChar = CHR(124)
BChar = CHR(35)
```

Drawing graphs on the screen is easy compared to drawing them on the printer. On the screen, we can draw them in a free-form fashion, moving up and down the screen freely. On the printer, each line on the graph must be created independently, since the printer can only move in a top-to-bottom fashion (unless you happen to have a plotter). The BarGraph.PRG procedure assumes you are using a standard dot-matrix printer (though the temptation to revert to a plotter nagged me for a while before I wrote this little chunk of code).

The routine below sets up the x-axis line (XLine), bar, and blank spaces (Blanks) to be used in printing the graph (the Blanks variable contains blank spaces equal to the width of a single bar, and is printed above the top of completed bars):

```
* – – – Create x-axis, bar, and blanks for printed graph.
XLine = REPLICATE(XChar,(No_Col*Col_Width) – 1)
Bar = REPLICATE(BChar,Col_Width – 1)
Blanks = SPACE(Col_Width – 1)
```

The procedure then clears the screen, sets the printer on, and prints the graph title, which has already been sufficiently padded with leading blanks to be centered on the graph:

```
* – – – Center title on printer graph.
CLEAR
SET PRINT ON
? Title
?
```

Next the procedure creates and initializes three variables; LCount (Line Count), CCount (Column Count), and BCount (Bar Count):

```
* – – – – Start graph loops.
LCount = 1
CCount = 1
BCount = 0
```

Each line to be printed is created in the two nested loops below, and stored in a variable named GLine (for Graph Line). Since there are 20 lines in the printed graph, the outer loop runs from 1 to 20.

GLine initially receives five spaces followed by the YChar variable (the y-axis graphics character). However, if the current line is evenly divisible by 4, or is equal to 1, and is still less than 20, then GLine is recalculated so that the number to the left of the y-axis is added to the left of the y-axis character. As in the screen version of the graph, the number to display to the left of the y-axis is calculated using the BCount variable:

```
* – – – – Build printed graph line (GLine).
DO WHILE LCount<21
   GLine = SPACE(5) + YChar
   IF (((LCount – 1)/4 = INT((LCount – 1)/4))
   .OR.LCount = 1).AND.LCount<20
      GLine = STR(Hr – ((BCount/5)∗Hr),5) + YChar
      BCount = BCount + 1
   ENDIF (lcount)
```

Another loop repeats once for each column (bar) in the graph. The CCount variable keeps track of the number of passes through the loop. Within the loop, the variable VName is assigned the name of the column currently being processed (i.e., Col1, Col2, Col3, and so forth) using the same technique that was used in the screen version of the graph:

```
DO WHILE CCount< = No_Col
   VName = 'Col' + LTRIM(STR(CCount,2))
```

Now the procedure needs to determine whether the line that is to be printed (GLine) should have a bar in the current column, or just blanks. Succinctly stated, if the line count (LCount) is greater than 20 (the height of the graph in lines) minus twice the current value being plotted (&VName) divided by the divisor we calculated earlier (Div), then GLine should have the Bar characters added to it (to print a bar). Otherwise, it should just have blanks (the Blanks variable) and an extra blank to maintain the width of the original Bar characters added to it. The line below makes this decision:

```
GLine = IIF(LCount>20 – (2*(&VName/Div)),GLine + Bar,
GLine + Blanks) + ' '
```

Once that's decided, the column count (CCount) variable can be incremented by 1, and the inner loop repeated for the next column:

```
   CCount = CCount + 1
ENDDO (for ccount)
```

When the inner loop is done, the GLine variable for printing a single line of the printed graph is complete, so the procedure prints it. Then it resets the column count variable to 1, increments the line count by 1, and closes the outermost loop:

```
   * – – – Print graph line     (GLine) and proceed through loop.
   ? GLine
   CCount = 1
   LCount = LCount + 1
ENDDO (lcount)
```

When those two nested loops are finished, the main body of the graph is printed. So the procedure prints the x-axis line (XLine) preceded by the lowest value on the y-axis (Lr), and prints the bottom-line titles (BLine) preceded by a blank space:

```
   * – – – – – – Print bottom titles and x-axis.
   ? STR(Lr,5) + " " + XLine
```

```
? ' ' + BLine
EJECT
SET PRINT OFF
RETURN
```

The BarGraph procedure is somewhat complicated and may take a bit of study to fully understand. Fortunately, it is very easy to use, as discussed in the next sections.

PLOTTING THE BAR GRAPH

Figure 5.11 shows a sample command file named EZGraf.PRG that accesses the BarGraph routine.

Note that 12 columns of data, Col1 to Col12, and 12-column titles, Title1 to Title12, are first assigned data as memory variables. The variables GTitle (graph title), Columns (number of columns), Col_Width (column width), Lowest (lowest y-axis value), and Highest (highest y-axis value) are also assigned values, and are passed to the BarGraph routine through the DO. . .WITH command. Figure 5.12 shows you how the resulting bar graph appears on the screen. Press any key after viewing the graph, and the program will ask if you want a printed copy of the graph. Answer "Y" if you want to print the bar graph.

PLOTTING DATA FROM A DATABASE

More often than not, you'll probably want to plot data directly from a database. That way, you can add, change, or delete data at your whim, and replot the new data with little effort. (Those of you who create custom systems in dBASE can make displaying data on a bar graph a simple menu selection for end users.)

Let's look at an example. Figure 5.13 shows a sample database, named Sales2.DBF (slightly different from the Sales.DBF file in Chapter 4). Note that the Date column contains dates throughout the year 1986. Though our sample database only contains 16 records, there is no limit to the size of the database you can use.

Figure 5.14 shows a sample command file named GrafTest that calculates the total sales (Qty * U_Price) for each quarter. The SUM commands, used to calculate the data, include FOR commands that limit each sum to a range of data reflecting each quarter in the year. These calculated values are stored in the variables Col1 through Col4. The variables Title1 through Title4 are also assigned data.

```
********************************* EZGRaf.PRG
*-- Sample program to call the bar-graph routine.

*-- Define graph data.
*-- MUST use variable name Col1, Col2... ColNN.
*-- Titles use Title1, Title2... TitleNN, as shown:
Col1 = 5
Title1 = "Jan"
Col2 = 10
Title2 = "Feb"
Col3 = 15
Title3 = "Mar"
Col4 = 25
Title4 = "Apr"
Col5 = 35
Title5 = "May"
Col6 = 40
Title6 = "Jun"
Col7 = 50
Title7 = "Jul"
Col8 = 60
Title8 = "Aug"
Col9 = 70
Title9 = "Sep"
Col10 = 80
Title10 = "Oct"
Col11 = 90
Title11 = "Nov"
Col12 = 100
Title12 = "Dec"

*-- Define graph parameters.
GTitle = "Sample Graph"
Columns = 12
Col_Width = 6
Lowest = 0
Highest = 100

DO BarGraph WITH GTitle,Columns,Col_Width,Lowest,Highest

RETURN
```

Figure 5.11: Sample command file for plotting a bar graph

Since it is not possible to specify a specific upper limit in advance for the y-axis of every graph, the GrafTest program calculates one with a simple series of IF commands. The variable Hr is assigned an initial value of 100. Each of the four items of data to be plotted, Col1 through Col4, is compared to the current value of Hr. If the Col to be plotted is greater than Hr, Hr receives that higher value. By the time all four IF clauses are considered, Hr is equal to the highest of the four values.

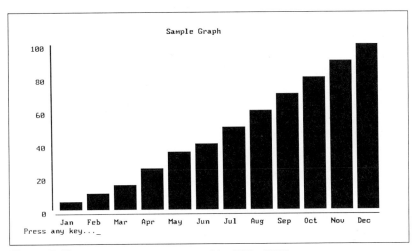

Figure 5.12: Sample bar graph created by EZGraf.PRG

RECORD#	PARTNO	PARTNAME	QTY	U_PRICE	DATE
1	A-123	Microprocessor	100	55.55	01/01/86
2	B-222	Laser Engine	2	1234.56	02/01/86
3	C-333	Color Terminal	5	400.00	02/01/86
4	D-444	Hard Disk	25	500.00	03/02/86
5	E-555	Disk Controller	50	200.00	04/15/86
6	F-666	Graphics Board	20	249.00	05/15/86
7	G-777	Modem	5	249.00	05/15/86
8	H-888	SemiDisk	25	600.00	06/15/86
9	A-123	Microprocessor	10	55.55	07/30/86
10	B-222	Laser Engine	8	1234.56	07/31/86
11	A-123	Microprocessor	10	55.00	08/30/86
12	E-555	Disk Controller	25	200.00	09/01/86
13	E-555	Disk Controller	100	180.00	10/01/86
14	F-666	Graphics Board	5	200.00	11/01/86
15	A-123	Microprocessor	20	50.00	11/15/86
16	H-888	SemiDisk	50	600.00	12/15/86

Figure 5.13: Sample Sales database

```
*********************************** GrafTest.PRG
*-- Test bar-graph procedure using Sales database.
CLEAR
? "Working..."
SET TALK OFF

*--- Sample.DBF includes the numeric fields Qty and U_Price.
USE Sales2

*--- Sum data for plotting (must use subscripted names
*--- such as Col1, Col2... Title1, Title2...).

*--- Store first-quarter total in Col1 variable.
SUM (Qty*U_Price) FOR Month(Date) <= 3 TO Col1
Title1 = "1st Quarter"

*--- Store second-quarter total in Col2 variable.
SUM (Qty*U_Price) FOR Month(Date) >= 4 .AND. MONTH(Date) <= 6 TO Col2
Title2 = "2nd Quarter"

*--- Store third-quarter total in Col3 variable.
SUM (Qty*U_Price) FOR Month(Date) >= 7 .AND. MONTH(Date) <= 9 TO Col3
Title3 = "3rd Quarter"

*--- Store fourth-quarter total in Col4 variable.
SUM (Qty*U_Price) FOR Month(Date) > 9 TO Col4
Title4 = "4th Quarter"

*--- Determine highest value for highest x-axis value (XTop).
XTop = 100
XTop = IIF (Col1 > XTop, Col1, XTop)
XTop = IIF (Col2 > XTop, Col2, XTop)
XTop = IIF (Col3 > XTop, Col3, XTop)
XTop = IIF (Col4 > XTop, Col4, XTop)

*---- Round highest y-axis value upward.
Digits = LEN(LTRIM(STR(XTop,12,0)))
Zeros = REPLICATE("0",Digits-3)
RoundUp = XTop + VAL("5"+Zeros)
XTop = ROUND(RoundUp,-1*(Digits-2))

*----- Turn off status bar and set up colors.
SET STATUS OFF
IF ISCOLOR()
   SET COLOR TO W+/B+,GR+/N, R+
ENDIF (iscolor)
CLEAR

*-------------- Send parameters to bar-graph routine.

DO BarGraph WITH "Quarterly Data from Sales",4,15,0,XTop

*-------------- All done.
RETURN
```

Figure 5.14:   The GrafTest program

You might want to round the highest y-axis value upward to an even number (such as 32,000 rather than 31,984), if you prefer that your graph display more evenly rounded numbers next to the y-axis. The routine shown below (and in GrafTest.PRG) will round any number upward by 100. You might want to experiment with other techniques for rounding the highest value on the y-axis, or you might prefer to leave the rounding routine out altogether.

```
* - - Round highest y-axis value upward.
Digits = LEN(LTRIM(STR(XTop,12,0)))
Zeros = REPLICATE("0",Digits-3)
RoundUp = XTop + VAL("5"+Zeros)
XTop = ROUND(RoundUp, -1*(Digits-2))
```

The last line of the program:

DO BarGraph WITH "Quarterly Data from Sales",4,15,0,Hr

plots the bar graph with the title "Quarterly Data from Sales", four columns, each 15 characters wide, with 0 as the lowest y-axis value, and the current contents of the Hr variable as the highest y-axis value. Figure 5.15 shows the resulting bar graph as it appears on the screen.

In the interest of maximizing both speed and flexibility, the BarGraph program has no built-in error-trapping capabilities. Therefore, it is up to you to

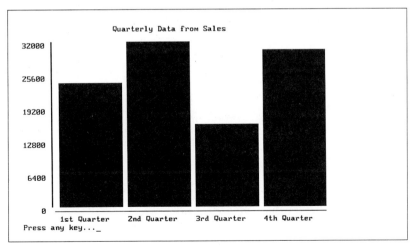

Figure 5.15: Sample graph printed with GrafTest.PRG

```
********************************* GTest2.PRG
*-- Test bar-graph procedure using Sales database.
CLEAR
? "Working..."
SET TALK OFF

*--- Sample.DBF includes the numeric fields Qty and U_Price.
USE Sales2

*--- Sum data for plotting (must use subscripted names
*--- such as Col1, Col2... Title1, Title2...).

*--- Store first-quarter total in Col1 variable.
SUM (Qty*U_Price) FOR Month(Date) <= 3 TO Col1
Title1 = "1st Quarter"
Col1 = Col1/100

*--- Store second-quarter total in Col2 variable.
SUM (Qty*U_Price) FOR Month(Date) >= 4 .AND. MONTH(Date) <= 6 TO Col2
Title2 = "2nd Quarter"
Col2 = Col2 / 100

*--- Store third-quarter total in Col3 variable.
SUM (Qty*U_Price) FOR Month(Date) >= 7 .AND. MONTH(Date) <= 9 TO Col3
Title3 = "3rd Quarter"
Col3 = Col3/100

*--- Store fourth-quarter total in Col4 variable.
SUM (Qty*U_Price) FOR Month(Date) > 9 TO Col4
Title4 = "4th Quarter"
Col4 = Col4/100

*--- Determine highest value for highest x-axis value (XTop).
XTop = 100
XTop = IIF (Col1 > XTop, Col1, XTop)
XTop = IIF (Col2 > XTop, Col2, XTop)
XTop = IIF (Col3 > XTop, Col3, XTop)
XTop = IIF (Col4 > XTop, Col4, XTop)

*-- (Not rounded here, so data are
*--  more literal on the graph.)

*----- Turn off status bar and set up colors.
SET STATUS OFF
IF ISCOLOR()
   SET COLOR TO W+/B+,GR+/N,R+
ENDIF (iscolor)
CLEAR

*-------------- Send parameters to bar-graph routine.
DO BarGraph WITH "Quarterly Data from Sales",4,15,0,XTop

*-------------- All done.
RETURN
```

Figure 5.16: Modified version of the GrafTest program

ensure that reasonable data is passed to the program. For example, if the highest value to be plotted on a graph is 1,234, and the Hr value for the y-axis is only 1,000, the program will probably crash. Similarly, if you attempt to plot 12 columns, each ten characters wide, you'll get a mess on the screen, because 12 * 10 is 120, and the screen is only 80 characters wide. You must take into consideration that the numbers to the left of the y-axis take up five characters of space, and the axis itself takes up a column. Therefore, the product of the number of columns and the column width should not exceed 72. The column titles must be sized accordingly too.

On the bar graph with 12 columns, we assigned a width of six characters to each column (12 * 6 = 72), and used abbreviated column titles (Jan, Feb, Mar, and so on) for a good fit. Remember that there are two spaces surrounding each column, so the actual bar is two characters less than the column width.

If you attempt to plot very large numbers, your data might overflow the five-digit maximum for numbers along the y-axis. You can rectify this situation by dividing all data to be plotted by a constant. Figure 5.16 shows a modified version of the GrafTest program, which divides each of the values to be plotted (Col1 through Col4) by 100 prior to calculating the highest range on the graph and printing the graph.

Dividing data to be plotted might make a better-looking graph anyway, because the data along the y-axis will not be so "literal." Since dBASE has no high-resolution capability, plotted data are rounded to the nearest row anyway. Therefore rounding will probably have no effect on the accuracy of the graph.

GENERAL-PURPOSE
PROCEDURES

6

In this chapter we'll discuss some general-purpose procedures for managing dBASE III PLUS data. You may want to add some of these procedures to your existing procedure files, or store them separately in a procedure file named GenProcs.PRG that we will develop in this chapter. The complete GenProcs.PRG procedure is shown in Figure 6.1.

```
*********************************** GenProcs.PRG
*-------------------- General-purpose procedures.

***************************** List duplicates.
PROCEDURE DupCheck
PARAMETERS FieldName
  SET HEADING OFF

  *-------------------- Sort by FieldName.
  CLEAR
  ? "Presorting for duplication check..."
  INDEX ON &FieldName TO Temp

  *---------------- Clear screen and print title.
  CLEAR
  ? "Possible Duplications"+SPACE(50)+DTOC(DATE())
  ?
  ? "Record #"
  ?
  *----- Loop through database until end of file.
  GO TOP
  DO WHILE .NOT. EOF()
     Compare = &FieldName
     SKIP
     *------ If two records match...
     IF &FieldName = Compare
        *--- then skip back one record...
        SKIP -1
        *--- and list identical records.
        LIST WHILE &FieldName = Compare
        ?
     ENDIF (&FieldName = Compare)
  ENDDO (while not eof)
  SET INDEX TO
RETURN

****************** Mark duplicates for deletion.
PROCEDURE DupDel
PARAMETERS FieldName

  *-------------------- Sort by FieldName.
  CLEAR
  ? "Presorting for duplication deletion..."
  INDEX ON &FieldName TO Temp

  *---------------- Clear screen and print title.
  CLEAR
  ? "Deleting..."
```

Figure 6.1:   The GenProcs.PRG procedure file

```
      *------- Loop through database until end of file.
      GO TOP
      DO WHILE .NOT. EOF()
         Compare = &FieldName
         SKIP
         *------ If two records match...
         IF &FieldName = Compare
            *--- delete identical records.
            DELETE WHILE &FieldName = Compare
         ENDIF (&FieldName = Compare)
      ENDDO (while not eof)

      *----------------- Done.
      CLEAR
      TEXT

         Duplicate records are marked for deletion.

         Make all index files active before packing.

      ENDTEXT
      SET INDEX TO
   RETURN

   ****************** Capitalize first letter only.
   PROCEDURE Proper
   PARAMETERS String
         String = UPPER(LEFT(String,1)) + ;
         LOWER(RIGHT(String,LEN(String)-1))
   RETURN

   ********** Capitalize first letter of every word.
   PROCEDURE FullProp
   PARAMETERS String
   String = UPPER(LEFT(String,1)) + ;
    LOWER(RIGHT(String,LEN(String)-1))
   BSearch = 1
   CapSpot = 1
   DO WHILE BSearch > 0
      BSearch = AT(" ",SUBSTR(String,CapSpot,;
      LEN(TRIM(String))-CapSpot))
      IF BSearch > 0
         CapSpot = BSearch + CapSpot
         String = STUFF(String,CapSpot,1,;
         UPPER(SUBSTR(String,CapSpot,1)))
      ENDIF
   ENDDO (bsearch)

   ********************** Word wrap long strings.
   PROCEDURE WordWrap
   PARAMETERS String, Left, Right, LF
     Length = LEN(TRIM(String))
     *---------------- Set up loop through string.
     DO WHILE Length > Right-Left
        Place = Right-Left

        *-- Find blank nearest right margin (Place).
```

Figure 6.1: The GenProcs.PRG procedure file (continued)

```
      DO WHILE SUBSTR(String,Place,1) # " "
         Place = Place - 1
      ENDDO (until blank space found)

      *- Print portion, and assign rest to String.
      ? SPACE(Left)+LTRIM(LEFT(String,Place-1))
      String = SUBSTR(String,Place+1,Length-Place)
      Length = LEN(TRIM(String))
      LF = LF + 1
   ENDDO (while length > margin)

   *------ Print remainder of String, then return.
   ? SPACE(Left)+LTRIM(String)
   LF = LF + 1
RETURN


********************** Translate date to English.
*------- Make Eng_Date public in calling program.
PROCEDURE TransDat
PARAMETERS PDate
   PDay = STR(DAY(PDate),IIF(DAY(PDate)<10,1,2))
   Eng_Date = CMONTH(PDate) + " " + PDay + ", " ;
      + STR(YEAR(PDate),4)
RETURN


******** Convert a number to English equivalent.
* Make Eng_Num variable public in calling program.
* Must have access to English.MEM variables.

PROCEDURE Translat
PARAMETERS Amount

*---------- Set up memory variables.
Counter = 1
Start = 1
String = STR(Amount,9,2)
Eng_Num = " "

*-------- Loop through thousands and hundreds.
DO WHILE Counter < 3

   *------ Split out hundreds, tens, and ones.
   Chunk = SUBSTR(String,Start,3)
   Hun = SUBSTR(Chunk,1,1)
   Ten = SUBSTR(Chunk,2,2)
   One = SUBSTR(Chunk,3,1)

   *------ Handle hundreds portion.
   IF VAL(Chunk) > 99
      Eng_Num = Eng_Num + U&Hun + ' HUNDRED '
   ENDIF (chunk > 99)

   *------ Handle second two digits.
   T = VAL(Ten)
   IF T > 0
```

Figure 6.1:   The GenProcs.PRG procedure file (continued)

```
        DO CASE
           *-- Handle even tens and teens.
           CASE (INT(T/10.0)=T/10.0).OR. ;
                (T>9.AND.T<20)
                Eng_Num = Eng_Num + U&Ten

           *-- Handle greater than 10, but not evenly divisible.
           CASE T > 9 .AND. (INT(T/10.0)#T/10.0)
                Ten = SUBSTR(Ten,1,1) +'0'
                Eng_Num = Eng_Num + U&Ten+' '+U&One

           *-- Handle less than 10.
           CASE T < 10
                Eng_Num = Eng_Num + U&One

        ENDCASE
     ENDIF (T > 0)

     *-- Add "Thousand" if necessary.
     IF Amount > 999.99 .AND. Counter = 1
        Eng_Num = Eng_Num +' THOUSAND '
     ENDIF (need to add "thousand")

     *-- Prepare for pass through hundreds.
     Start = 4
     Counter = Counter + 1

  ENDDO (while counter < 3)

  *----- Tack on cents.
  IF INT(Amount) > 0
     Eng_Num = Eng_Num + " AND "
  ENDIF

  Eng_Num = Eng_Num + SUBSTR(String,8,2)+"/100"

  *-------- End procedure.
  RETURN
```

Figure 6.1: The GenProcs.PRG procedure file (continued)

⊙CHECKING FOR DUPLICATE RECORDS

The first procedure in the GenProcs.PRG file displays duplicate records in a database. It allows you to display records with either a single field in common (for example, all records with identical part numbers), or several fields in common (such as all records with identical zip codes, addresses, and last names). It will not actually delete any records, just display the duplicates so that you can decide what to do with them.

We'll use a sample database, named Mail.DBF, to test the procedures. The structure for the Mail database is shown in Figure 6.2. Sample data stored in the Mail database are displayed in Figure 6.3.

```
Structure for database : C:Mail.dbf

      Field    Field name    Type         Width    Dec
        1      LNAME         Character      10
        2      FNAME         Character      10
        3      ADDRESS       Character      15
        4      CITY          Character      10
        5      STATE         Character       2
        6      ZIP           Character       5
```

Figure 6.2:   Structure of the sample Mail database

	LNAME	FNAME	ADDRESS	CITY	STATE	ZIP
1	Smith	Bertha	333 Grape St.	San Diego	CA	92122
2	Rosielli	Richard	444 K St.	Glendora	CA	91740
3	Kenney	Dave	371 Brill St.	La Jolla	CA	92112
4	Jones	Cecilia	280 Z St.	La Jolla	CA	92038
5	Miller	George	371 Brill St.	La Jolla	CA	92112
6	Schumack	Susita	1086 Crest Dr.	Encinitas	CA	92345
7	Doe	John	239 Ascii Ave.	Culver City	CA	92745
8	Miller	George	371 Brill St.	La Jolla	CA	92112
9	Aronson	George	101 256th St.	Sunnyvale	CA	92424
10	Schumack	Susita	5328 Bragg St.	San Diego	CA	92122
11	Pulver	Jonathan	273 Ash Ave.	Bellevue	WA	98009
12	Eprom	Edna	471 B St.	Las Vegas	NE	88888
13	Jones	Ralph	280 Z St.	La Jolla	CA	92038
14	Schumack	Susita	5328 Bragg St.	San Diego	CA	92122
15	Miller	George	371 Brill St.	La Jolla	CA	92112
16	Smith	Georgia	321 Bunny Lane	La Jolla	CA	92037

Figure 6.3:   Sample data stored in the Mail database

   Figure 6.4 shows the DupCheck procedure that checks for records that are duplicates in one or more fields. This figure also shows the opening lines of the GenProcs.PRG procedure file. If you are following along on line, use the MODIFY COMMAND editor or your word processor to create the GenProcs.PRG procedure file, and type in the procedure as shown in Figure 6.4.

```
******************************* GenProcs.PRG
*-------------------- General-purpose procedures.

****************************** List duplicates.
PROCEDURE DupCheck
PARAMETERS FieldName
   SET HEADING OFF

   *------------------- Sort by FieldName.
   CLEAR
   ? "Presorting for duplication check..."
   INDEX ON &FieldName TO Temp

   *---------------- Clear screen and print title.
   CLEAR
   ? "Possible Duplications"+SPACE(50)+DTOC(DATE())
   ?
   ? "Record #"
   ?
   *----- Loop through database until end of file.
   GO TOP
   DO WHILE .NOT. EOF()
      Compare = &FieldName
      SKIP
      *------ If two records match...
      IF &FieldName = Compare
         *--- then skip back one record...
         SKIP -1
         *--- and list identical records.
         LIST WHILE &FieldName = Compare
         ?
      ENDIF (&FieldName = Compare)
   ENDDO (while not eof)
   SET INDEX TO
RETURN
```

Figure 6.4:   The DupCheck procedure in the GenProcs procedure file

Let's take a moment to discuss how the procedure works. The parameter FieldName will contain the name of the field (or combination of fields) in the database to analyze for duplications. The procedure sets the HEADING parameter off, then clears the screen and displays a message, as below:

```
********************************************* GenProcs.PRG
*-------------------- General-purpose procedures.

****************************** List duplicates.
PROCEDURE DupCheck
PARAMETERS FieldName
   SET HEADING OFF

   *----------------- Sort by FieldName.
   CLEAR
   ? "Presorting for duplication check. . ."
```

Next, the procedure creates an index file named Temp.NDX by using the command below:

```
INDEX ON &FieldName TO Temp
```

This command puts the records in the database into a sorted order according to the field(s) being analyzed. This makes the rest of the procedure easier, because any duplicates will be adjacent to each other in the sorted order.

Once the index file is created, the procedure clears the screen, displays a heading with the date, and begins a DO WHILE loop that reads each record in the database:

```
*---------------- Clear screen and print title.
CLEAR
? "Possible Duplications" + SPACE(50) + DTOC(DATE( ))
?
? "Record #"
?
*----- Loop through database until end of file.
GO TOP
DO WHILE .NOT. EOF( )
```

The contents of the specified field(s) in the current record in the database are stored in a memory variable named Compare. Then, the SKIP command moves the record pointer to the next record. An IF clause checks to see if the specified field(s) in the current record (&FieldName) match those in the previous record (Compare):

```
Compare = &FieldName
SKIP
*------ If two records match. . .
IF &FieldName = Compare
```

If the two records match, then the command file skips back one record and displays duplicate records from that point on (LIST WHILE. . .). The ENDDO command marks the end of the DO WHILE loop, which repeats the comparisons for each record in the database:

```
*--- then skip back one record. . .
SKIP  −1
*--- and list duplicate records.
LIST WHILE &FieldName = Compare
?
```

ENDIF (&FieldName = Compare)
ENDDO (while not eof)

Before returning from the procedure, the SET INDEX TO command detaches the Temp index file from the database:

SET INDEX TO
RETURN

Before we test the DupCheck procedure, let's add the DupDel procedure, which is similar to the DupCheck procedure, except that it actually marks duplicate records for deletion. It is shown in Figure 6.5.

```
****************** Mark duplicates for deletion.
PROCEDURE DupDel
PARAMETERS FieldName

   *------------------ Sort by FieldName.
   CLEAR
   ? "Presorting for duplication deletion..."
   INDEX ON &FieldName TO Temp

   *--------------- Clear screen and print title.
   CLEAR
   ? "Deleting..."

   *------- Loop through database until end of file.
   GO TOP
   DO WHILE .NOT. EOF()
      Compare = &FieldName
      SKIP
      *------ If two records match...
      IF &FieldName = Compare
         *--- delete identical records.
         DELETE WHILE &FieldName = Compare
      ENDIF (&FieldName = Compare)
   ENDDO (while not eof)

   *----------------- Done.
   CLEAR
   TEXT

      Duplicate records are marked for deletion.

      Make all index files active before packing.

   ENDTEXT
   SET INDEX TO
RETURN
```

Figure 6.5: The DupDel procedure in the GenProcs procedure file

Like DupCheck, DupDel uses a single parameter named FieldName that contains the name of the field(s) used for comparison. The procedure creates an index file of the chosen field(s) named Temp.NDX:

```
* * * * * * * * * * * * * * * * * * * * * * * * * * * * * Mark duplicates for deletion.
PROCEDURE DupDel
PARAMETERS FieldName

    *------------------- Sort by FieldName.
    CLEAR
    ? "Presorting for duplication deletion. . ."
    INDEX ON &FieldName TO Temp
```

Then the procedure displays a message (*Deleting. . .*) and begins a DO WHILE loop through the indexed database. As with DupCheck, the procedure compares records for identical values, but uses the DELETE WHILE command, rather than LIST WHILE, to delete matching records. Also, the SKIP −1 command is left out so that the first of the identical records is not deleted:

```
    *---------------- Clear screen and print title.
    CLEAR
    ? "Deleting. . ."

    *------- Loop through database until end of file.
    GO TOP
    DO WHILE .NOT. EOF( )
       Compare = &FieldName
       SKIP
       *------ If two records match. . .
       IF &FieldName = Compare
          *--- delete identical records.
          DELETE WHILE &FieldName = Compare
       ENDIF (&FieldName = Compare)
    ENDDO (while not eof)
```

When done marking duplicates for deletion, the lines below display a message reminding you to make any index files active prior to packing the database so as to keep them updated. (If you are using this procedure in a custom system, you'll probably want to remove this message, and instead put the appropriate commands directly into the calling program.)

```
    *------------------ Done.
    CLEAR
```

```
      TEXT
         Duplicate records are marked for deletion.
         Make all index files active before packing.
      ENDTEXT
      SET INDEX TO
   RETURN
```

Suppose you access the DupDel procedure from a mailing system that uses a database named Mail.DBF, and retains two active index files named Names.NDX and Zips.NDX. The following commands will remove all records with identical zip codes, addresses, and last names (duplicate mailings), and also ensure that both the Names and Zips index files are properly updated:

```
   SET PROCEDURE TO GenProcs
   USE Mail
   DO DupDel WITH "Zip + Address + LName"
   USE Mail INDEX Names,Zips
   PACK
```

If you've created the Mail database mentioned earlier in this chapter and have added some data, you can experiment with these two procedures. First, be sure to save the procedure file, and enter the following commands at the dot prompt:

```
   SET PROCEDURE TO GenProcs
   USE Mail
```

to open the procedure file and use the Mail database.

You will probably want to add the commands SET TALK OFF and SET SAFETY OFF to the command files that call the DupCheck and DupDel procedures. These will prevent extraneous messages from being printed on the screen, and will also stop dBASE from asking for permission to overwrite the temporary file, Temp.NDX. Optionally, you can place the SET TALK OFF and SET SAFETY OFF commands near the top of the Dup-Check and DupDel procedures themselves.

Now, when accessing either DupCheck or DupDel, the general syntax is

```
   DO Procedure WITH "FieldName(s)"
```

For example, to view records with identical last names, type

```
   DO DupCheck WITH "LName"
```

The screen will clear, you'll see a brief message as the index file is created, and then you'll see the display shown in Figure 6.6.

You will notice, however, that this report does not actually give you an accurate display of duplicate mailings, because LName alone is not a stringent enough criteria. You need to check for identical zip codes and addresses, together with names, for a more rigid test. When combining field names in the WITH portion of the DO DupCheck command, you must join the field names with plus (+) signs. For example, to test for identical Zip, Address, and LName fields, type

DO DupCheck WITH "Zip + Address + LName"

The screen will display duplicates as in Figure 6.7.

An even more rigid criterion would be to include first names in the duplications search, using the following command:

DO DupCheck WITH "Zip + Address + LName + FName"

You might want to experiment with several possibilities when using the DupCheck procedure with your own databases.

Possible Duplications						09/05/85	
Record #							
4	Jones	Cecilia	280 Z St.	La Jolla	CA	92038	
13	Jones	Ralph	280 Z St.	La Jolla	CA	92038	
5	Miller	George	371 Brill St.	La Jolla	CA	92112	
8	Miller	George	371 Brill St.	La Jolla	CA	92112	
15	Miller	George	371 Brill St.	La Jolla	CA	92112	
6	Schumack	Susita	1086 Crest Dr.	Encinitas	CA	92345	
10	Schumack	Susita	5328 Bragg St.	San Diego	CA	92122	
14	Schumack	Susita	5328 Bragg St.	San Diego	CA	92122	
1	Smith	Bertha	333 Grape St.	San Diego	CA	92122	
16	Smith	Georgia	321 Bunny Lane	La Jolla	CA	92037	

Figure 6.6:   Identical last names in the Mail database

Possible Duplications				09/05/85		
Record #						
4	Jones	Cecilia	280 Z St.	La Jolla	CA	92038
13	Jones	Ralph	280 Z St.	La Jolla	CA	92038
5	Miller	George	371 Brill St.	La Jolla	CA	92112
8	Miller	George	371 Brill St.	La Jolla	CA	92112
15	Miller	George	371 Brill St.	La Jolla	CA	92112
10	Schumack	Susita	5328 Bragg St.	San Diego	CA	92122
14	Schumack	Susita	5328 Bragg St.	San Diego	CA	92122

Figure 6.7:   Records with identical zips, addresses, and last names

There is, however, one catch to watch out for when using multiple fields in the WITH part of the DO DupCheck command. All the fields must be of the same data type. Hence, if the Zip field was created as numeric data, you first have to convert to character data with the STR function, as shown below:

DO DupCheck WITH "STR(Zip,5,0) + Address + LName"

Similarly, if a Date field were to be included in the WITH part of the command, you would need to use the DTOC (Date-to-Character) function, as shown below:

DO DupCheck WITH "City + DTOC(Exp_Date)"

Figure 6.8 shows a command file named TestDup.PRG that tests the DupCheck and DupDel procedure files from within a command file. It uses the Mail database as an example. You could use techniques similar to those presented in the example to access these procedures from your own command files.

Once you've entered the TestDup.PRG command file, you can test it by entering the DO TestDup command. You'll notice that the records marked for deletion by the DupDel procedure are displayed on the screen when the program ends, as shown in Figure 6.9. This is because of the LIST FOR DELETED( ) command in the TestDup.PRG command file; it is not a built-in function of the DupDel procedure. You'll also note that not all identical records are deleted. One out of each group of identical records is retained in the database, because only the redundant records are marked for deletion.

```
*************************************** TestDup.PRG
*-- Test duplicates procedures with Mail database.

*-- Open appropriate database.
USE Mail

*-- Allow printer option.
CLEAR
ToPrint = " "
@ 10,5 SAY "Send data to printer? (Y/N) " ;
       GET ToPrint PICTURE "!"
READ
IF ToPrint = "Y"
   SET PRINT ON
ENDIF

CLEAR
*-- Open procedure file.
SET PROCEDURE TO GenProcs

*-- Do check-for-duplicates with
*-- zip code, address, and last name.
DO DupCheck WITH "Zip + Address + LName"

WAIT "Press any key to test DupDel..."

*-- Do delete-duplicates with zip code,
*-- address, and last name.
DO DupDel WITH "Zip + Address + LName"

*-- Display records marked for deletion.
?
LIST FOR DELETED()

*-- End of sample program.
SET PRINT OFF
CLOSE PROCEDURE
```

Figure 6.8:   The TestDup.PRG program to test duplicates procedures

---

Duplicate records are marked for deletion.

Make all index files active before packing.

8	*Miller	George	371 Brill St.	La Jolla	CA	92112
13	*Jones	Ralph	280 Z St.	La Jolla	CA	92038
14	*Schumack	Susita	5328 Bragg St.	San Diego	CA	92122
15	*Miller	George	371 Brill St.	La Jolla	CA	92112

Figure 6.9:   Records marked for deletion by the DupDel procedure

⊙PROPER CASE IN CHARACTER STRINGS

The next two procedures in the GenProcs.PRG procedure file can convert any character strings to proper case. The Proper procedure converts the first letter to uppercase and all following letters to lowercase. For example if a variable named Test1 contains the character string "this WaS a BIt of a MeSs", the command DO Proper WITH Test1 converts the contents of the Test1 variable to "This was a bit of a mess".

The FullProp procedure converts the first letter of each word to upper-case and all others to lowercase. For example, if the variable Test2 contains "DR. ADAM P. JONES", then the command DO FullProp WITH Test2 converts the contents of the Test2 variable to "Dr. Adam P. Jones". Figure 6.10 shows both the Proper and FullProp procedures.

The Proper procedure expects one parameter named String. This parameter contains the character string to be operated on. The procedure capitalizes the first letter of the character string using the expression

UPPER(LEFT(String,1))

Then it concatenates the rest of string, converted to lowercase, to the capitalized first letter using the expression

+LOWER(RIGHT(String,LEN(String) – 1))

```
******************* Capitalize first letter only.
PROCEDURE Proper
PARAMETERS String
     String = UPPER(LEFT(String,1)) + ;
     LOWER(RIGHT(String,LEN(String)-1))
RETURN

********** Capitalize first letter of every word.
PROCEDURE FullProp
PARAMETERS String
String = UPPER(LEFT(String,1)) + ;
 LOWER(RIGHT(String,LEN(String)-1))
BSearch = 1
CapSpot = 1
DO WHILE BSearch > 0
   BSearch = AT(" ",SUBSTR(String,CapSpot,;
   LEN(TRIM(String))-CapSpot))
   IF BSearch > 0
      CapSpot = BSearch + CapSpot
      String = STUFF(String,CapSpot,1,;
      UPPER(SUBSTR(String,CapSpot,1)))
   ENDIF
ENDDO (bsearch)
```

Figure 6.10: The Proper and FullProp procedures

The FullProp procedure is a little trickier than the Proper procedure. It begins by capitalizing the first letter and converting the rest of the letters to lowercase using the same technique used in the Proper procedure. Two variables named BSearch (for Blank Search) amd CapSpot (the place in the string to capitalize a letter) are each initialized to the value 1, as shown below:

```
BSearch = 1
CapSpot = 1
```

A DO WHILE loop repeats a routine to search for and replace lowercase letters at the start of each word. Within the loop, the variable BSearch takes on a value representing the position of the next blank space in String (beginning at the last CapSpot). If another blank space is found (BSearch > 0), then the STUFF function is used to replace the lowercase letter following the blank space with the uppercase equivalent of that letter. The DO WHILE loop, shown below, repeats until there are no blank spaces left in String:

```
DO WHILE BSearch > 0
   BSearch = AT(" ",SUBSTR(String,CapSpot,;
   LEN(TRIM(String)) – CapSpot))
   IF BSearch > 0
     CapSpot = BSearch + CapSpot
     String = STUFF(String,CapSpot,1,;
        UPPER(SUBSTR(String,CapSpot,1)))
   ENDIF
ENDDO (bsearch)
```

To test the procedures after keying them into the GenProcs procedure file, you can enter the commands below directly at the dot prompt:

```
SET TALK OFF

SET PROCEDURE TO GenProcs

Test1 = "THIS WAS ALL UPPERCASE"

Test2 = "this was all lowercase"

DO Proper WITH Test1

DO FullProp WITH Test2
```

When you then enter the command

```
? Test1
```

you'll see that Test1 now has an initial capital letter, as below:

This was all uppercase

When you enter the command

? Test2

you'll see that all words have an initial capital letter, as below:

This Was All Lowercase

Of course, like all procedures in this book, you can call Proper and FullProp from within a command file using the basic techniques shown above. If the string to be converted is stored in a database field, store a copy of the field in a memory variable and pass the name of the memory variable to the procedure.

⊙WORD WRAPPING

Managing long character strings in dBASE has always been somewhat awkward. dBASE III PLUS offers Memo fields that automatically *word wrap* long strings, but the large storage requirements of Memo fields are not necessary in cases where you need only 254 characters or fewer. The WordWrap procedure, shown in Figure 6.11, can wrap any normal Character field with a maximum width of 254 characters.

The WordWrap procedure is called with the general syntax

DO WordWrap WITH *String,Left Margin,Right Margin,Lines*

where String is the name of the memory variable containing the long character string to be formatted, Left Margin and Right Margin are the left and right margins to use when wrapping the string, and Lines is a variable that keeps track of the number of lines printed. We'll see some practical applications of the WordWrap procedure in a moment.

The procedure begins, as usual, with the PROCEDURE name and PARAMETERS statement, as shown below:

```
*********************** Word wrap long strings.
PROCEDURE WordWrap
PARAMETERS String, Left, Right, LF
```

```
************************ Word wrap long strings.
PROCEDURE WordWrap
PARAMETERS String, Left, Right, LF
   Length = LEN(TRIM(String))
   *---------------- Set up loop through string.
   DO WHILE Length > Right-Left
      Place = Right-Left

      *-- Find blank nearest right margin (Place).
      DO WHILE SUBSTR(String,Place,1) # " "
         Place = Place - 1
      ENDDO (until blank space found)

      *- Print portion, and assign rest to String.
      ? SPACE(Left)+LTRIM(LEFT(String,Place-1))
      String = SUBSTR(String,Place+1,Length-Place)
      Length = LEN(TRIM(String))
      LF = LF + 1
   ENDDO (while length > margin)

   *------ Print remainder of String, then return.
   ? SPACE(Left)+LTRIM(String)
   LF = LF + 1
RETURN
```

Figure 6.11: The WordWrap procedure

A variable named Length is assigned the length of the passed character string with any trailing blanks removed:

    Length = LEN(TRIM(String))

A DO WHILE loop is set up to keep breaking the loop String as long as the length of the String being word wrapped is longer than the space allotted (determined by subtracting the left-margin setting from the right-margin setting). Within this loop, the variable Place receives the true value of the right margin (again, the left-margin value subtracted from the right-margin value):

    * – – – – – – – –- Set up loop through string.
    DO WHILE Length > Right – Left
       Place = Right – Left

The word-wrapping procedure cannot arbitrarily break the String at the Place location, however, because this position might be in the middle of the word. Therefore, the DO WHILE loop below starts searching String backwards, from the right margin, until it finds a blank space. With each pass through the loop, the Place variable is decremented by 1:

```
* - Find blank nearest right margin (Place).
DO WHILE SUBSTR(String,Place,1) # " "
   Place = Place - 1
ENDDO (until blank space found)
```

When the small DO WHILE loop is done, the Place variable contains a number representing the blank space nearest but not greater than the right margin. Hence, the procedure prints enough blank spaces to fill in the requested left margin, followed by the left side of String up to the first blank space nearest the right margin:

```
*- Print portion, and assign rest to String.
? SPACE(Left) + LTRIM(LEFT(String,Place - 1))
```

The printed part of String is removed from the String variable, and the Length variable is reset to the size of the remaining String. Since a line has been printed, the LF variable, which counts line feeds (printed lines) is incremented by 1. Then the ENDDO command repeats the routine, assuming that the remaining length of string is wider than the margin space allotted:

```
String = SUBSTR(String,Place + 1,Length - Place)
Length = LEN(TRIM(String))
LF = LF + 1
ENDDO (while length > margin)
```

When the remaining part of String is short enough to be displayed within the allotted margins, the procedure prints that remaining part (preceded by the left-margin spaces), increments the line feed counter by 1 again, and returns control to the calling program:

```
* - - - Print remainder of    String, then return.
? SPACE(Left) + LTRIM(String)
LF = LF + 1
RETURN
```

Like some other procedures in this book, word wrapping is much easier to use than it is to explain. For example, suppose you have a field named Abstract in a database, which you want to display, word wrapped, on the screen or printer with a left margin of 5 and a right margin of 50. Assuming you've already opened the GenProcs procedure, you would first need to store a copy of the Abstract field in a memory variable

    Temp = Abstract

then call the WordWrap procedure with the appropriate parameters

    DO WordWrap WITH Temp,5,50,0

When the procedure is done, the character string in Abstract will be neatly displayed on the screen, with a left margin of 5 spaces and a right margin of 50. In this case, we just passed a zero as the line-feed parameter, but we'll see a practical application of this parameter in a moment.

Figure 6.12 shows a sample command file named TestStr.PRG that you can type in to run and test the WordWrap procedure. Notice that it initially sets a variable named Lines to 0, and passes this as the fourth parameter.

```
*********************************** TestStr.PRG
*-------- Program to test the WordWrap procedure.
SET TALK OFF
SET PROCEDURE TO GenProcs
CLEAR

*------------------- Get data from screen.
Left = 0
Right = 0
Lines = 0
LString = SPACE(254)

@ 2,1 SAY "Enter left margin " GET Left PICTURE "99"
@ 4,1 SAY "Enter right margin " GET Right PICTURE "99"
@ 6,1 SAY "Enter a long string " GET LString
READ

*---- Display string before word wrap.
CLEAR
? "Before WordWrap: "
?
? LString
?
?
? "After Word Wrap: "
?
DO WordWrap WITH LString,Left,Right,Lines
?
? "There were "+STR(Lines,2)+" lines printed above."
?
CLOSE PROCEDURE
RETURN
```

Figure 6.12:   The TextStr.PRG command file

When you DO TestStr, the screen will ask that you fill in a left-margin number, a right-margin number, and a long character string to wrap. Figure 6.13 shows the screen that TestStr displays with some sample data filled in.

Figure 6.14 shows the results of TestStr.PRG. Notice that the top part shows how arbitrarily dBASE displays the character string without word wrapping. The middle part of the screen shows the sample character string word wrapped within the requested margins. The last line shows the number of lines that were printed in the word-wrapped display.

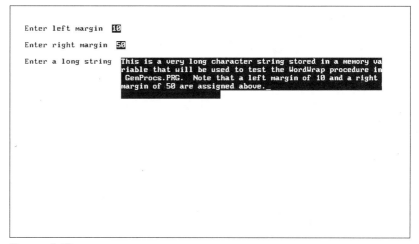

```
Enter left margin   10

Enter right margin  50

Enter a long string  This is a very long character string stored in a memory va
                     riable that will be used to test the WordWrap procedure in
                     GenProcs.PRG.  Note that a left margin of 10 and a right
                     margin of 50 are assigned above._
```

Figure 6.13: TestStr screen filled in with sample data

```
Before WordWrap:

This is a very long character string stored in a memory variable that will be us
ed to test the WordWrap procedure in GenProcs.PRG.  Note that a left margin of 1
0 and a right margin of 50 are assigned above.


After Word Wrap:

        This is a very long character string
        stored in a memory variable that will
        be used to test the WordWrap procedure
        in GenProcs.PRG.  Note that a left
        margin of 10 and a right margin of 50
        are assigned above.

There were 6 lines printed above.



   · _
```

Figure 6.14: Results of the Test.Str.PRG command file

A more practical application of the WordWrap procedure would be to use it with printed reports that display a long character field. Figure 6.15 shows the structure of a hypothetical database with a long field named Abstract that consists of 250 characters. Figure 6.16 shows a sample command file, named TestStr2.PRG, that prints a formatted report from the Library.DBF database. Note that the command file opens the Library database and the GenProcs procedure file.

```
Structure for database : C:LIBRARY.dbf

    Field   Field name    Type        Width     Dec
      1     AUTHOR        Character      30
      2     TITLE         Character      60
      3     PUB           Character      40
      4     LOCATION      Character      40
      5     PAGES         Character      10
      6     ABSTRACT      Character     250
    ** Total **                        431
```

Figure 6.15:   Structure for hypothetical Library.DBF database

The sample command file also keeps track of the number of lines printed on each page, using the variable LF. This variable is passed to the WordWrap procedure in the DO WordWrap WITH M_Abstract,8,68,LF command. Passing LF to the WordWrap procedure in this fashion ensures that lines printed during word wrap are also included in this line counter.

The routine in TestStr2.PRG that performs page breaks is shown below. Note that whenever 55 or more lines have been printed on the page, the EJECT command advances the paper in the printer to the top of the next page. The routine then prints the report title and a blank line at the top of the next page, and resets the line counter (LF) to 2.

```
* – –- If 55 or more lines printed, start on
* – –- new page, print heading, and reset LF.
IF LF > = 55
EJECT
? " Reference Listing"
?
LF = 2
ENDIF
```

```
****************************************** TestStr2.PRG
*- Test modified WordWrap procedure with Library data.
SET TALK OFF

*--- Open database.
USE Library

*-- Make LF variable public, and open procedure file.

SET PROCEDURE TO GenProcs

*-- Print heading.
SET PRINT ON
? "                         Reference Listing"
?
*-- Start LineFeed Counter.
LF = 2

*-- Loop through database.
GO TOP
DO WHILE .NOT. EOF()
    ? "Author:     ",Author
    ? "Title :     ",Title
    ? "Publisher: ",TRIM(Pub)+", "+Location
    ?
    ? "Abstract:   "
    *--- Increment LineFeed counter (LF).
    LF = LF + 5
    *--- Print abstract with margins of 10 and 68.
    M_Abstract = TRIM(Abstract)
    DO WordWrap WITH M_Abstract,8,68,LF
    ?
    ?
    LF = LF + 2

    *----- If 55 or more lines printed, start on
    *----- new page, print heading, and reset LF.
    IF LF >= 55
        EJECT
        ? "                         Reference Listing"
        ?
        LF = 2
    ENDIF
    *---- Skip to next record and continue loop.
    SKIP
ENDDO

CLOSE PROCEDURE
SET PRINT OFF
RETURN
```

Figure 6.16: Sample program to print data from Library database

Figure 6.17 shows two sample records printed from the Library.DBF database using the TestStr.PRG command file. The general techniques used in TestStr2.PRG can easily be used to print long fields from any database.

```
                        Reference Listing
Author:      Simpson, Alan
Title :      Advanced Techniques in dBASE III PLUS
Publisher:   SYBEX, Berkeley, CA

Abstract:
        This book presents numerous techniques for designing and
        developing custom systems written in dBASE III PLUS.
        Includes mailing list, inventory, and accounts receivable
        systems.  Also discusses maximizing speed of custom systems.

Author:      Simpson, Alan
Title :      Understanding dBASE III PLUS
Publisher:   SYBEX, Berkeley, CA

Abstract:
        Written for the novice computer user, this book discusses
        general techniques for creating, sorting, searching,
        formatting, and editing data through dBASE III PLUS.
        Provides an introduction to developing custom systems with
        command files.
```

Figure 6.17:   Sample display from Library database

⊙TRANSLATING DATES TO ENGLISH

The TransDat procedure translates dBASE III PLUS Date data from the MM/DD/YY format to English (for example, January 1 1986). The procedure, named TransDat, uses the parameter PDate and the public variable Eng_Date. Figure 6.18 shows the procedure, which you can add to the GenProcs procedure file in the usual manner.

The TransDat procedure is not terribly complex. The data passed to it must be of the Date data type. An IF clause converts the day part of the date to either a one- or two-character string, depending on whether the day is greater than nine. Then the Eng_Date variable is assigned the English month (CMONTH), the day followed by a comma and a space, and the year converted to a character string.

```
*********************** Translate date to English.
*------- Make Eng_Date public in calling program.
PROCEDURE TransDat
PARAMETERS PDate
   PDay = STR(DAY(PDate),IIF(DAY(PDate)<10,1,2))
   Eng_Date = CMONTH(PDate) + " " + PDay + ", " ;
     + STR(YEAR(PDate),4)
RETURN
```

Figure 6.18:   The TransDat procedure

A simple test for the TransDat procedure is to store the current system date (DATE( )) in a memory variable, and translate it. From the dot prompt, open the procedure file and store the system date in some variable such as T_Date, as in the commands below:

```
SET PROCEDURE TO GenProcs
T_Date = DATE( )
```

If you print the T_Date variable, you'll see the current system date, as shown below:

```
? T_Date
```

09/05/85

To test out the TransDat procedure, make the Eng_Date variable public, then run the TransDat procedure with the T_Date variable, as shown below:

```
PUBLIC Eng_Date
DO TransDat WITH T_Date
```

To view the date in English format, print the contents of the Eng_Date variable, as below:

```
? Eng_Date
```

September 5, 1985

We'll test the TransDat procedure from within a command file later in this chapter.

⊙TRANSLATING NUMBERS TO ENGLISH

Chances are, if you write many dBASE III PLUS command files, you'll eventually have to write a program that prints checks. This can be a tricky problem when it comes time to translate the dollar amount (1234.76) to English (ONE THOUSAND TWO HUNDRED THIRTY FOUR AND 76/100). We will now write a procedure named Translat that can translate any number up to 999,999.99 to its proper English equivalent.

First, we need to have access to all the unique English equivalents for numbers. For convenience, I've stored these in a memory file named English.MEM. To create the English.MEM file, type in the English.PRG command file shown in Figure 6.19. Then run the program with the DO command, and it will create the English.MEM memory file for you.

```
**************************************** English.PRG
* Sets up memory file for storing English equivalents.

CLEAR
? "Creating English.MEM memory file..."
?
SET TALK ON
CLEAR MEMORY

U  = " "
U1  = "ONE"
U2  = "TWO"
U3  = "THREE"
U4  = "FOUR"
U5  = "FIVE"
U6  = "SIX"
U7  = "SEVEN"
U8  = "EIGHT"
U9  = "NINE"
U10 = "TEN"
U11 = "ELEVEN"
U12 = "TWELVE"
U13 = "THIRTEEN"
U14 = "FOURTEEN"
U15 = "FIFTEEN"
U16 = "SIXTEEN"
U17 = "SEVENTEEN"
U18 = "EIGHTEEN"
U19 = "NINETEEN"
U20 = "TWENTY"
U30 = "THIRTY"
U40 = "FORTY"
U50 = "FIFTY"
U60 = "SIXTY"
U70 = "SEVENTY"
U80 = "EIGHTY"
U90 = "NINETY"

*----- Save all variables to English.MEM file.
SAVE TO English
CLEAR
?
?
? "English.MEM now has English words for numbers."
SET TALK OFF
RETURN
```

Figure 6.19:   The English.PRG command file

After running the English.PRG command file, check to make sure it ran correctly by typing the commands:

```
RESTORE FROM English
DISPLAY MEMORY
```

You should see all of the English words stored in memory variables. Each memory variable name consists of the letter U, followed by the number that it represents (e.g., U20 is "TWENTY", U9 is "NINE", and so forth). We'll see how this naming scheme comes in handy in a moment. Figure 6.20 shows how the screen looks when you display the memory.

```
U       pub     C       " "
U1      pub     C       "ONE"
U2      pub     C       "TWO"
U3      pub     C       "THREE"
U4      pub     C       "FOUR"
U5      pub     C       "FIVE"
U6      pub     C       "SIX"
U7      pub     C       "SEVEN"
U8      pub     C       "EIGHT"
U9      pub     C       "NINE"
U10     pub     C       "TEN"
U11     pub     C       "ELEVEN"
U12     pub     C       "TWELVE"
U13     pub     C       "THIRTEEN"
U14     pub     C       "FOURTEEN"
U15     pub     C       "FIFTEEN"
U16     pub     C       "SIXTEEN"
U17     pub     C       "SEVENTEEN"
U18     pub     C       "EIGHTEEN"
U19     pub     C       "NINETEEN"
U20     pub     C       "TWENTY"
U30     pub     C       "THIRTY"
U40     pub     C       "FORTY"
U50     pub     C       "FIFTY"
U60     pub     C       "SIXTY"
U70     pub     C       "SEVENTY"
U80     pub     C       "EIGHTY"
U90     pub     C       "NINETY"


   28 variables defined,   209 bytes used
   228 variables available, 5791 bytes available
```

Figure 6.20:   Memory variables restored from English.MEM

Creating these English variables solves several problems for us. For example, to see the English equivalent for the number 11, you merely need to enter the command

? U11

and dBASE displays

ELEVEN

To see the English equivalent for 99, enter the command

? U90,U9

and dBASE displays

NINETY NINE

Of course, we can't store English equivalents for every single possible number, but we can build long English translations from the elements in memory variables. The Translat procedure performs just this task. You can add the Translat procedure to the GenProcs procedure file using the usual method.

NOTE: If you are using the dBASE MODIFY COMMAND editor to create the GenProcs.PRG procedure file, the Translat procedure will be a tight squeeze. There are four alternative ways to solve the problem of getting too many characters into the MODIFY COMMAND editor:

1. Remove all comments and blank lines from the GenProcs procedure file to make as much room as possible,

2. Put the Translat procedure in its own procedure file,

3. Leave out some other procedure from the GenProcs procedure file, or

4. Use some word processor or text editor other than MODIFY COM-MAND to create the GenProcs procedure file.

Figure 6.21 shows the entire Translat procedure. Within the first few lines, a single parameter, Amount, is passed to the procedure. Amount must be a memory variable containing the number to be translated as numeric data:

```
*********************** Convert a number to English equivalent.
* Make Eng_Num variable public in calling program.
```

```
* Must have access to English.MEM variables.
PROCEDURE Translat
PARAMETERS Amount
```

Next, several variables used within the procedure are initialized. Most importantly, the variable String is assigned the character equivalent of the Amount passed, using a fixed format of nine digits (counting the decimal point) with two decimal places:

```
*---------- Set up memory variables.
Counter = 1
Start = 1
String = STR(Amount,9,2)
Eng_Num = " "
```

Next a loop is set up to make two passes through the number.

```
*-------- Loop through thousands and hundreds.
DO WHILE Counter < 3
```

To follow the logic of the program, assume that the number passed to the program was 123405.67. During the first pass through the loop, the Start variable equals 1. So the next commands figure out the values of the first three numbers:

```
*------ Split out hundreds, tens, and ones.
Chunk = SUBSTR(String,Start,3)
Hun = SUBSTR(Chunk,1,1)
Ten = SUBSTR(Chunk,2,2)
One = SUBSTR(Chunk,3,1)
```

and come up with the following variables:

```
Chunk = "123"
Hun = "1"
Ten = "23"
One = "3"
```

Next, the command file checks to see if the value of the Chunk variable is greater than 99. If so, it adds U&Hun plus the word "HUNDRED" to the Eng_Num variable:

```
*------ Handle hundreds portion.
IF VAL(Chunk) > 99
```

```
    Eng_Num = Eng_Num + U&Hun + ' HUNDRED '
ENDIF (chunk > 99)
```

In this example, the value of Chunk is greater than 99. The Hun variable contains 1, so U&Hun translates it to U1, or ONE. At this point, the Eng_Num variable contains the words ONE HUNDRED.

The second two digits of the Chunk variable are harder to handle because there are different rules for numbers under ten, teens, and numbers evenly divisible by ten. A DO CASE clause embedded in an IF clause decides how to handle the tens part of the number. First the command file checks to make sure that the tens part of the number is indeed greater than 0:

```
*------ Handle second two digits.
T = VAL(Ten)
IF T > 0
```

If so, several possibilities are considered. The first possibility is that the tens part of the number is either in the teens or is evenly divisible by ten. If so, the English equivalent for the tens part is attached to the Eng_Num variable, as shown below:

```
DO CASE

* Handle even tens and teens.
CASE (INT(T/10.0) = T/10.0).OR.(T>9.AND.T<20)
    Eng_Num = Eng_Num + U&Ten
```

Another possibility is that the tens part is indeed greater than 20, but is not evenly divisible by 10. Our sample number, 23, falls into this category. So the appropriate CASE statement peels the first digit off the tens variable (2 in this example) and tacks a 0 onto it (so the tens variable contains 20). Then, the case statement adds U20 and U3, (or TWENTY THREE) to the Eng_Num variable:

```
* Handle greater than 10, but not evenly divisible.
CASE T > 9 .AND. (INT(T/10.0)#T/10.0)
    Ten = SUBSTR(Ten,1,1) + '0'
    Eng_Num = Eng_Num + U&Ten + ' ' + U&One
```

At this point with our sample number, the Eng_Num variable contains ONE HUNDRED TWENTY THREE.

The third case handles the possibility that the tens part of the number is less than ten, in which case only the ones part is translated and added to the Eng_Num variable:

```
* Handle less than 10.
   CASE T < 10
      Eng_Num = Eng_Num + U&One
   ENDCASE
ENDIF (T > 0)
```

The next routine checks for two things:

1. If the number stored in Amount is greater than 999.99, and

2. If this is the first pass through the loop (Counter = 1).

If both conditions are true, as with our sample number, the word "THOU-SAND" is added to the information in the Eng_Num variable in the following lines:

```
*-- Add "Thousand" if necessary.
IF Amount > 999.99 .AND. Counter = 1
   Eng_Num = Eng_Num +' THOUSAND '
ENDIF (need to add "thousand")
```

At this point, Eng_Num is "ONE HUNDRED TWENTY THREE THOUSAND".

At this point, the Start variable is reset to 4, so that the next chunk of numbers begins with the fourth digit. The Counter variable is incremented by 1 (for the second pass through the loop), and the loop is repeated. The second three digits in the integer portion of the Amount are then translated using the same routines:

```
*-- Prepare for pass through hundreds.
Start = 4
Counter = Counter + 1

ENDDO (while counter < 3)
```

After the second pass through the DO WHILE loop, the entire integer part of the amount has been translated. If the Amount variable is greater than a dollar, the word *AND* is tacked onto the Eng_Num variable:

```
*----- Tack on cents.
IF INT(Amount) > 0
```

```
        Eng_Num = Eng_Num + " AND "
ENDIF
```

Then the pennies part, plus the /100 symbol, is added to the
Eng_Num variable, and the procedure is done:

```
        Eng_Num = Eng_Num + SUBSTR(String,8,2) + "/100"
```

```
        *-------- End procedure.
RETURN
```

```
********* Convert a number to English equivalent.
* Make Eng_Num variable public in calling program.
* Must have access to English.MEM variables.

PROCEDURE Translat
PARAMETERS Amount

*---------- Set up memory variables.
Counter = 1
Start = 1
String = STR(Amount,9,2)
Eng_Num = " "

*-------- Loop through thousands and hundreds.
DO WHILE Counter < 3

   *------ Split out hundreds, tens, and ones.
   Chunk = SUBSTR(String,Start,3)
   Hun = SUBSTR(Chunk,1,1)
   Ten = SUBSTR(Chunk,2,2)
   One = SUBSTR(Chunk,3,1)

   *------ Handle hundreds portion.
   IF VAL(Chunk) > 99
       Eng_Num = Eng_Num + U&Hun + ' HUNDRED '
   ENDIF (chunk > 99)

   *------ Handle second two digits.
   T = VAL(Ten)
   IF T > 0

      DO CASE
         *-- Handle even tens and teens.
         CASE (INT(T/10.0)=T/10.0).OR. ;
             (T>9.AND.T<20)
             Eng_Num = Eng_Num + U&Ten

         *-- Handle greater than 10, but not evenly divisible.
         CASE T > 9 .AND. (INT(T/10.0)#T/10.0)
             Ten = SUBSTR(Ten,1,1) +'0'
             Eng_Num = Eng_Num + U&Ten+' '+U&One
```

Figure 6.21:   The Translat procedure

```
              *-- Handle less than 10.
              CASE T < 10
                    Eng_Num = Eng_Num + U&One

          ENDCASE
        ENDIF (T > 0)

        *-- Add "Thousand" if necessary.
        IF Amount > 999.99 .AND. Counter = 1
           Eng_Num = Eng_Num +' THOUSAND '
        ENDIF (need to add "thousand")

        *-- Prepare for pass through hundreds.
        Start = 4
        Counter = Counter + 1

     ENDDO (while counter < 3)

     *----- Tack on cents.
     IF INT(Amount) > 0
        Eng_Num = Eng_Num + " AND "
     ENDIF

     Eng_Num = Eng_Num + SUBSTR(String,8,2)+"/100"

     *-------- End procedure.
     RETURN
```

Figure 6.21:   The Translat procedure (continued)

Once the procedure is added to the procedure file, it is easy to test. You need to perform three steps to use the translation procedure:

1. Open the GenProcs procedure file,

2. Call in the English memory variables, and

3. Make the Eng_Num variable public.

The commands to do so are displayed below. Type them in at the dot prompt.

```
SET PROCEDURE TO GenProcs
RESTORE FROM English
PUBLIC Eng_Num
```

From here, you can access the Translat procedure with a literal number, as in the command below:

```
DO Translat WITH 1234.56
```

To see the English translation, print the Eng_Num variable:

  ? Eng_Num

dBASE displays the proper translation:

  ONE THOUSAND TWO HUNDRED THIRTY FOUR AND 56/100

You can pass the number to be translated as a variable if you prefer. For example, the commands below assign a number to the variable X, translate the number, and display it on the screen:

  STORE 555.55 TO Z
  DO Translat WITH Z
  ? Eng_Num

dBASE displays:

  FIVE HUNDRED FIFTY FIVE AND 55/100

More often then not, of course, you'll want to use the TransDat and Translat procedures with data from a database. For an example we'll use the database with data for printing checks shown in Figure 6.22.

Structure for database : C:checks.dbf

Field	Field name	Type	Width	Dec
1	CHECKNO	Character	4	
2	C_DATE	Date	8	
3	TO_WHOM	Character	20	
4	AMOUNT	Numeric	12	2
Total			45	

Figure 6.22:   Structure for the Checks.DBF database

Let's assume that the Checks.DBF database contains the following data:

RECORD#	CHECKNO	C_DATE	TO_WHOM	AMOUNT
1	1001	06/01/86	Alfred P. Wonka	101.56
2	1002	06/15/86	General Utilities Co.	1230.99
3	1003	06/15/86	Astro Electronics	123456.78

Figure 6.23 shows a command file named TestTran.PRG that can print checks from this database, using the TransDat and Translat procedures to convert the dates and numbers to English.

Notice that the TestTran.PRG command file opens the GenProcs procedure, restores variables from the English.MEM memory file (using the ADDITIVE option to keep existing memory variables from being erased), and declares the Eng_Date and Eng_Num variables as public.

A DO WHILE loop steps through each record in the Checks database, translates the dates and amounts, and uses ? statements to format and print checks. Figure 6.24 shows a sample printout from the TestTran.PRG command file.

```
********************************* TestTran.PRG
*- Command file to test the translation procedure.

*--------------------------- Set procedure file.
SET TALK OFF
SET PROCEDURE TO GenProcs

*--------------------------- Get English words.
RESTORE FROM English ADDITIVE

*------------------------ Make variables public.
PUBLIC Eng_Date,Eng_Num

*------------------ Use database with check info.
USE Checks

*--- Loop through file.
CLEAR
GO TOP
DO WHILE .NOT. EOF()
   M_Date = C_Date
   DO TransDat WITH M_Date
   M_Amount = Amount
   DO Translat WITH M_Amount
   ? SPACE(5) + CheckNo
   ?? SPACE(36)+Eng_Date
   ?
   ? SPACE(5)+To_Whom
   ?? SPACE(20),Amount
   ?
   ? SPACE(4)+Eng_Num
   ?
   ?
   ?
   SKIP
ENDDO

CLOSE PROCEDURE
RELEASE Eng_Num
RETURN
```

Figure 6.23: The TestTran.PRG command file

```
1001                              June 1, 1986

Alfred P. Wonka                              101.56

ONE HUNDRED ONE AND 56/100


1002                              June 15, 1986

General Utilities Co.                       1230.99

ONE THOUSAND TWO HUNDRED THIRTY AND 99/100


1003                              June 15, 1986

Astro Electronics                         123456.78

ONE HUNDRED TWENTY THREE THOUSAND FOUR HUNDRED FIFTY SIX AND 78/100
```

Figure 6.24:   Output from the TestTran.PRG command file

Of course, this sample program probably won't print checks in exactly the format you need. You will need to modify the spaces and blank lines in the printing parts (? commands) to accommodate the format of your particular blank checks. (I suggest using photocopies of your checks while trying to get the program to fill them in properly.)

These general-purpose procedures should be useful in your own applications. One important point to keep in mind is that the English.MEM memory file needs to be readily accessible if you wish to use the Translat procedure. Public variables in use are noted in comments in the procedures themselves.

If you've been following along chapter by chapter, you are no doubt beginning to think that it might be nice to mix and match the procedures we've discussed so far into a variety of procedure files, each best suited to a particular application. In the next chapter, we'll discuss some advanced techniques that you can use with the MODIFY COMMAND editor to move procedures from one file to another.

MANAGING
PROCEDURES

7

At this point you might want to copy and move procedures from file to file to have quicker and more convenient access to particular procedures. For example, you might want to include the Log10 procedure, from the FinProcs.PRG procedure file, with the procedures in the StatProc procedure file. You can avoid retyping procedures by copying and moving chunks of files from one file to another.

With the MODIFY COMMAND editor, you have to be careful not to go beyond the 5,000-character limit. So in our examples with MODIFY COMMAND, we'll use temporary files to move procedures.

⊙MOVING PROCEDURES WITH THE MODIFY COMMAND EDITOR

Let's move a copy of the Log10 procedure from the FinProcs.PRG procedure file to the StatProc.PRG procedure file. First, make sure all procedure files are closed by entering the CLOSE PROCEDURE command. Then, call up the FinProcs procedure file by typing

    MODIFY COMMAND FinProcs

You'll see the FinProcs procedure file appear in the dBASE text editor. Now, make a copy of the entire procedure by typing ^KW.

dBASE will ask that you enter a file name. Use a unique file name, so that you don't accidentally destroy an important command file or procedure file. In this example, enter the file name Chunk.TXT, and press the Return key.

Now there is an exact duplicate of the FinProcs.PRG procedure file under the file name Chunk.TXT. Since we have not actually made any changes to the FinProcs procedure file, exit from the file by typing ^Q to "abandon edit."

Now we need to isolate the Log10 procedure. First, enter the command

    MODIFY COMMAND Chunk.TXT

to bring the Chunk.TXT file into the MODIFY COMMAND editor. Next, you need to delete all the lines except those composing the Log10 procedure. Type ^Y about 23 times, so that all the lines above the Log10 procedure are deleted, and the Log10 procedure is at the top of the procedure file, as in Figure 7.1. (NOTE: Pressing the F1 key toggles the MODIFY COMMAND editor help screen on and off.)

Next, press the down-arrow or ^X to move the cursor to the line beneath the last line of the Log10 procedure (one line below the RETURN command).

```
Edit: C:Chunk.TXT
                                                                        <
*--Log10 calculates the base 10 logarithm of a number.                  <
PROCEDURE Log10                                                         <
PARAMETERS Number                                                       <
   NatLog = LOG(Number)                                                 <
   IF NatLog >= 0                                                       <
      Con=(NatLog * .43429448)-INT(NatLog*.43429448)                    <
      LRound= ROUND(Con,6)                                              <
      Log10= (INT(NatLog*.43429448)+LRound)                             <
   ELSE                                                                 <
      Con=((NatLog*.43429448)-INT(NatLog*.43429448))*-1                 <
      LRound= ROUND(Con,6)                                              <
      Log10= (INT(NatLog*.43429448)-LRound)                             <
   ENDIF (natlog >=0)                                                   <
RETURN                                                                  <
                                                                        <
*------Cagr calculates the compound annual growth rate.                 <
*------Uses Log10 procedure for log base 10.                            <
PROCEDURE Cagr                                                          <
PARAMETERS Present, Future, Years                                       <
   *--- Get log of present and future values.                          <
   DO Log10 WITH Present                                                <
   PLog = Log10                                                         <
```

Figure 7.1: The Log10 procedure at the top of the Chunk.TXT file

You'll now need to delete all lines beneath the procedure by typing ^Y about 12 times. When you are done, you should see only the Log10 procedure on the screen, as in Figure 7.2.

Now type ^W to save this version of Chunk.TXT. The Chunk.TXT file now contains only the Log10 procedure. To read that procedure into the StatProc procedure file, enter the command

MODIFY COMMAND StatProc

which brings the StatProc procedure onto the screen for editing. Keep pressing PgDn (or ^C) and the down-arrow until the cursor is at the far left beneath the very last line in the procedure file (one line below the last RETURN command). Press the Return key a few times so that there is a little space between the last procedure and the cursor position, as in Figure 7.3.

Now, type ^KR. When the requested file is read in, it will be placed at the current cursor position in the StatProc file. When the screen asks for the name of the file to read in, enter the file name Chunk.TXT and press Return. You should see the Log10 procedure on the screen, as in Figure 7.4. Save the procedure file now by typing ^W.

To verify that the procedure works, first set the TALK option off, open the procedure file, and make the Log10 variable public:

SET TALK OFF
SET PROCEDURE TO StatProc
PUBLIC Log10

```
Edit: C:Chunk.TXT                                                 <
                                                                  <
*--Log10 calculates the base 10 logarithm of a number.            <
PROCEDURE Log10                                                   <
PARAMETERS Number                                                 <
  NatLog = LOG(Number)                                            <
  IF NatLog >= 0                                                  <
     Con=(NatLog * .43429448)-INT(NatLog*.43429448)               <
     LRound= ROUND(Con,6)                                         <
     Log10= (INT(NatLog*.43429448)+LRound)                        <
  ELSE                                                            <
     Con=((NatLog*.43429448)-INT(NatLog*.43429448))*-1            <
     LRound= ROUND(Con,6)                                         <
     Log10= (INT(NatLog*.43429448)-LRound)                        <
  ENDIF (natlog >=0)                                              <
RETURN                                                            <
                                                                  <
  _
```

Figure 7.2:   The Log10 procedure isolated on the screen

```
Edit: C:StatProc.prg                                              <
  *-- Multiply differences.                                       <
  DifDif = DifSqX * DifSqY                                        <
  DifRoot = SQRT(DifDif)                                          <
  *-- Calculate Pearson R.                                        <
  Pearson = RNum/DifRoot                                          <
RETURN                                                            <
                                                                  <
  _                                                               <
```

Figure 7.3:   Cursor beneath the last procedure in StatProc.PRG

If you now call the Log10 procedure with a simple command such as

    DO log10 WITH 1000

then enter the command

    ? Log10

```
Edit: C:StatProc.prg
   *-- Multiply differences.                                    <
   DifDif = DifSqX * DifSqY                                     <
   DifRoot = SQRT(DifDif)                                       <
   *-- Calculate Pearson R.                                     <
   Pearson = RNum/DifRoot                                       <
RETURN                                                          <
                                                                <
                                                                <
*--Log10 calculates the base 10 logarithm of a number.         <
PROCEDURE Log10                                                 <
PARAMETERS Number                                              <
   NatLog = LOG(Number)                                         <
   IF NatLog >= 0                                               <
      Con=(NatLog * .43429448)-INT(NatLog*.43429448)            <
      LRound= ROUND(Con,6)                                      <
      Log10= (INT(NatLog*.43429448)+LRound)                     <
   ELSE                                                         <
      Con=((NatLog*.43429448)-INT(NatLog*.43429448))*-1         <
      LRound= ROUND(Con,6)                                      <
      Log10= (INT(NatLog*.43429448)-LRound)                     <
   ENDIF (natlog >=0)                                           <
RETURN                                                          <
                                                                <
```

Figure 7.4:   The Log10 procedure read into the StatProc procedure file

you should see the results of the computation, as below:

3.0000000000

The most important advantage to combining procedures in a single procedure file is speed. Calling a single procedure with a DO...WITH command takes almost no time at all. However, the SET PROCEDURE command takes quite a while to locate the procedure file on disk and load it into RAM (particularly on floppy-disk-based computers). By combining all the necessary procedures for a given application into a single procedure file, you can eliminate repetitive SET PROCEDURE commands, and thereby make the entire application run a little faster.

When moving procedures from file to file, remember that MODIFY COMMAND has a 5,000-character limit. If you go over this limit, MODIFY COMMAND will simply cut the file off at about the 5,000th character. For this reason, it is a good idea to always append new procedures to the bottoms of existing procedures, so that none of the original procedures are accidentally cut off if you run over the 5,000-character limit. Also, keep in mind that a maximum of 32 procedures is allowed in one procedure file.

One way to avoid the 5,000-character limit of the MODIFY COMMAND editor, as well as to facilitate moving procedures from one file to another, is to use an external word processor instead of MODIFY COMMAND. As an example, I will now discuss techniques for using the WordStar package to create and edit procedure files.

⊙MANAGING PROCEDURES WITH WORDSTAR

When using an external word processor such as WordStar, it is important that you always use the nondocument or unformatted mode. If you don't specify the appropriate mode, the special formatting codes used by your word processor will wreak havoc on a command file or program.

To use WordStar, you simply type in the letters WS at the DOS A> or C> prompt. Optionally, if you have 380K RAM or more, and your Word-Star is accessible from the same disk as your dBASE III PLUS program, you can also run WordStar from the dBASE dot prompt by typing

RUN WS

In this example, we will once again move a copy of the Log10 procedure from the FinProcs.PRG procedure file into the StatProc.PRG procedure file.

From the WordStar main menu, type the letter N to select nondocument mode. When WordStar asks for the name of the file to edit, type FinProcs-.PRG. (You must specify file name extensions such as .PRG with external word processors, because they are not automatically supplied.) The FinProcs-.PRG procedure file will appear on the screen, ready for editing.

To locate the Log10 procedure quickly, enter the command ^QF. Word-Star will ask what you want to find. Type in Log10 and press the Return key. WordStar will then ask what options you wish to use. Type the letter U (to ignore upper- and lowercase), and press Return.

The cursor will move to the first occurrence of the word Log10 in the procedure file. This one is still up in the comments section of the proce-dure file, so type ^L to locate the next occurrence. This time the cursor will find its way to the top of the Log10 procedure. Type ^A to move the cursor to the first character on the first line of the Log10 procedure.

Now you need to mark the procedure as a block. Type ^KB to mark the beginning of the block. Next, type the down-arrow (or ^X) 14 times to move the cursor to the bottom of the procedure, one line below the RETURN command. Type ^KK to mark the end of the block. You should see the Log10 procedure darken on the screen, indicating that it is now marked as a block.

Now you can create a separate file containing a copy of the Log10 pro-cedure. Enter the command ^KW to write a copy of the marked block to a file. When WordStar asks for a file name, use a file name that has not been used before so you don't overwrite an existing procedure or command file. In this example, enter the file name Chunk.TXT and press Return.

If the selected file name does already exist, WordStar will display the following message:

FILE CHUNK.TXT EXISTS — OVERWRITE? (Y/N):

If it is safe to overwrite the existing file, enter the letter Y. (Otherwise, enter N, and type in another file name.)

At this point, the file Chunk.TXT contains the Log10 procedure. Leave the GenProcs.PRG command file by entering the command ^KQ. You will be returned to the WordStar main menu.

From the WordStar main menu, select nondocument (N) to edit the StatProc procedure file. Enter the file name StatProc.PRG when requested.

Once the procedure file appears on the screen, type ^QC to move the cursor to the bottom of the file. Press Return a couple of times to make room if necessary.

To read in the Log10 procedure, enter the command ^KR. When the screen asks for the name of the file to read, enter the file name Chunk.TXT, and press Return. The Log10 procedure will appear at the bottom of the procedure file.

You might notice that on the top of the screen, WordStar displays some statistics. If you type ^QC to move to the bottom of the file, the FC statistic tells you how many characters are in the entire file. If that number is below 5,000, it is still safe to edit the file with the MODIFY COMMAND editor.

Once you've read the Log10 procedure into the StatProc.PRG procedure file, save the file and exit WordStar by entering the command ^KX.

If you entered WordStar from the DOS prompt, you will be returned to the DOS prompt. If you entered WordStar with the command RUN WS from the dBASE dot prompt, you will be returned to the dBASE dot prompt.

When you are using an external word processor, dBASE will not insist that you close the procedure file before editing it. However, any changes that you make to an open procedure file will not work until you close the file and reopen it with the SET PROCEDURE command. That's because an open procedure file is stored in RAM, and the word processor edits only the copy stored on disk.

Most word processors have commands like the WordStar ^QF, ^KB, ^KK, ^KW, and ^KK commands for locating, marking, and moving blocks of text. However, the specific commands used to perform these tasks vary. Check your word-processing manual for details.

TECHNIQUES FOR
REPORTS AND FORMS

8

In this chapter we'll look at advanced methods for printing reports and for creating data-entry and editing techniques. I'll assume you are already familiar with the basic dBASE report generator and the screen painter. In this chapter, we'll focus on techniques that exceed the capabilities of these built-in dBASE features.

⊙UNLIMITED SUBTOTALS IN REPORTS

The dBASE III PLUS report generator allows you to print reports with subtotals and subsubtotals (i.e., two levels of *grouping*). With some programming, you can bypass the report generator and develop your own reports with just about any number of subtotals. While there is no quick-and-easy procedure that you can develop to handle this job, there are some basic, straightforward programming techniques you can use.

In this section we'll build a program with three levels of subtotals, starting with a program with only one level of subtotals. By building the program in this manner, you should be able to see how each level of subtotaling uses basically the same logic or *algorithm*.

Figure 8.1 shows the SubTots.DBF database we'll be using with the sample programs we develop. The database contains the fields PartNo, PartName, SalesMan (which contains salespersons' initials), Qty, UnitPrice, and Date. To show the potential for subtotaling, the file is sorted by part number, by salesperson within each part number, and by date within each salesperson.

Now, let's discuss the basic technique for printing subtotals. First of all, the file must be indexed (or sorted) on the field being used to define subtotal groups. Hence, if you are printing a report with subtotals based upon part number, the database must be indexed or sorted on the part number field.

Next, for each subtotal group you need a DO WHILE loop that has the basic structure shown in English below:

```
Store subtotal group identifier in a memory variable
Initialize subtotal accumulator to zero
Print subtotal heading (if any)
Start loop to repeat while still in subtotal group
    Print record from the database
    Increment the subtotal by current record amount
    Skip to next record in database
End loop when this subtotal group ends
Print subtotal
```

Each subtotal group will be represented by a loop, like the one above, in a command file. Furthermore, each of the subtotal loops must be nested inside

PARTNO	PARTNAME	SALESMAN	QTY	UNITPRICE	DATE
A-111	Floppy Drive	ABC	10	150.00	01/01/87
A-111	Floppy Drive	ABC	11	150.00	01/01/87
A-111	Floppy Drive	ABC	1	150.00	01/01/87
A-111	Floppy Drive	ABC	3	150.00	01/01/87
A-111	Floppy Drive	ABC	9	150.00	01/02/87
A-111	Floppy Drive	ABC	11	150.00	01/02/87
A-111	Floppy Drive	ZEM	12	150.00	01/01/87
A-111	Floppy Drive	ZEM	11	150.00	01/01/87
A-111	Floppy Drive	ZEM	5	150.00	01/01/87
A-111	Floppy Drive	ZEM	5	150.00	01/02/87
A-111	Floppy Drive	ZEM	7	150.00	01/02/87
A-111	Floppy Drive	ZEM	13	150.00	01/02/87
A-111	Floppy Drive	ZEM	15	150.00	01/02/87
B-222	Hard Disk	ABC	1	1495.00	01/01/87
B-222	Hard Disk	ABC	5	1495.00	01/01/87
B-222	Hard Disk	ABC	4	1495.00	01/01/87
B-222	Hard Disk	ABC	4	1495.00	01/02/87
B-222	Hard Disk	ABC	6	1495.00	01/02/87
B-222	Hard Disk	ABC	14	1495.00	01/02/87
B-222	Hard Disk	ZEM	2	1495.00	01/01/87
B-222	Hard Disk	ZEM	4	1495.00	01/01/87
B-222	Hard Disk	ZEM	4	1495.00	01/02/87
B-222	Hard Disk	ZEM	10	1495.00	01/02/87
B-222	Hard Disk	ZEM	2	1495.00	01/02/87

Figure 8.1:   Contents of the SubTots.DBF database

a single DO WHILE .NOT. EOF() that ensures that all records from the database will be printed.

ONE-LEVEL SUBTOTALS

Let's look at a sample program that prints subtotals based upon the PartNo field. Of course, the dBASE report generator can do the same thing this program can do, since the program displays only one level of subtotals. However, this program is only the first step in demonstrating how to develop programs that can print many levels of subtotals.

Figure 8.2 shows a sample program, named SubTot1.PRG, to print a single level of subtotals based upon the PartNo field. The output from the SubTot1.PRG program is shown in Figure 8.3.

Let's analyze the program line-by-line. Since PartNo is the field that defines subtotal groups, the database must be indexed on at least the

```
**************************************** SubTot1.PRG
*---- Displays subtotals based upon the PartNo field.

*-- File must be indexed on the PartNo field.
USE SubTots INDEX SubTots
GO TOP
CLEAR

*-- GrandTot variable accumulates grand total.
GrandTot = 0

*----------- Outermost loop does entire file.
DO WHILE .NOT. EOF()

   *--------- Loop to print first subtotal.
   *--------- Initialize subtotal field and value.
   ThisPart = PartNo
   PartTot = 0
   *--------- Subtotal heading (optional).
   ? "---Part Number "+ThisPart+" : "+PartName
   ?

   DO WHILE PartNo = ThisPart .AND. .NOT. EOF()
      *---- Print a record from the database.
      ? PartNo," ",SalesMan," ",Date,Qty,UnitPrice,;
        (Qty*UnitPrice)
      *---- Increment grand total and subtotals.
      GrandTot = GrandTot + (Qty * UnitPrice)
      PartTot = PartTot + (Qty * UnitPrice)
      SKIP
   ENDDO (part number subtotal)

   *----- Print subtotal.
   ? SPACE(40),"-----------"
   ? "Part &ThisPart total:",SPACE(20),PartTot
   ?
   ?
ENDDO (entire file)
*--- Print grand total.
? SPACE(40),"-----------"
? "Grand total:",SPACE(25),GrandTot
RETURN
```

Figure 8.2: The SubTot1.PRG command file

PartNo field. The first commands in the command file, shown below, open the SubTots database with the SubTots index file (previously created with the command INDEX ON PartNo TO SubTots). The GO TOP command ensures that the record pointer is at the top of the database:

* – Displays subtotals based upon the PartNo field.

* – File must be indexed on the PartNo field.
USE SubTots INDEX SubTots

```
--Part Number A-111 : Floppy Drive
    A-111       ABC        01/01/87      10      150.00        1500.00
    A-111       ABC        01/01/87      11      150.00        1650.00
    A-111       ABC        01/01/87       1      150.00         150.00
    A-111       ABC        01/01/87       3      150.00         450.00
    A-111       ABC        01/02/87       9      150.00        1350.00
    A-111       ABC        01/02/87      11      150.00        1650.00
    A-111       ZEM        01/01/87      12      150.00        1800.00
    A-111       ZEM        01/01/87      11      150.00        1650.00
    A-111       ZEM        01/01/87       5      150.00         750.00
    A-111       ZEM        01/02/87       5      150.00         750.00
    A-111       ZEM        01/02/87       7      150.00        1050.00
    A-111       ZEM        01/02/87      13      150.00        1950.00
    A-111       ZEM        01/02/87      15      150.00        2250.00
                                               Part A-111 total:    16950.00

--Part Number B-222 : Hard Disk
    B-222       ABC        01/01/87       1     1495.00        1495.00
    B-222       ABC        01/01/87       5     1495.00        7475.00
    B-222       ABC        01/01/87       4     1495.00        5980.00
    B-222       ABC        01/02/87       4     1495.00        5980.00
    B-222       ABC        01/02/87       6     1495.00        8970.00
    B-222       ABC        01/02/87      14     1495.00       20930.00
    B-222       ZEM        01/01/87       2     1495.00        2990.00
    B-222       ZEM        01/01/87       4     1495.00        5980.00
    B-222       ZEM        01/02/87       4     1495.00        5980.00
    B-222       ZEM        01/02/87      10     1495.00       14950.00
    B-222       ZEM        01/02/87       2     1495.00        2990.00
                                               Part B-222 total:    83720.00


                                               Grand total:       100670.00
```

Figure 8.3:   Report printed by the SubTot1.PRG program

```
GO TOP
CLEAR
```

The program then initializes a variable named GrandTot, which accumulates the grand total of all records displayed in the report:

```
* - GrandTot variable accumulates grand total.
GrandTot = 0
```

Now, the outermost DO WHILE loop begins, using the condition WHILE
.NOT. EOF() to ensure that all records in the database are printed:

```
* – – – – –- Outermost loop does entire file.
DO WHILE .NOT. EOF()
```

Before actually printing any records, however, the program needs
another DO WHILE loop to control the subtotal group. As in the English
version discussed previously, this DO WHILE loop stores the part number
of the current record in the database in a memory variable (named This-
Part in this example). The variable to accumulate the subtotal, named Part-
Tot in this example, is initialized as 0:

```
* – – – – –- Loop to print first subtotal.
* – – – – –- Initialize subtotal field and value.
ThisPart = PartNo
PartTot = 0
```

At this point, you can display a heading for the subtotal group, though it
is not absolutely necessary to do so. This routine prints a heading for the
subtotal group, consisting of the part number, part name, and some text:

```
* – – – – –- Subtotal heading (optional).
? "--Part Number " + ThisPart + " : " + PartName
?
```

Now the inner DO WHILE loop to control the part number subtotal
begins. Notice that the loop repeats so long as the current record has the
same part number that began this group (PartNo = ThisPart), and that the
loop also repeats the condition of the previous loop (.NOT. EOF()). The
most common mistake people make when developing programs that print
subtotals is forgetting this rule: *Each nested loop in a subtotaling program
must repeat the conditions stated in all previous loops.* We have not forgotten
the rule in this example:

```
DO WHILE PartNo = ThisPart .AND. .NOT. EOF()
```

Within this loop, the program prints a record from the database (which is
a row on the report), and then increments the grand total and subtotal
values by the amount being totaled and subtotaled (total sale, or quantity
times the unit price in this example):

```
* – – Print a record from the database.
```

```
? PartNo," ",SalesMan," ",Date,Qty,UnitPrice,;
   (Qty*UnitPrice)
* – – Increment grand total and subtotals.
GrandTot = GrandTot + (Qty * UnitPrice)
PartTot = PartTot + (Qty * UnitPrice)
```

With the job of printing the record and incrementing the total and sub-total done, the program can skip to the next record in the database:

```
SKIP
```

The process of printing a record and incrementing the total and subtotal continues until a new part number is encountered in the database (because of the condition WHILE PartNo = ThisPart stated in the inner DO WHILE loop):

```
ENDDO (part number subtotal)
```

When the innermost loop is done, all the records for the current part number have been printed and accumulated in the total and subtotal variables. Hence, the program can now print something beneath the subtotal group. In this example, it prints an underline beneath the totals in the right column of the report, some text, and the subtotal for the current part number (stored in the PartTot variable):

```
* – –- Print subtotal.
? SPACE(40)," – – – – –-"
? "Part &ThisPart total:",SPACE(20),PartTot
?
?
```

The report is not done, however, because only a single part number group has been printed. However, the closing ENDDO loop keeps printing records because the outermost loop has the condition WHILE .NOT. EOF():

```
ENDDO (entire file)
```

This outermost ENDDO command causes processing to resume at the lines within the outermost DO WHILE loop. These lines reset the ThisPart variable to the new current part number, and reset the PartTot accumulating variable to 0. Hence, the innermost loop prints the next subtotal group and subtotal amount. This process continues until all the records in the database have been printed.

When all the records in the database have been printed, the outermost
DO WHILE .NOT. EOF() loop terminates, and the program prints the grand
total at the bottom of the report:

```
* -- Print grand total.
? SPACE(40),"- - - - - -"
? "Grand total:",SPACE(25),GrandTot
```

I've intentionally left out some frills like a report heading and pagination
so we could concentrate on the logic used in the subtotaling. We can add
some frills later in the chapter.

TWO-LEVEL SUBTOTALS

So how do we add a second level of subtotaling to the report that Sub-
Tot1.PRG is printing? Well, basically we need to nest another DO WHILE
inside the currently innermost loop. This new loop will look very much like
the loop for subtotaling part numbers, and use the same technique discussed in the English version of the algorithm.

The new subtotal group will be based upon salespersons' initials (stored
in the SalesMan field). So the report will display subtotals by part number,
and within each part number it will display subtotal by salesperson. In view
of this, the database must be sorted by part number, and by salesperson
within each part number. Hence, the SubTots.NDX index file now needs to
be created with the command

```
INDEX ON PartNo + SalesMan TO SubTots
```

Figure 8.4 shows the SubTot2.PRG program, which has the new loop for
subtotaling on the SalesMan field nested within the original SubTot1.PRG
command file.

Only the following lines have been added to the original SubTot1.PRG
command file to create the SubTot2.PRG command file. First, nested within
the loop to subtotal part numbers are the commands to store the salesperson's initials from the current record in a variable named ThisPerson.
Second, a command creates a variable named PersonTot, which will be
used to accumulate the salesperson's subtotal. PersonTot is initialized as 0:

```
* - - Next loop handles subtotals for salesperson.
ThisPerson = SalesMan
PersonTot = 0
```

```
********************************** SubTot2.PRG
*- This program adds a DO WHILE loop to calculate
*- and display subtotals based upon the SalesMan field.

*-- File must be indexed on the
*-- PartNo and SalesMan fields.
USE SubTots INDEX SubTots
GO TOP
CLEAR
*-- GrandTot variable accumulates grand total.
GrandTot = 0
*---------- Outermost loop does entire file.
DO WHILE .NOT. EOF()
   *--------- Loop to print first subtotal.
   *--------- Initialize subtotal field and value.
   ThisPart = PartNo
   PartTot = 0
   *--------- Subtotal heading (optional).
   ? "---Part Number "+ThisPart+" : "+PartName
   ?
   DO WHILE PartNo = ThisPart .AND. .NOT. EOF()

      *-- Next loop handles subtotals for salesperson.
      ThisPerson = SalesMan
      PersonTot = 0
      DO WHILE SalesMan = ThisPerson .AND. ;
         PartNo = ThisPart .AND. .NOT. EOF()
         *---- Print a record from the database.
         ? PartNo," ",SalesMan," ",Date,Qty,UnitPrice,;
           (Qty*UnitPrice)
         *---- Increment grand total and subtotals.
         GrandTot = GrandTot + (Qty * UnitPrice)
         PartTot = PartTot + (Qty * UnitPrice)
         PersonTot = PersonTot + (Qty * UnitPrice)
         SKIP
      ENDDO (salesperson subtotal)
      ? SPACE(39),"------------"
      ? "  Salesperson &ThisPerson Part &ThisPart subtotal:",PersonTot
      ?

   ENDDO (part number subtotal)
   *----- Print subtotal.
   ? SPACE(40),"-----------"
   ? "Part &ThisPart total:",SPACE(20),PartTot
   ?
   ?
ENDDO (entire file)
*--- Print grand total.
? SPACE(40),"-----------"
? "Grand total:",SPACE(25),GrandTot
RETURN
```

Figure 8.4:   The SubTot2.PRG command file

Next the DO WHILE loop to print and accumulate a subtotal for a single salesperson begins. As before, the loop states its own condition (SalesMan = ThisPerson) to isolate a current salesperson, and also repeats the conditions of all previous loops (PartNo = ThisPart .AND. .NOT. EOF()), as shown below:

```
DO WHILE SalesMan = ThisPerson .AND. ;
     PartNo = ThisPart .AND. .NOT. EOF()
```

The innermost loop then performs the task of printing a record from the database and accumulating all subtotals and totals. To accumulate the subtotal for salesperson, SubTot2.PRG has the new line

```
PersonTot = PersonTot + (Qty * UnitPrice)
```

When all the records representing the current salesperson have been printed, the loop ends and the program prints some text and the subtotal for the current salesperson:

```
ENDDO (salesperson subtotal)
? SPACE(39)," – – – – – –"
? " Salesperson &ThisPerson Part &ThisPart subtotal:",PersonTot
?
```

Everything else in the program is exactly as it was in the original Sub-Tot1.PRG program.

Figure 8.5 shows the report printed by the SubTot2.PRG command file. Notice that subtotals for each part number still appear on the report, but there are also subtotals for each salesperson within each part number.

THREE-LEVEL SUBTOTALS

Now we can finally do something the REPORT FORM (the report generator) cannot do. We can add a third subtotal level to the report. We'll use the Date field as the third subtotal field, so that subtotals will be displayed by part number, by salesperson within each part number, and by date within each salesperson.

Since there are three levels of subtotals, there now need to be three sort levels—PartNo, SalesMan, and Date. So now the command to create the SubTots index file must be

```
INDEX ON PartNo + SalesMan + DTOC(Date) TO SubTots
```

```
--Part Number A-111 : Floppy Drive
      A-111      ABC       01/01/87      10       150.00         1500.00
      A-111      ABC       01/01/87      11       150.00         1650.00
      A-111      ABC       01/01/87       1       150.00          150.00
      A-111      ABC       01/01/87       3       150.00          450.00
      A-111      ABC       01/02/87       9       150.00         1350.00
      A-111      ABC       01/02/87      11       150.00         1650.00
                           Salesperson ABC Part A-111 subtotal:   6750.00


      A-111      ZEM       01/01/87      12       150.00         1800.00
      A-111      ZEM       01/01/87      11       150.00         1650.00
      A-111      ZEM       01/01/87       5       150.00          750.00
      A-111      ZEM       01/02/87       5       150.00          750.00
      A-111      ZEM       01/02/87       7       150.00         1050.00
      A-111      ZEM       01/02/87      13       150.00         1950.00
      A-111      ZEM       01/02/87      15       150.00         2250.00
                           Salesperson ZEM Part A-111 subtotal:  10200.00


                                         Part A-111 total:       16950.00


--Part Number B-222 : Hard Disk
      B-222      ABC       01/01/87       1      1495.00         1495.00
      B-222      ABC       01/01/87       5      1495.00         7475.00
      B-222      ABC       01/01/87       4      1495.00         5980.00
      B-222      ABC       01/02/87       4      1495.00         5980.00
      B-222      ABC       01/02/87       6      1495.00         8970.00
      B-222      ABC       01/02/87      14      1495.00        20930.00
                           Salesperson ABC Part B-222 subtotal:  50830.00


      B-222      ZEM       01/01/87       2      1495.00         2990.00
      B-222      ZEM       01/01/87       4      1495.00         5980.00
      B-222      ZEM       01/02/87       4      1495.00         5980.00
      B-222      ZEM       01/02/87      10      1495.00        14950.00
      B-222      ZEM       01/02/87       2      1495.00         2990.00
                           Salesperson ZEM Part B-222 subtotal:  32890.00


                                         Part B-222 total:       83720.00


                                         Grand total:           100670.00
```

Figure 8.5: Report printed by SubTot2.PRG

The DTOC function is necessary to combine the Date data type used for the date field with the Character data types of PartNo and SalesMan.

Notice that the order of the fields in the INDEX statement matches the levels of grouping in the report: from outermost level to innermost. The sort order *must* match the grouping order in this manner.

Figure 8.6 shows the SubTot3.PRG command file, which contains the new inner loop to subtotal by Date. Notice that all other parts of the program are identical to the SubTot2.PRG command file.

```
*************************************************** SubTot3.PRG
*-- This program adds a DO WHILE loop to calculate
*-- and display subtotals based upon the Date field.

*-- File must be indexed on the
*-- PartNo, SalesMan, and Date fields.
USE SubTots INDEX SubTots
GO TOP
CLEAR
*-- GrandTot variable accumulates grand total.
GrandTot = 0
*----------- Outermost loop does entire file.
DO WHILE .NOT. EOF()
    *--------- Loop to print first subtotal.
    *--------- Initialize subtotal field and value.
    ThisPart = PartNo
    PartTot = 0
    *--------- Subtotal heading (optional).
    ? "---Part Number "+ThisPart+" : "+PartName
    ?
    DO WHILE PartNo = ThisPart .AND. .NOT. EOF()
        *-- Next loop handles subtotals for salesperson.
        ThisPerson = SalesMan
        PersonTot = 0
        DO WHILE SalesMan = ThisPerson .AND. ;
            PartNo = ThisPart .AND. .NOT. EOF()

            *-- Next loop handles subtotals for date.
            ThisDate = Date
            DateTot = 0
            DO WHILE Date = ThisDate .AND. ;
                    SalesMan = ThisPerson .AND. ;
                    PartNo = ThisPart .AND..NOT. EOF()
            *---- Print a record from the database.
            ? PartNo," ",SalesMan," ",Date,Qty, ;
              UnitPrice,(Qty*UnitPrice)
            *---- Increment grand total and subtotals.
            GrandTot = GrandTot + (Qty * UnitPrice)
            PartTot = PartTot + (Qty * UnitPrice)
            PersonTot = PersonTot + (Qty * UnitPrice)
            DateTot = DateTot + (Qty * UnitPrice)
            SKIP
```

Figure 8.6:   The SubTot3.PRG command file

```
        ENDDO (date subtotal)
        ? SPACE(40),"-----------"
        ? SPACE(9),ThisPart,ThisPerson,ThisDate ,"subtotal:",DateTot
        ?

     ENDDO (salesperson subtotal)
     ? SPACE(39),"------------"
     ? "  Salesperson &ThisPerson Part &ThisPart subtotal:",PersonTot
     ?
  ENDDO (part number subtotal)
  *----- Print subtotal.
  ? SPACE(40),"-----------"
  ? "Part &ThisPart total:",SPACE(20),PartTot
  ?
  ?
ENDDO (entire file)
*--- Print grand total.
? SPACE(40),"-----------"
? "Grand total:",SPACE(25),GrandTot
RETURN
```

Figure 8.6: The SubTot3.PRG command file (continued)

Once again, the new inner loop follows the basic principles discussed throughout this section. The first new lines in the program are nested inside the previous innermost loop, and those lines store the current value of Date in a variable named ThisDate, and initialize a variable, named DateTot in this example, to accumulate the Date subtotal:

```
*- Next loop handles subtotals for date.
ThisDate = Date
DateTot = 0
```

The DO WHILE loop for the Date subtotal uses the expression WHILE Date = ThisDate, and also repeats the conditions stated in all the previous DO WHILE loops:

```
DO WHILE Date = ThisDate .AND. ;
   SalesMan = ThisPerson .AND. ;
   PartNo = ThisPart .AND..NOT. EOF()
```

The commands to print a line and increment the total and subtotals are now within this new innermost DO WHILE loop. SubTot3.PRG needs the additional command to increment the Date subtotal, as shown below:

```
DateTot = DateTot + (Qty * UnitPrice)
```

To mark the bottom of the new innermost DO WHILE loop, the program needs an ENDDO command, as well as commands to print the date subtotal (stored on the DateTot variable):

```
ENDDO (date subtotal)
? SPACE(40)," – – – – –-"
? SPACE(9),ThisPart,ThisPerson,ThisDate ,"subtotal:",DateTot
?
```

The report printed by the SubTot3.PRG command file is shown in Figure 8.7. The subtotal line for each date uses some abbreviated text to identify the total at a glance. For example, the line

A-111 ABC 01/01/87 subtotal: 3750.00

indicates that the subtotal of $3,750.00 is for part number A-111, for salesperson ABC, on January 1, 1987.

From this point on, you should be able to follow the techniques presented here to add more levels of subtotals, or to develop your own subtotaling programs. The only real limitation you need to be concerned with

```
--Part Number A-111 : Floppy Drive
    A-111        ABC        01/01/87        10        150.00        1500.00
    A-111        ABC        01/01/87        11        150.00        1650.00
    A-111        ABC        01/01/87         1        150.00         150.00
    A-111        ABC        01/01/87         3        150.00         450.00
                            A-111 ABC 01/01/87 subtotal:            3750.00

    A-111        ABC        01/02/87         9        150.00        1350.00
    A-111        ABC        01/02/87        11        150.00        1650.00
                            A-111 ABC 01/02/87 subtotal:            3000.00


                    Salesperson ABC Part A-111 subtotal:            6750.00

    A-111        ZEM        01/01/87        12        150.00        1800.00
    A-111        ZEM        01/01/87        11        150.00        1650.00
    A-111        ZEM        01/01/87         5        150.00         750.00
                            A-111 ZEM 01/01/87 subtotal:            4200.00
```

Figure 8.7:   Report printed by the SubTot3.PRG program

A-111	ZEM	01/02/87	5	150.00	750.00
A-111	ZEM	01/02/87	7	150.00	1050.00
A-111	ZEM	01/02/87	13	150.00	1950.00
A-111	ZEM	01/02/87	15	150.00	2250.00

A-111 ZEM 01/02/87 subtotal: 6000.00

Salesperson ZEM Part A-111 subtotal: 10200.00

Part A-111 total: 16950.00

--Part Number B-222 : Hard Disk

B-222	ABC	01/01/87	1	1495.00	1495.00
B-222	ABC	01/01/87	5	1495.00	7475.00
B-222	ABC	01/01/87	4	1495.00	5980.00

B-222 ABC 01/01/87 subtotal: 14950.00

B-222	ABC	01/02/87	4	1495.00	5980.00
B-222	ABC	01/02/87	6	1495.00	8970.00
B-222	ABC	01/02/87	14	1495.00	20930.00

B-222 ABC 01/02/87 subtotal: 35880.00

Salesperson ABC Part B-222 subtotal: 50830.00

B-222	ZEM	01/01/87	2	1495.00	2990.00
B-222	ZEM	01/01/87	4	1495.00	5980.00

B-222 ZEM 01/01/87 subtotal: 8970.00

B-222	ZEM	01/02/87	4	1495.00	5980.00
B-222	ZEM	01/02/87	10	1495.00	14950.00
B-222	ZEM	01/02/87	2	1495.00	2990.00

B-222 ZEM 01/02/87 subtotal: 23920.00

Salesperson ZEM Part B-222 subtotal: 32890.00

Part B-222 total: 83720.00

Grand total: 100670.00

Figure 8.7: Report printed by the SubTot3.PRG program (continued)

is the 256-character length limit that dBASE imposes on command lines. At a certain point, the DO WHILE conditions for an inner loop might exceed that length because each loop needs to repeat the conditions of the previous line.

You can conserve space in the DO WHILE command lines by using use brief variable names (e.g., L1, L2, and so forth), instead of the long variable names used in these examples (e.g., ThisPart, ThisPerson).

Just remember that the database must be in properly sorted order for the subtotaling programs to work. I've seen people waste hours trying to figure out what was wrong with their subtotaling program, only to discover that the program was fine. It was the index order that was wrong!

SOME FINISHING TOUCHES

We can add some finishing touches to the SubTot3 program to make it print a report total, and to properly paginate the report. Figure 8.8 shows

```
********************************************* SubTot4.PRG
*-- Same as SubTot3.PRG, but includes routines to
*-- print a heading and to paginate.

*-- File must be indexed on the
*-- PartNo, SalesMan, and Date fields.
USE SubTots INDEX SubTots
GO TOP
CLEAR

*------------ Print report heading.
SET PRINT ON
? "                Sales Report"
?
? "Part   Sales                   Unit        Total"
? " No.    man   Date    Qty    Price        Sale"
?
*------------ Set line feed and page counters.
LF = 5
PgCount = 1

*-- GrandTot variable accumulates grand total.
GrandTot = 0

*------------ Outermost loop does entire file.
DO WHILE .NOT. EOF()

    *--------- Loop to print first subtotal.
    *--------- Initialize subtotal field and value.
    ThisPart = PartNo
    PartTot = 0
    *--------- Subtotal heading (optional).
```

Figure 8.8:   Heading and pagination routines in SubTot3.PRG

```
? "---Part Number "+ThisPart+" : "+PartName
?
LF = LF + 2
DO WHILE PartNo = ThisPart .AND. .NOT. EOF()
   *-- Next loop handles subtotals for salesperson.
   ThisPerson = SalesMan
   PersonTot = 0
   DO WHILE SalesMan = ThisPerson .AND. ;
      PartNo = ThisPart .AND. .NOT. EOF()

      *-- Next loop handles subtotals for date.
      ThisDate = Date
      DateTot = 0
      DO WHILE Date = ThisDate .AND. ;
               SalesMan = ThisPerson .AND. ;
               PartNo = ThisPart .AND..NOT. EOF()
         *---- Print a record from the database.
         ? PartNo," ",SalesMan," ",Date,Qty, ;
           UnitPrice,(Qty*UnitPrice)

         *---- Start on a new page if necessary.
         LF = LF + 1
         IF LF >= 55
            ?
            ? SPACE(30),PgCount
            EJECT
            PgCount = PgCount + 1
            LF = 1
         ENDIF (1f)

         *---- Increment grand total and subtotals.
         GrandTot = GrandTot + (Qty * UnitPrice)
         PartTot = PartTot + (Qty * UnitPrice)
         PersonTot = PersonTot + (Qty * UnitPrice)
         DateTot = DateTot + (Qty * UnitPrice)
         SKIP
      ENDDO (date subtotal)
      ? SPACE(40),"-----------"
      ? SPACE(9),ThisPart,ThisPerson,ThisDate ,"subtotal:",DateTot
      ?
      LF = LF + 3
   ENDDO (salesperson subtotal)
   ? SPACE(39),"------------"
   ? "  Salesperson &ThisPerson Part &ThisPart subtotal:",PersonTot
   ?
   LF = LF + 3
ENDDO (part number subtotal)
*----- Print subtotal.
? SPACE(40),"-----------"
? "Part &ThisPart total:",SPACE(20),PartTot
?
?
LF = LF + 4
ENDDO (entire file)
*--- Print grand total.
? SPACE(40),"-----------"
? "Grand total:",SPACE(25),GrandTot
EJECT
SET PRINT OFF
```

Figure 8.8:   Heading and pagination routines in SubTot3.PRG (continued)

the SubTot3.PRG program modified to print page headings and eject the paper from the printer after 55 lines have been printed.

The routine to set the printer on, print the report heading, and initialize the LF (line feed counter) and PgCount (page counter) variables is shown below:

```
* − − − − − − Print report heading.
SET PRINT ON
? "  Sales Report"
?
?" Part  Sales              Unit  Total"
?" No.  man   Date Qty  Price Sale"
?
* − − − − − − Set line feed and page counters.
LF = 5
PgCount = 1
```

Wherever lines are printed with the ? command in the program, the LF variable is incremented by the appropriate number of lines. When 55 or more lines have been printed, the IF clause below prints a blank line and the page number centered on the page. The EJECT command advances the paper in the printer, and the page count variable (PgCount) is incremented by 1:

```
IF LF > = 55
   ?
   ? SPACE(30),PgCount
   EJECT
   PgCount = PgCount + 1
   LF = 1
ENDIF (If)
```

The program ends with the new commands EJECT and SET PRINT OFF, which ensure that the paper advances to the top of the next page in the printer, and that future printing commands go to the screen rather than the printer.

⊙MULTIPLE-COLUMN ALPHABETIZED REPORTS

Everyone knows how to use a phone book. The entries are in alphabetical order from beginning to end, and also in alphabetical order in three or more columns on each page. In the two-page example in Figure 8.9, page 1 lists last names beginning with the letters A through O, and page 2 lists last names beginning with P through Z.

Adams	Franklin	Kellerman
Baker	Gomer	Lambert
Carlson	Harris	Morris
Davis	Iglew	Nautach
Edwards	Johnson	Orasco

Page number: 1

Peterson	Trible	Xavier
Quincy	Ungulat	Young
Rasputin	Vista	Zeppo
Schumack	Walters	

Page number: 2

Figure 8.9: Alphabetical listing broken into columns

The ColRept.PRG command file, shown in Figure 8.10, can get data from any dBASE database into the "phone book" format shown in Figure 8.9. In addition, the program allows you to define the number of columns you want on each page, the number of rows on each page, and the width of each column.

Let's first discuss how to use the program, then we'll discuss how it works. First, assume you have a database named NameList.DBF that has a field called LName containing last names. You want the names displayed in 3 columns, with 50 lines (rows) per page, and a width of 20 characters per column.

Your first step is to ensure that the names are in alphabetical order. If an index file specifying this order does not exist, you can create one using the simple commands

USE NameList

INDEX ON LName TO NameList

When the sort order is set up, you just DO the ColRept.PRG command file with the appropriate parameters, as shown below:

DO ColRept WITH 3,50,20,"LName"

The ColRept program takes over from there, and prints the report you want. Note that in the WITH portion of the command, 3 is the number of

```
*********************************** ColRept.PRG
* Prints data in alphabetical order divided into
* columns on a page.  Assumes database file is
* open and indexed if necessary.

PARAMETERS Cols,Rows,ColWidth,FieldNam

*--------- Make a copy of the database to be printed.
SET SAFETY OFF
GO TOP
COPY TO Temp

*----------- Pad for an even number of records.
USE Temp
DO WHILE MOD(RECCOUNT(),Cols) # 0
   APPEND BLANK
ENDDO
GO TOP

*--------- Page counter and number of items
*--------- printed are initialized below.
PgCount = 1
Printed = 0

*--------- Outermost loop counts records printed.
SET PRINT ON
DO WHILE Printed < RECCOUNT()
   OnThisPage = MIN(Rows*Cols,RECCOUNT()-Printed)
   Rows = MIN(Rows,(OnThisPage/Cols))
   ThisRow = 1
   *-------- Middle loop controls rows.
   DO WHILE ThisRow <= Rows .AND. Printed <= RECCOUNT()
      ThisCol = 1
      ? LEFT(&FieldNam,ColWidth)+ ;
        SPACE(MAX(0,ColWidth-LEN(&FieldNam)))
      Printed = Printed + 1
      *------- Inner loop controls columns.
      DO WHILE ThisCol < Cols .AND. Printed <= RECCOUNT()
         SKIP Rows
         ?? LEFT(&FieldNam,ColWidth)+ ;
            SPACE(MAX(0,ColWidth-LEN(&FieldNam)))
         ThisCol = ThisCol + 1
         Printed = Printed + 1
      ENDDO (columns)
      ThisRow = ThisRow + 1
      SKIP (((Cols-1)*Rows)-1) * -1
   ENDDO (rows)
   ?
   ?  "Page number: ",PgCount
   EJECT
   PgCount = PgCount + 1
   SKIP ((Cols-1)*Rows)
ENDDO (records)
*--------------------- Done printing report.
SET PRINT OFF
CLOSE DATABASES
ERASE Temp.DBF
RETURN
```

Figure 8.10:   The ColRept.PRG command file

columns per page, 50 is the number of lines per page, 20 is the width of each column, and LName is the name of the field being printed on the report.

You can combine two or more fields in a single column of the report. For example, suppose the NameList database contains the fields LName and FName. To ensure a proper sort order, the database is indexed with the command

INDEX ON LName + FName TO NameList

To print a two-column report, with 55 lines per page and 35 characters per column, displaying the LName and FName fields with a space between each column, run the ColPrint.PRG program with the command

DO ColRept WITH 2,55,35,"TRIM(LName) + ' ' + FName"

You can also use numeric data in the report if you convert the numbers to character strings using the dBASE STR function. The command below prints the fields named LName and Number on a three-column report with 45 lines per page, and a width of 20 characters per column:

DO ColRept WITH 3,45,20,"LName + STR(Number,3,2)"

Similarly, you can include dates in the report as long as you use the DTOC function to convert Date data to the character data type, as in the command

DO ColRept WITH 2,55,35,"DTOC(Date) + ' ' + LName"

Let's take a look at the ColRept.PRG command file and see how it works. The opening lines, as usual, are comments. The first executable line is the PARAMETERS command. This command accepts the number of columns in the report (Cols), the number of rows per page (Rows), the width of each column (ColWidth), and the names of field(s) from the database to print (FieldNam), as shown below:

```
* * * * * * * * * * * * * * * * * * * * * * * * * * * * * * * * * * * * ColRept.PRG
* Prints data in alphabetical order divided into
* columns on a page. Assumes database file is
* open and indexed if necessary.

PARAMETERS Cols,Rows,ColWidth,FieldNam
```

The next lines set the safety off, go to the top of the currently open data-base, and copy its records to a database named Temp.DBF. Since the pro-gram assumes that the database is already open and has the appropriate index file active, the Temp.DBF file will be created in properly sorted order:

```
* – – – –- Make a copy of the database to be printed.
SET SAFETY OFF
GO TOP
COPY TO Temp
```

The Temp.DBF database needs to have enough records to be evenly divisible by the number of columns in the report (otherwise, end-of-file errors will occur near the end of the file when the program tries to jump ahead to the next record to print). Therefore, the DO WHILE loop below adds blank records to the end of Temp.DBF until the number of records in the database is evenly divisible by the number of columns in the report:

```
* – – – –- Pad for an even number of records.
USE Temp
DO WHILE MOD(RECCOUNT(),Cols) # 0
   APPEND BLANK
ENDDO
GO TOP
```

Variables for counting the number of printed pages (PgCount) and the number of items printed (Printed) are initialized in the next lines, and the printer is set on:

```
* – – – –- Page counter and number of items
* – – – –- printed are initialized below.
PgCount = 1
Printed = 0

* – – – –- Outermost loop counts records printed.
SET PRINT ON
```

Three nested loops are then used to print the report. The outermost loop repeats once for each record in the database. Within this loop, the OnThis-Page variable calculates how many records are to be printed on the current page. This is equal to either the number of rows times the number of columns, or the number of records remaining on the database, whichever is less. The Rows variable calculates how many rows to print on the current page. This is either the number of rows originally specified, or the number of items left to print divided by the number of columns in the report:

```
DO WHILE Printed < RECCOUNT()
OnThisPage = MIN(Rows*Cols,RECCOUNT() – Printed)
   Rows = MIN(Rows,(OnThisPage/Cols))
```

The next loop repeats once for each printed row on the current page. The variable ThisRow keeps track of which row is being printed. The loop repeats as long as the row being printed is less than or equal to the number of rows to be printed, and as long as the number of records printed does not exceed the number of records in the database:

```
ThisRow = 1
* – – – – Middle loop controls rows.
DO WHILE ThisRow < = Rows .AND. Printed < = RECCOUNT()
```

The innermost loop repeats once for each column in a row. The variable ThisCol keeps track of which column is being printed. For each row, the field of interest is printed with the ? command. The LEFT function is used to truncate the data to be printed if it is too long, and the SPACES function adds sufficient spaces to fill out the field to the requested column width if necessary. When the item is printed, the Printed variable is incremented by 1:

```
ThisCol = 1
? LEFT(&FieldNam,ColWidth) + ;
   SPACE(MAX(0,ColWidth – LEN(&FieldNam)))
Printed = Printed + 1
```

Remaining columns in the row are printed with a DO WHILE loop that repeats as long as there are still columns to be printed, and as long as the number of records printed does not exceed the number of records in the database. Within this loop, the command SKIP Rows tells dBASE how far to skip down in the database to get the next record to print. The ?? command prints the data, and the ThisCol and Printed variables are incremented by 1:

```
* – – –- Inner loop controls columns.
DO WHILE ThisCol < Cols .AND. Printed < = RECCOUNT()
   SKIP Rows
```

```
?? LEFT(&FieldNam,ColWidth) + ;
   SPACE(MAX(0,ColWidth – LEN(&FieldNam)))
ThisCol = ThisCol + 1
Printed = Printed + 1
ENDDO (columns)
```

When the innermost loop is done, all the columns for a single row are printed. The ThisRow variable is incremented by 1, indicating that another row has been printed. The SKIP command uses the formula $(((Cols-1)*Rows)-1) * -1$ to determine the number of records to skip backwards to access the next record to be printed:

```
ThisRow = ThisRow + 1
SKIP ((((Cols – 1)*Rows) – 1) * – 1
ENDDO (rows)
```

When the middle loop finishes its job, a single page has been printed. The commands below print the page number, eject the page from the printer, increment the page counter, and calculate how far back to skip in the database to begin printing the next page. The ENDDO marks the bottom of the outermost loop, which repeats once for each printed page:

```
?
? "Page number: ",PgCount
EJECT
PgCount = PgCount + 1
SKIP ((Cols – 1)*Rows)
ENDDO (records)
```

When all three nested loops have completed their jobs, the remaining lines set the printer off, close the open database, erase the Temp.DBF temporary database, and return control to the calling program or dot prompt:

```
* – – – – – – – – – -- Done printing report.
SET PRINT OFF
CLOSE DATABASES
ERASE Temp.DBF
RETURN
```

While the ColPrint.PRG command file is flexible and can be used with any database with any number of records, it may not be perfect for every application. You may need to experiment with it to get precisely the report you want. Nonetheless, it solves the problem of creating reports that are alphabetized in a telephone-book fashion, and will probably need only minor adjustments for similar types of reports.

⊙PRESS ANY KEY TO STOP THE PRINTER

If you use a command file rather than REPORT FORM to print a report, you can also add a feature to stop the printer by pressing any key. In this example, the screen displays the message

Press any key to abort print job...

while the report is being printed. Pressing any key displays the message

Print job aborted...

and terminates printing.

To add this feature to a program that prints reports, you can add a routine near the top of the program that asks if the report should be displayed on the printer. If the user answers Yes, then the program should print a message about pressing any key to stop the printer, and perform a few other tasks as shown below:

```
*— — —- Ask if report should be printed.
Printer = " "
@ 2,1 SAY "Send report to printer? (Y/N) " ;
    GET Printer PICTURE "!"
READ
*— — —- If printer requested, get prepared.
IF Printer = "Y"
    *— — — — — — — —- Allow for printer abort.
    CLEAR
    @ 23,1 SAY "Press any key to abort print job..."
    CLEAR TYPEAHEAD
    ON KEY DO PrinStop
    SET CONSOLE OFF
    SET PRINT ON
ENDIF
```

The CLEAR command clears the screen, and the @ sign displays the *Press any key to abort print job* message. Then the CLEAR TYPEAHEAD command clears out any extraneous keystrokes from the typeahead buffer.

(Every time you press a key, it first goes into a "holding tank" called the typeahead buffer. To ensure that the next command in the program, ON KEY, works, it's best to make sure the typeahead buffer is clear.)

The command ON KEY DO PrinStop will run a program named Prin-Stop.PRG (which we'll write in a moment) that in turn will stop all printing. The command SET CONSOLE OFF keeps the printed report from appearing on the screen, so that the *Press any key to abort print job* message doesn't disappear.

At the bottom of the program that prints the report, you'll need the lines

```
* – – –- Done; return to main menu.

SET CONSOLE ON
ON KEY
CLEAR TYPEAHEAD
SET PRINT OFF
RETURN
```

These commands will be executed only if the user does *not* press any key to abort printing, after the entire report is printed. The SET CONSOLE ON command returns the screen to normal. (Forgetting this command leaves the screen permanently blank, unless you successfully type in the command SET CONSOLE ON without being able to see what you're typing.) The ON KEY command disables the previous ON KEY DO PrinStop command, so the next keypress does not run the PrinStop.PRG program. CLEAR TYPEAHEAD clears out any extraneous keystrokes, and is just a precautionary measure in this case.

Figure 8.11 shows the PrinStop.PRG program, which is accessed only if the user presses any key to stop the printer.

PrinStop.PRG immediately sets the console back on, turns off the printer, and clears the screen. Then it displays the message *Print job aborted*. Then

```
*-------------------------------- PrinStop.PRG
*--------- Halt printer and return to main menu.
SET CONSOLE ON
SET PRINT OFF
CLEAR
? "Print job aborted..."
CLEAR TYPEAHEAD
ON KEY
RETURN TO MASTER
```

Figure 8.11:   The PrinStop.PRG program

the program clears the typeahead buffer, releases the previous ON KEY DO PrinStop command, and returns control to the highest-level program in your application.

Let's look at an example of the PrinStop routine in action. Assume that Director.PRG, shown in Figure 8.12, is used to print data from a database named Mail.DBF. Furthermore, Director.PRG is called from a higher-level menu program named MainMenu.PRG (not shown, but a basic menu program). And also you must assume that PrinStop.PRG is stored on the same disk and directory as MainMenu.PRG and Director.PRG.

You can see the routine near the top of the program for setting up the printer abort (particularly the line ON KEY DO PrinStop). Also, the necessary lines for terminating the "press any key to stop printer" option appear at the bottom of the command file, as discussed earlier.

You can, of course, store the PrinStop routine as a procedure inside a procedure file. Just make sure the procedure file is open before running the program to print the report.

⊙CUSTOM SCREENS WITH REPEAT DATA OPTION

Usually when entering records into a database using the APPEND command, you fill in a blank record, press Return, and fill in the next blank record. If you use the SET CARRY ON command before the APPEND command, each time the screen scrolls around for you to enter the next record, the data from the last record will automatically be displayed in the new record. This is a handy technique if you must repeatedly enter records into a database with similar data.

In most real-life situations, though, adding a record is neither a matter of always carrying data from the previously entered record into the new record, nor of never carrying over the data. Instead, you'd probably want to occasionally carry data from one new record to the next. For example, you may use a single database to enter several individuals who work at the same company (and therefore have the same address), or several orders for a single individual.

Let's look at an example. A small mail-order business stores all its orders in a database named Orders.DBF with the structure shown below:

Structure for Database: Orders.DBF

Field	Field Name	Type	Width	Dec
1	NAME	Character	35	
2	COMPANY	Character	35	
3	ADDRESS	Character	35	

```
********************************* Director.PRG
*   Print Mail.DBF with "any key" abort.
*   Called from hypothetical MainMenu.PRG.

USE Mail
*------ Initialize LF, PgCount, and Title variables.
LF = 2
PgCount = 1
Title = "Membership Directory"

*------- Start at top of database.
GO TOP

* -------------- Ask about printer.
Printer = " "
CLEAR
@ 5,5 SAY "Send report to printer? (Y/N) ";
  GET Printer PICTURE "!"
READ

*----------------- Allow for printer abort.
IF Printer = "Y"
   CLEAR
   @ 23,1 SAY "Press any key to abort print job"
   CLEAR TYPEAHEAD
   ON KEY DO PrinStop
   SET CONSOLE OFF
   SET PRINT ON
ENDIF

*------- Print report title.
? SPACE(20),Title
?
*------- Loop through each record in database.
DO WHILE .NOT. EOF()
   ? TRIM(LName)+" " + FName
   ? Address+SPACE(10)
   ? TRIM(City) + ", "+State+" "+Zip
   ?
   LF = LF + 4
   *--- If report being printed, handle pagination.
   IF Printer = "Y" .AND. LF >= 50
       ?
       ? SPACE(35),PgCount
       EJECT
       ? Title
       ?
       PgCount = PgCount + 1
       LF = 2
   ENDIF (printer and lf)
   SKIP
ENDDO (while not eof)

*------- Done; return to main menu.
SET CONSOLE ON
ON KEY
CLEAR TYPEAHEAD
SET PRINT OFF
RETURN
```

Figure 8.12:   The Director.PRG command file

4	CITY	Character	25
5	STATE	Character	5
6	ZIP	Character	10
7	COUNTRY	Character	35
8	PRODUCT	Numeric	2
9	DATE	Date	8
10	PRINTED	Logical	1

The Product field stores a number representing the product the customer ordered. The Printed field is either .F. if the order has not been filled, or .T. if the order has been filled. The purposes of the other fields are obvious. The business's needs do not require anything more complicated. Operators enter the information into the database, use the data to print receipts and mailing labels, and also keep a record of each order. Most of their business is from first-time customers, so they do not maintain a customer list with customer numbers.

Figure 8.13 shows a custom screen that the operators might use when entering data. Notice that the last field to complete on the screen gives three options: press up-arrow to make corrections to the order entered, press Return to complete the order and enter an entirely new order, or press R to carry the data from this order over to the next. If a customer orders several products, the operator can simply press R to repeat the name and address on the next new record, then fill in the product number for the new record.

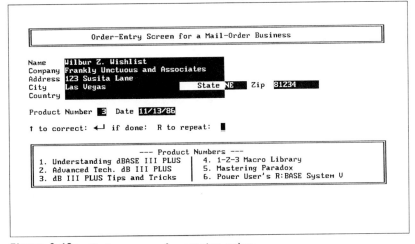

Figure 8.13: Custom screen for entering orders

When done entering records, the operator can press the usual dBASE ^W, ^End, or even the PgDn key when a blank entry form is on the screen. Doing so will terminate the program and of course save all the newly added records.

The first step in developing a data-entry system like this is to develop the screen for entering data. To simplify matters, you can use the dBASE III PLUS screen painter to develop most of the screen. Figure 8.14 shows how the custom screen looks when initially laid out on the screen painter. Notice that one line, preceded by asterisks, has been placed on the form. Later, this line will be replaced with a line to display instructions (with graphics characters) and the last entry field.

The screen was created by first entering the commands

USE Orders

CREATE SCREEN Orders

Then the usual screen painter commands and techniques were used to design the screen.

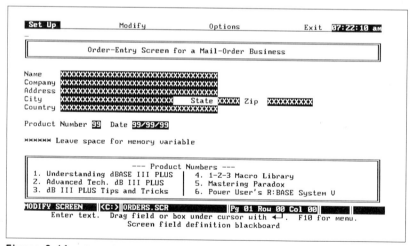

Figure 8.14:   Sample custom screen on the screen painter

When you save the screen, dBASE will create a format file, named Orders-.FMT in this example.

The next step is to add instructions with graphics characters, and a GET command for the last field on the screen to the format file. To do so, you can either use the command MODIFY COMMAND Orders.FMT directly at the dot prompt, or use an external word processor or text editor. Either way, be sure to use the entire file name, including the .FMT extension, when trying to access the format file.

Once the format file is on your screen, you'll need to change the "temporary" line

@ 13,0 SAY "***** Save space for memory variable"

to a line with some instructions, perhaps some graphics characters, and a GET command with a variable name, as in the example

@ 13,0 SAY Up+" to correct: "+Ret+" if done: R to repeat: ";
    GET Rep PICT "!"

(Note that the row numbers in the left column on your format file may differ, depending on how you design your screen.) The variables Up and Ret will later be assigned graphics characters for an up-arrow and a Return key symbol. The variable Rep will also be assigned a value, and will be used to determine whether to carry values from the last-entered record over to the next new record.

Now we need to develop a command file to use the Orders.FMT format file, and give the user the option to carry data over from one new record to the next with the press of a key. Figure 8.15 shows the command file, named Orders.PRG, in its entirety.

```
************************************** Orders.PRG
* Sample program to allow appending with optional
* repeat.

*--- Set parameters.
SET TALK OFF
SET SAFETY OFF

*---- Leave off any index files for the time being.
USE Orders

*-------------- Set up graphics character and
*-------------- "option to repeat" variable.
Ret = CHR(17)+CHR(196)+CHR(217)   && Return key
Up  = CHR(24)                     && Up arrow
Rep = " "                         && Form variable

************** Set up screen with Rep variable.
SET FORMAT TO Orders

*-------------- Add first blank record with dummy
*-------------- address "X" to get into loop below.
```

Figure 8.15: The Orders.PRG command file

```
APPEND BLANK
REPLACE Address WITH "X "
*---- Fill in today's date.
REPLACE Date WITH DATE()

*-------------- Get data from user until done.
DO WHILE Address # "  "

   *--- Clear out dummy address.
   IF Address = "X "
      REPLACE Address WITH "  "
   ENDIF (address)

   *----------- Read data from Orders.FMT screen.
   READ

   *-- Assume that if Address field left blank,
   *-- entire record was left blank.
   IF Address = "  "
      LOOP
   ENDIF (blank record)

   *-- If repeat requested, copy data to
   *-- the next new record.
   IF Rep = "R"
      COPY TO Temp NEXT 1
      APPE FROM Temp
      *--- Otherwise just add a new blank record,
      *--- and fill in the dummy address.
   ELSE
      APPEND BLANK
      REPLACE Address WITH "X "
   ENDIF

   *---- Fill in today's date.
   REPLACE Date WITH DATE()
   Rep = " "

ENDDO (while record not left blank)

*--------- Done adding records.
CLEAR
? "Please wait a moment while I update the database..."

*--- Delete any blank records (again assuming that
*--- a blank Address field implies a blank record).
SET TALK ON
DELETE ALL FOR Address = "  "
PACK

*--- If any index files are used, update them all here.
*USE Orders INDEX <every index file here>
*REINDEX
SET TALK OFF

*--- All done.
CLOSE FORMAT
CLEAR
RETURN
```

Figure 8.15:   The Orders.PRG command file (continued)

Now keep in mind that Orders.PRG is just a sample program. It is not a general-purpose procedure that can be used with any database. As we describe the logic of the program line-by-line below, you'll see why Orders-.PRG cannot actually be made into a universal procedure to handle all database and format (.FMT) files.

The Orders.PRG command file begins with the usual opening comments and a couple of SET commands, as shown below:

```
* * * * * * * * * * * * * * * * * * * * * * * * * * * * * * * * * * * * Orders.PRG
* Sample program to allow appending with optional
* repeat.

* -- Set parameters.
SET TALK OFF
SET SAFETY OFF
```

To ensure accuracy when carrying data from one record to the next during data entry, the program must use the database (.DBF) file without any active index files. The reason is that any active index files will cause an immediate resorting that might throw things out of whack farther down the line. Anyway, leaving index files inactive for the time being will probably increase the speed of data entry in general. Orders.PRG leaves off index files as below:

```
* - - Leave off any index files for the time being.
USE Orders
```

The index files can be updated later in the program.

Now, as you may recall, the custom screen used in this example (Orders-.FMT) uses the memory variables Up, Ret, and Rep. These variables are all created in the routine below. If you've read the chapter on dBASE graphics in this book, the Up and Ret variables may look familiar to you. They store the graphics characters for the up-arrow and Return keys on the keyboard. The Rep variable is initialized as a blank space. We'll see the role of the Rep variable a little later:

```
* - - - - - - - Set up graphics character and
* - - - - - - - "option to repeat" variable.
Ret = CHR(17)+CHR(196)+CHR(217)        && Return key
Up = CHR(24)                           && Up arrow
Rep = " "                              && Form variable
```

Next the command file sets up the Orders.FMT format file that we created and discussed a short time ago. Ensuing READ commands will use
the Orders.FMT screen because of the SET FORMAT command:

```
* * * * * * * * * * * * * * * Set up screen with Rep variable.
SET FORMAT TO Orders
```

Since the program is designed to allow the user to enter new records,
the command below adds a blank record to the bottom of the Orders.DBF
database:

```
* – – – – – – – Add first blank record with dummy
* – – – – – – – address "X" to get into loop below.
APPEND BLANK
```

Later, the command file will use a loop to allow the user to repeatedly enter
records until done. In this program, we'll assume that if a record is left blank,
the user is indicating that he or she is finished. However, rather than testing to
see if every single field in the record has been left blank, we'll just assume that
if the Address field has been left blank, then the entire record has been left
blank. (This is a reasonable assumption in this application, but other applications will no doubt need to use other assumptions.)

There is a small problem here though. Since the condition of the loop
states that records can be added while the Address field is not left blank
(Address # " "), and we just added a blank record to the database, the loop
will not even get started (because the Address field in the newly added
record is blank). To solve this dilemma, the command file sneaks a dummy
address into the Address of the blank record, which then passes control to
the inside of the DO WHILE loop:

```
REPLACE Address WITH "X "
```

As an added convenience to the user, the command file also fills in the
Date field on the Orders.DBF database with the system date:

```
* – – Fill in today's date.
REPLACE Date WITH DATE()
```

The next command begins the loop that allows the user to keep entering
records until he or she leaves a record blank (or actually, in this example,
until he or she leaves the Address field blank on a record):

```
* – – – – – – – Get data from user until done.
DO WHILE Address # " "
```

Because the program stuck the X character into the Address field just to get the ball rolling here, it now needs to take it out so that the user doesn't see an X in the address field when the Orders.FMT screen appears. The routine below takes the X out of the Address field:

```
* -- Clear out dummy address.
IF Address = "X "
   REPLACE Address WITH " "
ENDIF (address)
```

Now the READ command displays the Orders.FMT format on the screen, and allows the user to enter new data into the blank record appended to the bottom of the database file:

```
* - - - - - -   Read data from Orders.FMT screen.
READ
```

Once the data are filled in on the screen, the command file needs to decide what to do next. If the Address field was left blank, then the command file can reasonably assume (in this application) that the entire record was left blank, which indicates that the user is done entering records for the time being. This being the case, the command file simply bypasses all commands between the current command and the ENDDO command using the LOOP command:

```
* - Assume that if Address field left blank,
* - entire record was left blank.
IF Address = " "
   LOOP
ENDIF (blank record)
```

If the Address field was not left blank, then the user must have entered a record. So now the command file needs to decide what to do based upon the entry in the last field on the custom screen (the Rep variable). If the user presses the up-arrow to correct the current record, the command file doesn't have to do anything because the dBASE READ command moves the cursor up the screen automatically.

If the user entered R (to Repeat data) as the last entry on the screen, then the command file must copy the data from the current record to the next record to be entered into the database. It accomplishes this task by copying the current record to a database named Temp, then appending the copied record from the Temp database into the Orders.DBF database, as shown below:

```
* - If repeat requested, copy data to
* - the next new record.
IF Rep = "R"
   COPY TO Temp NEXT 1
   APPEND FROM Temp
```

If the user entered nothing in the last field (Rep) in the custom screen, then he or she must not have wanted to copy the data from the present record into the next record. Therefore, the command file just appends a new blank record to the Orders.DBF database and puts the dummy address into the Address field to keep the DO WHILE loop rolling:

```
* -- Otherwise just add a new blank record,
* -- and fill in the dummy address.
ELSE
   APPEND BLANK
   REPLACE Address WITH "X "
ENDIF
```

Before presenting the next record on the screen, the command file puts the system date (DATE()) into the Date field as a convenience to the user, and sets the Rep variable back to a blank. The ENDDO command marks the end of the loop to keep entering records as long as the Address field is not left blank:

```
* - - Fill in today's date.
   REPLACE Date WITH DATE()
   Rep = " "
ENDDO (while record not left blank)
```

When the user has finished entering records, then the DO WHILE loop is done and processing continues at the line below. First the command file clears the screen and displays a message:

```
* - - - -- Done adding records.
CLEAR
? "Please wait a moment while I update the database..."
```

Now, since the user exited by "saving" a blank record, the database has a useless blank record appended to it. The next lines delete any and all blank records from the database (again, assuming that a blank Address field indicates a blank record). So that the user sees some activity on the screen while the deletion is taking place, the TALK parameter is set on:

```
* –- Delete any blank records (again assuming that
* –- a blank Address field implies a blank record).
SET TALK ON
DELETE ALL FOR Address = " "
PACK
```

Now, any index files the system uses regularly must be updated because of the newly added records. To update index files, just USE the database with all index files (or use the SET INDEX command), and REINDEX:

```
* –- If any index files are used, update them all here.
*USE Orders INDEX <every index file here>
*REINDEX
SET TALK OFF
```

This example assumes no index files are used, so the lines above are treated as comments, and serve only as a reminder.

When the blank records are deleted and any index files are updated, the command file is done. The closing lines close the format file, clear the screen, and return control to the calling program or dot prompt:

```
* –- All done.
CLOSE FORMAT
CLEAR
RETURN
```

You might want to use a slightly different technique for indicating when the user is done entering records. Rather than saving a blank record by typing ^End or ^W, the user can place an X in the last field on the screen. This is a little bit simpler, and also frees you from having to select a single field for indicating a blank record.

Of course, you'll need to put the instructions on how to exit on-screen. Hence, you'll want to change the line in the Orders.FMT format file

```
@ 13,0 SAY Up +" to correct: " + Ret +" if done: R to repeat: ";
    GET Rep PICT "!"
```

to something like

```
@ 13,0 SAY Up+" to correct: "+Ret+" if done: R to repeat: "
@ 13,41 SAY "or X to exit " GET Rep PICT "!"
```

Then you'll want to use a command file like the one shown in Figure 8.16 to enter records. The program, named Orders2.PRG, is very similar to Orders.PRG, except that it uses the condition WHILE Rep # "X" in the DO WHILE loop for entering records, and the condition IF Rep = "X" to determine when the user is done entering records. Since the program uses the status of the Rep variable, rather than a field, to determine when the user is done entering records, there is no need to place dummy values in any of the fields in the database.

```
************************************** Orders2.PRG
* Sample program to allow appending with optional
* repeat.

*--- Set parameters.
SET TALK OFF
SET SAFETY OFF

*---- Leave off any index files for the time being.
USE Orders

*-------------- Set up graphics character and
*-------------- "option to repeat" variable.
Ret = CHR(17)+CHR(196)+CHR(217)   && Return key
Up  = CHR(24)                     && Up arrow
Rep = " "                         && Form variable

*************** Set up screen with Rep variable.
SET FORMAT TO Orders

*-------------- Add first blank record with dummy
*-------------- address "X" to get into loop below.
APPEND BLANK
*---- Fill in today's date.
REPLACE Date WITH DATE()

*-------------- Get data from user until done.
DO WHILE Rep # "X"

   *----------- Read data from Orders.FMT screen.
   READ

   *---- If exit selected, done entering records.
   IF Rep = "X"
      LOOP
   ENDIF (blank record)
```

Figure 8.16: Modified version of the Orders.PRG command file

```
        *-- If repeat requested, copy data to
        *-- the next new record.
        IF Rep = "R"
            COPY TO Temp NEXT 1
            APPEND FROM Temp
            *--- Otherwise just add a new blank record,
            *--- and fill in the dummy address.
        ELSE
            APPEND BLANK
        ENDIF

        *---- Fill in today's date.
        REPLACE Date WITH DATE()
        Rep = " "

ENDDO (while not exiting)

*--------- Done adding records.
CLEAR
? "Please wait a moment while I update the database..."

*--- Delete any blank records (again assuming that
*--- a blank Address field implies a blank record).
*--- In this version of the program, the next
*--- three command lines can be left out, but
*--- there is a slim chance that blank records
*--- might be left on the database.
SET TALK ON
DELETE ALL FOR Address = "    "
PACK

*--- If any index files are used, update them all here.
*USE Orders INDEX <every index file here>
*REINDEX
SET TALK OFF

*--- All done.
CLOSE FORMAT
CLEAR
RETURN
```

Figure 8.16: Modified version of the Orders.PRG command file (continued)

⊙SKIPPING FIELDS IN FORMS

A student once asked me to devise a scheme that would allow him to skip through five or ten fields on a custom data-entry (or data-editing) screen with a single keystroke. Apparently, personnel in his company were so fast, and so accustomed to the data-entry screens that they worked with regularly, they knew when they needed to press the Return key ten times to get to a particular field on the screen. Only they wanted to press one key to get there, instead.

Adding this capability to a custom screen is quite simple. You can assign two Return key presses to the F2 key, three Return key presses to the F3 key, four Return key presses to the F4 key, and so on, right up to the F10 or F12 key. The routine to set up the function keys in this manner is

```
SET FUNCTION 2 TO ";;"
SET FUNCTION 3 TO ";;;"
SET FUNCTION 4 TO ";;;;"
SET FUNCTION 5 TO ";;;;;"
SET FUNCTION 6 TO ";;;;;;"
SET FUNCTION 7 TO ";;;;;;;"
SET FUNCTION 8 TO ";;;;;;;;"
SET FUNCTION 9 TO ";;;;;;;;;"
SET FUNCTION 10 TO ";;;;;;;;;;"
```

You can place these commands at the top of your data-entry and/or data-editing programs. Once assigned, the function keys stay in effect until you specifically reassign them with the SET FUNCTION commands. The F1 function key is always used to call up dBASE help screens, and is not programmable with SET FUNCTION.

Keep in mind that the function keys will work exactly like the Return key on a form. Hence, if you are on the last field of a screen and press the F10 key, the cursor will immediately jump to the tenth field of the next record, or will stop appending or editing if there is no next record to skip to.

I hope that you find some of the tips and tricks presented in this chapter useful in your own applications. In the next chapter, we'll develop some procedures to overcome the limitations inherent in dBASE III PLUS data structures, particularly the limitations of 128 fields and 4,000 characters per record.

HANDLING
VERY LARGE DATA
REQUIREMENTS

As you probably know, dBASE III PLUS allows you to have up to 128 fields and 4,000 characters per record in a database. In this chapter we'll deal with a question many have asked when trying to develop exceptionally large databases: What does one do when the 128 fields and 4,000 characters that dBASE allows are simply not enough? The best solution is to string records across several databases. By keeping several related files open simultaneously, you can increase the database size limits ten times to 1,280 fields and 40,000 characters per record. We'll discuss general techniques for *linking* files in this way and develop some sample procedures that can help manage these extremely large databases.

⊙DESIGNING LARGE DATABASES

For our example database, let's assume that we need 384 fields per record. Since dBASE III PLUS allows a maximum of 128 fields per record, we'll need to string three databases together, each with 128 fields (see Figure 9.1). To solve the problem, a single record is spread across the three databases BigFile.DBF, BigFile.EX1, and BigFile.EX2.

For our examples in this chapter, we will set up three databases in a fashion similar to the one shown in Figure 9.1. However, to save a lot of work, we'll only put three fields on each database. (Obviously, we wouldn't normally spread just nine fields across three databases; this is just to simplify the example. Try to imagine that BigFile.DBF contains 128 fields, BigFile.EX1 contains another 128 fields, and BigFile.EX3 contains yet

Record No.	BigFile.DBF	BigFile.Ex1	BigFile.Ex2
1	128 fields	128 fields	128 fields
2	128 fields	128 fields	128 fields
3	128 fields	128 fields	128 fields
4	128 fields	128 fields	128 fields
5	128 fields	128 fields	128 fields
	Fields 1–128	Fields 129–256	Fields 257–384

Figure 9.1:   Five 384-field records linked across three databases

more fields.) At the dot prompt, use the CREATE command to create the BigFile.DBF database with the structure shown in Figure 9.2.

To better demonstrate the use of related files, we'll create a couple of index files for this database by entering the command

INDEX ON Code TO BigCodes

Again, at the dot prompt, create an index file of names by entering the command

INDEX ON UPPER(LName) + UPPER(FName) TO BigNames

Once you've created the BigFile.DBF, the BigCodes.NDX, and the Big-Names.NDX files, use the CREATE command to create the BigFile.EX1 database. You'll need to specify the file name extension in this case; otherwise dBASE will use the default .DBF extension. Enter the command

CREATE BigFile.EX1

at the dot prompt to create the database. Enter the database structure as shown in Figure 9.3.

```
Structure for database : Bigfile.DBF
     Field    Field name    Type        Width    Dec
       1      CODE          Numeric        5
       2      LNAME         Character     12
       3      FNAME         Character     12
```

Figure 9.2: Structure for the BigFile.DBF database

```
Structure for database : Bigfile.EX1
     Field    Field name    Type        Width    Dec
       1      CHILD1        Character     12
       2      CHILD2        Character     12
       3      CHILD3        Character     12
```

Figure 9.3: Structure for the BigFile.EX1 database

Finally, create the third database, BigFile.EX2, by typing

CREATE BigFile.EX2

at the dot prompt. Give it the structure shown in Figure 9.4.

```
Structure for database : BigFile.EX2
   Field    Field name      Type        Width    Dec
     1      GRANCHILD1      Character     12
     2      GRANCHILD2      Character     12
     3      GRANCHILD3      Character     12
```

Figure 9.4:   Structure for the BigFile.EX2 database

For convenience, I've used the same file name for each database, distinguishing the additional files by the extensions EX1 (Extension 1) and EX2 (Extension 2). There is no rule in dBASE III PLUS that requires you to name linked databases in this manner. But doing so makes it easier to manage the files through general-purpose procedures, and the procedures presented in this chapter assume this pattern in the file names.

⊙LINKING THE DATABASES

If we wish to manage these three separate databases as though they were one database with very long records, the key is to open all three files simultaneously, and set up a relationship based upon record number. Setting up such a relationship ensures that any movement through the first database automatically causes exactly the same movement in the other databases. To simplify the task of opening all three databases and setting up the necessary relationships, we will develop a procedure file called ThreeDbs.PRG. It is listed in its entirety in Figure 9.5.

To begin creating the ThreeDbs.PRG file, enter the command

MODIFY COMMAND ThreeDbs

and then type in the opening lines

```
*********************************************** ThreeDbs.PRG
*-- Procedure to manage three related databases.
```

```
********************************* ThreeDbs.PRG
*-- Procedure to manage three related databases.

*---------------------- Open three related files
*------- and set relation based on record number.
PROCEDURE ThreeFil
PARAMETERS DBName, IndFiles
   *--- Set up file names.
   MainFile = DBName + ".DBF"
   BFile = DBName + ".EX1"
   CFile = DBName + ".EX2"
   SELECT A
   USE &MainFile Alias First
   SET INDEX TO &IndFiles
   SELECT B
   USE &BFile ALIAS Second
   SELECT A
   *-- Set relation from A into B.
   SET RELATION TO RECNO() INTO Second
   SELECT C
   USE &CFile ALIAS Third
   SELECT B
   *-- Set relation from second into third.
   SET RELATION TO RECNO() INTO Third
   SELECT A
RETURN

*---------- Append a blank record across three files.
*- Three related files must already be open with
*- the ThreeFil procedure (or similar technique).
PROCEDURE AppBlank
   SELECT A
   APPEND BLANK
   SELECT B
   APPEND BLANK
   SELECT C
   APPEND BLANK
   SELECT A
RETURN

*--- Procedure to handle multiple screens.

PROCEDURE PgChange
PARAMETERS RootName, Tot_Pages

   *---------- Set up loop for pagination.
   IPage = SPACE(1)
   Page = 1
   DO WHILE Page <= Tot_Pages .AND. IPage # "E"

      *--- Create page subscript.
      Sub = LTRIM(STR(Page,2))

      *----- Generate screen file name.
      ScreenFile = RootName + ".P"+Sub

      *----- Display screen.
      CLEAR
      DO &ScreenFile
      READ
```

Figure 9.5: The ThreeDbs.PRG procedure file

```
*---------------- Display page menu.
@ 21,0 CLEAR
IPage = SPACE(4)
@ 22,0 SAY "RETURN - Next page"
@ 22,23 SAY "R - Repeat this page"
@ 22,47 SAY "P - Previous page"
@ 23,0 SAY "F - Forward one rec"
@ 23,23 SAY "B - Backward one rec"
@ 23,47 SAY "# = Record no. - "
@ 24,0 SAY "E - Exit"
@ 24,23 SAY "Enter Choice: " ;.
        GET IPage PICT "!!!!"
READ

*---------------- Respond to user's entry.
DO CASE

    *--------------- Record number entered.
    CASE VAL(IPage) > 0
        *-- Always select A when moving.
        SELECT A
        GOTO &IPage

    *------------------- Return pressed.
    CASE IPage = " "
        Page = Page + 1

    *------------ Previous page requested.
    CASE IPage = "P"
        Page = Page -1
    *---- Make sure page 0 not attempted.
        IF Page < 1
           @ 20,5 SAY "No previous page! "
           ?? CHR(7)
           Page = 1
        ENDIF

    *----------------- Forward one record.
    CASE IPage = "F"
        *-- Always select A when moving.
        SELECT A
        SKIP
        *- Make sure not skipping off end.
        IF EOF()
           @ 20,5 SAY "Can't go forward! "
           ?? CHR(7)
           SKIP -1
        ENDIF

    *----------------- Backward one record.
    CASE IPage = "B"
        *-- Always select A when moving.
        SELECT A
        SKIP -1
        IF BOF()
           @ 20,5 SAY "Can't go backward!"
           ?? CHR(7)
        ENDIF
```

Figure 9.5:   The ThreeDbs.PRG procedure file (continued)

```
                *-------------------- Exit requested.
                CASE IPage = "E"
                        CLEAR

            ENDCASE
        ENDDO (page <= tot_pages)
        *--- Return to A file before returning.
    SELECT A
RETURN

*------------ Mark records for deletion across
*------------ three related files.
PROCEDURE DelAcross
    SELECT A
    LOCATE FOR DELETED()
    DO WHILE .NOT. EOF()
        SELECT B
        DELETE
        SELECT C
        DELETE
        SELECT A
        *---- Continue locating and deleting.
        CONTINUE
    ENDDO (not eof)
    *------- Reselect file A before returning.
    SELECT A
RETURN

*------------------ Pack deleted records across
*------------------ three related files.
PROCEDURE PakAcross
    SELECT A
    PACK
    SELECT B
    PACK
    SELECT C
    PACK
    *------- Reselect file A before returning.
    SELECT A
RETURN
```

Figure 9.5:   The ThreeDbs.PRG procedure file (continued)

The first procedure in the ThreeDbs.PRG procedure file is called ThreeFil. It opens the three databases, along with index files, and sets up the appropriate relationships. Type in the procedure as shown in Figure 9.6 and save it in the usual manner.

Let's discuss how the procedure works. Two parameters are passed to the procedure, DBName and IndFiles, that contain the root database name (in this case, BigFile) and the index file names (in this case, BigCodes and BigNames, but the program will accommodate up to seven):

PARAMETERS *DBName, IndFiles*

```
*----------------------- Open three related files
*------- and set relation based on record number.
PROCEDURE ThreeFil
PARAMETERS DBName, IndFiles
   *--- Set up file names.
   MainFile = DBName + ".DBF"
   BFile = DBName + ".EX1"
   CFile = DBName + ".EX2"
   SELECT A
   USE &MainFile ALIAS First
   SET INDEX TO &IndFiles
   SELECT B
   USE &BFile ALIAS Second
   SELECT A
   *-- Set relation from A into B.
   SET RELATION TO RECNO() INTO Second
   SELECT C
   USE &CFile ALIAS Third
   SELECT B
   *-- Set relation from second into third.
   SET RELATION TO RECNO() INTO Third
   SELECT A
RETURN
```

Figure 9.6:   The ThreeFil procedure

In the next four lines, three memory variables are assigned file names. Main-File receives the root name and the extension .DBF (BigFile.DBF). BFile receives the root name plus .EX1 (BigFile.EX1). CFile receives BigFile.EX2.

```
*--- Set up file names.
MainFile = DBName + ".DBF"
BFile = DBName + ".EX1"
CFile = DBName + ".EX2"
```

Then, through the use of the SELECT and SET RELATION commands, all three files are opened simultaneously, and related based upon record numbers. First, MainFile is opened in work area A, and "First" is assigned as the alias file name. (Aliases are used in this procedure because an error occurs if you try to simultaneously open several files with the same first name.) The index file names passed in the IndFiles parameter are then attached to the MainFile:

```
SELECT A
USE &MainFile ALIAS First
SET INDEX TO &IndFiles
```

Next, the .EX1 database is opened in work area B, with the alias name "Second". Then, a relationship is set up between MainFile and the .EX1 file, based upon record numbers (RECNO( )). Note that the relationship is set from MainFile (SELECT A) into BFile. The relationship is easiest to work with if always done from A into B, B into C, and so forth.

```
SELECT B
USE &BFile ALIAS Second
SELECT A
*-- Set relation from A into B.
SET RELATION TO RECNO( ) INTO Second
```

Next, a relationship is set up between CFile (.EX2) and BFile, again based on record number:

```
    SELECT C
    USE &CFile ALIAS Third
    SELECT B
    *-- Set relation from second into third.
    SET RELATION TO RECNO( ) INTO Third
    SELECT A
RETURN
```

and that marks the end of the procedure.

Since the relationship is set from MainFile into BFile, any movement in the MainFile will cause the same movement in the BFile. Likewise, since there is a relationship from the BFile into the CFile, any movement through the BFile will cause the same movement in the CFile. Therefore, it follows to reason that any movement through MainFile will cause the same movement through both the BFile and CFile, and hence the three files are now joined in such a way as to be, in effect, one database with very long records.

If you need an even larger database, you can revise the procedure to accommodate more files (e.g., EX3, EX4, EX5), and continue stringing them together in the same fashion using SELECT D, SELECT E, SELECT F, and so on. You can open up to ten databases at a time, so theoretically you can have ten simultaneous relationships (up to SELECT J), which would allow 1,280 fields per record!

To test the procedure, first open the procedure file by typing

```
SET PROCEDURE TO ThreeDbs
```

at the dot prompt.

The general syntax for the ThreeFil procedure is

```
DO ThreeFil WITH "Root Database Name","Index Files"
```

The procedure assumes that the three databases all have the same first name, and the extensions .DBF, .EX1, and .EX2. Index file names, if any, must be contained in the second parameter, separated from each other by commas, and all of them together enclosed in a pair of quotation marks. If no index files are to be used, the second parameter must be a blank space enclosed in quotation marks, as shown below:

DO ThreeFil WITH "Sample"," "

To open and link the three BigFile databases with the BigCodes and BigNames index files, enter the command

DO ThreeFil WITH "BigFile","BigCodes, BigNames"

Not much will appear to happen; the dot prompt will simply reappear. You can verify that the files are opened and related, however, by entering the command

DISPLAY STATUS

at the dot prompt. You'll see a display like the one shown in Figure 9.7.

Note that the currently selected database is BigFile.DBF, which has the alias name First. Two index files are active—BigCodes and BigNames—and the file is related to Second through the common RecNo().

BigFile.EX1 is open in Select area 2 (same as B), with the alias name Second. This database is related to the database Third. BigFile.EX2 is open

```
Currently Selected Database:
Select area:  1, Database in Use: C:BigFile.DBF   Alias: FIRST
    Master index file:  C:BigCodes.ndx  Key: Code
            Index file:  C:BigNames.ndx  Key: UPPER(LName) + UPPER(FName)
    Related into: SECOND
    Relation: RECNO()

Select area:  2, Database in Use: C:BigFile.EX1   Alias: SECOND
    Related into: THIRD
    Relation: RECNO()

Select area:  3, Database in Use: C:BigFile.EX2   Alias: THIRD

Press any key to continue...
```

Figure 9.7: Part of the STATUS display with the three databases open in Select area 3 (same as C). Since there are no files "below" BigFile.EX2, it is not related to any files.

For those of you who wonder if any of this relates to dBASE View (.VUE) files, the answer is yes. In fact, we have created a view here. If, after running the ThreeFil procedure to set up the links between the databases, you were to enter the command

CREATE VIEW BigFile FROM ENVIRONMENT

dBASE would create a file named BigFile.VUE. The BigFile.VUE file would, in turn, contain basically the same instructions as the ThreeFil procedure. However, after creating the view file you'd have the option to use the command

SET VIEW TO BigFile

to open and relate the three big files. In this chapter, however, we'll avoid the redundancy of the view file and use the existing ThreeFil procedure to open the databases and set up the relationships.

⊙ADDING DATA TO LINKED DATABASES

Adding new records to linked databases can be a bit of a chore because the APPEND command only adds records to the currently selected database. Hence, if you issue the command SELECT A before APPEND, only the database in the A work area will receive new data.

A second consideration is that you are no doubt going to need several "pages" of screens for entering and editing data on the large database. It is not too likely that more than 128 fields of information will fit on a single screen.

The easiest way around these problems is to develop several screens for entering and editing information. The screen painter allows you to have up to ten pages in a given format file, but it assumes that all fields on all ten pages are being stored in a single .DBF file. Since we will be using multiple linked databases we'll also develop our own procedure to handle the multiple screens.

To simplify matters the procedure will assume that the screens all have the same file name followed by the extension .P1 for page 1, .P2 for page 2, .P3 for page 3, and so forth up to a maximum of .P99. Hence, in this example, the file BigFile.P1 is the first screen for the BigFile databases, BigFile.P2 is the second page for the databases, and so forth.

SCREENS FOR THE LINKED DATABASES

Figure 9.8 shows the first screen for entering data into the three linked databases. The file is named BigFile.P1. Within the command file is the instruction SELECT A, so that dBASE "knows" which database the fields used in GET statements are in. The @ SAY GET commands read in data for the fields Code, LName, and FName. (Since this is such a simple screen, you can just create it with MODIFY COMMAND or another text editor exactly as it appears in the figure.)

Figure 9.9 shows the second-page screen for the linked databases. This screen displays information from the first screen (i.e., A->Code and A->LName) to help the user remember what was entered on the first page. The fields that BigFile.P2 GETs are all from the B database. Hence, the

```
*********************** BigFile.P1
*-- Custom screen for first page of
*-- data entry/editing.

*------ These fields are all on the A database.
SELECT A

@  5,70 SAY "Page 1"
@  8,5 SAY "Code " GET Code
@ 10,5 SAY "Last Name " GET LName
@ 12,5 SAY "First Name " GET FName
```

Figure 9.8:   The BigFile.P1 screen file

```
******************** BigFile.P2
*-- Second page of screens for BigFile.DBF.

@ 2,1 SAY "Code: "
@ 2,8 SAY A->Code
@ 2,15 SAY "Last Name: "+A->LName
@ 2,70 SAY "Page 2"

*----- These fields are on the B database.
SELECT B
@ 10,5 SAY "1st Child " GET Child1
@ 12,5 SAY "2nd Child " GET Child2
@ 14,5 SAY "3rd Child " GET Child3
```

Figure 9.9:   The BigFile.P2 screen file

command SELECT B is placed above the GET statements to ensure that dBASE knows where to put the incoming data. Notice that the file reads in information for the Child1, Child2, and Child3 fields.

The third screen for the BigFile databases is named BigFile.P3, and is shown in Figure 9.10. Like the second-page screen, it redisplays some basic information from the first screen (A->Code and A->LName) as a reminder to the user. Then it SELECTS the C database to read in data for the GranChild1, GranChild2, and GranChild3 fields.

```
******************** BigFile.P3
*-- Third page of screens for BigFile.DBF.
@ 2,1 SAY "Code: "
@ 2,8 SAY A->Code
@ 2,15 SAY "Last Name: "+A->LName
@ 2,70 SAY "Page 3"

*--------- These fields are on the C database.
SELECT C
@ 10,5 SAY "1st GrandChild " GET GranChild1
@ 12,5 SAY "2nd GrandChild " GET GranChild2
@ 14,5 SAY "3rd GrandChild " GET GranChild3
```

Figure 9.10:   The BigFile.P3 screen file

It does not matter how you develop the screens, or which fields you place on each screen, as long as you use the appropriate SELECT command above the GET commands that read in data.

If you use the dBASE III PLUS screen painter to develop the screens, you'll need to manipulate file names a bit, and also add the appropriate SELECT commands to the files after the screens are fully developed. For example, suppose you want to develop some screens for the BigFile.EX2 database using the screen painter. Furthermore, suppose you've already developed four pages of screens for the BigFile.DBF database, and so will now begin developing page five.

Your first step is to make a temporary copy of the BigFile.EX1 database with a .DBF extension, because the screen painter will not recognize the .EX1 extension. You can assign any name to this temporary copy, so long as it has the .DBF extension. We'll use the name Temp1.DBF in this example.

To ensure that the database is not already open, enter the command CLOSE DATABASES at the dot prompt. Then enter the command

    USE BigFile.EX1

Now to make the copy, enter the command

    COPY TO Temp1.DBF

Now you can use the screen painter to create the screen. Use a file name that will be easy to remember. Because this is the fifth page of screens, perhaps you'd want to use the file name Page5, as shown below:

    MODIFY SCREEN Page5

When the screen painter appears on the screen, select the menu option Select Database File, and specify Temp1.DBF as the database to use. Then, select the menu option Select Fields, and use the usual techniques to select fields to display on the current screen. You can design the screen to your liking. (You may want to leave a few blank rows at the top to display information from other screens later).

Two points to keep in mind when developing screens for our upcoming procedure, however, are discussed below. First, do not extend any fields beyond the first page of the screen painter. Keep an eye on the cursor position noted at the bottom-right corner of the screen, as shown below:

    Pg 01 Row 01 Col 00

Do not extend any single page of screens beyond Pg 01. Second, rows 21 to 24 will later be erased to make room for a bottom menu when the procedure is used to manage the screens. Therefore, you might want to leave these bottom rows blank on your custom screens.

When you've designed the screen, call up the screen painter menu and select Exit and Save. You'll be returned to the dot prompt. The screen painter has created a format file named Page5.FMT. Now you need to rename this screen so that it follows the convention of adding the file name extensions .P1, .P2, and so forth, and also make sure that the correct SELECT command is embedded in the screen file.

To do so, first use the RENAME (or COPY) FILE command directly from the dot prompt to rename or copy the Page5.FMT file to BigFile.P5. Using the RENAME command, you would enter

    RENAME Page5.FMT TO BigFile.P5

Now that the screen file has the appropriate name, you can use MODIFY COMMAND or another editor to call up the BigFile.P5 screen and type in the appropriate SELECT command (SELECT B in this example). Be sure to place the SELECT command above the GET commands in the file. (You might also want to enter SAY A-> statements for displaying data from the first screen, as in the BigFile.P2 and BigFile.P3 examples above.)

You'll need to repeat these processes for each page of screens in your application. Any given linked database may have any number of screens associated with it, up to a maximum of 99 screens for all the linked databases combined.

PROCEDURE FOR MANAGING MULTIPLE SCREENS

To manage the screens, you can use the flexible PgChange procedure in the ThreeDBS.PRG procedure file, which is also shown in Figure 9.11. To use the procedure, you call it with the root name of the screens and the number of pages the screens comprise.

For example, in this sample application we created three pages of screens, named BigFile.P1, BigFile.P2, and BigFile.P3. To have the PgChange procedure handle the screens for us, we'd call the procedure with the command

    DO PgChange WITH "BigFile",3

In another application, you might create 11 pages of screens with the root name Tax. Hence, your screens would be named Tax.P1, Tax.P2, Tax.P3, and so forth up to Tax.P11. To have PgChange manage this set of screens, you'd call the PgChange procedure with the command

    DO PgChange WITH "Tax",11

Let's take a look at how PgChange works. The procedure name and parameters statements are at the top of the procedure as usual. The passed parameters are named *RootName* (the root file name of the screens), and Tot_Pages (total number of screens, or pages):

    PROCEDURE PgChange
    PARAMETERS RootName, Tot_Pages

The variable IPage stores the user's response in a menu displayed at the bottom of each screen. The Page variable keeps track of which page of screens is to be displayed next. Then a loop begins displaying individual pages of screens as long as the next page to be displayed is less than or

```
*--- Procedure to handle multiple screens.

PROCEDURE PgChange
PARAMETERS RootName, Tot_Pages

    *---------- Set up loop for pagination.
    IPage = SPACE(1)
    Page = 1
    DO WHILE Page <= Tot_Pages .AND. IPage # "E"

        *--- Create page subscript.
        Sub = LTRIM(STR(Page,2))

        *----- Generate screen file name.
        ScreenFile = RootName + ".P"+Sub

        *----- Display screen.
        CLEAR
        DO &ScreenFile
        READ

        *---------------- Display page menu.
        @ 21,0 CLEAR
        IPage = SPACE(4)
        @ 22,0 SAY "RETURN - Next page"
        @ 22,23 SAY "R - Repeat this page"
        @ 22,47 SAY "P - Previous page"
        @ 23,0 SAY "F - Forward one rec"
        @ 23,23 SAY "B - Backward one rec"
        @ 23,47 SAY "# = Record no. - "
        @ 24,0 SAY "E - Exit"
        @ 24,23 SAY "Enter Choice: " ;
                GET IPage PICT "!!!!"
        READ

        *---------------- Respond to user's entry.
        DO CASE

            *--------------- Record number entered.
            CASE VAL(IPage) > 0
                *-- Always select A when moving.
                SELECT A
                GOTO &IPage

            *------------------- Return pressed.
            CASE IPage = " "
                Page = Page + 1

            *------------- Previous page requested.
            CASE IPage = "P"
                Page = Page -1
            *---- Make sure page 0 not attempted.
                IF Page < 1
                   @ 20,5 SAY "No previous page! "
                   ?? CHR(7)
                   Page = 1
                ENDIF

            *------------------ Forward one record.
```

Figure 9.11: The PgChange procedure

```
              CASE IPage = "F"
                    *-- Always select A when moving.
                    SELECT A
                    SKIP
                    *- Make sure not skipping off end.
                    IF EOF()
                        @ 20,5 SAY "Can't go forward! "
                        ?? CHR(7)
                        SKIP -1
                    ENDIF

                *----------------- Backward one record.
              CASE IPage = "B"
                    *-- Always select A when moving.
                    SELECT A
                    SKIP -1
                    IF BOF()
                        @ 20,5 SAY "Can't go backward!"
                        ?? CHR(7)
                    ENDIF

                *------------------- Exit requested.
              CASE IPage = "E"
                    CLEAR

          ENDCASE
       ENDDO (page <= tot_pages)
       *--- Return to A file before returning.
       SELECT A
    RETURN
```

Figure 9.11:   The PgChange procedure (continued)

equal to the total number of pages of screens, and the user does not select
E to exit:

```
*- - - - - - Set up loop for pagination.
IPage = SPACE(1)
Page = 1
DO WHILE Page < = Tot_Pages .AND. IPage # "E"
```

The next routine determines the number of the next page to display and
stores this as a character string, with leading blanks removed, in a variable
named Sub:

```
*-- Create page subscript.
Sub = LTRIM(STR(Page,2))
```

The name of the file containing the next page to display is then stored in
a variable named ScreenFile. The name is calculated by concatenating the

root file name with ".P" and the next page number. Hence, if page three is to be displayed next, the ScreenFile variable will contain the text "Big-File.P3" in this example:

```
* – –- Generate screen file name.
ScreenFile = RootName + ".P" + Sub
```

The next commands clear the screen, DO the appropriate screen file, and read in the information the user wants to enter:

```
* – –- Display screen.
CLEAR
DO &ScreenFile
READ
```

When the user is done entering data for one page, the menu for new options appears at the bottom of the screen. The options presented are summarized in Table 9.1.

The routine to display the bottom menu and store the user's selection in the IPage variable is shown below:

```
* – – – – – – – –- Display page menu.
@ 21,0 CLEAR
IPage = SPACE(4)
@ 22,0 SAY "RETURN - Next page"
@ 22,23 SAY "R - Repeat this page"
@ 22,47 SAY "P - Previous page"
@ 23,0 SAY "F - Forward one rec"
@ 23,23 SAY "B - Backward one rec"
@ 23,47 SAY "# = Record no. - "
@ 24,0 SAY "E - Exit"
@ 24,23 SAY "Enter Choice: " ;
    GET IPage PICT "!!!!"
READ
```

When the user makes a selection, the rest of the procedure decides what to do next. If the user enters a number, then the procedure assumes that he or she wants to move to the record with that number. Hence, it selects the A database, so that the pointer will move evenly through all the linked files, and uses the GOTO command to move to the requested record number:

```
* – – – – – – – – Respond to user's entry.
DO CASE
```

Option	Effect
R	Makes more changes to the current page
Return	Moves to the next page
P	Skips to the previous page
F	Stays on this page, but skips to next record
B	Stays on this page, but skips to previous record
#	Stays on this page, but goes to new record
E	Stops entering/editing data

Table 9.1: Page-management options

```
* — — — — — — —- Record number entered.
CASE VAL(IPage) > 0
   * — Always select A when moving.
   SELECT A
   GOTO &IPage
```

If the user just presses Return, then he or she wants to move to the next page. This being the case, the procedure increments the Page number variable by 1:

```
* — — — — — — — — — Return pressed.
CASE IPage = " "
   Page = Page + 1
```

If the user presses P to skip back a page, the procedure subtracts 1 from the current page number. However, if the user tries to skip back beyond page one, the procedure beeps and displays the error message "No previous page!". Then it resets the page number to 1:

```
* — — — — — —- Previous page requested.
CASE IPage = "P"
   Page = Page −1
   * — — Make sure page 0 not attempted.
   IF Page < 1
      @ 20,5 SAY "No previous page! "
      ?? CHR(7)
      Page = 1
   ENDIF
```

If the user enters an F to stay on the same page but move forward one record in the database, the procedure skips to the next record (again, selecting database A first to ensure even movement of the record pointer). If SKIP causes the pointer to go beyond the end of the database, the procedure beeps, displays an error message, and skips back to the previous record:

```
*  — — — — — — — — —  Forward one record.
CASE IPage = "F"
   * — Always select A when moving.
   SELECT A
   SKIP
   *- Make sure not skipping off end.
   IF EOF()
      @ 20,5 SAY "Can't go forward! "
      ?? CHR(7)
      SKIP  − 1
   ENDIF
```

If the user enters B to stay on the same page but skip back one record, then the procedure attempts to skip back one record. If there is no record to skip back to, the procedure beeps and displays an error message:

```
*  — — — — — — — — —  Backward one record.
CASE IPage = "B"
   * — Always select A when moving.
   SELECT A
   SKIP  − 1
   IF BOF()
      @ 20,5 SAY "Can't go backward!"
      ?? CHR(7)
   ENDIF
```

If the user opts to exit by typing in the letter E, then the procedure simply clears the screen and terminates the DO WHILE loop for displaying screens:

```
*  — — — — — — — — — —-  Exit requested.
CASE IPage = "E"
   CLEAR

ENDCASE
ENDDO (page  < = tot_pages)
* —- Return to A file before returning.
```

Before returning control to the calling program, the procedure selects the A database, to maintain consistency and to keep the record pointer in line:

```
SELECT A
RETURN
```

USING PGCHANGE TO ADD NEW RECORDS

The PgChange procedure is primarily designed for editing records in a database, which is why its bottom menu offers so many options. To use it for entering new records, you need to first append a new blank record to the bottom of each of the three linked databases. The procedure named AppBlank in the ThreeDbs.PRG command file takes care of this job. Figure 9.12 shows the entire AppBlnk procedure.

```
*---------- Append a blank record across three files.
*- Three related files must already be open with
*- the ThreeFil procedure (or similar technique).
PROCEDURE AppBlank
   SELECT A
   APPEND BLANK
   SELECT B
   APPEND BLANK
   SELECT C
   APPEND BLANK
   SELECT A
RETURN
```

Figure 9.12:   The AppBlank procedure

As you can see in the figure, the AppBlank procedure adds a blank record to the bottom of each linked database file, then reselects the A database.

Now let's test the procedures. Enter the commands below to close all files and procedures (just to ensure that we're starting from scratch) and open the procedure file.

```
CLOSE PROCEDURE
CLOSE DATABASES
SET PROCEDURE TO ThreeDbs
```

Now, open the three BigFile databases by entering the command

DO ThreeFil WITH "BigFile","BigCodes,BigNames"

To add a blank record to the bottom of all three related files, enter the command

DO AppBlank

To begin adding data, call the PgChange procedure with the root file name (BigFile in this example), and 3 for the number of pages in the combined databases, as below:

DO PgChange WITH "BigFile",3

Fill in the first screen as shown in Figure 9.13.

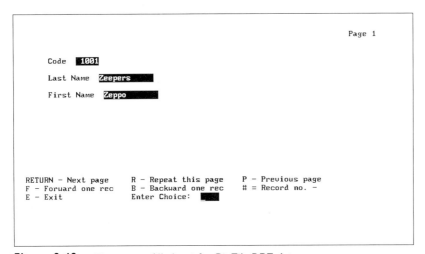

Figure 9.13:   First screen filled out for BigFile.DBF data

When the submenu appears, press Return to proceed to the next page, enter the data in Figure 9.14, and then go on to the next page and enter the data in Figure 9.15.

When the submenu appears, press Return once again and you'll be returned to the dot prompt. (Enter the CLEAR command to clear the screen, if necessary.)

Let's add a few more records to the BigFile database so that we can get some practice managing it. At the dot prompt, enter the command

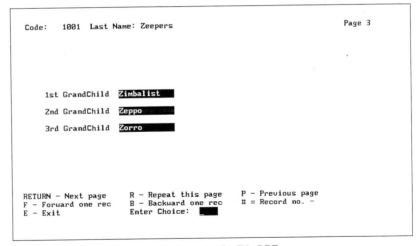

Figure 9.14: Second screen filled out for BigFile.DBF

Figure 9.15: Third screen filled out for BigFile.DBF

    DO AppBlank

to add a blank record to each database. Then enter the command

    DO PgChange WITH "BigFile",3

once again to add data, and fill in data as shown below:

Code	1002
Last Name	Miller
First Name	Mindy
1st Child	Mandy
2nd Child	Moe
3rd Child	Marie
1st Grandchild	Morris
2nd Grandchild	Mason
3rd Grandchild	Michael

Add another record by again entering the commands

```
DO AppBlank
DO PgChange WITH "BigFile",3
```

and adding the data listed below:

Code	1003
Last Name	Adams
First Name	Andy
1st Child	Anita
2nd Child	Arthur
3rd Child	Anne
1st Grandchild	Antoinette
2nd Grandchild	Allen
3rd Grandchild	Albert

We'll replace this somewhat awkward procedure for adding records with a command file later in the chapter. For now, let's see how to access the data we've just plugged in.

⊙ACCESSING DATA FROM LINKED DATABASES

You will notice that if you enter the LIST command, you'll see only the data from the BigFile.DBF database, shown below:

RECORD#	Code	LName	FName
1	1001	Zeepers	Zeppo
2	1002	Miller	Mindy
3	1003	Adams	Andy

If you wish to view data from the related files, you must specify the field names with the B—> and C—> symbols. (Enter the arrow symbol by typing a hyphen followed by a greater-than (>) sign.) For example, to see the Child1 field from the second file, and GranChild1 field from the third file, enter the following command:

LIST Code,LName,FName,B—>Child1,C—>GranChild1

dBASE will display the fields you requested:

Record#	Code	LName	FName	B—>Child1	C—>GranChild1
1	1001	Zeepers	Zeppo	Zori	Zimbalist
2	1002	Miller	Mindy	Mandy	Morris
3	1003	Adams	Andy	Anita	Antoinette

Notice that if you change the sort order by making the BigNames index primary (by listing it first in the SET INDEX command) with the command

SET INDEX TO BigNames,BigCodes

and list the data

LIST LName,FName,B—>Child1,C—>GranChild1,Code

the records will be displayed in the requested order, with the records from the three files "in synch" with one another, as shown here:

Record#	LName	FName	B—>Child1	C—>GranChild1	Code
3	Adams	Andy	Anita	Antoinette	1003
2	Miller	Mindy	Mandy	Morris	1002
1	Zeepers	Zeppo	Zori	Zimbalist	1001

The B—> and C—> arrow specifiers can be used almost anytime: in command files, with the REPORT FORM and LABEL FORM commands, and so forth. The point to remember is that you must use SELECT A when using any command that moves through the database (such as LIST, DIS-PLAY, REPORT, LABEL, SKIP, GO, and GOTO). All the procedures in the ThreeDbs procedure file return control to A before returning to the calling program or dot prompt. If ever in doubt about which file is currently selected, just enter the SELECT A command before attempting to move through the linked databases. (The DISPLAY STATUS command will show you the currently selected database.)

While we're on the subject of keeping everything aligned in the three linked databases, remember that you must never use the SORT command to organize any of the linked databases. You're sure to get the records out of order. It's OK to index though, as long as you select A before creating the index file. You need only index the A database, and use that index to display records across all linked files in the indexed order.

If there are more than three databases active, you just need more symbols, such as D—>, E—>, up to J—>.

⊙DELETING ACROSS LINKED DATABASES

Another possible problem to keep in mind when managing linked files is making sure that when you delete and pack records, the same action takes place across all the linked databases. As the program stands now, deleting records can cause major confusion in your database. For example, try typing

DELETE RECORD 2

to delete the second record from the database. If you enter the LIST command, you'll see the second record marked for deletion:

RECORD#	Code	LName	FName
3	1003	Adams	Andy
2 *	1002	Miller	Mindy
1	1001	Zeepers	Zeppo

However, if you enter the commands

SELECT B
LIST
SELECT C
LIST

you'll see that the records on the linked database are not marked for deletion:

SELECT B
LIST

RECORD#	CHILD1	CHILD2	CHILD3
1	Zori	Zelda	Zuzita
2	Mandy	Moe	Marie
3	Anita	Arthur	Anne

```
SELECT C
LIST
RECORD#    GRANCHILD1    GRANCHILD2    GRANCHILD3
       1   Zimbalist     Zeppo         Zorro
       2   Morris        Mason         Michael
       3   Antoinette    Allen         Albert
```

This would prove disastrous should you decide to pack the databases, because the alignment of the records across the three databases would be thrown off.

This problem can be handled easily with a couple of procedures. To add the necessary procedures begin by closing all open procedures so you can use the MODIFY COMMAND editor to edit the ThreeDbs.PRG procedure file. Move the cursor to the bottom of the procedure file, and add the DelAcross and PakAcross procedures shown in Figures 9.16 and 9.17. Save each one when you finish.

At the dot prompt, enter the command

SET PROCEDURE TO ThreeDbs

to reopen the procedure file. At the dot prompt, make sure all three files are still open by entering the DISPLAY STATUS command. If the three files are not still open, enter the command

DO ThreeFil WITH "BigFile","BigCodes,BigNames"

to reopen the files.

```
*------------ Mark records for deletion across
*------------ three related files.
PROCEDURE DelAcross
   SELECT A
   LOCATE FOR DELETED()
   DO WHILE .NOT. EOF()
      SELECT B
      DELETE
      SELECT C
      DELETE
      SELECT A
      *---- Continue locating and deleting.
      CONTINUE
   ENDDO (not eof)
*------- Reselect file A before returning.
SELECT A
RETURN
```

Figure 9.16:   The DelAcross procedure

```
*------------------ Pack deleted records across
*------------------ three related files.
PROCEDURE PakAcross
   SELECT A
   PACK
   SELECT B
   PACK
   SELECT C
   PACK
   *------- Reselect file A before returning.
   SELECT A
RETURN
```

Figure 9.17:   The PakAcross procedure

You can now delete as many records as you wish using the DELETE command (or ^U when Editing or Browsing). When you're done, enter the command

DO DelAcross

to delete appropriate records across the linked databases. You may want to try this now, and use the SELECT B, SELECT C, and LIST commands to verify the deletions, as shown below:

SELECT A
LIST

RECORD#		Code	LName	FName
3		1003	Adams	Andy
2	*	1002	Miller	Mindy
1		1001	Zeepers	Zeppo

SELECT B
LIST

RECORD#		CHILD1	CHILD2	CHILD3
1		Zori	Zelda	Zuzita
2	*	Mandy	Moe	Marie
3		Anita	Arthur	Anne

SELECT C
LIST

RECORD#	GRANCHILD1	GRANCHILD2	GRANCHILD3
1	Zimbalist	Zeppo	Zorro

2	*	Morris	Mason	Michael
3		Antoinette	Allen	Albert

SELECT A

When packing records marked for deletion, you must be sure to pack all three databases. To do so, enter the command

DO PakAcross

when the ThreeDbs.PRG procedure file is open. Check to see if it has worked by typing

LIST Code,LName,B—>Child1,C—>GranChild1

You'll see that the second record has been deleted across all three files:

RECORD#	Code	LName	B—>Child1	C—>GranChild1
2	1003	Adams	Anita	Antoinette
1	1001	Zeepers	Zori	Zimbalist

In its entirety, the ThreeDbs.PRG procedure file is not quite as universal as the others we have developed, because it is specifically designed to handle three linked databases and your application may require fewer or more. Each procedure would have to be modified accordingly.

⊙USING YOUR LINKED DATABASES

In this section we'll develop some sample command files to demonstrate techniques for using both the linked databases and the associated procedures.

ADDING

Figure 9.18 shows a sample command file named AddBig.PRG that allows a user to enter new records into the three linked databases. Note that the command file declares the IPage variable as public so that it can be passed from the PgChange procedure back to the AddBig.PRG command file when necessary.

AddBig.PRG first accesses the ThreeFil procedure to open the three databases and set up the relationships. A DO WHILE loop repeatedly performs the AppBlank procedure to add new blank records to the bottoms of all

```
*********************************** AddBig.PRG
*-- Sample program to add data to the BigFile.DBF
*-- data file(s) using many screens and PgChange.
CLEAR
SET TALK OFF

*-- Declare IPage variable from PgChange
*-- procedure public to help with loop.
PUBLIC IPage
SET PROCEDURE TO ThreeDbs

*-- Open three-across database, no index files.
DO ThreeFil WITH "BigFile"," "

*---------- Keep adding until exit requested.
IPage = " "
DO WHILE IPage # "E"
   DO AppBlank
   DO PgChange WITH "BigFile",3
ENDDO (ipage # e)

*--- Get rid of extra blank record
*--- and reindex database.
CLEAR
? "Resorting with new data: Please wait..."
DELETE ALL FOR Code = 0 .AND. ;
   LName = " "

*---- Delete and pack across all three files.
DO DelAcross
DO PakAcross
SET INDEX TO BigCodes, BigNames
SET TALK ON
REINDEX
SET TALK OFF

CLOSE PROCEDURE
RETURN
```

Figure 9.18: The AddBig command file

three linked databases, and the PgChange procedure to allow the user to type in the new data. The DO WHILE loop repeats until the user selects E to exit (WHILE IPage # "E").

When the user is done entering records, there may be one or more blank records left on the database. The AddBig.PRG command file deletes these records by assuming that any record with a zero in the Code field, and a blank in the LName field, (Code = 0 .AND. LName = " ") is probably a blank record. The command file then uses the DelAcross and PakAcross procedures to permanently remove these blank records from the database.

Before terminating, the AddBig.PRG command file reactivates the Big-Codes.NDX and BigNames.NDX index files, and uses the REINDEX command to update both index files.

EDITING

The EdBig.PRG command file, shown in Figure 9.19, allows the user to look up any given record in the database and make changes to that record. EdBig.PRG is very similar to AddBig.PRG, except that rather than appending blank records to the linked databases, it asks the user to enter the code number or last name of the record to edit. Then it attempts to find the appropriate record. If it can find the requested record, it allows the user to make changes via the PgChange procedure.

```
*************************************** EdBig.PRG
* Sample program to edit data on the BigFile.DBF
* data file using many screens and PgChange.
CLEAR
SET TALK OFF

*-- Declare IPage variable from PgChange
*-- procedure public to help with loop.
PUBLIC IPage
SET PROCEDURE TO ThreeDbs

*-- Open three-across database and index files.
CLOSE DATABASES
DO ThreeFil WITH "BigFile","BigCodes,BigNames"

*-- Ask for code number, Name, or Exit.
Start_Rec = "X"
DO WHILE Start_Rec # " "
   CLEAR

   *------ Make sure starting in A file with
   *------ Big codes index file primary.
   SELECT A
   SET INDEX TO BigCodes,BigNames

   Start_Rec = SPACE(15)
   @ 10,2 SAY "Enter code number or last name, "
   @ 12,2 SAY "or <--' to Exit " ;
          GET Start_Rec
   READ

   *----- Trim and make uppercase.
   Start_Rec = UPPER(TRIM(Start_Rec))

   *----- Respond to entry.
   DO CASE

      *---- If number entered, seek it.
      CASE VAL(Start_Rec) > 0
           SEEK VAL(Start_Rec)

      *--- If name entered, locate it.
```

Figure 9.19: The EdBig.PRG command file

```
        CASE ASC(Start_Rec) >= 65
             SET INDEX TO BigNames,BigCodes
             SEEK Start_Rec

      *--- Otherwise, exit.
      OTHERWISE
             Start_Rec = " "
             LOOP

   ENDCASE

   *---- Make sure record exists.
   IF EOF()
      @ 15,5 SAY "Can't Find " + Start_Rec
      ? CHR(7)
      WAIT "Press any key to try again..."
      LOOP
   ENDIF (eof)

   *---------- Keep editing until exit requested.
   IPage = " "
   DO WHILE IPage # "E"
      DO PgChange WITH "BigFile",3
   ENDDO (ipage # e)

ENDDO (exit from program)

*--- Close up and end program.
CLOSE PROCEDURE

RETURN
```

Figure 9.19:   The EdBig.PRG command file (continued)

DELETING

The DelBig.PRG command file allows the user to delete records from the three linked databases. The general techniques used to isolate, delete, and recall records before packing should be somewhat obvious to most dBASE programmers. The comments in the program describe what the various routines do. Figure 9.20 shows the DelBig.PRG command file.

PRINTING

Finally, the PrintBig.PRG command file shows a technique for printing data from the three related databases. Note that data from the linked files are displayed with the usual B—> and C—> symbols. The LF memory variable keeps track of lines printed. The command file includes a routine to eject the page in the printer when LF reaches 48 lines or pause the

```
********************************** DelBig.PRG
* Sample program to delete data on
* the BigFile.DBF linked databases.
CLEAR
SET TALK OFF

SET PROCEDURE TO ThreeDbs

*-- Open three-across database and index files.
CLOSE DATABASES
DO ThreeFil WITH "BigFile","BigCodes,BigNames"

*-- Ask for code number or Exit.
Start_Rec = 999
DO WHILE Start_Rec # 0
    CLEAR

    Start_Rec = 0
    @ 10,2 SAY "Enter code number of record "
    @ 12,2 SAY "to delete or <--' to Exit " ;
           GET Start_Rec PICT "99999"
    READ

    *----- Respond to entry.
    DO CASE

        *---- If not exiting, look up.
        CASE Start_Rec > 0
             SEEK Start_Rec

        *--- Otherwise, exit.
        OTHERWISE
             LOOP

    ENDCASE

    *---- Make sure record exists.
    IF EOF()
        @ 15,5 SAY "Can't Find " + STR(Start_Rec,5)
        ? CHR(7)
        WAIT "Press any key to try again..."
        LOOP
    ENDIF (eof)

    *-- If found, display and ask for permission.
    CLEAR
    DISPLAY Code,LName,FName,B->Child1,C->GranChild1
    ?
    WAIT "Delete this record? (Y/N) " TO YesNo

    IF UPPER(YesNo) = "Y"
        DELETE
        DO DelAcross
    ENDIF (yesno = y)

ENDDO (exit from program)

*-- Final check before permanent deletion.
*-- Count how many records marked for deletion
```

Figure 9.20: The DelBig.PRG command file

```
*-- and store in memory variable No_Dels.
COUNT FOR DELETED() TO No_Dels

CLEAR
Permiss = "N"
DO WHILE Permiss = "N" .AND. No_Dels > 0
   CLEAR
   ?
   DISPLAY OFF ALL Code,LName,FName, ;
        B->Child1,C->GranChild1 FOR DELETED()
   ?
   Permiss = " "
   @ ROW(),5 SAY "Ok to delete all these? (Y/N) " ;
     GET Permiss PICTURE "!"
   READ
   *--- If not OK to delete all, find out which.
   IF Permiss # "Y"
      CodeRec = 0
      @ ROW(),0 CLEAR
      @ ROW(),5 SAY "Recall which code number: ";
        GET CodeRec PICT "99999"
      READ
      SEEK CodeRec
      *--- If found, recall.
      IF .NOT. EOF() .AND. DELETED()
         RECALL
         SELECT B
         RECALL
         SELECT C
         RECALL
         SELECT A
         No_Dels = No_Dels - 1
      *--- Otherwise, warn user.
      ELSE
         @ 20,2
         ? "No such record to recall!"
         WAIT
      ENDIF (eof())
   ENDIF (permiss # y)
ENDDO (permiss and No_dels)

*--- Pack across three files.
DO PakAcross

*-- Done.
CLOSE PROCEDURE
RETURN
```

Figure 9.20:   The DelBig.PRG command file (continued)

screen when LF reaches 20 or more lines. (Otherwise there will not be
enough room for the next complete record.) Figure 9.21 shows the entire
PrintBig.PRG command file.

Each command file in these examples closes all databases, opens the
ThreeDbs.PRG procedure file, and opens all databases using the ThreeFil
procedure. This is not a very efficient technique, because there is a delay at

```
******************************* PrintBig.PRG
* Sample program to display data from three
* linked files in Code field order.
CLEAR
SET TALK OFF

SET PROCEDURE TO ThreeDbs

*-- Open three-across database and index files.
CLOSE DATABASES
DO ThreeFil WITH "BigFile","BigCodes,BigNames"

*-- Ask about printer.
CLEAR
ToPrint = " "
@ 10,5 SAY "Send report to printer? (Y/N) ";
       GET ToPrint PICTURE "!"
       READ

*-- Turn on printer, if requested.
IF ToPrint = "Y"
   SET PRINT ON
ENDIF

*--- Start line counter.
LF = 0

*--- Loop through linked databases.
CLEAR
SELECT A
GO TOP
DO WHILE .NOT. EOF()
   ? "Code:",STR(Code,5)
   ?? SPACE(5) + "Last Name:",LName
   ?? SPACE(5) + "First Name:",FName
   ?
   ? "  First Child : ",B->Child1
   ? "  Second Child: ",B->Child2
   ? "  Third Child : ",B->Child3
   ?
   ? "     First Grandchild : ",C->GranChild1
   ? "     Second Grandchild: ",C->GranChild2
   ? "     Third Grandchild : ",C->GranChild3
   ?
   ?
   ?
   *-- Increment line counter.
   LF = LF + 12
   *-- Check printer lines printed.
   IF ToPrint = "Y" .AND. LF >= 48
      EJECT
      LF = 0
   ENDIF (48 or more lines printed).

   *-- Check screen lines displayed.
   IF ToPrint # "Y" .AND. LF >= 20
      WAIT
      CLEAR
      LF = 0
   ENDIF (20 or more lines displayed)
```

Figure 9.21: The PrintBig.PRG command file

```
     SKIP
 ENDDO (not eof)
 EJECT
 SET PRINT OFF
 CLOSE PROCEDURE
 RETURN
```

Figure 9.21:   The PrintBig.PRG command file (continued)

the start of each command file while these commands are being executed. I've only designed the programs this way to keep them independent.

If these command files were linked through a single main menu program, you could open the ThreeDbs procedure file and "DO" the ThreeFil procedure once when the main menu program was first run. Then, you could delete the lines that perform these tasks from the subordinate command files to make everything run faster. (Just be sure that you don't use the CLOSE DATABASES command in any of the subordinate command files.)

Again, let me emphasize that managing linked files in this fashion is a somewhat tricky business, and the procedures in this chapter are not universal to every possible application. However, the general techniques for opening, linking, and managing linked files are universal. With a little practice and ingenuity, you'll be able to handle many linked files to overcome dBASE III PLUS's database size limitations.

☉AN ALTERNATIVE METHOD FOR MANAGING SCREENS

Before leaving this topic of managing multiple linked databases and their custom screens, I should mention that there is an alternative method for managing the separate screens used for entering and editing data. And that is, rather than storing them as separate files with the extensions .P1, .P2, .P3, and so forth on disk, you can store them as procedures in a procedure file with procedures named P1, P2, P3, P4.

The advantage to storing the separate screens in a single procedure file is that each screen is displayed more quickly as the user switches from one page to the next.

To add the various screen file pages to the ThreeDbs.PRG procedure file, you'll need to use something other than the MODIFY COMMAND editor, because the procedures already in ThreeDbs.PRG are pushing the 5,000-character limit. You'll also need to change the PgChange procedure slightly, as we'll discuss in a moment.

Suppose you wanted to use this alternative method with the BigFile.P1, BigFile.P2, and BigFile.P3 databases. To begin with, you'd need to load the ThreeDbs.PRG procedure file into your word processor and move the cursor to the bottom of the file. Then you'd need to read in each screen file and convert it to a procedure. For example, if using WordStar, you'd type ^KR to read in an external file, and specify BigFile.P1 as the file to read in. Then you'd need to add the command

PROCEDURE P1

to the top of the new procedure, and the command

RETURN

to the bottom of the procedure.

To read in the next screen file, use the appropriate command, and specify BigFile.P2 as the file to read in. Name the new procedure P2, and add the RETURN command to the bottom of the procedure. You'll want to repeat this process for each screen file in your application. Make sure each new procedure begins with the PROCEDURE command followed by the correct procedure name (i.e., P1, P2, P3, P4, and so forth), and each procedure ends with RETURN, as shown in the example below:

```
* – Custom screen for first page.

PROCEDURE P1
    *- These fields are all on the A database.
    SELECT A
    @ 5,70 SAY "Page 1"
    @ 8,5 SAY "Code " GET Code
    @ 10,5 SAY "Last Name " GET LName
    @ 12,5 SAY "First Name " GET FName
RETURN

* –- Second page of screens for BigFile.DBF.

PROCEDURE P2
    @ 2,1 SAY "Code: "
    @ 2,8 SAY A->Code
    @ 2,15 SAY "Last Name: " + A->LName
    @ 2,70 SAY "Page 2"
```

```
* — These fields are on the database.
SELECT B
@ 10,5 SAY "1st Child " GET Child1
@ 12,5 SAY "2nd Child " GET Child2
@ 14,5 SAY "3rd Child " GET Child3
RETURN

* — Third page of screens for BigFile.DBF.

PROCEDURE P3

@ 2,1 SAY "Code: "
@ 2,8 SAY A->Code
@ 2,15 SAY "Last Name: " + A->LName
@ 2,70 SAY "Page 3"

* – – – –- These fields are on the C Database.
SELECT C
@ 10,5 SAY "1st Grandchild " GET GranChild1
@ 12,5 SAY "2nd Grandchild " GET GranChild2
@ 14,5 SAY "3rd Grandchild " GET GranChild3
RETURN
```

The only change you need to make to the PgChange procedure to use this alternative technique is to change the lines

```
* – –- Generate screen file name.
ScreenFile = RootName + ".P" + Sub
```

to

```
* – –- Generate page name.
ScreenFile = "P" + Sub
```

That way, with each pass through the DO WHILE loop, the DO &Screen-File command will DO P1, P2, or P3 rather than BigFiles.P1, BigFiles.P2, and so forth. (Actually, you wouldn't even need to pass the RootName parameter if you made this change.) Keep in mind that you can have only 32 procedures in a procedure file. Therefore, if you have too many screens to fit in a procedure file, you'll need to use the original PgChange procedure file to manage custom screens.

⊙OTHER USES OF THE SET RELATION COMMAND

In this chapter we've used the SET RELATION command to link several databases with equal numbers of records, so that moving the record number pointer through one database causes equal movements through the other. Before closing this chapter, I should mention that this is not the only use of the SET RELATION command.

Linking parallel databases by record numbers is certainly valuable, but the SET RELATION command is more commonly used to set up *one-to-many relationships* among databases. This allows you to avoid uneccessary repetitions of data, and therefore save disk space and typing effort.

For example, look at the database in Figure 9.22, named AR.DBF, which stores data for an Accounts Receivable system. It contains fields for storing the date and amount of various invoices, as well as the name and address of the billed customer.

```
Structure for database : AR.DBF
    Field   Field name    Type        Width    Dec
      1     BILL_DATE     Date          8
      2     AMOUNT        Numeric      10        2
      3     CUSTOMER      Character    20
      4     ADDRESS       Character    20
      5     CITY          Character    15
      6     STATE         Character     2
      7     ZIP           Character     5
```

Figure 9.22:   The AR.DBF database structure

This particular design is not very practical for this application because there may be hundreds of billings to only a few customers. The customer name and address would have to be stored repeatedly and redundantly, throughout the database, as in Figure 9.23.

A better approach would be to simply store the billing date and amount on one database, and the individual customer names and addresses on another. Then, use a code to *relate* the two databases to each other.

For example, you could use a Customer database to store the customer number, name, address, and other relevant information, using the structure shown in Figure 9.24. An example of data for several customers is shown in Figure 9.25.

Next, you could create a second database to store individual charge transactions on (Figure 9.26). It would contain only the customer number (which relates it to the full name and address in the Customer database), the date, amount, and a brief description of each charge transaction (Figure 9.27).

The only repetitive data in two such separate databases is the small Cust_No field. No disk space is wasted by repeating the customer name and address with every charge.

Now, the question is, how do we inform dBASE III PLUS of the relationship between these two databases? You cannot relate them by record numbers; it is the Cust_No field that relates the two databases to each other. When such a

BILL_DATE	AMOUNT	CUSTOMER	ADDRESS	CITY	STATE	ZIP
03/25/60	734.75	American Iceberg Co.	345 No. Pole St.	Gnome	AL	00001
03/25/60	8456.32	Thompson Twins, Inc.	466 Chesapeake Way	San Francisco	CA	91121
03/25/60	2956.70	Logitek Microcode	256 Eprom Blvd.	Van Nuys	CA	93323
03/25/60	624.88	DBMS Software	256 K. St.	Solana Beach	CA	93221
07/24/60	1115.60	Antioch Petroleum	8776 Fossil St.	Denver	CO	55555
07/24/61	534.94	Hockleed Aeronautics	1777 Cannard Blvd.	Augusta	GA	32212
03/26/70	4236.54	Hockleed Aeronautics	1777 Cannard Blvd.	Augusta	GA	32212
03/26/70	2352.54	DBMS Software	256 K. St.	Solana Beach	CA	93221
08/24/70	3426.43	Thompson Twins, Inc.	466 Chesapeake Way	San Francisco	CA	91121
07/24/71	8351.76	American Iceberg Co.	345 No. Pole St.	Gnome	AL	00001
07/24/71	6342.75	Logitek Microcode	256 Eprom Blvd.	Van Nuys	CA	93323
02/23/72	946.38	Antioch Petroleum	8776 Fossil St.	Denver	CO	55555
03/25/80	684.34	Logitek Microcode	256 Eprom Blvd.	Van Nuys	CA	93323
04/26/81	12354.34	DBMS Software	256 K. St.	Solana Beach	CA	93221
07/24/81	1234.56	American Iceberg	345 No. Pole St.	Gnome	AL	00001
07/24/81	232.12	Thompson Twins, Inc.	466 Chesapeake Way	San Francisco	CA	91121
07/24/81	877.43	Antioch Petroleum	8776 Fossil St.	Denver	CO	55555
03/26/82	3214.45	Hockleed Aeronautics	1777 Cannard Blvd.	Augusta	GA	32212

Figure 9.23: Listing from the AR.DBF database

Structure for database : Customer.DBF

Field	Field name	Type	Width	Dec
1	CUST_NO	Character	5	
2	CUSTOMER	Character	20	
3	ADDRESS	Character	20	
4	CITY	Character	15	
5	STATE	Character	5	
6	ZIP	Character	10	

Figure 9.24: The Customer.DBF database structure

CUST_NO	CUSTOMER	ADDRESS	CITY	STATE	ZIP
1001	American Iceberg Co.	345 No. Pole St.	Gnome	AL	00001
1002	Antioch Petroleum	8776 Fossil St.	Denver	CO	55555
1003	DBMS Software	256 K. St.	Solana Beach	CA	93221
1004	Hockleed Aeronautics	1777 Cannard Blvd.	Augusta	GA	32212
1005	Logitek Microcode	256 Eprom Blvd.	Van Nuys	CA	93323
1006	Thompson Twins, Inc.	466 Chesapeake Way	San Francisco	CA	91121

Figure 9.25: Listing from the Customer.DBF database

Structure for database : Charges.DBF

Field	Field name	Type	Width	Dec
1	CUST_NO	Character	5	
2	BILL_DATE	Date	8	
3	AMOUNT	Numeric	12	2
4	DESCRIPT	Character	20	

Figure 9.26: The structure of the Charges database

common field is used to relate two databases, it is often called the *key field*. To set up a relationship, the key field should first be indexed for rapid access. To create an index of the Cust_No field for the Customer database named Customer.NDX, use the commands

```
USE Customer
INDEX ON Cust_No TO Customer
```

To create an index file of the Cust_No field for the Charges database, use the commands

```
USE Charges
INDEX ON Cust_No TO Charges
```

Now, you can set up a relationship between the two files. First use the SELECT command that allows the two databases to be open at the same time:

```
SELECT A
USE Charges INDEX Charges
SELECT B
Use Customer Index Customer
```

CUST_NO	BILL_DATE	AMOUNT	DESCRIPT
1003	12/12/85	123.45	Floppy Disks
1001	04/01/85	322.60	Printer Paper
1002	03/15/85	233.20	Monitors
1001	03/01/85	45.00	Cable
1004	03/05/85	90.00	Cables
1002	03/25/85	444.44	Drive Controller
1003	03/15/85	623.45	Color Monitor
1003	03/15/85	623.45	Color Monitor
1001	04/01/85	212.10	Monitor
1004	02/15/85	90.00	Switch Box
1002	01/01/85	55.00	Tech Manual

Figure 9.27:   Transactions on the Charges.DBF database

Then, use the SET RELATION command to set up a relationship between Charges and Customer, as below:

```
SELECT A
SET RELATION TO Cust_No INTO Customer
```

Note that we first select the Charges database (SELECT A), then set a relationship, based on the Cust_No field, into the Customer database (SET RELATION TO Cust_No INTO Customer).

Now we have full access to both databases. Whenever dBASE is positioned to a Charge transaction in the Charges databases, it automatically looks up the appropriate record in the Customer database, so that the customer name and address are readily available.

Let's look at an example. If you type the LIST or the DISPLAY ALL command, the contents of the Charges database are displayed as they normally would be, shown below:

RECORD#	CUST_NO	BILL_DATE	AMOUNT	DESCRIPT
2	1001	04/01/85	322.60	Printer Paper
4	1001	03/01/85	45.00	Cable
9	1001	04/01/85	212.10	Monitor
3	1002	03/15/85	233.20	Monitors
6	1002	03/25/85	444.44	Drive Controller
11	1002	01/01/85	55.00	Tech Manual
1	1003	12/12/85	123.45	Floppy Disks

7	1003	03/15/85	623.45	Color Monitor
8	1003	03/15/85	623.45	Color Monitor
5	1004	03/05/85	90.00	Cables
10	1004	02/15/85	90.00	Switch Box

However, if you specify fields from the Customer database to be included in the display, then dBASE automatically displays, along with the Charges data, the data from the Customer database appropriate to each Charge record. Since the Customer database was opened using the SELECT B command, you can specify fields from this database by preceding the field name with the usual B—> symbol. Note the LIST command below:

LIST OFF Cust_No,Bill_Date,Amount,B—>Customer,B—>Address

All the fields from the Charges database are specified, and the Customer and Address fields from the Customer database are specified. The resulting listing looks like Figure 9.28.

Of course, you can list any combination of fields from the two databases. The point is, you can produce reports that appear as though the Charges database has the name and address of every customer included in it, without wasting the space or time required actually to repeat every name and address with every transaction.

When designing databases with one-to-many relationships, it is important to make sure the *master file* (the "one" database of the one-to-many pair)

Cust_No	Bill_Date	Amount	B—>Customer	B—>Address
1001	04/01/85	322.60	American Iceberg Co.	345 No. Pole St.
1001	03/01/85	45.00	American Iceberg Co.	345 No. Pole St.
1001	04/01/85	212.10	American Iceberg Co.	345 No. Pole St.
1002	03/15/85	233.20	Antioch Petroleum	8776 Fossil St.
1002	03/25/85	444.44	Antioch Petroleum	8776 Fossil St.
1002	01/01/85	55.00	Antioch Petroleum	8776 Fossil St.
1003	12/12/85	123.45	DBMS Software	256 K. St.
1003	03/15/85	623.45	DBMS Software	256 K. St.
1003	03/15/85	623.45	DBMS Software	256 K. St.
1004	03/05/85	90.00	Hockleed Aeronautics	1777 Cannard Blvd.
1004	02/15/85	90.00	Hockleed Aeronautics	1777 Cannard Blvd.

Figure 9.28: Joint listing from the Customer and Charges databases

has a unique item in each record of the key field. For example, if more that one customer in the Customer.DBF database had the customer number 1001, then there would be no way to tell *which* customer number 1001 a particular charge from the Charges database is to be billed to. But, if each customer has a unique number (or some other identifying code), there is no chance for a mix-up.

Since, in this book, we're focusing on procedures to expand the capabilities of dBASE III PLUS rather than discussing its inherent capabilities, I won't pursue this topic any further. If you are interested in these one-to-many relationships, or an Accounts Receivable system in general, these are covered extensively in my book *Advanced Techniques in dBASE III PLUS,* published by SYBEX. The book contains a complete Accounts Receivable system, as well as tutorials on general dBASE III PLUS programming techniques.

A DEBUGGING AID 10

Every programmer knows that if anything is certain in this world, it is that command files rarely work right the first time. It is not unusual for a programmer, particularly a beginner, to spend more time getting the bugs out of a program than he or she spends creating it. Some bugs in programs are easy to find, but the more subtle errors are not so easy.

Two of the biggest impediments to the debugging process are

- Lack of proper indentations, which makes it difficult to see "chunks" of logic at a glance, and

- Missing ENDDO, ENDIF, and ENDCASE commands, which dBASE III PLUS is incapable of telling you about.

In this chapter, we'll develop a command file that can put proper indentations into any command file, and will also inform you of any missing or extraneous ENDIF, ENDDO, or ENDCASE commands. The program will also list all calls to other programs.

⊙USING THE DEBUG PROGRAM

The entire Debug.PRG command file is listed in Figure 10.1. The second half of this chapter explains the code thoroughly. First, however, you will learn how to use this program to debug programs of your own.

To run this command file simply enter the command

DO Debug

at the dot prompt. When the program begins running, the screen asks you to enter the name of the command file to debug. If the file that you wish to debug already has the extension .PRG, you can type in just the first name (e.g., EXAMPLE for a command file named EXAMPLE.PRG). Otherwise, specify the extension. The screen will display the message *Working. . .* and then will display each line of the command file as it puts in the proper indentations.

Next, the program displays a count of all commands that involve "clauses," as in Figure 10.2.

Note that the screen points out an unmatched DO WHILE. . .ENDDO pair. Calls to other programs are listed beneath the clause statements. Also, the new command file with proper indentations is now stored under the original file name, EXAMPLE.PRG, and the original program is stored under the file name EXAMPLE.OLD.

```
***************************************** Debug.PRG
*_  Test for unmatched clauses in command files,
*_  and correct indentations.
*_  Requires the Debug.DBF database.
SET TALK OFF
SET EXACT OFF
SET SAFETY OFF
CLEAR

*----------------------- Make sure Debug.DBF is available.
IF .NOT. FILE("Debug.DBF")
    ? CHR(7)
    ? "Sorry, can't find the Debug.DBF database on this drive."
    ?
    ? "COPY Debug.DBF to this drive, then try again."
    ?
    ? "Exiting the debugger..."
    ?
    CANCEL
ENDIF (no file)

*------- Get name of program to debug.
FileName = SPACE(14)
@ 5,5 SAY "Enter name of command file to analyze"
@ 7,5 SAY "The .PRG extension is assumed unless you"
@ 8,5 SAY "specify otherwise (e.g. MyProg.CMD)."
@ 10,5 SAY "The currently logged drive is assumed "
@ 11,5 SAY "unless you specify otherwise (e.g. B:MyProg)"
@ 13,5 GET FileName
READ

CLEAR
? "Working..."
*------- Add .PRG extension if necessary.
IF .NOT. "." $(FileName)
    FileName = TRIM(FileName) + ".PRG"
ENDIF

*------- Make sure file exists.
IF .NOT. FILE(FileName)
    ? CHR(7)
    ?
    ? "Sorry, can't find a file named "+UPPER(FileName)
    ?
    ? "Exiting the debugger..."
    ?
    CANCEL
ENDIF

*------- Store file name without extension to FName.
FileName = UPPER(FileName)
FName = SUBSTR(FileName,1,AT(".",FileName)-1)

*------- Pull a copy of the program into DEBUG.DBF.
CLOSE DATABASES
USE Debug
ZAP
APPEND FROM &FileName SDF
GO TOP
```

Figure 10.1: The Debug.PRG command file

```
*------- Start counters for clause commands.
STORE 0 TO Indent, Amt, DoWhile, NewIf, DoCase, ;
           CEndDo, CEndIf, CEndCase, PCount

*------- Loop through each line of the command file.
DO WHILE .NOT. EOF()
   MemVar = TRIM(Line)
   *------ Peel off leading blanks.
   MemVar = LTRIM(MemVar)

   *------- Set flags to false.
   STORE .F. TO Increase, Decrease, NewElse, ;
             NewCase, NewText

   *------- Check for clause commands and
   *------- handle counters and indents.
   DO CASE

      CASE UPPER(Memvar) = "DO WHIL"
           DoWhile = DoWhile + 1
           Amt = 3
           Increase = .T.

      CASE UPPER(Memvar) = "IF "
           NewIf = NewIf + 1
           Amt = 3
           Increase = .T.

      CASE UPPER(Memvar) = "DO CASE"
           DoCase = DoCase + 1
           Amt = 8
           Increase = .T.

      CASE UPPER(Memvar) = "CASE" .OR. Memvar = "OTHE"
           NewCase = .T.

      CASE UPPER(Memvar) = "ENDD"
           CEndDo = CEndDo + 1
           Indent = Indent - 3

      CASE UPPER(Memvar) = "ENDI"
           CEndIf = CEndIf + 1
           Indent = Indent - 3

      CASE UPPER(Memvar) = "ENDC"
           CEndCase = CEndCase + 1
           Indent = Indent - 8

      CASE UPPER(Memvar) = "ELSE"
           NewElse = .T.

      CASE UPPER(Memvar) = "TEXT"
           NewText = .T.

      *------- Note calls to another program.
      CASE UPPER(Memvar) = "DO " .OR. ;
           UPPER(MemVar) = "SET PROC" .OR. ;
           UPPER(MemVar) = "CALL" .OR. ;
           UPPER(MemVar) = "LOAD "
```

Figure 10.1:   The Debug.PRG command file (continued)

```
                 PCount = PCount + 1
                 PSub = LTRIM(STR(PCount,3))
                 PCall&Psub = TRIM(MemVar)

      ENDCASE

      *------- Add new indent to line.
      REPLACE Line WITH SPACE(MAX(Indent,0)) + MemVar

      *------- If command was "ELSE", unindent the one line.
      IF NewElse
         Indent = Indent - Amt
         REPLACE Line WITH SPACE(MAX(Indent,0)) + MemVar
         Indent = Indent + Amt
      ENDIF

      *------- If command was a CASE or OTHERWISE, unindent.
      IF NewCase
         Indent = Indent - 5
         REPLACE Line WITH SPACE(MAX(Indent,0)) + MemVar
         Indent = Indent + 5
      ENDIF

      *------- If remaining lines to be indented,
      *------- increase indent.
      IF Increase
         Indent = Indent + Amt
      ENDIF

      REPLACE Line WITH TRIM(Line)
      ? TRIM(Line)

      *------- Don't modify anything in
      *------- TEXT...ENDTEXT block.
      IF NewText
         SKIP
         DO WHILE .NOT. "ENDT" $ (UPPER(Line))
            ? TRIM(Line)
            SKIP
         ENDDO
      *------- Otherwise, skip to next line.
      ELSE
         SKIP
      ENDIF (NewText)

      ENDDO (while not eof)

      *------- Store original command file
      *------- with .OLD as the extension.
      Oldname = FName + ".OLD"
      IF FILE(Oldname)
         ERASE &Oldname
      ENDIF
      RENAME &FileName TO &Oldname

      *------- Copy new version of program
      *------- to original file name.
      COPY TO &FileName DELIM WITH BLANK
      CLOSE DATABASES
```

Figure 10.1:   The Debug.PRG command file (continued)

```
*------- Display command file stats.
CLEAR
ToPrint = " "
WAIT "Send statistics to printer? (Y/N) " TO ToPrint
ToPrint = UPPER(ToPrint)
IF ToPrint = "Y"
   SET PRINT ON
ENDIF

CLEAR
Whoops = "  <--- Whoops!  Unmatched pair."
? "Command file statistics for: "+FileName
?

*------- Print DO WHILE...ENDDO stats.
? "DO WHILE statements  :", DoWhile
? "ENDDO statements     :", CEndDo
IF DoWhile # CEndDo
   ?? Whoops
ENDIF
?

*------- Print IF...ENDIF stats.
? "IF statements        :", NewIf
? "ENDIF statements     :", CEndIf
IF NewIf # CEndIf
   ?? Whoops
ENDIF
?

*------- Print DO CASE...ENDCASE stats.
? "DO CASE statements   :", DoCase
? "ENDCASE statements   :", CEndCase
IF DoCase # CEndCase
   ?? Whoops
ENDIF
?
?
? "Calls to other programs:"
Row = 14
IF PCount = 0
   ?? " None"
ELSE
   ?
   Counter = 1
   DO WHILE Counter <= PCount
      PSub = LTRIM(STR(Counter,3))
      ? PCall&Psub
      Counter = Counter + 1
      Row = Row + 1
      IF ToPrint = "Y" .AND. Row > 56
         EJECT
         Row = 1
      ENDIF (printer)
      IF ToPrint # "Y" .AND. Row > 21
         ?
         WAIT
         ?
         Row = 2
```

Figure 10.1:   The Debug.PRG command file (continued)

```
      ENDIF (screen)
   ENDDO (counter)
ENDIF (pcount = 0)

*------- Print closing statements.
?
? "The original command file is now stored under &OldName"
?
? "The modified, indented version is stored under &FileName"
IF ToPrint = "Y"
   SET PRINT OFF
   EJECT
ENDIF (to print)
```

Figure 10.1:   The Debug.PRG command file (continued)

```
Command file statistics for: EXAMPLE.PRG

DO WHILE statements  :        1
ENDDO statements     :        0  <--- Whoops!  Unmatched pair.

IF statements        :        0
ENDIF statements     :        0

DO CASE statements   :        1
ENDCASE statements   :        1

Calls to other programs:

DO SubMenu1
DO SubMenu2
DO SubMenu3

The original command file is now stored under EXAMPLE.OLD

The modified, indented version is stored under EXAMPLE.PRG


  . _
```

Figure 10.2:   Screen from the Debug.PRG command file

To test the Debug program we'll use a program named TestDbug-.PRG. Figure 10.3 displays the program before it is run through the Debug program (it's a mess, I know).

After you run the TestDbug.PRG command file through the Debug program, the screen displays the information shown in Figure 10.4.

You can now see that this command file is missing an ENDCASE command. To fix this error, just edit the command file using the MODIFY COMMAND editor. You'll have to determine for yourself where to place the missing ENDCASE command. Then save the command file.

```
         ******************************* TestDbug.PRG
      *--------------- Test the Debug.PRG program.
      SET TALK OFF

           *-------- Display menu and get user's choice.
      Choice = 0
      DO WHILE Choice # 5
      CLEAR
      TEXT

                    Membership System Main Menu

                         1. Add new members
                         2. Print membership information
                         3. Change/delete data
                         4. Check for duplicates

                         5. Exit membership system

      ENDTEXT
             @ 12,22 SAY "Enter choice (1-5) " GET Choice
          READ

      *------------ Branch to appropriate program.
          DO CASE

      CASE Choice = 1
                  DO AddNew

      CASE Choice = 2
      DO Reports

          CASE Choice = 3
      DO EditDel

      CASE Choice = 4
             SET PROCEDURE TO GenProcs
          DO DupCheck WITH "Zip + Address + LName"
      CLOSE PROCEDURE

              ENDDO (while choice < 5)
      CLOSE DATABASES
          QUIT
```

Figure 10.3: TestDbug.PRG before the debugging program

If you wish to have Debug reindent the program lines to take into consideration the new ENDCASE command, just enter the DO Debug command again, and specify TestDbug as the command file.

After Debug makes its second pass at the TestDbug.PRG command file and informs you that there are no more unmatched "clause" commands, you might want to see how the command file looks with proper indentations. Just use the dBASE TYPE or MODIFY command to view the TestDbug.PRG command file. Figure 10.5 shows the TestDbug.PRG command file after the Debug program has cleaned it up.

```
Command file statistics for: TESTDBUG.PRG

DO WHILE statements  :          1
ENDDO statements     :          1

IF statements        :          0
ENDIF statements     :          0

DO CASE statements   :          1
ENDCASE statements   :          0   <--- Whoops!  Unmatched pair.

Calls to other programs:

DO AddNew
DO Reports
DO EditDel
SET PROCEDURE TO GenProcs
DO DupCheck WITH "Zip + Address + LName"

The original command file is now stored under TESTDBUG.OLD

The modified, indented version is stored under TESTDBUG.PRG

 · _
```

Figure 10.4: TestDbug.PRG statistics

As you can see, Debug put in all the proper indentations. There may be other errors in the program, since Debug only looks for unmatched clauses. But most other errors are of the type that dBASE will spot immediately and inform you of at the dot prompt.

The Debug.PRG program uses a database named Debug.DBF that has the structure shown in Figure 10.6. You'll need to use the dBASE CREATE command to create this database before using the Debug.PRG command file. Notice that the file contains only one field named Line, which is 254 characters wide. When the Debug.PRG program is run, each record in this database will contain a command line from the command file being debugged.

⊙THE DEBUG.PRG COMMAND FILE

Let's now discuss how the program does what it does. First, it sets up some parameters and clears the screen, as shown below:

```
* * * * * * * * * * * * * * * * * * * * * * * * * * * * * * * * * * * * * Debug.PRG
*--- Test for unmatched clauses in command files,
*--- and correct the indentations.
*--- Requires the Debug.DBF database.
SET TALK OFF
SET EXACT OFF
SET SAFETY OFF
CLEAR
```

```
******************************* TestDbug.PRG
*--------------- Test the Debug.PRG program.
SET TALK OFF

*--------- Display menu and get user's choice.
Choice = 0
DO WHILE Choice # 5
    CLEAR
    TEXT

              Membership System Main Menu

                    1. Add new members
                    2. Print membership information
                    3. Change/delete data
                    4. Check for duplicates

                    5. Exit membership system

    ENDTEXT
    @ 12,22 SAY "Enter choice (1-5) " GET Choice
    READ

    *------------ Branch to appropriate program.
    DO CASE

        CASE Choice = 1
             DO AddNew

        CASE Choice = 2
             DO Reports

        CASE Choice = 3
             DO EditDel

        CASE Choice = 4
             SET PROCEDURE TO GenProcs
             DO DupCheck WITH "Zip + Address + LName"
             CLOSE PROCEDURE
    ENDCASE

ENDDO (while choice < 5)
CLOSE DATABASES
QUIT
```

Figure 10.5: TestDbug.PRG cleaned up by the debugging program

```
Structure for database : C:DEBUG.dbf
     Field    Field name    Type          Width     Dec
       1       LINE         Character      254
```

Figure 10.6: Structure of the Debug.DBF database

Next, Debug.PRG makes sure that the Debug.DBF database is available. If the database is not available, the program beeps [CHR(7)], displays an error message, and returns control to the dot prompt (CANCEL):

```
* – – – – – – – – – – – Make sure Debug.DBF is available.
IF .NOT. FILE("Debug.DBF")
   ? CHR(7)
   ? "Sorry, can't find the Debug.DBF database on this drive."
   ?
   ? "COPY Debug.DBF to this drive, then try again."
   ?
   ? "Exiting the debugger..."
   ?
   CANCEL
ENDIF (no file)
```

Next, Debug.PRG displays instructions for entering the name of the command file to debug, and stores the user's answer in a variable named FileName:

```
* – – –- Get name of program to debug.
FileName = SPACE(14)
@ 5,5 SAY "Enter name of command file to analyze"
@ 7,5 SAY "The .PRG extension is assumed unless you"
@ 8,5 SAY "specify otherwise (e.g. MyProg.CMD)."
@ 10,5 SAY "The currently logged drive is assumed "
@ 11,5 SAY "unless you specify otherwise (e.g. B:MyProg)"
@ 13,5 GET FileName
READ
```

Now the program clears the screen and displays the message *Working. . ..* An IF clause checks to see if a period is embedded in the file name. If not, the command file adds the extension .PRG to the file name:

```
CLEAR
? "Working. . . . ."

*------- Add .PRG extension if necessary.
IF .NOT. "." $(FileName)
   FileName = TRIM(FileName) + ".PRG"
ENDIF
```

The command file next makes sure that the program the user wants to debug is available on disk. If it is not, Debug beeps, displays an error message, and returns to the dot prompt:

```
* – – –- Make sure file exists.
IF .NOT. FILE(FileName)
    ? CHR(7)
    ?
    ? "Sorry, can't find a file named " + UPPER(FileName)
    ?
    ? "Exiting the debugger..."
    ?
    CANCEL
ENDIF
```

Then, the variable FName is assigned the first part of the command file name (without the .PRG extension) using a slightly tricky maneuver with the SUBSTR and AT functions:

```
*---- Store file name without extension to FName.
FileName = UPPER(FileName)
FName = SUBSTR(FileName,1,AT(".",FileName) – 1)
```

The program then closes any open databases (just as a safety measure), and opens the Debug.DBF database. Any data in the Debug.DBF database is quickly eliminated (ZAP), and the contents of the indicated command file are read into the Debug.DBF database, each line as a separate record. The SDF (Structured Data Format) option informs dBASE that the incoming data are coming from a "straight" ASCII file with no header or special symbols, rather than in dBASE III PLUS format. (All command files are stored as straight ASCII files.)

```
*----- Pull a copy of the program into DEBUG.DBF.
CLOSE DATABASES
USE Debug
ZAP
APPEND FROM &FileName SDF
GO TOP
```

Next, several variables are initialized to 0. The Indent and Amt variables help keep track of how far to indent a line in the command file. The other variables act as counters for clause statements, such as DO WHILE, IF, and so forth:

```
* – – –- Start counters for clause commands.
STORE 0 TO Indent, Amt, DoWhile, NewIf, DoCase, ;
     CEndDo, CEndIf, CEndCase, PCount
```

Now a DO WHILE loop starts reading each record from the Debug.DBF file (which contains the command file being debugged). Each line is first assigned to the memory variable MemVar, with leading and trailing blanks trimmed off:

```
* – – –- Loop through each line of the command file.
DO WHILE .NOT. EOF()
   MemVar = TRIM(Line)
   * – – – Peel off leading blanks.
   MemVar = LTRIM(MemVar)
```

Now, several flags (variables) are set to False (.F.). These flags determine whether or not to increase or decrease the indentation, and they also detect new ELSE, CASE, and TEXT commands.

```
*------- Set flags to false.
STORE .F. TO Increase, Decrease, NewElse;
     NewCase, NewText
```

A series of CASE statements then determine if a clause statement such as DO WHILE, DO CASE, or IF starts the current command line. Any CASE statement that proves True increments a counter, and alerts variables that control the size of the indentation necessary for proper formatting.

```
* – – –- Check for clause commands and
* – – –- handle counters and indents.
DO CASE

   CASE UPPER(Memvar) = "DO WHIL"
      DoWhile = DoWhile + 1
      Amt = 3
      Increase = .T.

   CASE UPPER(Memvar) = "IF "
      NewIf = NewIf + 1
      Amt = 3
      Increase = .T.
```

```
    CASE UPPER(Memvar) = "DO CASE"
       DoCase = DoCase + 1
       Amt = 8
       Increase = .T.

    CASE UPPER(Memvar) = "CASE" .OR. Memvar = "OTHE"
       NewCase = .T.

    CASE UPPER(Memvar) = "ENDD"
       CEndDo = CEndDo + 1
       Indent = Indent - 3

    CASE UPPER(Memvar) = "ENDI"
       CEndIf = CEndIf + 1
       Indent = Indent - 3

    CASE UPPER(Memvar) = "ENDC"
       CEndCase = CEndCase + 1
       Indent = Indent - 8

    CASE UPPER(Memvar) = "ELSE"
       NewElse = .T.

    CASE UPPER(Memvar) = "TEXT"
       NewText = .T.
```

Debug.PRG also checks to see if there is a call to another program in the current program line. If there is, it increments the PCount variable by 1, converts it to a character string with leading blanks removed, and stores the entire line in a variable with the prefix PCall. (Hence, the first line is stored in PCall1, the second in PCall2, and so forth.)

```
    *----- Note calls to another program.
    CASE UPPER(MemVar) = "DO " .OR. ;
       UPPER(MemVar) = "SET PROC" .OR. ;
       UPPER(MemVar) = "CALL" .OR. ;
       UPPER(MemVar) = "LOAD "
       PCount = PCount + 1
       PSub = LTRIM(STR(PCount,3))
       PCall&Psub = TRIM(MemVar)

    ENDCASE
```

At this point, the number of spaces to indent the line has been calculated. However, if a clause statement is missing, the calculated indentation might be a negative number. Therefore, the line below replaces the original program line with either the appropriate number of blank spaces, or no blank spaces, whichever is larger:

```
* − − −- Add new indent to line.
REPLACE Line WITH SPACE(MAX(Indent,0)) + MemVar
```

If the line currently being debugged is an ELSE command, the program line is unindented by three spaces for proper indentation, then the indentation is reset to its previous width:

```
* − − −- If command was "ELSE", unindent the one line.
IF NewElse
   Indent = Indent − Amt
   REPLACE Line WITH SPACE(MAX(Indent,0)) + MemVar
   Indent = Indent + Amt
ENDIF
```

If a CASE or OTHERWISE command appears in the current program line, indentations are again handled accordingly:

```
* − − −- If command was a CASE or OTHERWISE, unindent.
IF NewCase
   Indent = Indent − 5
   REPLACE Line WITH SPACE(MAX(Indent,0)) + MemVar
   Indent = Indent + 5
ENDIF
```

If the Increase flag was set to true during the previous CASE statements, the amount of the indentation is increased by the number specified in the Amt variable:

```
*------- If remaining lines to be indented,
*------- increase Indent.
IF Increase
   Indent = Indent + Amt
ENDIF
```

The current contents of the Line variable are now placed into the record with trailing blanks trimmed off. The line just analyzed is displayed on the screen:

```
REPLACE Line WITH TRIM(Line)
? TRIM(Line)
```

If a TEXT command is encountered, all lines within the TEXT. . .ENDTEXT commands are not modified, since this would throw off the screen display of the text:

```
*------- Don't modify anything in
*------- TEXT. . .ENDTEXT block.
IF NewText
   SKIP
   DO WHILE .NOT. "ENDT" $ (UPPER(Line))
      ? TRIM(Line)
      SKIP
ENDDO
```

However, if the TEXT command is not encountered, the program simply skips to the next record in the database (the next command in the command file) and analyzes it using the same process:

```
*------- Otherwise, skip to next line.
ELSE
   SKIP
ENDIF (Newtext)

ENDDO (while not eof)
```

When the DO WHILE .NOT. EOF( ) loop is done, the entire program has been analyzed and properly indented. The variable Oldname is assigned the original file name plus the extension .OLD. If that file name already exists, the original one is erased from the disk and the command file being analyzed is renamed to the Oldname file name:

```
*------- Store original command file with
*------- .OLD as the extension.
Oldname = FName + ".OLD"
IF FILE(Oldname)
   ERASE &Oldname
ENDIF
RENAME &FileName TO &Oldname
```

Now we need to get the modified command file out of Debug.DBF, and back into a normal command file with the original name. The COPY TO command, along with the DELIM WITH BLANK option, copies the contents of the Debug.DBF database to a straight ASCII file with the original file name.

```
*------- Copy new version of program to
*------- original file name.
COPY TO &FileName DELIM WITH BLANK
CLOSE DATABASES
```

Now the counters for the various clause commands are displayed on either the screen or hard copy. If there is an unequal pair of DO WHILE. . . ENDDO, IF. . .ENDIF, or DO CASE. . .ENDCASE commands, the Whoops variable, which contains an error message, is printed next to the faulty pair:

```
* – – –- Display command file stats.
CLEAR
ToPrint = " "
WAIT "Send statistics to printer? (Y/N) " TO ToPrint
ToPrint = UPPER(ToPrint)
IF ToPrint = "Y"
   SET PRINT ON
ENDIF


CLEAR
Whoops = " < –- Whoops! Unmatched pair."
? "Command file statistics for: "+FileName
?


* – – –- Print DO WHILE...ENDDO stats.
? "DO WHILE statements :", DoWhile
? "ENDDO statements     :", CEndDo
IF DoWhile # CEndDo
   ?? Whoops
ENDIF
?


* – – –- Print IF...ENDIF stats.
? "IF statements      :", NewIf
? "ENDIF statements :", CEndIf
IF NewIf # CEndIf
   ?? Whoops
ENDIF
?


* – – –- Print DO CASE...ENDCASE stats.
? "DO CASE statements :", DoCase
? "ENDCASE statements :", CEndCase
```

```
IF DoCase # CEndCase
   ?? Whoops
ENDIF
```

Debug next lists all lines that call other programs. The PCount variable kept track of how many calls were made, and the calls themselves were stored in an array of variables named PCall. The routine below displays all the lines that called other programs:

```
?
?
? "Calls to other programs:"
Row = 14
IF PCount = 0
   ?? " None"
ELSE
   ?
   Counter = 1
   DO WHILE Counter < = PCount
      PSub = LTRIM(STR(Counter,3))
      ? PCall&Psub
      Counter = Counter + 1
      Row = Row + 1
      IF ToPrint = "Y" .AND. Row > 56
         EJECT
         Row = 1
      ENDIF (printer)
      IF ToPrint # "Y" .AND. Row > 21
         ?
         WAIT
         ?
         Row = 2
      ENDIF (screen)
   ENDDO (counter)
ENDIF (pcount = 0)
```

The Debug program is done at this point. It ends by displaying both the file name for the modified version of the program, and the file name for the original undebugged version. If the command file statistics were sent to the printer, Debug turns off the printer and ejects the page:

```
* – – –- Print closing statements.
?
? "The original command file is now stored under &OldName"
?
? "The modified, indented version is stored under &FileName"
```

```
IF ToPrint = "Y"
   SET PRINT OFF
   EJECT
ENDIF (to print)
```

When you type in the Debug program, don't use it on a "real" command file until your typed version of Debug is itself fully tested and debugged. You should first make a test program simply to run it through Debug.PRG. Once the test program is created, copy it with the command

```
COPY FILE TEST.PRG TO TEST.BAK
```

Then, when you run the Debug program, enter TEST as the name of the program to debug. If the Debug program "crashes," you can just correct your error and enter the DO Debug command again. In this example, you can get your original command file back by entering the commands

```
ERASE Test.PRG
RENAME Test.BAK TO Test.PRG
```

Keep in mind that the Debug program calculates the amount of indentation based upon the commands in the program you are debugging. So, if your program is missing an ENDDO, ENDIF, or ENDCASE command, the indentations will probably be inaccurate in the newly indented program. Therefore, an inaccurate indentation may point you to the exact spot in a program where the missing ENDIF, ENDCASE, or ENDDO command belongs.

You can run any command file through the Debug program as many times as you wish. However, each time you do, the .OLD program will represent the previous revision, rather than the original .PRG program.

In the next chapter, we'll develop some procedures that replace routines commonly used in command files. These can speed programming and debugging by replacing several line of code with a single DO WITH command.

A PROGRAM
GENERATOR

11

A program generator, or *application generator,* is a program that writes programs. More specifically, a program generator is a program that asks you questions about a custom system you are developing, then writes all or some of the programs for that custom system.

Historically, most program generators have achieved only minor popularity because they are typically marketed as devices that allow users with no programming experience to develop sophisticated custom software systems. Unfortunately, this is not truly the case. No program generator is powerful or flexible enough to replace hard-earned human programming skill, because no computer is as smart or as creative as a skilled human programmer.

Nonetheless, a program generator is a great tool for individuals with intermediate-to-advanced programming skills, because it can do the "drudgery" of creating all the basic programs for managing a database through user-friendly menus. The experienced programmer can then refine and embellish the generated programs into precisely the custom system he or she has in mind.

But why would an experienced programmer want to bother with a program generator in the first place? There is a very obvious answer to this question: The average program generator can produce about 350 lines of custom, error-free code per minute (on an IBM PC/AT with an 8 MHz clock). Needless to say, the generator works quite a bit faster than even the fastest human programmers.

You may already be familiar with the application generator that came with your dBASE III PLUS package, or one of the many other program generators available from third-party vendors. And perhaps you've already found that one of these generators suits your needs. If this is the case, you might not be particularly interested in reading the rest of this chapter.

On the other hand, if you are interested in creating your own program generator, or in trying out a new one, you should read on. In this chapter we're going to discuss a general-purpose dBASE III PLUS program generator, as well as the general techniques that were used to create it.

This program generator is one I've written for my own work. The generated system allows novice users to easily add new data to a database, locate records to edit or delete, print reports with selected sort orders and query conditions, and optionally to print a report of probable duplicate records on a database. As a consultant, I can use it to generate a user-friendly, fully customized, bug-free system for a client in a matter of minutes. The client with no dBASE experience can use this custom system immediately to easily enter and maintain records on the database while I create the more complex parts of the system, if any.

I've named this program generator PlusGen, because it generates dBASE III PLUS programs. (It's also written entirely in dBASE III PLUS, of course.)

Before we begin discussing the technical aspects of the PlusGen program generator, let's discuss how it is used.

⊙USING PLUSGEN

PlusGen builds a system of menus around an existing database (.DBF) file and its related format (.FMT) files, report (.FRM) files, and mailing-label (.LBL) files. Optionally, if you use custom command (.PRG) files to print certain reports, these can be included in the generated system. PlusGen allows one database file, up to two format files (one for adding data and one for editing data), up to four multiple-field sort orders, and up to eight different reports.

Even though PlusGen develops programs for a single database, it can help you produce custom systems with multiple databases. After all, even a custom system with multiple databases requires that the user add data, edit and delete data, and print reports from each database. You can use PlusGen to develop the basic programs for managing individual databases, then create your own higher-level menu, updating, and other programs to link the various pieces created by PlusGen into a larger integrated system.

In this first example we'll use PlusGen to create a custom application to manage a basic club membership database. Let's take it from the first step: creating the database structure, screen formats, and report formats.

STEP 1:
DEVELOPING THE DATABASE, FORMS, AND REPORTS

As mentioned earlier, you need to create all the "nonprogram" files for your custom system before using PlusGen. Of course, you'll want to start with your database file.

Creating the Database

The sample system we'll develop in this chapter will manage a simple database named ClubMem.DBF. Figure 11.1 shows the structure of the sample ClubMem database, created with the usual dBASE CREATE command.

Creating the Custom Screens

PlusGen allows up to two custom screens for entering and editing data on the database (if you leave out the custom screens, PlusGen will use the standard APPEND and EDIT screens). In this example, I've used the dBASE

Structure for database: C:ClubMem.dbf

Field	Field Name	Type	Width	Dec
1	LNAME	Character	20	
2	FNAME	Character	20	
3	COMPANY	Character	25	
4	ADDRESS	Character	25	
5	CITY	Character	20	
6	STATE	Character	2	
7	ZIP	Character	10	
8	PHONE	Character	13	
9	EXP_DATE	Date	8	
10	EXP_MONTH	Numeric	2	
✶✶ Total ✶✶			146	

Figure 11.1: Structure of the sample ClubMem.DBF database

III PLUS screen painter to create a custom screen for entering data. To draw the screen, I entered the command

MODIFY SCREEN AdScreen

at the dot prompt, and used the usual screen painter techniques to lay out the screen shown in Figure 11.2.

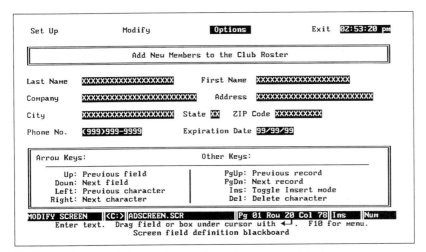

Figure 11.2: The AdScreen format file on the screen painter

After drawing the custom screen on the screen painter and saving it, dBASE creates a format file named AdScreen.FMT.

To create a second screen for editing data that is similar to the screen for entering data, I first copied the screen painter AdScreen.SCR file by entering the command below at the dBASE dot prompt:

COPY FILE AdScreen.SCR TO EdScreen.SCR

Then to modify the editing screen, I entered the command

MODIFY SCREEN EdScreen

at the dot prompt. Then I used the usual screen painter techniques to make a few minor changes. Figure 11.3 shows the editing screen on the screen painter.

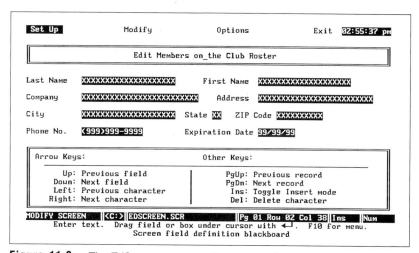

Figure 11.3:   The EdScreen screen on the screen painter

After saving the new screen, dBASE created a format file named EdScreen.FMT.

So now the sample system has one database file, ClubMem.DBF, and two format files, AdScreen.FMT and EdScreen.FMT. Next we need to develop some reports for this database.

Creating the Reports

PlusGen allows you to use up to eight existing report formats in your custom system. For this example, however, I've created only three. The first

is a report named Director (short for directory). To create the report I began
with the usual dot prompt commands

    USE ClubMem
    MODIFY REPORT Director

Using the usual report generator techniques, I designed the report with
the format shown in Figure 11.4. After designing the report format, I exited
the report generator, saved the format, and dBASE thereby created a
report format file named Director.FRM.

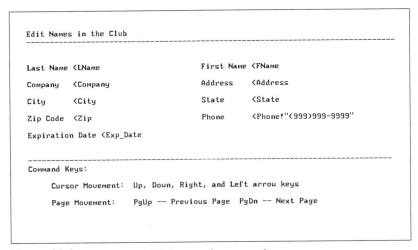

Figure 11.4:   The Director.FRM report format on the screen

The second report prints mailing labels. To create the mailing label format I entered the commands

    USE ClubMem
    MODIFY LABEL ClubLab

at the dot prompt. Using the usual techniques, I created the mailing label
format shown in Figure 11.5.

When finished designing the label format, I exited and saved my work,
and dBASE created the mailing label format file named ClubLab.LBL.

For the third report in the sample system, I wanted to produce a file that
could be accessed by WordStar's MailMerge capability to print form letters.
Since neither the report generator nor the mailing form generator can help

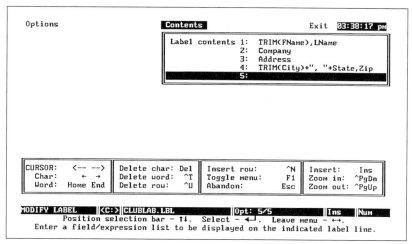

Figure 11.5: Mailing label format for the sample system

with this, I wrote a custom command file named WSMerge.PRG, shown in Figure 11.6. WSMerge.PRG is a rather simple command file that asks for the name of the file to create, and then copies records from the Club-Mem.DBF database to the named file. The DELIMITED option in the COPY command creates an ASCII delimited file, which is the format MailMerge uses.

So now all the basic files for the custom sample system are created. There is one database file, ClubMem.DBF, two format files, AdScreen.FMT and EdScreen.FMT, and three report-producing files, Director.FRM, ClubLab.LBL, and WSMerge.PRG. Of course, you can use any files you wish with PlusGen; these are only examples.

```
******************************** WSMerge.PRG
*---------------- Make a WordStar MailMerge file.
Filename = SPACE(14)
SET CONFIRM ON
@ 5,0 CLEAR
@ 15,5 SAY "Enter name of form-letter file ";
GET Filename
READ
SET CONFIRM OFF
SET TALK ON
COPY TO &Filename DELIMITED
SET TALK OFF
RETURN
```

Figure 11.6: The WSMerge.PRG command file

The next step is to use PlusGen to write all the programs to integrate the various files into a custom, menu-driven system. This step assumes you have either already keyed in the PlusGen program generator shown at the end of the chapter, or purchased the disk containing all the files in this book.

STEP 2: RUNNING PLUSGEN

Now we'll see how PlusGen asks questions about the system you are trying to develop. When you first enter the command

    DO PlusGen

at the dot prompt to get things running, PlusGen displays the opening page shown in Figure 11.7. It reminds you that you should have already created the basic files for the system, and asks if you want to continue. In this example, we've created the basic files, so you can type in a Y to continue.

The next page asks some basic questions about where everything is stored. The first question asks where the .DBF, .FMT, and other files for the generated system are stored. (Probably drive B on a floppy-based computer, and drive C on a hard disk.) The second question asks where you want to store the generated code (again, probably drive B or C).

The third question asks for a unique abbreviation to name the files in the generated system. This abbreviation can be up to four characters long

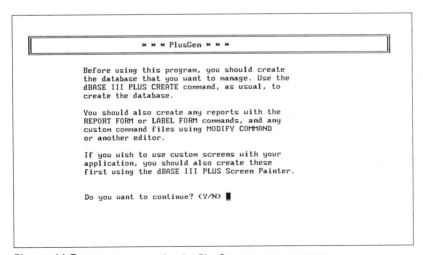

Figure 11.7: Opening page for the PlusGen program generator

(though it should not be "PLUS" because the program generator files all begin with those four letters). In the example shown in Figure 11.8, I've designated hard disk drive C as the drive for all files, and have assigned the four-letter abbreviation Club to the system to be generated.

The third page in PlusGen asks for the name of the database (.DBF) file the generated system will use, and a title for the system. As shown in Figure 11.9, I've entered the database name ClubMem. I've assigned the name

```
            PlusGen: A dBASE III PLUS Program Generator

     Default drive that the generated system will use (B or C)  C

     Drive for storing generated code [must be the same
     drive that contains the database (.DBF) file ]  C

     Enter unique abbreviation -- up to four characters long
     (Do not use PLUS as abbreviation)  Club


     Press UP arrow to make corrections,
     or press any key to continue...  ▮
```

Figure 11.8:   Second page that PlusGen displays

```
     Record No.       10    ClubStr
     FIELD_NAME COMMON----------------------------
     LNAME      Last Name
     FNAME      First Name
     COMPANY    Company
     ADDRESS    Address
     CITY       City
     STATE      State
     ZIP        Zip Code
     PHONE      Phone Number
     EXP_DATE   Expiration Date
     EXP_MONTH  Expiration Month
```

Figure 11.9:   Third page of PlusGen

Club to the main menu program so that I can later enter the command DO Club to run the entire generated system. Note that when entering the database and main menu program names, you should not use the extension or a drive designator (e.g., enter ClubMem and Club instead of ClubMem.DBF or B:Club.PRG).

On this same page, I've also entered "Club Membership Management System" as the overall system title.

The fourth page that PlusGen displays asks if you plan to use custom screens with your system. If so, you can enter their names on this page. In this example, we've already created the AdScreen.FMT and EdScreen.FMT format files, so I've entered their names as shown in Figure 11.10.

```
    If you are using custom screens (.FMT files) for
    adding or editing data, enter the file names
    below.  If the same format file is to be used
    for both adding and editing records, enter name
    twice.  If no format files will be used, leave
    both options blank.


    Format file for Appending   AdScreen

    Format file for Editing     EdScreen
```

Figure 11.10:   Fourth page of PlusGen

The fifth page asks for the name of the field that will most likely be used for looking up a particular record. In this example, the user would most likely use a person's last name to find an individual record to edit or delete. In another database, it might be a customer number, a part number, an account number, or some other field (any data type is allowed).

The fifth page also asks for a "plain English" description of the field. As shown in Figure 11.11, I've entered LName as the field for looking up information, and "Last Name" as the plain English description of this field. (Note also that PlusGen displays the names of all the database fields at the top of the page, for your reference.)

The sixth page of PlusGen displays some instructions for specifying sort orders, as shown in Figure 11.12.

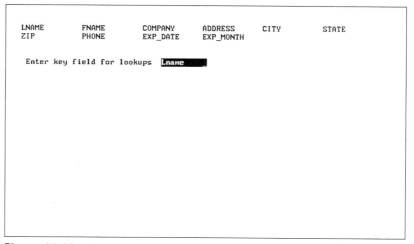

Figure 11.11:   Fifth page of PlusGen

```
LNAME          FNAME          COMPANY        ADDRESS        CITY         STATE
ZIP            PHONE          EXP_DATE       EXP_MONTH

    Sort Menu Option                        Field(s)

    1.   Last Name                     Lname

    2.   Name and Zip Code             LName      FName      Zip

    3.   Zip Code                      Zip        LName

    4.   Expiration Date               Exp_Date   LName      FName
```

Figure 11.12:   Sixth page of PlusGen

The seventh page of PlusGen, shown in Figure 11.13, displays all field names at the top of the screen, and asks you to enter English descriptions of sort orders in the left column, and the fields that contain those sort orders in the right columns. Note that the previously defined lookup field is already included, and cannot be altered.

In this example, I've filled in the page for three sort orders. The first sort order is by last and first name. The second sort order is by zip code and

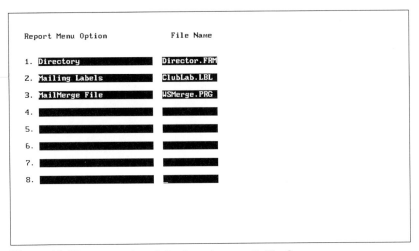

Figure 11.13:   Sort orders defined on the seventh PlusGen page

city (for bulk mailing), and the third sort order is by expiration date, last name, and first name. You can freely mix data types on this page without worrying about converting numbers or dates with the STR and DTOC functions. PlusGen will take care of all that automatically.

As soon as this page of PlusGen is complete, PlusGen will create the appropriate index files and show you its progress. Then it will move on to page eight.

Page eight of PlusGen displays instructions for entering report options, as Figure 11.14 shows. As the page points out, here you *do* want to include file name extensions with file names, so that PlusGen will know what type of report is being displayed.

Page nine of PlusGen then asks that you list up to eight English names for reports, and the names of the files that will produce these reports. In the example shown in Figure 11.15, I've specified the three reports created earlier. The Directory of Members is printed by Director.FRM, mailing labels are printed by ClubLab.LBL, and the MailMerge file is created by WSMerge.PRG. Again, notice that file name extensions are included on this page.

The tenth page of PlusGen asks the question

Include duplicates check option? (Y/N) :

For the sample membership system we're developing, I answered Yes.

If you answer Yes to page 10, PlusGen asks you to select fields that define a duplicate. In any mailing system, it is reasonable to assume that if

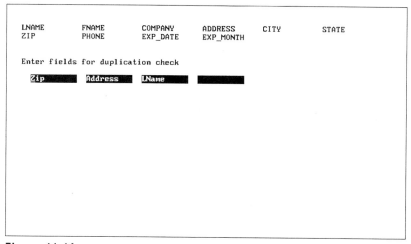

```
    LNAME         FNAME         COMPANY       ADDRESS       CITY        STATE
    ZIP           PHONE         EXP_DATE      EXP_MONTH

    Enter fields for duplication check

       Zip          Address       LName
```

Figure 11.14:   PlusGen instructions for defining report options

```
    Report Menu Option                 File Name

    1. Directory of Members            Director.FRM
    2. Mailing Labels                  ClubLab.LBL
    3. MailMerge File                  WSMerge.PRG
    4.
    5.
    6.
    7.
    8.
```

Figure 11.15:   Report options defined for sample system

two records have identical zip codes, addresses, and last names, then they are probably duplicates. For your own application you might use other fields to define duplicates.

When listing fields to define duplicates, list them from left to right, starting with the least specific and ending with the most specific. PlusGen will use the same algorithm to locate duplicates that the DupDel procedure in

Chapter 6 uses. If you are unclear about how to define these fields, you might want to brush up on Chapter 6. Figure 11.16 shows the eleventh page of PlusGen filled in with the fields Zip, Address, and LName defined for duplication check. (Again, you can freely mix data types on this page without using the STR and DTOC functions.)

At this point, PlusGen has everything it needs to create the custom system. After a pause and some status messages, you'll see the generated programs whiz by on the screen as PlusGen creates them. When done, PlusGen displays a screen describing the generated system as in Figure 11.17. (If the information does not fit on your screen, don't worry. It's also stored on disk for future reference or printing.)

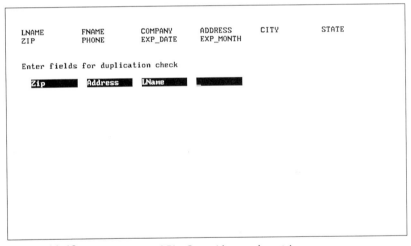

Figure 11.16:   Page eleven of PlusGen with sample entries

Notice that all the generated programs have file names with the abbreviation you originally supplied (Club in this example). The main menu program, however, has whatever name you originally requested back on page three of PlusGen. To view the contents of any of these files, you can use the DOS or dBASE TYPE command (e.g., TYPE ClubRep.PRG). In the next section, we'll take a quick look at the techniques for using the system PlusGen created.

```
The following files have been generated to
manage the Clubmem.DBF database:

Command Files           Task Performed

Club.PRG:           Main Menu program
  ClubRep.PRG:        Sort, search, and display reports
  ClubEdi.PRG:        Edit data
  ClubDel.PRG:        Delete data
  ClubDup.PRG:        Check for duplicates

Format Files accessed: AdScreen.FMT and EdScreen.FMT

The following index files have been created
for the generated system:

Index File         Contents

ClubNx1:       UPPER(LName) + UPPER(FName)
ClubNx2:       UPPER(Zip) + UPPER(City)
ClubNx3:       DTOC(Exp_Date) + UPPER(LName) + UPPER(FName)

These data files used by PlusGen only: C:ClubStr.dbf
                                       C:ClubPrm.dbf

Batch file for copying generated system: ClubCopy.BAT
This information is stored in:  ClubDoc.TXT

To run the generated system, use the command DO Club
at the dBASE dot prompt.
```

Figure 11.17:   PlusGen documentation for the generated system

⊙USING THE GENERATED PROGRAMS

You can use the generated programs right away. In this example we named the main menu program Club. So, on a hard disk system, you can just enter the command

DO Club

at the dBASE dot prompt. On a computer with two floppy disks, enter the command

DO B:Club

to run the system.

You'll first see the main menu for the custom system, as shown in Figure 11.18. The menu options are self-explanatory.

```
┌─────────────────────────────────────────────────────────────────┐
│                                                                   │
│   Club Membership Management System                               │
│   ──────────────────────────────────────────────────────────     │
│                                                                   │
│                                                                   │
│                   1. Add New Data                                 │
│                                                                   │
│                   2. Print Reports                                │
│                                                                   │
│                   3. Edit Data                                    │
│                                                                   │
│                   4. Delete Data                                  │
│                                                                   │
│                   5. Check for Duplicates                         │
│                                                                   │
│                   X. Exit                                         │
│                                                                   │
│                                                                   │
│                                                                   │
│   Enter choice  █                                                 │
│                                                                   │
└─────────────────────────────────────────────────────────────────┘
```

Figure 11.18:   Main menu for the generated program

ADDING NEW RECORDS

To add new records to the ClubMem database, select option 1. The custom screen, AdScreen, appears as in Figure 11.19. You can enter data into as many records as you wish. When done entering records, just press Return rather than entering data into the first field on the screen. You'll be returned to the main menu automatically.

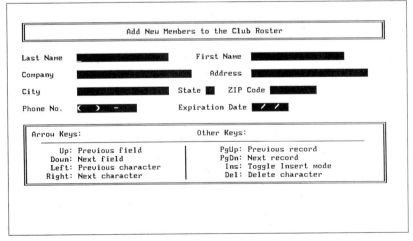

Figure 11.19:   Screen for entering new records

PRINTING REPORTS

To print reports, select option 2 from the main menu. The first submenu to appear will display the various types of reports you can print, as shown in Figure 11.20. Of course, these are exactly the options we specified when answering questions in PlusGen.

Once you've selected a report to print, another submenu will appear asking which sort order you want. The options displayed are exactly those you told PlusGen to include in the generated code, as shown in Figure 11.21. Select any option from the sort submenu.

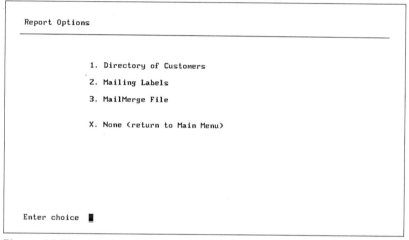

```
    Report Options
    _____


               1. Directory of Customers
               2. Mailing Labels
               3. MailMerge File

               X. None (return to Main Menu)




    Enter choice ▮
```

Figure 11.20: Screen for selecting a report to print

After you select a sorting option, the screen will ask

Print (A)ll records, or (Q)uery [Enter A or Q] :

To print all the records in the database, type A. To specify only certain records (such as NY residents, or people with expiration dates in December), type Q. If you type Q to query the database, the dBASE query form will appear on the screen, as in Figure 11.22. You can specify any query using the usual techniques that the query screen offers. In Figure 11.22, I've set up a query to display records with CA in the State field.

After filling in the query form, select the Exit and Save options from the top menu. The screen will ask

Send data to printer? (Y/N)

```
   Sort Options
   _____

                  1. Last Name

                  2. Zip Code

                  3. Expiration Date












   Enter choice  ▯
```

Figure 11.21:   Sort options displayed in the custom system

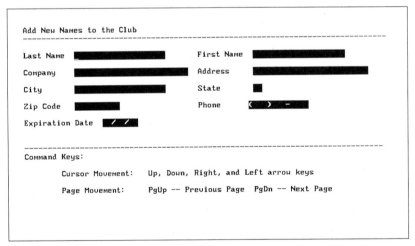

Figure 11.22:   Query form to display California residents only

If you type Y, the report will be displayed on the printer; otherwise the report will be displayed on the screen. (If you are printing mailing labels, you'll be given the opportunity to print several dummy labels until the labels are properly aligned in the printer.)

When the report is fully printed, you'll see the message

Press any key to return to menu...

Just press any key, and the main menu will reappear on the screen.

EDITING DATA

To edit information on the ClubMem database through the custom system generated by PlusGen, select option 3 from the main menu. The screen will ask that you

Enter Last name to Edit
or press < −' to Exit

Type in the last name of the person whose record you wish to edit (upper- or lowercase doesn't matter) and press Return. The custom system will respond in one of three ways. If you enter a last name that cannot be found on the database, the screen displays the message

Can't find: XXXXXX

where XXXXXX is the last name you attempted to find. You can then enter another last name to try again.

If you enter a last name for which there are several matches in the database, the screen displays the message

X matches found
Use PgDn, PgUp keys to scroll
Press any key to edit...

where X is the number of records on the database that share the same last name. Press any key to edit the first record on the database that has the requested last name. The first last name in the database that matches the last name you entered is displayed on the custom EdScreen screen we created earlier, ready for editing. You can use the PgUp and PgDn keys to scroll through other records in the database that have the same last name, and make whatever changes you wish to the records.

If only one person on the database has the last name you requested, that person's record is displayed on the EdScreen screen ready for editing.

When done editing a record, type ^W. You'll be given the opportunity to enter another last name, or just press Return to return to the main menu.

DELETING RECORDS

To delete records from the ClubMem database through the custom system PlusGen created, select option 4 from the main menu. The screen will ask that you

> Enter Last name to Delete
> or < −' to exit :

As with editing, you just type in the last name of the individual whose record you wish to delete, and press Return. If you type in a last name that does not exist in the database, the screen will inform you of this and give you an opportunity to try again.

If you type in a last name for which there is only one match in the database, the screen will display some of that person's data (and record number), and ask for permission to delete it, as below:

> 5 Wilson Wilbur
> OK to delete this record? (Y/N) :

Type Y to delete the record (temporarily), or N to change your mind and save the record.

Just in case you type in a last name for which there are several matches on the database, the custom program will display all individuals with that last name, and ask for more specific information, as below:

> 16   Smith   Albert
> 29   Smith   Marion
> 121   Smith   Susita
> Delete which one? (by record number) :

If you want to delete Marion Smith, just type in the record number (29) and press Return. If you do not want to delete any of the records shown, just press Return without entering a record number.

You'll be given the opportunity to delete as many records as you wish. When done deleting records, just press Return in lieu of typing in the last name of the person whose record you wish to delete.

As an added precaution, the program gives you a second chance to recall any individual records before permanently deleting them from the database. You'll see a display of all the records you selected to delete, along with a request for permission to delete, as in the example below:

> 5   Wilson   Wilbur
> 29   Smith   Marion
> OK to delete all these? (Y/N)

If you are sure you want to permanently delete all the records shown, enter a Y. Otherwise, type N. The screen will allow you to undelete any record, then redisplay the remaining records that are to be deleted and once again ask for permission to delete them all. This process will continue until you give permission to permanently delete all the records shown on the screen. At that point, the custom program will permanently delete all the selected records, then return control to the main menu.

CHECKING FOR DUPLICATE RECORDS

If you opt to include the check-for-duplicates feature in your custom system, you can select option 5 from the main menu to activate it. When you do so, the screen will ask

Send possible duplicates to printer? (Y/N)

If you answer Yes, a listing of possible duplicate records will be printed on paper. Otherwise, the records will be displayed only on the screen. Figure 11.23 shows a sample check-for-duplicates report. Numbers in the left column of the report are record numbers. Should you decide to delete any duplicates through the deletion option, these record numbers will help you select specific records to edit.

When the duplications report is completely printed, you'll see the message

Press any key to return to menu...

Just press any key to return to the main menu.

```
Possible Duplications                                      11/26/86


        1    92024         123 A St.            Watson
        6    92024         123 A St.            Watson

        3    92038         P.O. Box 2908        Adams
        4    92038         P.O. Box 2908        Adams
        5    92038         P.O. Box 2908        Adams

        1    88123         393 Pacific Hwy.     Zeppo
        6    88123         393 Pacific Hwy.     Zeppo
```

Figure 11.23:   Sample check-for-duplicates report

EXITING THE SYSTEM

To leave a custom system generated by PlusGen, select option X from the main menu. You'll be returned to the dBASE dot prompt.

⊙PROGRAMS GENERATED BY PLUSGEN

Now that we've discussed how to use the PlusGen program generator, and the programs that PlusGen creates, let's look at some more technical aspects, beginning with a quick view of the command files and other files that PlusGen created in this example.

THE GENERATED MAIN MENU PROGRAM

As you may recall, PlusGen creates a main menu program with whatever name you provided on the third page of PlusGen screens. In the example used in this chapter, I entered Club as the name for the main menu program, so PlusGen stored the main menu program in a file named Club-.PRG. Figure 11.24 shows the Club.PRG command file PlusGen created.

If you wonder how PlusGen created this custom program from the small amount of information we provided during the question-and-answer phase, I'll give you a hint right now. About 99 percent of the program is already written and stored in a "skeletal" program available to PlusGen. PlusGen just fills in a few "blank spaces" in the skeletal program, based upon the answers to the questions PlusGen posed.

For example, the comments at the top of the Club.PRG command file include the name and description I entered on page three of the PlusGen screens, as shown below:

```
* * * * * * * * * * * * * * * * * * * * * * * * * * * * * * * * * * Club.PRG
* -- Main Menu for Club Membership Management System.
```

The DO CASE clause in the generated Club.PRG program calls other programs that all begin with the letters I used for the four-letter abbreviation in this sample system, namely Club. PlusGen always uses this four-letter abbreviation for the first letters of every file it generates, followed by a three-letter extension describing the program. In this example, ClubRep-.PRG is the report program, ClubEdi.PRG is the editing program, Club-Del.PRG is the deletion program, and so forth.

The generated program also calls the AdScreen.FMT format file when the user requests to enter new records. PlusGen "knew" that AdScreen

```
*********************************** Club.PRG
*--- Main Menu for Club Membership Management System.
SET DEFAULT TO C
SET TALK OFF
SET HEADING OFF
SET STATUS OFF
SET SAFETY OFF

*-------------- Create underline variable, ULine.
ULine = REPLICATE("_",80)

*------------ Display menu and get user's choice.
Choice = " "
USE Clubmem INDEX ClubNx1, ClubNx2, ClubNx3
DO WHILE Choice # "X"
   CLEAR
   @ 1,1 SAY " Club Membership Management System "
   @ 2,0 SAY ULine
   ?
   ?
   TEXT
                      1. Add New Data

                      2. Print Reports

                      3. Edit Data

                      4. Delete Data

                      5. Check for Duplicates

                      X. Exit

   ENDTEXT
   @ 24,1 SAY "Enter choice " GET Choice PICT "!"
   READ

   *-------------- Branch to appropriate program.
   DO CASE
      CASE Choice = "1"
           SET FORMAT TO AdScreen
           APPEND
           CLOSE FORMAT
      CASE Choice = "2"
           DO ClubRep
      CASE Choice = "3"
           DO ClubEdi
      CASE Choice = "4"
           DO ClubDel
      CASE Choice = "5"
           DO ClubDup
   ENDCASE

ENDDO (Choice)

CLOSE DATABASES
*QUIT
```

Figure 11.24: The Club.PRG program created by PlusGen

was the name of the format file to use in this example because I told it so
on the fourth page of its questions. The DO CASE clause PlusGen created
for the ClubMem example is shown below:

```
*  – – – – – – Branch to appropriate program.
DO CASE
   CASE Choice = "1"
      SET FORMAT TO AdScreen
      APPEND
      CLOSE FORMAT
   CASE Choice = "2"
      DO ClubRep
   CASE Choice = "3"
      DO ClubEdi
   CASE Choice = "4"
      DO ClubDel
   CASE Choice = "5"
      DO ClubDup
ENDCASE
```

Almost everything else in the generated program is typical "main menu
program" material already available to PlusGen. As I mentioned before,
PlusGen simply used an existing "typical" main menu program, and filled
in the blanks that made the program specific to this particular application.

THE GENERATED REPORTS PROGRAM

The program PlusGen generated to display reports and the various associated options is named ClubRep.PRG in this example system (the four-
letter abbreviation plus Rep). ClubRep.PRG is shown in Figure 11.25.

As with the main menu program, PlusGen began with a "skeletal" program to display reports, and filled in the blanks from answers presented on
the pages. The menu displayed by ClubRep for this sample system was
generated from the list of English reports entered earlier:

1. Directory of Members
2. Mailing Labels
3. MailMerge File

X. None (return to Main Menu)

```
**************************************** ClubRep
*  Set up sort orders and search conditions,
*    then print the appropriate report.

CLEAR
@ 1,1 SAY "Report Options"
@ 2,0 SAY ULine
?
?
TEXT
                 1. Directory of Members

                 2. Mailing Labels

                 3. MailMerge File


                 X. None (return to Main Menu)
ENDTEXT

MChoice = " "
@ 24,1 SAY "Enter choice " GET MChoice PICT "!"
READ

IF MChoice = "X"
    RETURN
ENDIF

*------------------- Ask about sort order.
CLEAR
@ 1,1 SAY "Sort Options"
@ 2,0 SAY ULine
?
?
TEXT
                 1. Last Name

                 2. Zip Code

                 3. Expiration Date


ENDTEXT

SChoice = 0
@ 24,1 SAY "Enter choice " GET SChoice PICTURE "9"
READ

*------------------- Set up appropriate sort order.
DO CASE
     CASE SChoice = 1
          SET INDEX TO ClubNx1
     CASE SChoice = 2
          SET INDEX TO ClubNx2
     CASE SChoice = 3
          SET INDEX TO ClubNx3
ENDCASE

*------------------- Present query form if user requests.
```

Figure 11.25: The ClubRep.PRG program created by PlusGen

```
CLEAR
AllNone = " "
@ 5,2 SAY "Print (A)ll records, or (Q)uery [Enter A or Q] " ;
       GET AllNone PICT "!"
READ
IF AllNone = "Q"
   MODIFY QUERY Clubmem
   SET FILTER TO FILE Clubmem
ENDIF

*------------------- Print report based on previous MChoice.
CLEAR
STORE " " TO Printer, PMacro

@ 15,5 SAY "Send data to printer? (Y/N) " GET Printer PICT "!"
READ
IF Printer = "Y"
     PMacro = "TO PRINT"
     WAIT "Prepare printer, then press any key to continue..."
ENDIF

*------- Leave out records marked for deletion.
SET DELETED ON
CLEAR

DO CASE

   CASE MChoice = "1"
        REPORT FORM Director.FRM &PMacro
   CASE MChoice = "2"
        LABEL FORM ClubLab.LBL SAMPLE &PMacro
   CASE MChoice = "3"
        DO WSMerge.PRG

ENDCASE

*------------------ Done.  Return to main menu.
IF Printer = "Y"
     EJECT
ENDIF
SET DELETED OFF
SET FILTER TO
USE Clubmem INDEX ClubNx1, ClubNx2, ClubNx3
WAIT "Press any key to return to menu..."
RETURN
```

Figure 11.25:   The ClubRep.PRG program created by PlusGen (continued)

The menu of sort options was developed from the plain English entries made on the seventh page of PlusGen questions:

1. Last Name
2. Zip Code
3. Expiration Date

A DO CASE clause in the ClubRep program selects the appropriate index file based upon the user's menu selection. PlusGen created the index files and their names, and used them in the DO CASE clause, as shown below:

```
* – – – – – – – – Set up appropriate sort order.
DO CASE
   CASE SChoice = 1
      SET INDEX TO ClubNx1
   CASE SChoice = 2
      SET INDEX TO ClubNx2
   CASE SChoice = 3
      SET INDEX TO ClubNx3
ENDCASE
```

ClubRep.PRG always allows the user to set up a query before printing a report. It also allows the user to modify a query form named Club-Mem.QRY should he or she opt to perform a query, as shown below:

```
* – – – – – – – – Present query form if user requests.
CLEAR
AllNone = " "
@ 5,2 SAY "Print (A)ll records, or (Q)uery [Enter A or Q] " ;
   GET AllNone PICT "!"
READ
IF AllNone = "Q"
   MODIFY QUERY Clubmem
   SET FILTER TO FILE Clubmem
ENDIF
```

Finally, ClubRep.PRG uses a DO CASE clause to print the appropriate report based upon the user's earlier menu choice. PMacro is a variable that contains the words TO PRINT if the user opts to send the report to the printer (otherwise, PMacro is blank). PlusGen determines which command to use (e.g., REPORT FORM, LABEL FORM, or DO), based on the extension used in the file name when filling out page nine of PlusGen's questions:

```
DO CASE

   CASE MChoice = "1"
      REPORT FORM Director.FRM &PMacro
   CASE MChoice = "2"
      LABEL FORM ClubLab.LBL SAMPLE &PMacro
```

```
    CASE MChoice = "3"
        DO WSMerge.PRG

    ENDCASE
```

Most other parts of the generated ClubRep.PRG come from PlusGen's skeletal reports program.

THE GENERATED EDITING PROGRAM

The program generated by PlusGen to manage the ClubMem database is named ClubEdi.PRG. Like all the generated programs, most of Club-Edi.PRG came from a skeletal program. Parts that are custom-tailored to the ClubMem application include the prompt that asks the user to enter the last name of the individual whose record he or she wants to edit:

```
Search = SPACE(20)
@ 10,5 SAY "Enter Last name to Edit"
@ 12,5 SAY "or press < -' to Exit " GET Search
READ
```

ClubEdi.PRG counts how many records in the database have the requested last name:

```
Search = UPPER(TRIM(Search))
* - - -- Try to find the record.
SEEK Search
COUNT WHILE UPPER(Lname) = Search TO HowMany
```

If one or more names matching the last name are found in the database, then ClubEdit.PRG lets the user edit the record(s) using the EdScreen.FMT format file:

```
IF HowMany > 1
    @ 20,1 SAY STR(HowMany,3) + " matches found"
    @ 22,1 SAY "Use PgDn, PgUp keys to scroll"
    ?
    WAIT "Press any key to edit..."
ENDIF (howmany)
SEEK Search

* - - -- If found, edit. Otherwise, warn user.
IF FOUND()
    SET FORMAT TO EdScreen
```

```
    EDIT
    CLOSE FORMAT
```

If nobody has the requested last name, the program displays the message *Can't find:* followed by the last name that cannot be matched, and allows the user to try again:

```
    ELSE
        @ 22,0
        ? "Can't find: ",Search
        ?? CHR(7)
        WAIT
    ENDIF (found)

ENDDO (More)
```

Figure 11.26 shows the entire ClubEdi.PRG program as generated by PlusGen. Most of ClubEdi.PRG is from a skeletal program, but PlusGen filled in specific information like the lookup field (LName), the English description of the lookup field (Last Name), and the format file name (EdScreen) for this application.

PlusGen automatically handles any data type conversions that might be required in a lookup field in other applications.

THE GENERATED DELETION PROGRAM

The program PlusGen created to help the user delete records in the ClubMem application is named ClubDel.PRG. The program is shown in Figure 11.27. It uses the same routines that were used in the editing program to help the user locate a particular record. However, rather than allowing the user to edit the record, the ClubDel.PRG command file gives the user the opportunity to delete it.

Before permanently deleting records from the database with the PACK command, ClubDel.PRG gives the user the opportunity to recall any records marked for deletion. This last step is performed in the DO WHILE loop that uses the condition Permiss = "N" .AND. No_Dels > 0 (where Permiss is the user's permission to delete all records, and No_Dels is the number of records on the database that are marked for deletion).

Again, most of ClubDel.PRG is generated from a skeletal program within PlusGen, except that the particulars about the lookup field (entered on the fifth page of questions from PlusGen) are substituted where appropriate.

```
*********************************** ClubEdi
*------------------------ Edit data.
*------------------- Set up loop for editing.
More = .T.
DO WHILE More
    CLEAR
    @ 1,1 SAY "Edit Data"
    @ 2,0 SAY ULine
    Search = SPACE(20)
    @ 10,5 SAY "Enter Last name to Edit"
    @ 12,5 SAY "or press <--' to Exit " GET Search
    READ

    *------- Exit if nothing entered.
    IF Search = " "
        More = .F.
        LOOP
    ENDIF
    Search = UPPER(TRIM(Search))

    *------- Try to find the record.
    SEEK Search
    COUNT WHILE UPPER(Lname) = Search TO HowMany
    IF HowMany > 1
        @ 20,1 SAY STR(HowMany,3)+" matches found"
        @ 22,1 SAY "Use PgDn, PgUp keys to scroll"
        ?
        WAIT "Press any key to edit..."
    ENDIF (howmany)
    SEEK Search

    *------- If found, edit.  Otherwise, warn user.
    IF FOUND()
        SET FORMAT TO EdScreen
        EDIT
        CLOSE FORMAT
    ELSE
        @ 22,0
        ? "Cant find: ",Search
        ?? CHR(7)
        WAIT
    ENDIF (found)

ENDDO (More)

RETURN
```

Figure 11.26:   The ClubEdi.PRG program created by PlusGen

THE GENERATED DUPLICATES CHECK PROGRAM

The check-for-duplicates program is generated only if requested and specified on the last two pages of PlusGen questions. In this sample application, we did request this feature, and specified Zip, Address, and LName as the duplications fields. PlusGen used this information to generate the program named ClubDup.PRG, shown in Figure 11.28.

```
*********************************** ClubDel
* Delete Data for Club Membership Management System.
CLEAR
@ 1,1 SAY "Delete Data"
@ 2,0 SAY ULine

*----------------- Find highest record number.
USE Clubmem
GO BOTTOM
Max = RECNO()
USE Clubmem INDEX ClubNx1, ClubNx2, ClubNx3

*----------------- Ask for record or exit.
More = .T.
DO WHILE More
   @ 3,0 CLEAR
   Search = SPACE(20)
   @ 10,2 SAY "Enter Last name to Delete "
   @ 12,2 SAY "or <--' to exit " ;
          GET Search
   READ

   *----- Respond to entry.
   DO CASE

      *---- If not exiting, look up.
      CASE Search # " "
           Search = UPPER(TRIM(Search))
           SEEK Search

      *--- Otherwise, exit.
      OTHERWISE
           More = .F.
           LOOP
   ENDCASE

   *---- Make sure record exists.
   IF .NOT. FOUND()
      @ 20,0 CLEAR
      ? "Can't Find",Search
      ?? CHR(7)
      WAIT "Press any key to try again..."
      LOOP
   ENDIF (not found)

   *-- If found, count and display.
   COUNT WHILE UPPER(Lname) = SEARCH TO HowMany
   IF HowMany > 1
      @ 3,0 CLEAR
      SEEK Search
      DISPLAY Lname,Fname WHILE ;
             UPPER(Lname) = Search
      Recno = 0
      @ 23,2 SAY "Delete which one (by record number) " ;
        GET Recno PICTURE "9999"
      READ
      IF Recno <= Max .AND. Recno > 0
         DELETE RECORD Recno
      ELSE
         @ 20,0 CLEAR
```

Figure 11.27: The ClubDel.PRG program created by PlusGen

```
            @ 22,1 SAY "No such record: "+STR(Recno,4)
            ? CHR(7)
            WAIT "Press any key to try again..."
         ENDIF
     ELSE
        SEEK Search
        @ 3,0 CLEAR
        DISPLAY Lname,Fname
        Maybe = " "
        @ 23,1 SAY "Delete this record? (Y/N) ";
             GET MayBe PICTURE "!"
        READ
        IF UPPER(Maybe) = "Y"
           DELETE
        ENDIF (maybe)
   ENDIF (howmany)
ENDDO (More)

*-- Final check before permanent deletion.
*-- Count records marked for deletion
*-- and store in memory variable No_Dels.
COUNT FOR DELETED() TO No_Dels

Permiss = "N"
DO WHILE Permiss = "N" .AND. No_Dels > 0
   @ 3,0 CLEAR
   ?
   DISPLAY Lname,Fname FOR DELETED()
   ?
   Permiss = " "
   @ 23,5 SAY "Ok to delete all these? (Y/N) " ;
     GET Permiss PICTURE "!"
   READ

   *--- If not OK to delete all, find out which.
   IF Permiss # "Y"
      RecNo = 0
      @ 20,0 CLEAR
      @ 23,5 SAY "Recall which one (record number): ";
        GET RecNo PICT "99999"
      READ
      IF Recno > 0 .AND. Recno <= Max
         GOTO RecNo
         IF DELETED()
            RECALL
            No_Dels = No_Dels - 1
         ENDIF (deleted)
      ELSE
         @ 20,0 CLEAR
         @ 22,1 SAY "No such record: "+STR(RecNo,4)
         ? CHR(7)
         WAIT
      ENDIF (recno)
   ENDIF (permiss # y)
ENDDO (permiss and No_dels)

*--- Pack and return.
PACK

RETURN
```

Figure 11.27: The ClubDel.PRG program created by PlusGen (continued)

```
*********************************** ClubDup
*  Scan database for possible duplicates.
SET HEADING OFF
SET DELETED ON

*------------------- Ask about printer.
CLEAR
@ 1,1 SAY "Duplicate Check"
@ 2,0 SAY ULine
Printer = " "
@ 10,5 SAY "Send possible duplicates to printer? (Y/N) ";
  GET Printer PICTURE "!"
READ

*------------------- Set printer on, if necessary.
IF Printer = "Y"
    WAIT "Prepare printer, then press any key to continue..."
    SET PRINT ON
ENDIF

*------------------- Clear screen and print title.
@ 3,0 CLEAR
USE Clubmem
? "Pre-sorting for duplications check..."
INDEX ON  UPPER(ZIP)+UPPER(ADDRESS)+UPPER(LNAME) TO Temp

CLEAR
? "Possible Duplications" + SPACE(38) + DTOC(DATE())
? ULine
?
?

*------- Loop through database until end of file, and
*------- compare records based on specified fields.

RecCheck = "  UPPER(ZIP)+UPPER(ADDRESS)+UPPER(LNAME) "
DO WHILE .NOT. EOF()
    Compare = &RecCheck
    SKIP
    IF &RecCheck = Compare
        SKIP -1
        LIST WHILE &RecCheck = Compare;
          Zip, Address,Lname
        ?
    ENDIF (&RecCheck = Compare)
ENDDO (while not eof)

*------------------- Done.  Return to menu.
IF Printer = "Y"
    EJECT
    SET PRINT OFF
ENDIF
SET DELETED OFF

*--- Reassign index files and return.
USE Clubmem INDEX ClubNx1, ClubNx2, ClubNx3
@ 22,0
WAIT "Press any key to return to menu..."
RETURN
```

Figure 11.28:   The ClubDup.PRG program created by PlusGen

Like all the other programs in this system, most of ClubDup.PRG comes from a predefined skeletal command file. To tailor the program to the ClubMem application, PlusGen creates the appropriate INDEX command, as shown below:

```
? "Pre-sorting for duplications check..."
INDEX ON UPPER(ZIP) + UPPER(ADDRESS) + UPPER(LNAME);
TO Temp
```

PlusGen also fills in the appropriate field names for comparing and displaying records, as shown below:

```
RecCheck = "UPPER(ZIP) + UPPER(ADDRESS) + UPPER(LNAME)"
DO WHILE .NOT. EOF()
   Compare = &RecCheck
   SKIP
   IF &RecCheck = Compare
      SKIP -1
      LIST WHILE &RecCheck = Compare;
         Zip, Address,Lname
      ?
   ENDIF (&RecCheck = Compare)
ENDDO (while not eof)
```

The logic used in the ClubDup.PRG program is virtually identical to the DupCheck procedure presented and discussed in Chapter 6.

THE GENERATED BATCH FILE

For the convenience of people who use floppy-disk systems, PlusGen also creates a DOS batch file to copy all the files in the generated system to the floppy disk in drive B. Like all DOS batch files, you run this one from the DOS prompt, not the dBASE dot prompt.

The batch file is named with the four-letter abbreviation followed by Copy.BAT. Hence, for the Club application, PlusGen created the batch file named ClubCopy.BAT, shown in Figure 11.29.

THE GENERATED DOCUMENTATION

PlusGen always creates a brief textual description of the programs it generates, as shown previously in Figure 11.17. This documentation is stored with the name beginning with the four-letter abbreviation followed by Doc.TXT.

```
COPY Clubmem.DBF  B:
COPY ClubNx*.NDX  B:
COPY Club.PRG  B:
COPY ClubRep.PRG  B:
COPY ClubEdi.PRG  B:
COPY ClubDel.PRG  B:
COPY ClubDup.PRG  B:
COPY AdScreen.FMT  B:
COPY EdScreen.FMT  B:
COPY ClubDoc.TXT  B:
COPY ClubCopy.BAT  B:
```

Figure 11.29:   The ClubCopy.BAT batch file generated by PlusGen

Therefore, if you want to view the documentation for the generated Club application, you can use the DOS or dBASE command TYPE ClubDoc.TXT, or use any text editor or word processor to view or print the file.

⊙MODIFYING THE GENERATED PROGRAMS

Before we begin developing the program generator, let's look at an example showing how easy it is to modify the generated program.

You can modify the command files generated by PlusGen as you would any others. For example, in the original ClubMem.DBF, we included a field named Exp_Month, which is the month of expiration for the member. Since this can be deduced directly from the Exp_Date field, I placed no prompt on the AdScreen or EdScreen screens for adding or editing this field. Instead, I'll add a couple of commands to the generated system to fill in the Exp_Month field automatically.

The Exp_Month field should be filled in whenever records are added or edited. The routine for adding new records is in the Club.PRG main menu. In this example, you merely need to enter the command

    MODIFY COMMAND Club

to call up the program, and then change the routine that reads

    CASE Choice = "1"
      SET FORMAT TO AdScreen
      APPEND
      CLOSE FORMAT

to

```
CASE Choice = "1"
   SET FORMAT TO AdScreen
   APPEND
   CLOSE FORMAT
   REPLACE ALL Exp_Month WITH MONTH(Exp_Date)
```

Similarly, you would need to ensure that the Exp_Month field is recalculated after the data are edited. To do so, enter the same REPLACE command above the RETURN command in the ClubEdi.PRG command file shown below:

```
ENDDO (More)
REPLACE ALL Exp_Month WITH MONTH(Exp_Date)
RETURN
```

These are just a couple of minor examples of how to change the generated system. The important point to remember, however, is that once PlusGen creates command files, they are no different from command files that you create yourself. They can be changed or edited in any way you desire.

If you wish to make more substantial changes, such as modifying the database structure, adding or deleting sort orders and reports, or changing the lookup field, you should use PlusGen to recreate the entire system. You can change the database structure or create reports using the usual commands from the dot prompt.

After changing to the database structure or reports, run PlusGen again exactly as before, and be sure to use the same four-letter abbreviation you used when you generated the system the first time. PlusGen will redisplay all your original answers, and allow you to change any of them. When you've completed all the pages of questions, PlusGen will regenerate the entire system using the original file names.

⊙THE PLUSGEN DATABASE FILES

Now we can get into the nitty-gritty technical aspects of the PlusGen program generator. While we cannot possibly discuss each and every line of code in PlusGen (because there are far too many of them), we can discuss the basic techniques used to create the program generator. As mentioned earlier, you might find it quite easy to use the same techniques to create a program generator of your own.

First of all, PlusGen needs some basic data, all stored on database files, to create a custom system. PlusGen needs

1. A "skeletal" custom system to build from;

2. Information describing field names, types, and widths on the database that the custom system is to manage; and

3. Answers to the questions PlusGen presents before generating the custom system.

Let's look at each database individually.

THE SKELETAL CUSTOM SYSTEM

The skeletal custom system that PlusGen uses to generate code is stored in a database named PlusGen.DBF. PlusGen.DBF has the simple structure shown below:

Structure for database: C:PlusGen.DBF

Field	Field Name	Type	Width	Dec
1	PROGRAM	Character	4	
2	LINE	Character	80	
** Total **			85	

The Line field holds a single line of code in the skeletal system, and the Program field holds the name of the program that the line is used in. PlusGen creates up to five programs: main menu, report, editing, deleting, and duplicates. The Program field contains one of the codes MENU, REPT, EDIT, DEL, or DUP to describe which program the line belongs in. Figure 11.30 shows the entire contents of the PlusGen.DBF database file.

In case you are wondering how I had the patience to key PlusGen.DBF line-by-line into a database: I didn't. Here is how PlusGen.DBF was created.

First, I took a "typical" custom system that was designed to manage a specific database, and removed those elements from the command files that made the typical system unique to the database. I replaced each specific field name, menu, data type, and other items with either a %% or %-symbol followed by a variable name. The %% symbols indicate where PlusGen must substitute a single piece of information into a line (such as %%MainTitle near the top of PlusGen.DBF). The %- symbols indicate where PlusGen needs to create entire routines (usually menus) in the skeletal program. Examples you can see in PlusGen.DBF are %-RepMenu where

```
 1   MENU    ********************************** %%ProgName
 2   MENU    *--- Main Menu for: %%MainTitle.
 3   MENU    SET DEFAULT TO %%M_Drive
 4   MENU    SET TALK OFF
 5   MENU    SET HEADING OFF
 6   MENU    SET STATUS OFF
 7   MENU    SET SAFETY OFF
 8   MENU
 9   MENU    *-------------- Create underline variable, ULine.
10   MENU    ULine = REPLICATE("_",80)
11   MENU
12   MENU    *------------ Display menu and get user's choice.
13   MENU    Choice = " "
14   MENU    USE %%FUllUse
15   MENU    DO WHILE Choice # "X"
16   MENU       CLEAR
17   MENU       @ 1,1 SAY " %%MainTitle "
18   MENU       @ 2,0 SAY ULine
19   MENU       ?
20   MENU       ?
21   MENU       TEXT
22   MENU                          1. Add New Data
23   MENU
24   MENU                          2. Print Reports
25   MENU
26   MENU                          3. Edit Data
27   MENU
28   MENU                          4. Delete Data
29   MENU
30   MENU                          %%DupOpt
31   MENU
32   MENU                          X. Exit
33   MENU       ENDTEXT
34   MENU       @ 24,1 SAY "Enter choice " GET Choice PICT "!"
35   MENU       READ
36   MENU
37   MENU       *-------------- Branch to appropriate program.
38   MENU       DO CASE
39   MENU          CASE Choice = "1"
40   MENU             %-AddOpt
41   MENU
42   MENU
43   MENU          CASE Choice = "2"
44   MENU             DO %%RepProg
45   MENU          CASE Choice = "3"
46   MENU             DO %%EdProg
47   MENU          CASE Choice = "4"
48   MENU             DO %%DelProg
49   MENU          %%DupCase1
50   MENU          %%DupCase2
51   MENU       ENDCASE
52   MENU
53   MENU    ENDDO (Choice)
54   MENU
55   MENU    CLOSE DATABASES
56   MENU    *QUIT
57   MENU
58   REPT    ********************************** %%RepProg
59   REPT    *  Set up sort orders and search conditions,
```

Figure 11.30: The PlusGen.DBF database

```
60   REPT   *        then print the appropriate report.
61   REPT
62   REPT   CLEAR
63   REPT   @ 1,1 SAY "Report Options"
64   REPT   @ 2,0 SAY ULine
65   REPT   ?
66   REPT   ?
67   REPT   TEXT
68   REPT                            %-RepMenu
69   REPT
70   REPT                     X. None (return to Main Menu)
71   REPT   ENDTEXT
72   REPT
73   REPT   MChoice = " "
74   REPT   @ 24,1 SAY "Enter choice " GET MChoice PICT "!"
75   REPT   READ
76   REPT
77   REPT   IF MChoice = "X"
78   REPT        RETURN
79   REPT   ENDIF
80   REPT
81   REPT   *------------------- Ask about sort order.
82   REPT   CLEAR
83   REPT   @ 1,1 SAY "Sort Options"
84   REPT   @ 2,0 SAY ULine
85   REPT   ?
86   REPT   ?
87   REPT   TEXT
88   REPT                         %-SortMenu
89   REPT
90   REPT   ENDTEXT
91   REPT
92   REPT   SChoice = 0
93   REPT   @ 24,1 SAY "Enter choice " GET SChoice PICTURE "9"
94   REPT   READ
95   REPT
96   REPT   *------------------- Set up appropriate sort order.
97   REPT   DO CASE
98   REPT                         %-SortCase
99   REPT   ENDCASE
100  REPT   *------------------- Present query form if user requests.
101  REPT   CLEAR
102  REPT   AllNone = " "
103  REPT   @ 5,2 SAY "Print (A)ll records, or (Q)uery [Enter A or Q] "
                GET AllNone PICT "!"
104  REPT   READ
105  REPT   IF AllNone = "Q"
106  REPT      MODIFY QUERY %%DBName2
107  REPT      SET FILTER TO FILE %%DBName2
108  REPT   ENDIF
109  REPT
110  REPT   *------------------- Print report based on previous MChoice.
111  REPT   CLEAR
112  REPT   STORE " " TO Printer, PMacro
113  REPT
114  REPT   @ 15,5 SAY "Send data to printer? (Y/N) " GET Printer PICT "!"
115  REPT   READ
116  REPT   IF Printer = "Y"
117  REPT        PMacro = "TO PRINT"
```

Figure 11.30: The PlusGen.DBF database (continued)

```
118   REPT            WAIT "Prepare printer, then press any key to continue..."
119   REPT       ENDIF
120   REPT
121   REPT       *------- Leave out records marked for deletion.
122   REPT       SET DELETED ON
123   REPT       CLEAR
124   REPT
125   REPT       DO CASE
126   REPT
127   REPT            %-RepCases
128   REPT
129   REPT       ENDCASE
130   REPT
131   REPT       *----------------- Done.  Return to main menu.
132   REPT       IF Printer = "Y"
133   REPT            EJECT
134   REPT       ENDIF
135   REPT       SET DELETED OFF
136   REPT       SET FILTER TO
137   REPT       USE %%FullUse
138   REPT       WAIT "Press any key to return to menu..."
139   REPT       RETURN
140   REPT
141   EDIT       ***************************************** %%EdProg
142   EDIT       *----------------------- Edit data.
143   EDIT       *------------------ Set up loop for editing.
144   EDIT       More = .T.
145   EDIT       DO WHILE More
146   EDIT            CLEAR
147   EDIT            @ 1,1 SAY "Edit Data"
148   EDIT            @ 2,0 SAY ULine
149   EDIT            Search = %%LookBeg
150   EDIT            @ 10,5 SAY "Enter %%LookComm to Edit"
151   EDIT            @ 12,5 SAY "or press <--' to Exit " GET Search
152   EDIT            READ
153   EDIT
154   EDIT            *------- Exit if nothing entered.
155   EDIT            IF Search = %%LookStop
156   EDIT                 More = .F.
157   EDIT                 LOOP
158   EDIT            ENDIF
159   EDIT            %%LookConv
160   EDIT            *------- Try to find the record.
161   EDIT            SEEK Search
162   EDIT            COUNT WHILE %%LookCount = Search TO HowMany
163   EDIT            IF HowMany > 1
164   EDIT                 @ 20,1 SAY STR(HowMany,3)+" matches found"
165   EDIT                 @ 22,1 SAY "Use PgDn, PgUp keys to scroll"
166   EDIT                 ?
167   EDIT                 WAIT "Press any key to edit..."
168   EDIT            ENDIF (howmany)
169   EDIT            SEEK Search
170   EDIT            *------- If found, edit.  Otherwise, warn user.
171   EDIT            IF FOUND()
172   EDIT                 %-EdDecide
173   EDIT
174   EDIT
175   EDIT            ELSE
176   EDIT                 @ 22,0
177   EDIT                 ? "Can't find: ",Search
```

Figure 11.30:   The PlusGen.DBF database (continued)

```
178  EDIT          ?? CHR(7)
179  EDIT          WAIT
180  EDIT        ENDIF (found)
181  EDIT
182  EDIT    ENDDO (More)
183  EDIT
184  EDIT    RETURN
185  EDIT
186  DEL    ******************************* %%DelProg
187  DEL    * Delete Data for %%MainTitle
188  DEL    CLEAR
189  DEL    @ 1,1 SAY "Delete Data"
190  DEL    @ 2,0 SAY ULine
191  DEL    *----------------- Find highest record number.
192  DEL    USE %%DBName2
193  DEL    GO BOTTOM
194  DEL    Max = RECNO()
195  DEL    USE %%FullUse
196  DEL    *----------------- Ask for record or exit.
197  DEL    More = .T.
198  DEL    DO WHILE More
199  DEL       @ 3,0 CLEAR
200  DEL       Search = %%LookBeg
201  DEL       @ 10,2 SAY "Enter %%LookComm to Delete "
202  DEL       @ 12,2 SAY "or <--' to exit " ;
203  DEL          GET Search
204  DEL       READ
205  DEL       *----- Respond to entry.
206  DEL       DO CASE
207  DEL          *---- If not exiting, look up.
208  DEL          CASE Search # %%LookStop
209  DEL             %%LookConv
210  DEL             SEEK Search
211  DEL
212  DEL          *--- Otherwise, exit.
213  DEL          OTHERWISE
214  DEL             More = .F.
215  DEL             LOOP
216  DEL       ENDCASE
217  DEL
218  DEL       *---- Make sure record exists.
219  DEL       IF .NOT. FOUND()
220  DEL          @ 20,0 CLEAR
221  DEL          ? "Can't Find",Search
222  DEL          ?? CHR(7)
223  DEL          WAIT "Press any key to try again..."
224  DEL          LOOP
225  DEL       ENDIF (not found)
226  DEL
227  DEL       *-- If found, count and display.
228  DEL       COUNT WHILE %%LookCount = SEARCH TO HowMany
229  DEL       IF HowMany > 1
230  DEL          @ 3,0 CLEAR
231  DEL          SEEK Search
232  DEL          DISPLAY %%SmallDisp WHILE ;
233  DEL             %%LookCount = Search
234  DEL          Recno = 0
235  DEL          @ 23,2 SAY "Delete which one (by record number) " ;
236  DEL             GET Recno PICTURE "9999"
237  DEL          READ
```

Figure 11.30: The PlusGen.DBF database (continued)

```
238  DEL            IF Recno <= Max .AND. Recno > 0
239  DEL                DELETE RECORD Recno
240  DEL            ELSE
241  DEL                @ 20,0 CLEAR
242  DEL                @ 22,1 SAY "No such record: "+STR(Recno,4)
243  DEL                ? CHR(7)
244  DEL                WAIT "Press any key to try again..."
245  DEL            ENDIF
246  DEL         ELSE
247  DEL            SEEK Search
248  DEL            @ 3,0 CLEAR
249  DEL            DISPLAY %%SmallDisp
250  DEL            Maybe = " "
251  DEL            @ 23,1 SAY "Delete this record? (Y/N) ";
252  DEL                    GET MayBe PICTURE "!"
253  DEL            READ
254  DEL            IF UPPER(Maybe) = "Y"
255  DEL                DELETE
256  DEL            ENDIF (maybe)
257  DEL         ENDIF (howmany)
258  DEL      ENDDO (More)
259  DEL
260  DEL      *-- Final check before permanent deletion.
261  DEL      *-- Count records marked for deletion
262  DEL      *-- and store in memory variable No_Dels.
263  DEL      COUNT FOR DELETED() TO No_Dels
264  DEL
265  DEL      Permiss = "N"
266  DEL      DO WHILE Permiss = "N" .AND. No_Dels > 0
267  DEL         @ 3,0 CLEAR
268  DEL         ?
269  DEL         DISPLAY %%SmallDisp FOR DELETED()
270  DEL         ?
271  DEL         Permiss = " "
272  DEL         @ 23,5 SAY "Ok to delete all these? (Y/N) " ;
273  DEL             GET Permiss PICTURE "!"
274  DEL         READ
275  DEL         *--- If not OK to delete all, find out which.
276  DEL         IF Permiss # "Y"
277  DEL            RecNo = 0
278  DEL            @ 20,0 CLEAR
279  DEL            @ 23,5 SAY "Recall which one (record number): ";
280  DEL                GET RecNo PICT "99999"
281  DEL            READ
282  DEL            IF Recno > 0 .AND. Recno <= Max
283  DEL                GOTO RecNo
284  DEL                IF DELETED()
285  DEL                    RECALL
286  DEL                    No_Dels = No_Dels - 1
287  DEL                ENDIF (deleted)
288  DEL            ELSE
289  DEL                @ 20,0 CLEAR
290  DEL                @ 22,1 SAY "No such record: "+STR(RecNo,4)
291  DEL                ? CHR(7)
292  DEL                WAIT
293  DEL            ENDIF (recno)
294  DEL         ENDIF (permiss # y)
295  DEL      ENDDO (permiss and No_dels)
```

Figure 11.30: The PlusGen.DBF database (continued)

```
296  DEL
297  DEL    *--- Pack and return.
298  DEL    PACK
299  DEL
300  DEL    RETURN
301  DUP    ************************************** %%DupProg
302  DUP    *  Scan database for possible duplicates.
303  DUP    SET HEADING OFF
304  DUP    SET DELETED ON
305  DUP
306  DUP    *------------------- Ask about printer.
307  DUP    CLEAR
308  DUP    @ 1,1 SAY "Duplicate Check"
309  DUP    @ 2,0 SAY ULine
310  DUP    Printer = " "
311  DUP    @ 10,5 SAY "Send possible duplicates to printer? (Y/N) ";
312  DUP       GET Printer PICTURE "!"
313  DUP    READ
314  DUP
315  DUP    *------------------- Set printer on, if necessary.
316  DUP    IF Printer = "Y"
317  DUP        WAIT "Prepare printer, then press any key to continue..."
318  DUP        SET PRINT ON
319  DUP    ENDIF
320  DUP
321  DUP    *------------------- Clear screen and print title.
322  DUP    @ 3,0 CLEAR
323  DUP    USE %%DBName2
324  DUP    ? "Pre-sorting for duplications check..."
325  DUP    INDEX ON %%DupComp TO Temp
326  DUP
327  DUP    CLEAR
328  DUP    ? "Possible Duplications" + SPACE(38) + DTOC(DATE())
329  DUP    ? ULine
330  DUP    ?
331  DUP    ?
332  DUP
333  DUP    *------- Loop through database until end of file, and
334  DUP    *------- compare records based on specified fields.
335  DUP
336  DUP    RecCheck = " %%DupComp "
337  DUP    DO WHILE .NOT. EOF()
338  DUP        Compare = &RecCheck
339  DUP        SKIP
340  DUP        IF &RecCheck = Compare
341  DUP           SKIP -1
342  DUP           LIST WHILE &RecCheck = Compare;
343  DUP              %%DupDisp
344  DUP           ?
345  DUP        ENDIF (&RecCheck = Compare)
346  DUP    ENDDO (while not eof)
347  DUP
348  DUP    *------------------- Done.  Return to menu.
349  DUP    IF Printer = "Y"
350  DUP        EJECT
351  DUP        SET PRINT OFF
352  DUP    ENDIF
353  DUP    SET DELETED OFF
```

Figure 11.30:   The PlusGen.DBF database (continued)

```
354  DUP    *--- Reassign index files and return.
355  DUP    USE %%Fulluse
356  DUP    @ 22,0
357  DUP    WAIT "Press any key to return to menu..."
358  DUP    RETURN
```

Figure 11.30:   The PlusGen.DBF database (continued)

the reports menu is generated, and %-SortMenu, where the sort menu options are generated.

After I placed the %% and %- signs in the original custom system, I used the APPEND FROM *file name* SDF command to read the custom command files into the PlusGen.DBF database. After reading in a particular program (such as the main menu or editing program), I used the REPLACE command to fill in the smaller Program field. All in all, it actually took only a few minutes to create the entire PlusGen.DBF database.

If you create your own program generator, you might want to use the same technique. If you want to use exactly the PlusGen program generator, you might have to type in each record of PlusGen.DBF yourself, or use the coupon at the end of this book to purchase a disk copy of the files.

THE DATABASE

Given the skeletal system to build upon, PlusGen needs answers to specific questions so it can substitute the right information for the various %% and %- symbols in the skeletal database. It gets the answers to these questions from the pages of screens it presents. It stores the answers on a file that we'll call the *parameters file.*

Each custom system that PlusGen creates will have its own parameters file, but you need to create the initial file structure using the usual dBASE CREATE command. Name the file PlusData.DBF, create it using the structure shown in Figure 11.31, then save the structure without adding any data to the file.

Later, when you create a custom system, PlusGen will create a database with the same structure as PlusData.DBF, but name it using the four-letter abbreviation for the system, followed by the letters Prm.DBF. For example, when creating the Club application, PlusGen created a database file named ClubPrm.DBF, and stored the answers to all the PlusGen questions on that database.

Structure for database: PlusData.DBF

Field	Field Name	Type	Width	Dec
1	DRIVE	Character	1	
2	MAINTITLE	Character	40	
3	MAINPROG	Character	8	
4	ABBREV	Character	4	
5	DATABASE	Character	8	
6	NO_FIELDS	Numeric	3	
7	FMTFILE1	Character	8	
8	FMTFILE2	Character	8	
9	LOOKUP	Character	10	
10	LOOKCOMM	Character	25	
11	OPTION1	Character	25	
12	OPTION2	Character	25	
13	OPTION3	Character	25	
14	OPTION4	Character	25	
15	SRTFLDA1	Character	10	
16	SRTFLDB1	Character	10	
17	SRTFLDC1	Character	10	
18	SRTFLDA2	Character	10	
19	SRTFLDB2	Character	10	
20	SRTFLDC2	Character	10	
21	SRTFLDA3	Character	10	
22	SRTFLDB3	Character	10	
23	SRTFLDC3	Character	10	
24	SRTFLDA4	Character	10	
25	SRTFLDB4	Character	10	
26	SRTFLDC4	Character	10	
27	REPOPT1	Character	25	
28	REPFILE1	Character	12	
29	REPOPT2	Character	25	
30	REPFILE2	Character	12	
31	REPOPT3	Character	25	
32	REPFILE3	Character	12	
33	REPOPT4	Character	25	
34	REPFILE4	Character	12	
35	REPOPT5	Character	25	
36	REPFILE5	Character	12	
37	REPOPT6	Character	25	
38	REPFILE6	Character	12	
39	REPOPT7	Character	25	
40	REPFILE7	Character	12	

Figure 11.31:   Structure of the PlusData.DBF database

```
Structure for database: PlusData.DBF

Field   Field Name        Type           Width   Dec
  41    REPOPT8           Character        25
  42    REPFILE8          Character        12
  43    REPOPT9           Character        25
  44    REPFILE9          Character        12
  45    DUPCHECK          Logical           1
  46    DUPEYN            Character          1
  47    DUPFLD1           Character         10
  48    DUPFLD2           Character         10
  49    DUPFLD3           Character         10
  50    DUPFLD4           Character         10

** Total **                                711
```

Figure 11.31:   Structure of the PlusData.DBF database (continued)

THE STRUCTURE FILE

The third and final database used by PlusGen is the database that holds information describing the structure of the database that the custom system will generate. Figure 11.32 shows the structure of this database, which you can create with the usual CREATE command. Name the database Plus-Stru, and do not add any records to it.

Let's look at an example of how PlusGen uses the PlusStru database. Recall that the Club application presented earlier in this chapter used a

```
Structure for database: C:PlusStru.DBF

Field   Field Name        Type           Width   Dec
   1    FIELD_NAME        Character        10
   2    FIELD_TYPE        Character         1
   3    FIELD_LEN         Numeric           3
   4    FIELD_DEC         Numeric           3
   5    COMMON            Character        30

** Total **                                 48
```

Figure 11.32:   Structure of the PlusStru.DBF database

database named ClubMem.DBF. For PlusGen to determine exactly how to handle data types in the generated system, it must "know" the data types, lengths, and decimals for each field in the database. The PlusStru.DBF database is a structure for storing this information.

When creating the Club application, PlusGen used this PlusStru.DBF database in conjunction with the dBASE COPY STRUCTURE EXTENDED command to create a file named ClubStr.DBF (by using the four-letter abbreviation followed by the letters Str.DBF). Once created, ClubStr.DBF contained all the information about each field in the ClubMem.DBF database, with each individual field in ClubMem.DBF stored on a separate record. Hence, if you were to LIST all the records in the ClubStr.DBF database, you would see the display below:

RECORD#	FIELD_NAME	FIELD _TYPE	FIELD _LEN	FIELD _DEC	COMMON
1	LNAME	C	20	0	Last name
2	FNAME	C	20	0	
3	COMPANY	C	25	0	
4	ADDRESS	C	25	0	
5	CITY	C	20	0	
6	STATE	C	0		
7	ZIP	C	10	0	
8	PHONE	C	13	0	
9	EXP_DATE	D	8	0	
10	EXP_MONTH	N	2	0	

To find the data type, length, decimals, or common English name for any field in the ClubMem.DBF database, PlusGen needs only to LOCATE the appropriate field name in the FIELD_NAME field of the ClubStr.DBF database. The FIELD_TYPE, FIELD_LEN, FIELD_DEC, and COMMON fields hold the rest of the information PlusGen might need from time to time.

In case this is a bit confusing, let me put it all another way. When you create custom programs, you probably sometimes refer to the DISPLAY STRUCTURE command on screen or on a printed copy to see which data types are in use. PlusGen cannot "look at" a DISPLAY STRUCTURE output to determine data types. However, it can look into a file that was created with the COPY STRUCTURE EXTENDED COMMAND to achieve the same result. In other words, the information that PlusGen gets from this structure file is identical to the information you would get from the DISPLAY STRUCTURE command.

⊙THE PLUSGEN PROCEDURE FILE

PlusGen uses a few predefined procedures to perform a few repetitive tasks while generating custom systems. These are all stored in a file named PlusProc.PRG. Figure 11.33 lists the entire PlusProc.PRG procedure file.

The first procedure in the procedure file, named Fldisp, displays field names at the top of the screen on certain pages of questions PlusGen presents to the user.

The second procedure in the PlusProc.PRG procedure file is named RepCreate. This procedure allows the user to develop a customer report format, mailing label format, or command file "on the fly," after he or she is already in PlusGen. Generally, it is better to create all these files before running PlusGen, to avoid trying to do too many things at once. But, just in case you feel like developing a new report while defining report options in PlusGen, the RepCreate procedure allows you to do so.

The final procedure in the PlusProc procedure file, named Proper, converts text to initial uppercase (e.g., ABC, abc, and aBc would all be converted to Abc). This procedure is used to add some consistency to data field and variable names being substituted into the skeletal custom system.

⊙THE PLUSGEN COMMAND FILES

PlusGen can be written as a single command file, but since the MODIFY COMMAND editor imposes a 5,000-character limit, I've broken PlusGen into seven smaller command files. Of these seven command files, only two are actually used to generate programs: PlusGen6.PRG and PlusGen7.PRG. All the other programs (named PlusGen.PRG through PlusGen5.PRG) present the pages of questions to the user, verify their entries, and in some cases make some minor conversions to speed the program generation phase.

PLUSGEN.PRG

The PlusGen.PRG command file, shown in Figure 11.34, displays the first three pages of questions to the user, verifies all answers, and stores the answers in the parameters database. This is also the command file that creates the parameters database for the custom system being generated. PlusGen uses the four-letter abbreviation to create a unique file name for the parameters database for each custom system. The name of the parameters file is stored in the variable named ParamFile. Hence, any time you

```
******************************* PlusProc.PRG
*---------- Procedures for the program generator.
PROCEDURE Fldisp
PARAMETERS DBName
   USE &DBName
   CLEAR
   ?
   DO WHILE .NOT. EOF()
      Counter = 1
      DO WHILE Counter <= 6 .AND. .NOT. EOF()
         ?? Field_Name + SPACE(3)
         SKIP
         Counter = Counter + 1
      ENDDO (counter)
      ?
   ENDDO (not eof)
RETURN

*------ Create reports on the fly.
PROCEDURE RepCreate
PARAMETERS DBName,RepFile
   USE &DBName
   Error = .T.
   DO WHILE Error
      Error = .F.
      RepFile = UPPER(RepFile)
      Spot = AT(".",RepFile)
      Exten = SUBSTR(RepFile,Spot+1,3)

      *--- Create appropriate report.
      DO CASE
         CASE Exten = "FRM"
               MODIFY REPORT &RepFile
         CASE Exten = "LBL"
               MODIFY LABEL &RepFile
         CASE Exten = "PRG"
               MODIFY COMMAND &RepFile
         OTHERWISE
               ? "Don't recognize &Exten extension"
               ? "Must be .FRM, .LBL, or .PRG"
               Error = .T.
               ? "Re-enter report file name -- "
               ACCEPT "with extension " TO RepFile
      ENDCASE
   ENDDO (error)
   CLOSE DATABASES
RETURN

*------ Convert to "proper" case (initial caps).
PROCEDURE Proper
PARAMETERS String
   String = UPPER(SUBSTR(String,1,1))+ ;
   LOWER(SUBSTR(String,2,LEN(String)-1))
RETURN
```

Figure 11.33: The PlusProc.PRG procedure file

```
*********************************** PlusGen.PRG
*------------------ dBASE III PLUS program generator.

*------- Set parameters and display instructions.
CLOSE DATABASES
CLEAR ALL
SET TALK OFF
SET SAFE OFF
SET STATUS OFF

*---- Set colors and draw opening screen.
IF ISCOLOR()
    SET COLOR TO GR+/B,W+/BR,RB
ENDIF
CLEAR
@ 1,1 TO 3,79 DOUBLE
IF ISCOLOR()
    SET COLOR TO R+*/BG,R+/B,RB
ENDIF
@ 2,26 SAY "* * * PlusGen * * *"
IF ISCOLOR()
    SET COLOR TO GR+/B,W+/BR,R
ENDIF
?
TEXT

            Before using this program, you should create
            the database you want to manage. Use the
            dBASE III PLUS CREATE command, as usual, to
            create the database.

            You should also create any reports with the
            REPORT FORM or LABEL FORM commands, and any
            custom command files using MODIFY COMMAND
            or another editor.

            If you wish to use custom screens with your
            application, you should also create these
            first using the dBASE III PLUS Screen Painter.

ENDTEXT
YesNo = " "
@ Row()+2,13 SAY "Do you want to continue? (Y/N)";
        GET YesNo PICTURE "!"
READ
IF YesNo # "Y"
    CANCEL
ENDIF (yesno)

*---------------------- Get general information.
SET PROCEDURE TO PlusProc
M_Drive = " "
G_Drive = " "
M_Abbrev = SPACE(4)

OK = " "
CLEAR
@ 1,12 SAY "PlusGen: A dBASE III PLUS Program Generator"
@ 3,1 SAY "Default drive that the generated system will use (B or C)"
```

Figure 11.34: The PlusGen.PRG command file

```
@ 3,60 GET M_Drive PICTURE "A"
@ 5,1 SAY "Drive for storing generated code [must be the same"
@ 6,1 SAY "drive that contains the database (.DBF) file ] ";
       GET G_Drive PICT "A"
@ 8,1 SAY "Enter unique abbreviation -- up to four characters long "
@ 9,1 SAY "(Do not use PLUS as abbreviation)"
@ 9,36 GET M_Abbrev PICTURE "AAAA"
@ 13,1 SAY "Press UP arrow to make corrections,"
@ 14,1 SAY "or press any key to continue..." ;
       GET OK PICTURE "!"
READ

*-------------- Disallow PLUS as abbreviation.
IF UPPER(M_Abbrev) = "PLUS"
   ? "Illegal abbreviation"
   CLEAR ALL
   CANCEL
ENDIF
IF G_Drive # " "
   G_Drive = UPPER(TRIM(G_Drive))+":"
ENDIF

M_Abbrev = TRIM(M_Abbrev)
DO Proper with M_Abbrev
M_Drive = UPPER(M_Drive)
ParamFile = G_Drive+TRIM(M_Abbrev) + "Prm.DBF"

*----- Create parameter file if not already available.
IF .NOT. FILE(ParamFile)
   USE PlusData
   COPY STRUCTURE TO &ParamFile
   USE &ParamFile
   APPEND BLANK
   REPLACE Abbrev WITH M_Abbrev
   REPLACE Drive WITH M_Drive
ENDIF
USE &ParamFile

*--------------------- Get database information.
CLEAR
OK = " "
@ 3,1 SAY "Enter Database Name (no drive or extension) " GET DataBase
@ 5,1 SAY "Enter name for main menu program"
@ 6,1 SAY "(8 letters max., no spaces, drive, or extension) ";
       GET MainProg PICTURE "AAAAAAAA"
@ 8,1 SAY "Enter overall system title"
@ 8,30 GET MainTitle
@ 18,1 SAY "Press UP arrow to make corrections,"
@ 19,1 SAY "or any key to continue " GET Ok
READ
M_MainProg = MainProg
DO Proper WITH M_MainProg

*--------------------- Verify database file name.
@ 22,0 SAY "Verifying..."
Valid = .F.
DO WHILE .NOT. Valid
   DBName = TRIM(DataBase)
   DO Proper WITH DBName
```

Figure 11.34: The PlusGen.PRG command file (continued)

```
        DBName = G_Drive+DBName + ".DBF"
        DBName2 = TRIM(DataBase)
        DO Proper WITH DBName2
        IF FILE(DBName)
           Valid = .T.
        ELSE
           CLEAR
           ? "Database File &DBName does not exist!"
           ?
           ? "Database must exist to generate programs."
           ?
           ? "Re-enter database name, or just press Return to quit "
           ?
           REPLACE DataBase WITH SPACE(8)
           @ 10,10 SAY "Enter database name (no drive or extension) ";
             GET DataBase
           READ
           IF LEN(TRIM(DataBase)) = 0
              CLOSE DATABASES
              QUIT
           ENDIF (len)
        ENDIF (file exists)
     ENDDO (not valid)

     *--------- Continue with PlusGen2.
     DO PlusGen2
```

Figure 11.34:   The PlusGen.PRG command file (continued)

see the command USE &ParamFile in the PlusGen programs, you'll know that PlusGen is opening the parameters file for the custom system currently being created.

As you can see in PlusGen.PRG, and throughout most of the PlusGen command files, there is a strong emphasis on trapping and correcting errors as they occur. Error trapping is important in any program generator, because any errors that slip through the question-and-answer part of program generation will no doubt show up as bugs in the generated custom system.

PLUSGEN2.PRG

The PlusGen2.PRG command file, shown in Figure 11.35, is a continuation of the PlusGen.PRG command file. PlusGen2 creates the structure file for the custom system being generated, using COPY STRUCTURE EXTENDED as we discussed earlier. The name of the structure file for a given system is stored in the variable StruFile. Therefore, PlusGen uses the command USE &StruFile to open the structure file when it needs to look up data types or lengths. Incidentally, PlusGen only creates a structure file if one does not already exist. Otherwise it uses the original structure file, and copies any new fields from the new database structure.

```
********************************* PlusGen2.PRG.
* Make "structure file" of field names and types.

*--- If structure file does not exist, create it.
StruFile = G_Drive+TRIM(M_Abbrev) + "Str.DBF"
IF .NOT. FILE(StruFile)
    ? "Creating Structure File: &StruFile..."
    USE &DBName
    COPY TO Temp STRUCTURE EXTENDED
    USE PlusStru
    COPY STRUCTURE TO &StruFile
    USE &StruFile
    APPEND FROM Temp
    ERASE Temp.DBF
ELSE
    *------------- Otherwise, recreate structure
    *---------------- file with old and new data.
    ? "Rebuilding Structure File: &StruFile..."
    USE &StruFile
    COPY TO Temp
    USE &DBName
    COPY TO Temp2 STRUCTURE EXTENDED
    USE &StruFile
    ZAP
    APPEND FROM Temp2
    SELECT A
    USE &StruFile
    SELECT B
    USE Temp
    INDEX ON Field_Name TO TempNdx
    SELECT A
    SET RELATION TO Field_Name INTO Temp
    REPLACE ALL Common WITH B->Common ;
            FOR Field_Name = B->Field_Name
    CLOSE DATABASES
    ERASE Temp.DBF
    ERASE Temp2.DBF
    ERASE TempNdx.NDX
ENDIF (not file)
USE &StruFile
COUNT TO No_Fields
USE &ParamFile
REPLACE No_Fields WITH M->No_Fields
REPLACE Drive WITH M_Drive
CLOSE DATABASES

*------------------------- Get format file names.
CLEAR
TEXT
    If you are using custom screens (.FMT files) for
    adding or editing data, enter the file names
    below.  If the same format file is to be used
    for both adding and editing records, enter the
    name twice.  If no format files will be used,
    leave both options blank.

    Do NOT include drive or .FMT extension in format file name.
ENDTEXT
OK = .F.
```

Figure 11.35: The PlusGen2.PRG command file

```
USE &ParamFile
DO WHILE .NOT. OK
    @ 12,0 CLEAR
    @ 12,5 SAY "Format file for Appending " ;
       GET FmtFilel
    @ 14,5 SAY "Format file for Editing ";
       GET FmtFile2
    READ
    @ 23,1 SAY "Verifying..."

    *--------------------- Make sure format files exist.
    OK = .T.
    IF FmtFilel # " "
       Check = G_Drive+TRIM(FmtFilel) + ".FMT"
       IF .NOT. FILE(Check)
          ? CHR(7)
          @ 16,5 SAY "No format file &Check"
          OK = .F.
       ENDIF (not file)
    ENDIF (fmtfile # " ")

    IF FmtFile2 # " "
       Check = G_Drive+TRIM(FmtFile2) + ".FMT"
       IF .NOT. FILE(Check)
          ? CHR(7)
          @ 18,5 SAY "No format file &Check"
          OK = .F.
       ENDIF (not file)
    ENDIF (fmtfile # " ")
    IF .NOT. Ok
       Answer = " "
       @ 19,0 CLEAR
       @ 19,1 SAY "********************************"
       @ 20,1 SAY "* Type X to exit...            *"
       @ 21,1 SAY "* or any other key to try again *" ;
          GET Answer PICTURE "!"
       @ 22,1 SAY "********************************"
       READ
       IF Answer = "X"
          CLOSE DATA
          CLOSE PROC
          CANCEL
       ENDIF (answer)
    ENDIF (not ok)
ENDDO (not ok)
CLOSE DATABASE

*----------------------- Get key (lookup) field.
OK = .F.
DO WHILE .NOT. OK
    CLEAR
    DO Fldisp with StruFile
    USE &ParamFile
    STORE LookComm TO TempComm
    @ ROW()+2,1 SAY "Enter key field for lookups " ;
       GET Lookup
    @ ROW()+2,1 SAY "Enter common name for field "
    @ ROW()+1,1 SAY "(e.g. Last Name for LName)" ;
       GET TempComm
    READ
```

Figure 11.35: The PlusGen2.PRG command file (continued)

```
*---- Verify that lookup field exists.
Lookup = UPPER(TRIM(Lookup))
FieldTypeA1 = " "
SrtFldA1 = " "
USE &StruFile
SET EXACT ON
LOCATE FOR Field_Name = Lookup
SET EXACT OFF
IF EOF()
   ?
   ? "No such field: &Lookup"
   ?
   WAIT "Press any key to try again..."
ELSE
   *------- If lookup field OK, then use it as
   *------- first field in first index file.
   OK = .T.
   IF TempComm = " "
      TempComm = LookUp
   ENDIF
   ? "Verifying..."
   DO Proper WITH TempComm
   REPLACE Common WITH TempComm
   LookComm = Common
   FldTypeA1 = Field_Type
   SrtFldA1 = Lookup

   *---- Get type and length of main lookup field.
   LookType = Field_Type
   LookLen = Field_Len
  ENDIF (eof)
ENDDO (not ok)
DO Proper WITH LookUp

*------ Put lookup field data into parameters file.
USE &ParamFile
REPLACE Lookup WITH M->Lookup
REPLACE LookComm WITH M->LookComm
REPLACE Option1 WITH M->LookComm
REPLACE SrtFldA1 WITH M->SrtFldA1

*------ Assign data type conversion for
*------ editing and deleting programs now.
IF LookType = "N"
   LookStart = "-1"
   LookStop = "0"
   LookBeg = "0"
   LookConv = " "
   LookCount = TRIM(M->LookUp)
   REPLACE SrtFldB1 WITH " "
   REPLACE SrtFldC1 WITH " "
ELSE
   LookStart = "X"
   LookStop = ' " "'
   LookBeg = "SPACE("+STR(LookLen,2)+")"
   LookConv = "Search = UPPER(TRIM(Search))"
   DO Proper WITH M->LookUp
   LookCount = "UPPER("+TRIM(M->LookUp)+")"
ENDIF
```

Figure 11.35:   The PlusGen2.PRG command file (continued)

```
IF LookType = "D"
   LookConv = "Search = CTOD(Search)"
   LookCount = M->Lookup
   REPLACE SrtFldB1 WITH " "
   REPLACE SrtFldC1 WITH " "
ENDIF

*------------- Continue with PlusGen3.PRG.
DO PlusGen3
```

Figure 11.35:   The PlusGen2.PRG command file (continued)

PlusGen2.PRG also displays instructions and prompts for entering format file names and the main lookup field. It verifies all the entries, and also determines the data type for the lookup field by checking the structure file.

PLUSGEN3.PRG

PlusGen3.PRG, shown in Figure 11.36, displays the instructions and prompts for entering sort order options and fields. All field names are verified and data types determined by checking the structure file.

```
********************************** PlusGen3.PRG
*--------------------------- Set up sort menu.
OK = .F.
DO WHILE .NOT. OK
   CLEAR
   TEXT
   On the next page, please fill in information for presenting sort
   orders to the user.  In the left column, place the menu option as it
   should read on the menu. In the right column, enter field names for
   sorting, as in the example below. Note that the Lookup field (menu option
   1) is already included as a sort option.  You can add more fields to
   the right of the lookup field ONLY if the first field is a character
   field.  You can freely mix data types in other index files (menu
   options 2 through 4).


      Sort Menu Option              Field(s)

      1. Customer Number        CustNo

      2. Names                  LName       FName

      3. Zip Code               Zip         CustNo       City

      4.
```

Figure 11.36:   The PlusGen3.PRG command file

```
ENDTEXT
?
WAIT
CLEAR

*---- Show field names, and have user fill in menu
*---- options and sorting fields.
DO FlDisp WITH StruFile
?
? " Sort Menu Option                    Field(s)"
Option1 = LookComm
USE &ParamFile
SrtFldA1 = Lookup
DO Proper WITH SrtFldA1
@ Row()+2,1 SAY " 1.   " + Option1
@ Row(),35 SAY SrtFldA1
IF LookType = "C"
   @ ROW(),47 GET SrtFldB1
   @ ROW(),59 GET SrtFldC1
ENDIF
Counter = 2
DO WHILE Counter <= 4
   Sub = STR(Counter,1)
   @ ROW()+1,1 SAY STR(Counter,2) + ". " ;
       GET Option&Sub
   @ ROW(),35 GET SrtFldA&Sub
   @ ROW(),47 GET SrtFldB&Sub
   @ ROW(),59 GET SrtFldC&Sub
   Counter = Counter + 1
ENDDO (counter <= 4)
READ
CLEAR
? "Creating index files..."

*-- Make memory variables from fields.
Counter = 1
DO WHILE Counter <= 4
   Sub = STR(Counter,1)
   Option&Sub = Option&Sub
   SrtFldA&Sub = SrtFldA&Sub
   SrtFldB&Sub = SrtFldB&Sub
   SrtFldC&Sub = SrtFldC&Sub
   Counter = Counter + 1
ENDDO (counter <= 4)

*-- Verify and get data types.
SET EXACT ON
OK = .T.
USE &StruFile
Counter = 1
DO WHILE Counter <= 4
   SUB = STR(Counter,1)
   FldCount&Sub = 0
   IF SrtFldA&sub # " "
      SrtFldA&Sub = UPPER(TRIM(SrtFldA&Sub))
      FldCount&Sub = FldCount&Sub + 1
      LOCATE FOR Field_Name = SrtFldA&Sub
      IF EOF()
         ? "No such field: "+SrtFldA&Sub
```

Figure 11.36: The PlusGen3.PRG command file (continued)

```
                 WAIT
                 OK = .F.
                 Counter = 5
                 LOOP
             ENDIF (eof)
             FldTypeA&Sub = Field_Type
          ENDIF
          IF SrtFldB&Sub # " "
             SrtFldB&Sub = UPPER(TRIM(SrtFldB&Sub))
             FldCount&Sub = FldCount&Sub + 1
             LOCATE FOR Field_Name = SrtFldB&Sub
             IF EOF()
                 ? "No such field: "+SrtFldB&Sub
                 WAIT
                 OK = .F.
                 Counter = 5
                 LOOP
             ENDIF (eof)
             FldTypeB&Sub = Field_Type
          ENDIF (srtfldBsub)
          IF SrtFldC&Sub # " "
             SrtFldC&Sub = UPPER(TRIM(SrtFldC&Sub))
             FldCount&Sub = FldCount&Sub + 1
             LOCATE FOR Field_Name = SrtFldC&Sub
             IF EOF()
                 ? "No such field: "+SrtFldC&Sub
                 WAIT
                 OK = .F.
                 Counter = 5
                 LOOP
             ENDIF (eof)
             FldTypeC&Sub = Field_Type
          ENDIF (srtfldc&sub)
          Counter = Counter + 1
       ENDDO (counter)
    ENDDO (ok)
    SET EXACT OFF

    *--------------- Continue with PlusGen4.PRG.
    DO PlusGen4
```

Figure 11.36:   The PlusGen3.PRG command file (continued)

Variable names for the indexed fields are constructed in a manner similar to an array. In the first index file, field names are stored in variables named SortFldA1, SortFldB1, SortFldC1. In the second index file, field names to index on are stored in variables named SrtFldA2, SrtFldB2, SrtFldC2. This same pattern is used in the third and fourth index files for the application.

PLUSGEN4.PRG
PlusGen4.PRG, shown in Figure 11.37, uses the variables created in PlusGen3.PRG to create index files. The data types that were determined in

```
****************************** PlusGen4.PRG
*-- Set up index file for lookup.
?
? "USE "+DBName
USE &DBName
IFile1 = M_Abbrev + "Nx1"
IFileNm1 = IFile1

*---------- Create index files.
Counter = 1
IndeString = " "

*----- This loop repeats once for each
*----- possible sort order.
DO WHILE Counter <= 4
   Sub = STR(Counter,1)

   *---- SorFldA is first field in index file.
   IF SrtFldA&Sub # " "
   DO CASE
      CASE FldTypeA&Sub = " "
           LOOP
      CASE FldTypeA&Sub = "C"
           SrtFldA&Sub = "UPPER("+SrtFldA&Sub+")"
      CASE FldTypeA&Sub = "N" .AND. Counter > 1
           SrtFldA&sub = "STR("+SrtFldA&Sub+",12,4)"
      CASE FldTypeA&Sub = "D" .AND. Counter > 1
           SrtFldA&sub = "DTOC("+SrtFldA&Sub+")"
   ENDCASE
   ENDIF

   *---- SorFldB is second field in index file.
   IF SrtFldB&Sub # " "
   DO CASE
      CASE FldTypeB&Sub = " "
           *-- Do nothing.
      CASE FldTypeB&Sub = "C"
           SrtFldB&Sub = "UPPER("+SrtFldB&Sub+")"
      CASE FldTypeB&Sub = "N"
           SrtFldB&sub = "STR("+SrtFldB&Sub+",12,4)"
      CASE FldTypeB&Sub = "D"
           SrtFldB&sub = "DTOC("+SrtFldB&Sub+")"
   ENDCASE
   ENDIF

   *---- SorFldC is third field in index file.
   IF SrtFldC&Sub # " "
   DO CASE
      CASE FldTypeC&Sub = " "
           *-- Do nothing.
      CASE FldTypeC&Sub = "C"
           SrtFldC&Sub = "UPPER("+SrtFldC&Sub+")"
      CASE FldTypeC&Sub = "N"
           SrtFldC&sub = "STR("+SrtFldC&Sub+",12,4)"
      CASE FldTypeC&Sub = "D"
           SrtFldC&sub = "DTOC("+SrtFldC&Sub+")"
   ENDCASE
   ENDIF
   *---- IndString is all fields in index file combined.
```

Figure 11.37: The PlusGen4.PRG command file

```
      IndString&Sub = SrtFldA&Sub
      IF SrtFldB&Sub # " "
          IndString&Sub = IndString&Sub +" + "+SrtFldB&Sub
      ENDIF
      IF SrtFldC&Sub # " "
          IndString&Sub = IndString&Sub +" + "+SrtFldC&Sub
      ENDIF
      FldName = IndString&Sub
      IFileNm&Sub = M_Abbrev + "Nx"+Sub
      IFileNm = IFileNm&Sub
      Check = G_Drive + IFileNm
      IF FldName # " "
          ? "INDEX ON "+FldName+" TO "+Check
          SET TALK ON
          INDEX ON &FldName TO &Check
          SET TALK OFF
          ?
          IF Counter = 1
              IndeString = IFileNm
          ELSE
              IndeString = TRIM(IndeString)+", "+IFileNm
          ENDIF
      ENDIF (FldName # " ")
      Counter = Counter + 1
ENDDO
CLOSE DATABASES

*-------------------------- Ask about reports.
OK = .F.
DO WHILE .NOT. OK
   CLEAR
   TEXT
The next page represents a menu for displaying reports.  In the
left column, enter the option as it is to appear on the reports
menu in the generated system.  In the right column, enter the
name of the file that displays the report, INCLUDING the file
name extension; (e.g., .FRM for REPORT, .LBL for LABEL, or .PRG
for command file).  Do NOT include drive designator.  Valid
examples are shown below:

    Report Menu Option              File Name

    1. Directory of Customers       Director.FRM

    2. Mailing Labels               TwoCol.LBL

    3. MailMerge File               MMerge.PRG

    4.

    5.

    ENDTEXT
    ?
    WAIT
    CLEAR
    ? "  Report Menu Option              File Name"
    ?
    Counter = 1
    USE &ParamFile
```

Figure 11.37: The PlusGen4.PRG command file (continued)

```
      DO WHILE Counter < 9
         Sub=STR(Counter,1)
         @ ROW()+2,1 SAY STR(Counter,2)+". "
         @ ROW(),5 GET RepOpt&Sub
         @ ROW(),32 GET RepFile&Sub
         Counter = Counter + 1
      ENDDO (counter < 10
      READ
      ? "Verifying..."

      *------------------ Verify entries and
      *------------------ create memory variables.
      Counter = 1
      OK = .T.
      DO WHILE Counter < 9
         Sub = STR(Counter,1)
         IF RepOpt&Sub = " "
            RepOpt&Sub = " "
            RepFile&Sub = " "
            Counter = Counter + 1
            LOOP
         ENDIF (blank option)
         RepOpt&Sub = TRIM(RepOpt&Sub)
         RepFile&Sub = TRIM(RepFile&Sub)

         IF .NOT. "." $ RepFile&Sub
            ? "No file name extension: "+RepFile&Sub
            WAIT "Press any key, then re-enter"
            OK = .F.
            Counter = 10
            LOOP
         ENDIF (no dot in file name)
         Check = G_Drive + RepFile&Sub
         IF .NOT. FILE(Check)
            ? CHR(7)
            ? "No file named "+Check
            WAIT "Create it now? (Y/N) " TO YesNo
            IF UPPER(YesNo) = "Y"
               DO RepCreate WITH DBName,RepFile&Sub
               USE &ParamFile
               DO Proper WITH RepFile&Sub
            ELSE
               ? "Will generate programs anyway, but"
               ? "you must eventually create a file named:"
               ?
               ? RepFile&Sub
               ?
               ? "using dBASE III PLUS"
               ?
               WAIT
            ENDIF
         ENDIF (not file)
         Counter = Counter + 1
      ENDDO (Counter < 10)
ENDDO (not ok)
RepOpt9 = " "
RepFile9 = " "

*------------------ Continue with PlusGen5.PRG.
DO PlusGen5
```

Figure 11.37: The PlusGen4.PRG command file (continued)

PlusGen3.PRG are used to determine data types in the index files. (You'll notice that indexed fields are all character strings: UPPER for text data, STR for numeric data, and DTOC for dates.) The command INDEX ON &FldName TO &Check creates the actual index file after the string of fields to index on is created.

PlusGen4.PRG also displays instructions and prompts for reports in the custom system. The program checks for the existence of all report names entered. If one does not exist, the user is given the opportunity to create it on the fly (with the help of the RepCreate procedure developed earlier).

After all report options and report names are entered and verified, PlusGen moves on to the PlusGen5.PRG command file.

PLUSGEN5.PRG

PlusGen5.PRG, shown in Figure 11.38, finishes up the question-and-answer period by asking about the check-for-duplicates option. If the user wants to add this feature to the custom application, PlusGen5.PRG requests field names to be used in the check, creates the appropriate index commands, and also creates a list of field names (in a variable named DupDisp) to display in the check-for-duplicates report.

```
******************************* PlusGen5.PRG.
*----------------- Ask about duplications check.
OK = .F.
DO WHILE .NOT. OK
    CLEAR
    USE &ParamFile
    REPLACE DupCheck WITH .F.
    Pmt = "Include duplicates check option? (Y/N)"
    @ 10,5 SAY Pmt GET DupeYn PICTURE "!"
    READ
    IF DupeYn = "N"
        OK = .T.
        Replace DupCheck WITH .F.
        DupCheck = .F.
        LOOP
    ELSE
        REPLACE DupCheck WITH .T.
        DupCheck = .T.
        DO FlDisp WITH StruFile
        ?
        ? "Enter fields for duplication check"
        ?
        ?
        USE &ParamFile
        @ Row(),2 GET DupFld1
```

Figure 11.38: The PlusGen5.PRG command file

```
        @ Row(),14 GET DupFld2
        @ Row(),26 GET DupFld3
        @ Row(),38 GET DupFld4
        READ
        *--------- Verify field names.
        ? "Verifying..."
        OK = .T.
        Counter = 1
        DO WHILE Counter <= 4
           USE &ParamFile
           Sub = STR(Counter,1)
           IF DupFld&Sub = " "
              Counter = 5
              LOOP
           ENDIF
           DupFld = UPPER(TRIM(DupFld&Sub))
           USE &StruFile
           SET EXACT ON
           LOCATE FOR Field_Name = DupFld
           SET EXACT OFF
           IF EOF()
              ? "No such field: "+DupFld
              WAIT "Press a key and re-enter"
              OK = .F.
              Counter = 5
              LOOP
           ELSE
              DupType&Sub = Field_Type
              DupLen&Sub = Field_Len
           ENDIF (eof)
           Counter = Counter + 1
        ENDDO (Counter <= 4)
     ENDIF (yesno)
ENDDO (ok)

*---------- Build indexing string and field names
*---------- for LIST command in duplicates check.
Counter = 1
DO Proper WITH LookUp
DupDisp = " "
DDispLen = LookLen
USE &ParamFile
DO WHILE DupCheck .AND. Counter <= 4
   Sub = STR(Counter,1)
   DupConv&Sub = " "
   IF DupFld&Sub # " "
     DupFld=UPPER(TRIM(DupFld&Sub))
     DupFld&Sub = DupFld
     DO CASE
        CASE DupType&Sub = "C"
             DupFld = "UPPER("+DupFld+")"
        CASE DupType&Sub = "N"
             DupFld = "STR("+DupFld+",12,4)"
        CASE DupType&Sub = "D"
             DupFld = "DTOC("+DupFld+")"
     ENDCASE
     DupConv&Sub = DupFld
     IF DDispLen + DupLen&Sub < 65 .AND. .NOT. ;
        UPPER(TRIM(DupFld&Sub)) $ UPPER(DupDisp)
```

Figure 11.38:   The PlusGen5.PRG command file (continued)

```
             DO Proper WITH DupFld&Sub
             IF DupDisp = " "
                  DupDisp=DupFld&Sub
             ELSE
                  DupDisp=TRIM(DupDisp)+", "+DupFld&Sub
             ENDIF (dupdisp = " ")
             DDispLen = DDispLen + DupLen&Sub
        ENDIF (DDisplen)
     ENDIF (dupfld&sub # " ")
     Counter = Counter + 1
ENDDO (counter <= 4 and dupcheck)
DupFld&Sub = " "

*------- Add some more fields to field names for
*------- LIST command if still under 66 characters.
IF DDispLen < 65 .AND. .NOT. UPPER(Lookup) $ UPPER(DupDisp)
     DupDisp = TRIM(DupDisp)+", "+TRIM(M->Lookup)
     DDispLen = DDispLen + LookLen
ENDIF
CLOSE DATABASES
USE &StruFile
DO WHILE DDispLen < 65 .AND. .NOT. EOF()
     IF Field_Len + DDispLen <= 65 .AND. .NOT. ;
             TRIM(Field_Name) $ UPPER(DupDisp)
             Add_On = Field_Name
             DO Proper WITH Add_On
        DupDisp = TRIM(DupDisp)+", "+Add_On
        DDispLen = DDispLen + Field_Len
     ENDIF
     SKIP
ENDDO
CLOSE DATABASES

*--------------------------- Done getting data.
*------------------------- Start generating code.
CLEAR
? "Working"

*------------------------ Create all file names.
USE &ParamFile
M_Drive = UPPER(Drive)
MainTitle = TRIM(MainTitle)
DO Proper WITH M_MainProg
ProgName = TRIM(M_MainProg)+".PRG"
DO Proper WITH LookUp
RepProg = TRIM(M_Abbrev) + "Rep"
EdProg = TRIM(M_Abbrev) + "Edi"
LookComm = TRIM(LookComm)
DelProg = TRIM(M_Abbrev) + "Del"
DupCheck = DupCheck

*----- Prepare for duplicates check if requested.
IF DupCheck
     DupCase1 = 'CASE Choice = "5"'
     DupCase2 = "     DO "+TRIM(M_Abbrev)+"Dup"
     Choices = "6"
     DupOpt = "5. Check for Duplicates"
     ExOpt = "6.  Exit"
     DupProg = TRIM(M_Abbrev)+"Dup"
```

Figure 11.38:   The PlusGen5.PRG command file (continued)

```
    ELSE
       Choices = "5"
       DupOpt = " "
       ExOpt = "5.  Exit"
       STORE " " TO DupCase1,DupCase2,DupProg
    ENDIF
    FullUse = DBName2 + " INDEX " + IndeString
    FmtFile1 = FmtFile1
    FmtFile2 = FmtFile2
    DO Proper WITH M->FmtFile1
    DO Proper WITH M->FmtFile2
    DO Proper WITH LookUp

    *------------------- Generate SmallDisp variable.
    SmallDisp = M->Lookup
    USE &StruFile
    LOCATE FOR Field_Name = UPPER(LookUp)
    DispLen = Field_Len
    GO TOP
    DO WHILE .NOT. EOF() .AND. DispLen < 65
       IF TRIM(Field_Name) # UPPER(LookUp)
           DispLen = DispLen + Field_Len
           IF DispLen < 65
               AddOn = TRIM(Field_Name)
               DO Proper WITH AddOn
               SmallDisp = TRIM(SmallDisp)+"," + AddOn
           ENDIF
       ENDIF
       SKIP
       ?? "."
    ENDDO

    *- Generate comparison string for duplicates check.
    Counter = 1
    DupComp = " "
    DO WHILE DupCheck .AND. Counter <= 4
       Sub = STR(Counter,1)
       IF DupConv&Sub # " "
           IF Counter > 1
               DupComp = TRIM(DupComp) + "+"
           ENDIF
           DupComp = DupComp + DupConv&Sub
       ENDIF
       Counter = Counter + 1
       ?? "."
    ENDDO
    CLOSE DATABASES

    *------------------- Continue with PlusGen6.PRG.
    DO PlusGen6
```

Figure 11.38:   The PlusGen5.PRG command file (continued)

After all the questions are answered, PlusGen5.PRG displays the message *working* and starts getting ready to generate programs. First it determines the names of the files in the application and assigns these names to the variables ProgName, RepProg, EdProg, DelProg, and DupProg. It also converts many file and field names to proper case, creates a few more pieces

of data to be used in the generated application, then moves on to the
PlusGen6.PRG program.

PLUSGEN6.PRG

PlusGen6.PRG, shown in Figure 11.39, begins substituting the
application-specific pieces into the skeletal structure of the custom system.
To do this, PlusGen first copies the entire skeletal program from
PlusGen.DBF to a file named ProgWrk.DBF. All substitutions take place
through the ProgWrk copy so that the original skeletal program is not
modified (it needs to remain unchanged so that future custom systems can
begin with the same skeletal structure).

```
****************************** PlusGen6.PRG
*-- Begin program generation.
*-- Do simple replacements first.
USE PlusGen
?
SET TALK ON

*- ProgWrk.DBF holds temporary copy of PlusGen.DBF.
COPY TO ProgWrk
SET TALK OFF
?
? "Still at it."
USE ProgWrk
LOCATE FOR "%%" $ Line
DO WHILE .NOT. EOF()
    Start = AT("%%",Line)
    VarLen = AT(" ",SUBSTR(Line,Start,80))-3
    Stop = (VarLen + Start)+2
    VarName = SUBSTR(Line,Start+2,VarLen)
    REPLACE Line WITH SUBSTR(Line,1,Start-1) + ;
    &VARNAME + SUBSTR(Line,Stop,80)
    CONTINUE
    ?? "."
ENDDO (not eof)

*-- Generate main menu command file.
?? "."
USE ProgWrk
COPY TO ProgHold FIELDS Line WHILE Program="MENU"
USE ProgHold

*-- Handle appends in main menu.
CLEAR
? "Creating Main Menu Program: &ProgName"
LOCATE FOR "%-AddOpt" $ Line
IF FmtFile1 = " "
    REPLACE Line WITH SPACE(11)+"APPEND"
    SKIP
```

Figure 11.39: The PlusGen6.PRG command file

```
      DELETE
      SKIP
      DELETE
   ELSE
      REPLACE LINE WITH SPACE(11) + ;
      "SET FORMAT TO " + FmtFile1
      SKIP
      REPLACE Line WITH SPACE(11) + "APPEND"
      SKIP
      REPLACE Line WITH SPACE(11) + "CLOSE FORMAT"
   ENDIF
   Check = G_Drive+ProgName
   COPY TO &Check DELIM WITH BLANK FOR .NOT. DELETED()
   TYPE &Check

   *-- Generate reports command file.
   ?
   ?
   RepProg = RepProg + ".PRG"
   ? "Generating Reports program: &RepProg"
   ? "(This one takes a while..."
   USE ProgWrk
   LOCATE FOR PROGRAM = "REPT"
   COPY TO ProgHold FIELDS Line WHILE .NOT. "%-RepMenu" $ Line
   SELECT A
   USE ProgHold
   ?? "."

   *-- Create reports menu.
   GO BOTT
   ?? "."
   Counter = 1
   DO WHILE Counter < 9
      ?? "."
      Sub = STR(Counter,1)
      IF RepOpt&Sub = " "
         Counter = 9
         LOOP
      ENDIF
      APPEND BLANK
      REPLACE Line WITH SPACE(15) + ;
      Sub + ". " + Repopt&Sub
      Counter = Counter + 1
      APPEND BLANK
      ?? "."
   ENDDO (counter < 9)

   *-- Create sort menu.
   USE ProgWrk
   LOCATE FOR "%-RepMenu" $ Line
   SKIP
   COPY TO ProgTemp FIELDS Line WHILE .NOT. "%-SortMenu" $ Line
   USE ProgHold
   APPEND FROM ProgTemp
   GO BOTT
   Counter = 1
   DO WHILE Counter <= 4
      Sub = STR(Counter,1)
      IF Option&Sub = " "
```

Figure 11.39: The PlusGen6.PRG command file (continued)

```
            Counter = 5
            LOOP
        ENDIF
    APPEND BLANK
    REPLACE Line WITH SPACE(15) + ;
        Sub + ". " + Option&Sub
    Counter = Counter + 1
    APPEND BLANK
    ?? "."
ENDDO (counter <= 4)

*--------------- Create sort cases.
USE ProgWrk
LOCATE FOR "%-SortMenu" $ Line
SKIP
COPY TO ProgTemp FIELDS Line WHILE .NOT. "%-SortCase" $ Line
USE ProgHold
APPEND FROM ProgTemp
GO BOTT
Counter = 1
DO WHILE Counter <= 4
    Sub = STR(Counter,1)
    IF Option&Sub = " "
        Counter = 5
        LOOP
    ENDIF
    APPEND BLANK
    REPLACE Line WITH SPACE(5) + ;
        "CASE SChoice = " + Sub
    APPEND BLANK
    REPLACE Line WITH SPACE(10) + ;
      "SET INDEX TO "  + IFileNm&Sub
    Counter = Counter + 1
    ?? "."
ENDDO (counter <= 4)

*--------------- Query form routine.
USE ProgWrk
LOCATE FOR "%-SortCase" $ Line
SKIP
COPY TO ProgTemp FIELDS Line WHILE .NOT. "%-RepCases" $ Line
USE ProgHold
APPEND FROM ProgTemp
GO BOTT

*---------- Generate reports CASE statements.
Counter = 1
DO WHILE Counter < 9
    Sub = STR(Counter,1)
    IF RepFile&Sub = " "
        Counter = 10
        LOOP
    ENDIF
    V1 = '    CASE MChoice = "'+Sub+'"'
    Ext=" "
    Ext = UPPER( SUBSTR(RepFile&Sub,AT(".",RepFile&Sub),4))
    IF Ext = ".FRM"
        V2 = SPACE(8)+"REPORT FORM "+TRIM(RepFile&Sub)+" &PMacro"
```

Figure 11.39:   The PlusGen6.PRG command file (continued)

```
           ENDIF
           IF Ext = ".LBL"
              V2 = SPACE(8)+"LABEL FORM "+TRIM(RepFile&Sub)+" SAMPLE &PMacro"
           ENDIF
           IF Ext = ".PRG"
              V2 = SPACE(8)+"DO "+TRIM(RepFile&Sub)
           ENDIF
           APPEND BLANK
           REPLACE Line WITH V1
           APPEND BLANK
           REPLACE Line WITH V2
           Counter = Counter + 1
           ?? "."
     ENDDO (counter < 9)
     USE ProgWrk
     LOCATE FOR "%-RepCases" $ Line
     SKIP
     COPY TO ProgTemp FIELDS Line WHILE PROGRAM = "REPT"
     USE ProgHold
     APPEND FROM ProgTemp
     CLOSE DATABASES
     USE ProgHold
     Check = G_Drive + RepProg
     COPY TO &Check DELIM WITH BLANK
     TYPE &Check
     CLOSE DATABASES
     ERASE ProgTemp.DBF

     *--------- Generate editing command file.
     ?
     EdProg = EdProg + ".PRG"
     ? "Generating Edit program: &EdProg"
     USE ProgWrk
     LOCATE FOR Program = "EDIT"
     COPY TO ProgHold FIELDS Line WHILE Program = "EDIT"
     USE ProgHold

     LOCATE FOR "%-EdDecide" $ Line
     IF FmtFile2 = " "
        REPLACE Line WITH SPACE(8)+"EDIT"
        SKIP
        DELETE
        SKIP
        DELETE
     ELSE
        REPLACE Line WITH SPACE(8) + ;
           "SET FORMAT TO "+FmtFile2
        SKIP
        REPLACE Line WITH SPACE(8)+ "EDIT"
        SKIP
        REPLACE Line WITH SPACE(8)+"CLOSE FORMAT"
     ENDIF
     Check = G_Drive+EdProg
     COPY TO &Check DELIM WITH BLANK FOR .NOT. DELETED()
     TYPE &Check

     *---------------- Continue with PlusGen7.PRG.
     Do PlusGen7
```

Figure 11.39:   The PlusGen6.PRG command file (continued)

To begin substituting, PlusGen first locates each place where the %% symbol appears in a record in the ProgWrk.DBF database. When it finds %% in a record, it isolates the characters attached to the %% sign. For example, PlusGen6.PRG will find the %% sign in the record below:

* -- Main Menu for: %%MainTitle.

The program then isolates the variable name attached to the %% sign (MainTitle in this example), finds out what is stored in the field named MainTitle on the Parameters database, then substitutes that into the record. In the Club application, the MainTitle field in the parameters database contains the character string

"Club Membership Management System"

After PlusGen6.PRG performs the substitution, the record in the Prog-Wrk.DBF database contains

* -- Main Menu for: Club Membership Management System.

All these basic substitutions are handled by the first DO WHILE .NOT. EOF() loop near the top of PlusGen6.PRG.

Once the basic substitutions are complete, PlusGen6.PRG begins building individual programs by substituting in larger routines (those identified by the %- symbol rather than %%). PlusGen6.PRG generates the main menu, reports, and editing programs for the custom application. Individual programs are copied from the ProgWrk.DBF database to an empty database named ProgHold.DBF to speed the development of the smaller individual programs.

You'll notice that after all substitutions take place, the command COPY TO *file name* DELIMITED WITH BLANK is used. This command copies individual records from the ProgWrk database to an ASCII file that has no special header or characters in it. Hence, the copied file is a straight ASCII file, just like one created with the MODIFY COMMAND editor or a word processor in nondocument (unformatted) mode. After PlusGen6.PRG creates its programs, it passes control to PlusGen7.PRG.

PLUSGEN7.PRG

PlusGen7.PRG, shown in Figure 11.40, completes the process of generating all the files for the application. It generates the deletions program, and

```
******************************** PlusGen7.PRG.
*--------------- Generate deletion program.
?
DelProg = DelProg + ".PRG"
? "Generating Deletion Program: &DelProg"
USE ProgWrk
LOCATE FOR Program = "DEL"
Check = G_Drive+DelProg
COPY TO &Check FIELDS Line ;
   WHILE Program = "DEL" DELIMITED WITH BLANK
TYPE &Check

*-- Generate check-for-duplicates program.
IF DupCheck
   ?
   DupProg = DupProg + ".PRG"
   ? "Generating Duplications Program: &DupProg"
   USE ProgWrk
   LOCATE FOR Program = "DUP"
   Check = G_Drive+DupProg
   COPY TO &Check FIELDS Line ;
      WHILE PROGRAM = "DUP" DELIMITED WITH BLANK
   TYPE &Check
ENDIF (dupcheck)

*-------------------- Make batch file.
?
?
? "Creating batch file for copying system to drive B"
USE ProgWrk
ZAP
DBName2 = TRIM(DBName2) + ".DBF"
DocFile = M_Abbrev+"Doc.TXT"
BatFile = M_Abbrev+"Copy.BAT"
APPEND BLANK
REPLACE Line WITH "COPY "+DBName2+" B:"
APPEND BLANK
REPLACE Line WITH "COPY "+M_Abbrev+"Nx*.NDX B:"
APPEND BLANK
REPLACE Line WITH "COPY "+ProgName+ " B:"
APPEND BLANK
REPLACE Line WITH "COPY "+RepProg+ " B:"
APPEND BLANK
REPLACE Line WITH "COPY "+EdProg+ " B:"
APPEND BLANK
REPLACE Line WITH "COPY "+DelProg+ " B:"
IF DupCheck
   APPEND BLANK
   REPLACE Line WITH "COPY "+DupProg+ " B:"
ENDIF                         ;
IF FmtFile1 # " "
   APPEND BLANK
   REPL Line WITH "COPY "+TRIM(FmtFile1)+".FMT B:"
ENDIF
IF FmtFile2 # " "
   APPEND BLANK
   REPL Line WITH "COPY "+TRIM(FmtFile2)+".FMT B:"
ENDIF (fmtfile)
APPEND BLANK
```

Figure 11.40: The PlusGen7.PRG command file

```
REPLACE LINE WITH "COPY "+DocFile+ " B:"
APPEND BLANK
REPLACE LINE WITH "COPY "+BatFile+ " B:"
Check = G_Drive + BatFile
COPY TO &Check DELIM WITH BLANK
TYPE &Check
?
?
WAIT "Press any key to see documentation..."
CLEAR
Check = G_Drive + DocFile
SET ALTERNATE TO &Check
SET ALTERNATE ON
? "The following files have been generated to manage the"
? "&DBName2 database:"
?
? "Command Files          Task Performed"
? ProgName +": Main Menu program"
? "  "+RepProg + ;
   ": Sort, Search, and Display Reports"
? "  "+EdProg + ": Edit data"
? "  "+DelProg + ": Delete data"
IF DupCheck
    ? "  "+DupProg + ": Check for Duplicates."
ENDIF
?
IF FmtFilel = " " .AND. FmtFile2 = " "
    FMFiles = "none"
ELSE
    FMFiles = TRIM(FmtFilel)+".FMT"
    IF FmtFile2 # " "
        FMFiles = FMFiles +" and "+TRIM(FmtFile2)+".FMT"
    ENDIF
ENDIF
? "Format Files accessed:",FMFiles
?
? "The following index files have been created for the"
? "generated system:"
? "Index File       Contents"
Counter = 1
DO WHILE Counter <= 4
    Sub = STR(Counter,1)
    IF IndString&Sub # " "
        ? IFileNm&Sub +":    ",IndString&Sub
    ENDIF
    Counter = Counter + 1
ENDDO
?
? "These data files used by PlusGen only: "
DO Proper WITH StruFile
DO Proper WITH ParamFile
?? StruFile + "  "
?? ParamFile
?
? "Batch file for copying generated system:",BatFile
? "This information is stored in: ",DocFile
?
DoComm = SUBSTR(ProgName,1,AT(".",ProgName)-1)
? "To run the generated system, use the command DO &DoComm "
```

Figure 11.40: The PlusGen7.PRG command file (continued)

```
? "at the dBASE dot prompt."
SET ALTERNATE OFF
CLOSE ALTERNATE
CLOSE DATABASES
CLOSE PROCEDURE
CLEAR ALL
ERASE ProgWrk.DBF
ERASE ProgHold.DBF

*-------------------- All done.
CANCEL
```

Figure 11.40:   The PlusGen7.PRG command file (continued)

optionally the check-for-duplicates program. For convenience, it also generates a DOS batch file for copying the generated system to drive A, and a small bit of documentation, as we discussed earlier in the chapter.

⊙LEARNING MORE ABOUT PLUSGEN

The PlusGen system is too large to describe every line in detail, so understanding every single routine will take some study. To make it easier to learn more about PlusGen, I suggest that you add the command

SAVE TO Thought

just above the CLEAR ALL command near the end of PlusGen7.PRG. This will store all the currently active memory variables in a file named Thought.MEM. Next, enter the command

RESTORE FROM Thought

to retrieve these memory variables, and type

SET PRINT ON
LIST MEMORY

to get a copy of these variables. Next USE the PlusGen.DBF database, and enter the LIST TO PRINT command to get a hard copy of the database. Then you can see where the variables, such as %%MainTitle, are substituted into the skeletal program.

Longer routines, such as %RepMenu, are generated by routines in the PlusGen6 and PlusGen7 command files. Viewing the memory variables will also help you see how these routines are generated. In addition, the Prm and Str databases are important. If you create a system with the abbreviation Mail, for example, enter the commands below (at the dot prompt) to see the contents of the databases involved:

```
SET PRINT ON
USE MailPrm
SET HEADING ON
DISPLAY STRUCTURE
LIST
EJECT
USE MailStr
LIST
EJECT
SET PRINT OFF
CLOSE DATABASES
```

Keep in mind that Mail is only the abbreviation for this example. If your abbreviation were Club, you would need to substitute the names ClubPrm and ClubStr in the commands above.

⊙TIPS ON USING THE PROGRAM GENERATOR

If you plan to use the program generator on a computer with two floppy disks, you'll need to juggle some disks around. I would suggest the following procedure. Copy the entire program generator to a blank formatted disk in drive B. (From the A> prompt, use the DOS command COPY PLUS∗.∗ B:.) Then, put your dBASE III PLUS disk in drive A, call up dBASE, and SET DEFAULT TO B. Next, create your database, screen files, reports, and additional command files. When that's done, enter the command DO PlusGen to have PlusGen generate a system.

When PlusGen is done (it will probably take five or ten minutes on a floppy disk), exit from dBASE to get back to the A> prompt. Remove the disk from drive B, and place it in drive A. Put a blank formatted disk in drive B, and execute the batch file to copy the generated system to drive B. (For example, if the abbreviated name for your system is MAIL, enter the command MAILCOPY at the A> prompt.) You might want to repeat this process to make two copies of your generated system.

Use the disk that has only the generated system on it for general work, but keep the disk with both PlusGen and the generated system for future modifications. If in the future you regenerate a system after adding data to the database, be sure not to overwrite the database containing data with the empty database on the PlusGen disk. Copy only the command files from the PlusGen disk onto your database disk, using your four-letter abbreviation and the .PRG extension, as below:

    COPY Mail∗.PRG B:

If you are using a hard-disk system, you can simply store everything on a single directory. Use data presented in the documentation file (e.g., Club-Doc.TXT) to help you move files around after generation.

I would strongly suggest practicing a bit with the PlusGen system before doing serious work with it. Generate your system, then use it to add a few records to the database. Try out all the options, and then decide if you want to make modifications. Make your modifications before adding a great deal of data to a database, and that way you won't lose much data should you make an error. And of course, keep backups of everything.

⊙CONCLUSION

I hope you find many of the procedures and systems we've developed throughout these chapters useful in your own work with dBASE III PLUS. I've used all the procedures and systems presented in this book at one time or another, and have found them to be very handy in a number of diverse applications. Keep disk copies of any routines you enter stored in a safe place. You never know when you'll need to use some old routine in a new application.

Once you have the routines on disk, you may occasionally need a quick reminder about command syntax, public variables, and so forth. You can refer to Appendix A, a complete summary of the procedure library. Then, if you need further information, turn back to the original discussion in the text.

SUMMARY OF PROCEDURES A

This appendix summarizes all the general-purpose procedures presented in this book. The procedures are categorized by the chapters in which they appear. After you've keyed in the procedures that you are likely to use in your own work, you can use this appendix as a quick-reference guide. Each summary includes the basic information needed to use the procedure, including the procedure name, parameters, public memory variables (if any), general syntax, and examples of use.

FINANCIAL PROCEDURES (CHAPTER 3)

Title: PAYMENT ON A LOAN

Procedure name: Pmt

Purpose: Calculates the payment on a loan.

Procedure file: FinProcs

Public memory variables: Pmt

Result stored in: Pmt

Parameters: Principal, Interest, Term

General syntax: DO Pmt WITH *Principal, Interest, Term*

Example: DO Pmt WITH 147000,.10/12,15*12

Remarks: All parameters are numeric, and can be memory variables in which data is stored. Calculates data on a monthly basis, so annual percentage rate (APR) should be divided by 12, and the term, if measured in years, multiplied by 12 (as in the example).

Title: FUTURE VALUE

Procedure name: FV

Purpose: Calculates future value.

Procedure file: FinProcs

Public memory variables: FV

Result stored in: FV

Parameters: Payment, Interest, Term

General syntax: DO FV WITH *Payment, Interest, Term*

Example: DO FV WITH 5000,.12/12,12*20

Remarks: All parameters are numeric, and can be memory variables in which data is stored. Calculates data on a monthly basis, so annual percentage rate (APR) should be divided by 12, and the term, if measured in years, multiplied by 12 (as in the example).

Title: PRESENT VALUE

Procedure name: PV

Purpose: Calculates present value.

Procedure file: FinProcs

Public memory variables: PV

Result stored in: PV

Parameters: Payment, Interest, Term

General syntax: DO PV WITH *Payment,Interest,Term*

Example: DO PV WITH 125,.125/12,2*12

Remarks: All parameters are numeric, and can be memory variables in which data is stored. Calculates data on a monthly basis, so annual percentage rate (APR) should be divided by 12, and the term, if measured in years, multiplied by 12 (as in the example).

Title: COMPOUND ANNUAL GROWTH RATE

Procedure name: Cagr

Purpose: Calculates compound annual growth rate.

Procedure file: FinProcs

Public memory variables: Cagr, Log 10

Result stored in: Cagr

Parameters: Present Value, Future Value, Years

General syntax: DO Cagr WITH *Present Value,Future Value,Years*

Example: DO Cagr WITH 5000, 10000, 15

Remarks: All parameters are numeric, and may be passed as memory variables. Determines interest rate necessary for current dollar amount (present value) to reach a goal (future value) within a specified time (years).

Title: LOGARITHM BASE 10

Procedure name: Log10

Purpose: Calculates logarithm base 10.

Procedure file: FinProcs

Public memory variables: Log10

Result stored in: Log10

Parameters: Number

General syntax: DO Log10 WITH *Number*

Example: DO Log10 WITH 128

Remarks: Item passed is numeric, and may be a number stored in a memory variable.

STATISTICAL PROCEDURES (CHAPTER 4)

Title: HIGHEST VALUE

Procedure name: Max

Purpose: Calculates highest value in a numeric field.

Procedure file: StatProc

Public memory variables: Max

Result stored in: Max

Parameters: Field name

General syntax: DO Max WITH *"FieldName"*

Example 1: DO Max WITH "Amount"

Example 2: DO Max WITH "Qty"

Remarks: FieldName is the name of the field being analyzed (must be numeric data). To analyze only a part of the database, you can use the MODIFY QUERY or SET FILTER commands to filter the database before calling the procedure with the DO command.

Title: LOWEST VALUE

Procedure name: Min

Purpose: Calculates lowest value in a numeric field.

Procedure file: StatProc

Public memory variables: Min

Result stored in: Min

Parameters: Field name

General syntax: DO Min WITH *"FieldName"*

Example 1: DO Min WITH "Amount"

Example 2: DO Min WITH "Qty"

Remarks: FieldName is the name of the field being analyzed (must be numeric data). To analyze only a part of the database, you can use the MODIFY QUERY or SET FILTER commands to filter the database before calling the procedure with the DO command.

Title: VARIANCE

Procedure name: Var

Purpose: Calculates variance of a numeric field.

Procedure file: StatProc

Public memory variables: Var

Result stored in: Var

Parameters: Field name

General syntax: DO Var WITH *"FieldName"*

Example 1: DO Var WITH "Amount"

Example 2: DO Var WITH "Qty"

Remarks: FieldName is the name of the field being analyzed (must be numeric data). To analyze only a part of the database, you can use the MODIFY QUERY or SET FILTER commands to filter the database before calling the procedure with the DO command.

Title: STANDARD DEVIATION

Procedure name: StD

Purpose: Calculates standard deviation of a numeric field.

Procedure file: StatProc

Public memory variables: StD

Result stored in: StD

Parameters: Field name

General syntax: DO StD WITH *"FieldName"*

Example 1: DO StD WITH "Amount"

Example 2: DO StD WITH "Qty"

Remarks: FieldName is the name of the field being analyzed (must be numeric data). To analyze only a part of the database, you can use the MODIFY QUERY or SET FILTER commands to filter the database before calling the procedure with the DO command.

Title: FREQUENCY DISTRIBUTION

Procedure name: FreDist

Purpose: Calculates and displays frequency distribution.

Procedure file: StatProc

Public memory variables: None

Result stored in: N/A

Parameters: Field Name

General syntax: DO FreqDist WITH *"FieldName"*

Example: DO FreqDist WITH "Zip"

Remarks: Parameter passed is the name of the field being used in the frequency distribution. In the example, a frequency distribution will be calculated and displayed for a field named Zip in the currently open database.

Title: PEARSON PRODUCT-MOMENT CORRELATION COEFFICIENT

Procedure name: Pearson

Purpose: Calculates Pearson Product-Moment Correlation Coeffecient.

Procedure file: StatProc

Public memory variables: Pearson

Result stored in: Pearson

Parameters: Column X, Column Y

General syntax: DO Pearson WITH *"Column X","Column Y"*

Example: DO Pearson WITH "Age","Score"

Remarks: Determines if there is a positive or negative correlation between two paired sets of numbers. Data passed are names of numeric fields in the currently open database. Result is returned in the public memory variable named Pearson.

GRAPHICS PROCEDURES (CHAPTER 5)

Title: DRAW A BAR

Procedure name: Bar

Purpose: Displays a bar of ASCII characters.

Procedure file: Graphics

Public memory variables: None

Result stored in: N/A

Parameters: ASCII Codes, Length

General syntax: DO Bar WITH *ASCII Code,Length*

Example: DO Bar WITH 10,80

Remarks: The ASCII Code parameter is a number between 0 and 255, representing an ASCII graphics character. The Length parameter is the number of columns long the bar should be. Bar is drawn starting at the current cursor position.

Title: DRAW A COLUMN

Procedure name: Column

Purpose: Displays a column of ASCII characters.

Procedure file: Graphics

Public memory variables: None

Result stored in: N/A

Parameters: ASCII Codes, Height

General syntax: DO Column WITH *ASCII Code,Height*

Example: DO Column WITH 10,80

Remarks: ASCII Code is a number between 0 and 255, representing an ASCII graphics character. Height is the number of rows high the bar should be. Column is drawn starting at the current cursor position.

Title: CENTER

Procedure name: Center

Purpose: Centers a character string on the screen or printer.

Procedure file: Graphics

Public memory variables: None

Result stored in: N/A

Parameters: String, Right Margin

General syntax: DO Center WITH *"String",Margin*

Example 1: DO Center WITH "Sample Title",80

Example 2: DO Center WITH RepTitle,RM

Remarks: String is either a literal character string enclosed in quotation marks (as in Example 1), or the name of a memory variable containing a character string (as in Example 2). The right margin is a number (80), or a numeric memory variable.

Title: KEY SYMBOLS

Procedure name: KeySigns

Purpose: Assigns special graphics characters to variable names, and makes them globally available.

Procedure file: Graphics

Public memory variables: Those listed below (assigned automatically)

Result stored in: Ret,Left,Right,Up,Down,Bullet,Solid,Degrees,Reverse, Blink,Standard

Parameters: None

General syntax: DO KeySigns

Example: DO KeySigns

Remarks: Resulting special symbols can be linked to character strings (e.g., Prompt = "Press " + Ret + "to continue") or as macros embedded in character strings (e.g., @ 10,10 SAY "Press &Ret to continue. . .").

Title: BAR GRAPH

Procedure name: BarGraph

Purpose: Draws a bar graph on the screen or the printer.

Procedure file: BarGraph

Public memory variables: None

Result stored in: N/A

Parameters: Graph Title, Columns, Column Width, Lowest, Highest

General syntax: DO BarGraph WITH *"Title", Columns, Width, Lowest, Highest*

Example 1: DO BarGraph WITH "Sample Graph",10,6,0,100

Example 2: DO BarGraph WITH GrafTitle, Cols,Col_Width,Low,High

Remarks: Data to be graphed must be preassigned to numeric variables Col1, Col2, Col3 and so on. Bar titles must be preassigned to character variables Title1, Title2,. . .TitleN. The Lowest and Highest variables are lowest and highest Y-axis values.

GENERAL-PURPOSE PROCEDURES (CHAPTER 6)

Title: CHECK FOR DUPLICATES

Procedure name: DupCheck

Purpose: Checks for duplicate records in a database.

Procedure file: GenProcs

Public memory variables: None

Result stored in: N/A

Parameters: Field Name

General syntax: DO DupCheck WITH *"FieldName(s)"*

Example 1: DO DupCheck WITH "Part_No"

Example 2: DO DupCheck WITH "STR(Zip,5) + Address + LName + FName"

Remarks: FieldName may be the name of a single field, or multiple fields from the currently open database. FieldName must be the same data type, or converted, as in Example 2 where the numeric Zip field is converted to a string.

Title: DELETE DUPLICATES

Procedure name: DupDel

Purpose: Marks duplicate records in a database for deletion.

Procedure file: GenProcs

Public memory variables: None

Result stored in: N/A

Parameters: Field Name

General syntax: DO DupDel WITH *"FieldName(s)"*

Example 1: DO DupDel WITH "Part_No"

Example 2: DO DupDel WITH "STR(Zip,5) + Address + LName + FName"

Remarks: FieldName can be the name of a single field, or multiple fields from the currently open database. FieldName must be the same data type, or converted, as in Example 2 where the numeric Zip field is converted to a string.

Title: FULL PROPER CASE

Procedure name: FullProp

Purpose: Converts the first letter of every word in a character string to uppercase, and all other characters to lowercase.

Procedure file: GenProcs

Public memory variables: None

Result stored in: Original variable name

Parameters: String

General syntax: DO FullProp WITH *Character Memory Variable*

Example: DO FullProp WITH M_LName

Remarks: Character string passed to the procedure must be stored in a memory variable.

Title: PROPER CASE

Procedure name: Proper

Purpose: Converts the first letter of a character string to uppercase, and all other characters to lowercase.

Procedure file: GenProcs

Public memory variables: None

Result stored in: Original variable name.

Parameters: String

General syntax: DO Proper WITH *Character Memory Variable*

Example: DO Proper WITH M_LName

Remarks: Character string passed to the procedure must be stored in a memory variable.

Title: WORDWRAP

Procedure name: WordWrap

Purpose: Displays long character strings within specified margins, breaking lines only between words. Counts and returns the number of lines printed.

Procedure file: GenProcs

Public memory variables: N/A

Result stored in: LF (line counter only)

Parameters: String, Left Margin, Right Margin, Line Counter

General syntax: DO WordWrap WITH *String,Left Margin,Right Margin,Line Counter*

Example: DO WordWrap WITH *Abstract,20,50,*LF

Remarks: In the example above, the character string Abstract must be stored in a memory variable, and LF must be a predefined numeric memory variable. The command will word wrap the contents of the Abstract variable within a left margin of 20, and a right margin of 50.

Title: TRANSLATE NUMBERS TO WORDS

Procedure name: TransLat

Purpose: Translates a number (1234.56) to words (ONE THOUSAND TWO HUNDRED THIRTY FOUR AND 56/100).

Procedure file: GenProcs

Public memory variables: Eng_Num

Result stored in: Eng_Num

Parameters: Amount

General syntax: DO TransLat WITH *Amount*

Example 1: DO TransLat WITH 1234.56

Example 2: DO TransLat WITH Payment

Remarks: Data passed must be a number (such as 999.99), or the name of a memory variable containing a number. Result is stored in a public memory variable named Eng_Num.

Title: TRANSLATE DATES TO ENGLISH

Procedure name: TransDat

Purpose: Translates MM/DD/YY date format to English format (for example, January 21, 1985).

Procedure file: GenProcs

Public memory variables: Eng_Date

Result stored in: Eng_Date

Parameters: Date

General syntax: DO TransDat WITH *Date*

Example 1: DO TransDat WITH DATE( )

Example 2: DO TransDat WITH CTOD("12/31/85")

Remarks: Date must be passed as Date data type, as in the examples. Result is stored as character data in the Eng_Date memory variable.

REPORTS AND FORMS (CHAPTER 8)

Title: COLUMNAR REPORT

Procedure name: ColRept

Purpose: Displays a field (or fields) from a database in an alphabetized columnar report similar to the format used in a telephone directory.

Procedure file: ColRept.PRG

Public memory variables: N/A

Result stored in: N/A

Parameters: Columns,Rows,Column Width,Field Name

General syntax: DO ColRept WITH *Cols,Rows,ColWidth,FieldName*

Example: DO ColRept WITH 3,55,30,"LName"

Remarks: In the example above, the LName field from the currently open database will be displayed, in alphabetical order per page, on a report with three columns across each page, 55 lines per page, with each column being 30 spaces wide.

MULTIPLE LINKED DATABASES (CHAPTER 9)

Title: MULTIPLE DATABASES

Procedure name: ThreeFil

Purpose: Opens three databases simultaneously, and keeps record pointer even across the three files. (Extends the dBASE III PLUS 128-field limit.)

Procedure file: ThreeDbs

Public memory variables: None

Result stored in: N/A

Parameters: Root Database Name, Index Files

General syntax: DO ThreeFil WITH *"Database","Indexes"*

Example: DO ThreeFil WITH *"BigFile","BigNames,BigCodes"*

Remarks: Though example in text demonstrates the use of three files open simultaneously, the procedure can be modified to use more or fewer files.

Title: ADD RECORDS TO LINKED FILES

Procedure name: AppBlank

Purpose: Appends a blank record across multiple linked files.

Procedure file: ThreeDbs

Public memory variables: None

Result stored in: N/A

Parameters: None

General syntax: DO AppBlank

Example: DO AppBlank

Remarks: Use in conjunction with the ThreeFil procedure to extend dBASE III PLUS's 128-field limit by as much as tenfold.

Title: DELETE RECORDS ACROSS LINKED FILES

Procedure name: DelAcross

Purpose: Marks the current record for deletion across multiple linked files.

Procedure file: ThreeDbs

Public memory variables: None

Result stored in: N/A

Parameters: None

General syntax: DO DelAcross

Example: DO DelAcross

Remarks: Use in conjunction with the ThreeFil procedure to extend dBASE III PLUS's 128-field limit by as much as tenfold.

Title: MULTIPLE-PAGE SCREENS

Procedure name: PgChange

Purpose: Allows scrolling through multiple custom screens associated with a large database.

Procedure file: ThreeFil

Public memory variables: lPage

Result stored in: lPage

Parameters: DBName, ToT_Pages

General syntax: DO PgChange WITH *"Database name"*,Pages

Example: DO PgChange WITH "Taxes",5

Remarks: Custom screens must have the extension ".P" followed by a page number. A maximum of 99 pages can be scrolled through.

Title: PACK RECORDS ACROSS LINKED FILES

Procedure name: PakAcross

Purpose: Permanently deletes records across multiple linked files.

Procedure file: ThreeDbs

Public memory variables: None

Result stored in: N/A

Parameters: None

General syntax: DO PakAcross

Example: DO PakAcross

Remarks: Use in conjunction with the ThreeFil procedure to extend dBASE III PLUS's 128-field limit by as much as tenfold.

dBASE III PLUS
COMPILERS

B

In this appendix we'll discuss *compilers,* which are primarily of interest to those who are either considering marketing the programs they create, or who need maximum speed and performance in their custom dBASE III PLUS systems. Compilers offer many advantages to the programmer who is considering marketing his or her software. Briefly, these advantages are:

- Better performance. Compiled dBASE programs run up to 20 times faster than dBASE command files (though in most applications, the speed increase will not be quite so dramatic).

- Stand-alone performance. Since a compiled program can be run directly from the DOS A> or C> prompt, a potential user need not own dBASE III PLUS. The compiled programs are completely independent.

- Program security. Since the compiled version of a dBASE command file contains only machine-language commands, unauthorized users cannot access the original dBASE program.

- More power. The compilers include additional commands and functions the original dBASE language does not offer. (However, they generally lack some dBASE commands as well, such as BROWSE and EDIT.)

At present, there are two compilers available for dBASE III PLUS. One is Clipper, manufactured by Nantucket Corporation in Culver City, CA. The other is Quicksilver, manufactured by WordTech Systems in Orinda, CA. We'll discuss each compiler in this appendix.

⊙HIGH- AND LOW-LEVEL LANGUAGES

Before we begin discussing the compilers, let's first discuss some of the basics of *assembly language, machine language,* and *compilation.*

A SAMPLE dBASE PROGRAM

Figure B.1 shows a dBASE III PLUS command file that can display all the ASCII characters, with a space between each, on the screen. The command file takes up about 215 bytes of disk space, and takes about 22 seconds to run. However, since you need to have dBASE readily available to run the program, the actual disk space required to run this program is closer to 451,275 bytes (or 440K).

```
*---------------------- ASCII.PRG
*---------------------- Display all ASCII codes.
SET TALK OFF
Counter = 0
DO WHILE Counter <= 255
   ?? STR(Counter,3),CHR(Counter)+" "
   Counter = Counter + 1
ENDDO (Counter = 0)
```

Figure B.1: dBASE program to display ASCII codes

A SAMPLE ASSEMBLY-LANGUAGE PROGRAM

Figure B.2 shows a program, written in assembly language, that also shows ASCII characters with blank spaces in between. The left column contains commands for the assembler, the middle column contains the assembly language proper (starting at the mov cx,100h command and ending at the int 20h command), and the lines preceded with semicolons are programmer comments. Even though the sample dBASE and assembly programs perform exactly the same task, they obviously look very different.

```
;---------------------- ASCII.ASM
;---------------------- Display all ASCII codes.
prog    segment          ;start of segment
        assume cs:prog   ;assume code segment
        mov cx,100h      ;start counter at 256 dec
        mov dl,0         ;start with 0 ASCII character
next:   mov ah,2         ;call DOS Output function
        int 21h          ;call to DOS function
        push dx          ;save last value in dx
        mov dl,20h       ;put in ASCII space
        int 21h          ;call DOS function
        pop dx           ;get back last dx value
        inc dl           ;next ASCII character
        loop next        ;repeat until done
        int 20h          ;return to DOS
prog    ends             ;end of segment
        end              ;end of assembly
```

Figure B.2: Assembly-language program to show ASCII characters

Before you can run the assembly-language program, you need to assemble it into machine language. The IBM ASM or MASM assemblers will take care of that process for you. Figure B.3 shows the assembly program after translation into machine language.

```
B90001
B200
B402
CD21
52
B220
CD21
5A
FEC2
E2F2
CD20
```

Figure B.3:   Machine-language program to show ASCII codes

The dBASE program must also be translated to machine language. The computer needs lots of help translating the English-like dBASE commands, and that extra help is provided by the dBASE III PLUS *interpreter*. The interpreter reads a single line from your dBASE program, checks it for errors, translates it to machine language, and then executes it. It repeats this process for every line in the command file. All these steps take time, and hence the program runs relatively slowly.

There are two very big advantages to the assembly-language version of the ASCII program, as opposed to the dBASE version. One advantage is that it uses only 21 bytes of disk space (as opposed to 451,275 in dBASE). The other is that it takes only about 1 second to run, as opposed to 22 seconds in dBASE. That's about 22 times faster using about 1/20,000th the disk space.

An assembled (machine language) program requires no overhead, and no translation. The computer (with the help of DOS) can read and execute the program immediately. You just type in the name of the program at the DOS A> or C> prompt, and the program runs.

A big disadvantage to assembly language, however, is that it is difficult to learn, read, and produce. While dBASE has many English-like commands, such as APPEND, EDIT, and UPDATE, assembly language has only very primitive commands like mov, int, push, and pop. Assembly language has no built-in commands for managing data files or even screen displays. To produce an assembly-language program to perform what dBASE does in a single command (like INDEX) could take days or even weeks.

So how do you gain the advantages of using assembly language, while avoiding the disadvantages? You use a compiler. A compiler takes your command file(s) and makes a copy that is, in essence, written in assembly language. Like all assembly-language programs, the compiled program can be run directly from the DOS prompt.

A compiled program is never quite as efficient as one that is actually written in assembly language. But, then again, it's much easier to write a program in dBASE and compile it (using two simple commands), then it is to write a program in assembly language. Therefore, the compiler acts as sort of a compromise between the convenience of a high-level language (like dBASE), and the efficiency of a low-level language (like assembly language).

THE IN-BETWEEN LANGUAGES

At the risk of digression, I might mention that there are many languages in between the high-level dBASE and low-level assembly language. Such languages do not generally offer an interpreter. You write your program using a text editor (like WordStar), and then you must compile it to run it, even the first time. Furthermore, these languages generally don't offer the high-level file- and screen-handling features of dBASE, like INDEX, @, SET FILTER, and so forth. You have to write such routines yourself, or purchase them from somebody who has already taken the time to do so.

The mid-level languages have the (perhaps familiar) names C, Pascal, CB86, CBASIC, COBOL, FORTRAN..., on and on. (In fact, there are some 250 documented programming languages floating about.)

Languages that are designed to be compiled generally compile and run more efficiently. For example, a sample program to display all the ASCII characters, written in Turbo Pascal, is shown in Figure B.4.

```
program PrintASCII;
{Print the characters for all the ASCII codes, 0 to 255.}
var i : integer;
begin
  for i := 0 to 255 do
    Write(i,' ',Chr(i),' ');
end.
```

Figure B.4:   Turbo Pascal version of the ASCII program

When compiled, this program takes up 8,074 bytes of disk space (about 8K), and about three seconds to run. The same program, written in C, would probably run faster and require less disk space (depending on the particular compiler used).

So now, why so many languages? Well, different languages are good for different things. Assembly language is especially well suited for writing real-time software to control external machines that require critical timing.

The C language is generally used for writing operating systems (like UNIX), compilers, spreadsheets, word processors, and database-management systems (dBASE is written in C). Languages like Pascal are also good for word processors and database managers, but are high-level enough to write applications software like general ledger and payroll systems. Database managers, like dBASE, are specifically designed for writing business applications software.

Another class of languages is designed for artificial intelligence applications. LISP and PROLOG fall into this category, and are used for expert systems and other programs that mimic human thinking and learning. LISP is an acronym for LISt Processor, and PROLOG an acronym for PROgramming in LOGic. Most versions of LISP are interpretive (like dBASE). Turbo PROLOG, by Borland, is compilable.

Of course, there is considerable overlap in the uses of the languages, but suffice it to say that you would probably not write a payroll system in C or assembly language. The long development time would not justify the quicker run-time speed. Clearly one pays a price for convenience in a language. Table B.1 shows the speed and size requirements of the ASCII character display program we've discussed using four languages: dBASE III PLUS, dBASE III PLUS compiled with Clipper, Turbo Pascal, and assembly language. (These are all based on performance on an IBM XT.) As you can see, going "down the ladder" from a very high-level language (dBASE) to a very low-level language (assembly) dramatically affects processing speed and storage requirements.

But enough digression. Now that we have an idea about high- and low-level languages, and what compilers are all about, let's get down to more specifics about using dBASE III PLUS with a compiler.

Language	Speed (in seconds)	File Size (in bytes)
dBASE III PLUS	22	440,000
dBASE compiled	10	127,872
Turbo Pascal	3	11,511
Assembly	1	21

Table B.1:   Comparison of dBASE III PLUS, compiled, Pascal, and assembly-language programs

⊙THE CLIPPER COMPILER

The Clipper compiler allows you to compile any command file, or group of command files, from the dBASE .PRG to the DOS .EXE executable format. Because Clipper is a true *native code* compiler (which means it generates .EXE files that require no further interpretation), significant increases in speed are virtually guaranteed. (The last section in this appendix provides examples of performance improvements.)

To compile a program with Clipper, you need to enter two commands at the DOS prompt. First, to compile a program named Test1.PRG, you would enter the command

CLIP Test1

The second step is to link the compiled program using the command

PLINK86 FILE Test1

You can compile and link groups of command files, procedure files, and *user-defined functions* into a single large file. (A user-defined function is similar to a normal dBASE function such as TRIM() or RECNO(), except you create and define it yourself.)

At the time this book was written, the Autumn 1986 version of Clipper was not quite ready for review. Therefore, you might want to check with Nantucket Corporation for the latest information on its features before making a purchase. However, information released by Nantucket indicates that the Autumn 1986 version will not be copy protected (unlike previous releases), will support networking, and will also make for use of expanded memory following the Lotus/Intel/Microsoft specification. Some of the features in the Autumn 1986 version are included in this discussion.

CLIPPER ENHANCEMENTS

Clipper provides more flexibility than dBASE III PLUS in several respects. Clipper allows up to 2,048 memory variables, 1,024 fields per record, and up to eight children to one parent in a SET RELATION definition (as opposed to one in dBASE). Clipper also provides the capability to add custom help screens the user can access by pressing F1.

Clipper enables you to store Memo fields in memory variables, which means you can search and manipulate the memo field. Clipper provides liberal use of macros, including macros as conditions in DO WHILE loops, and recursive macros. Macros cannot be used in place of commands (like USE, LIST, DISPLAY, and so forth).

User-defined functions provide more flexibility than procedures. For example, in Chapter 3 we created some business procedures that could accept parameters such as

    DO Pmt WITH (150000,.16/12,30*12)

In Clipper, you can easily change the procedure into a user-defined function, and treat it as you would any other function using the syntax

    Payment = PMT(15000,.16/12,30*12)

or

    ? PMT(15000,.16/12,30*12)

During editing on a screen, Clipper allows the user to press ^U to undo a change. For example, if during editing the user changes the part number A-111 to Z-999, typing ^U immediately converts the part number back to A-111.

Clipper can call assembly-language subroutines with up to seven parameters (as opposed to one in dBASE). Clipper can save and restore screens displayed with @ SAY commands, so that they "pop up" on the screen instantly.

The Clipper DECLARE statement allows you to use true arrays (subscripted variables) in your programs. For example, you could use the array

    DECLARE Day[7]
    Day[1] = "Sunday"
    Day[2] = "Monday"
    Day[3] = "Tuesday"
    Day[4] = "Wednesday"
    Day[5] = "Thursday"
    Day[6] = "Friday"
    Day[7] = "Saturday"

Once an array is declared, you can use numbers to access the array elements. For example

    ? Day[3]

displays "Tuesday". If variable XYZ = 7, then the command

? DAY[XYZ]

displays Saturday. An array can contain up to 2,048 elements.

CLIPPER FUNCTIONS

All the dBASE III PLUS functions are supported by Clipper, though some are supported through an external file you must link into your compiled program. (This is easily achieved.) Some additional functions that are unique to Clipper are listed below.

ALIAS()	Returns the alias assigned to a SELECT work area.
ALLTRIM()	Trims both leading and trailing blanks from a character string.
AMPM()	Displays time based on a 12-hour clock with "am" or "pm".
INDEXKEY()	Returns the key expression of an index file.
DAYS()	Calculates days based upon a number of seconds.
DTOS()	Converts a date to yyyymmdd format as a character string (e.g., 19861201). This is very useful for combining dates and character strings in index files.
ELAPTIME()	Calculates elapsed time between two times.
EMPTY()	Returns True (.T.) if a variable or expression is blank.
FCOUNT()	Returns the number of fields in the selected database.
LENNUM()	Returns the length of a number.
PCOUNT()	Returns the number of parameters passed.
PROCLINE()	Returns the line number of the current program or procedure file.
PROCNAME()	Returns the name of the current program or procedure file.
SECS()	Returns the number of seconds in a time string.
SETPRC()	Sets internal printer row and column positions to specific values.

SOUNDEX()	Returns the Soundex code for a word that helps find data of similar sound, but different spelling.
STRZERO()	Creates the string equivalent of a number with leading zeros rather than leading blanks.
TSTRING()	Converts seconds to a time string.
UPDATED()	Returns True if a value was changed during a READ command.

NETWORKING COMMANDS AND FUNCTIONS

The Autumn 1986 version of Clipper promises to offer several networking commands and functions. These are summarized below:

SET EXCLUSIVE ON/OFF	Controls access to an open database.
USE *File Name* EXCLUSIVE	Controls access to an open database file.
RLOCK()	Locks a record to prevent changes being made by other users.
FLOCK()	Locks a file to prevent changes being made by other users.
NETERR()	Returns information about the success of the APPEND BLANK and USE EXCLUSIVE commands on a network.
SET PRINTER TO	Directs the printer output to a device or a print file.
UNLOCK [ALL]	Releases the file or record lock in a SELECT area. The ALL option releases all current locks in all work areas.

UNSUPPORTED dBASE COMMANDS

Table B.2 shows the dBASE commands not supported by Clipper. Keep in mind that some of this information is likely to change with future releases of Clipper. As we'll discuss in a moment, most of the listed commands are excluded because they are virtually useless in a compiled program.

APPEND[a]	ON *Key, Escape, Error*
ASSIST	RELEASE MODULE
BROWSE	RETRY
CHANGE	RETURN TO MASTER
CREATE *File Name*[b]	SET
CLEAR FIELDS	SET CARRY
CLEAR TYPEAHEAD	SET DATE
CREATE/MODIFY LABEL	SET DEBUG
CREATE/MODIFY QUERY	SET DOHISTORY
CREATE/MODIFY REPORT	SET ECHO
CREATE/MODIFY SCREEN	SET FIELDS
CREATE/MODIFY VIEW	SET HEADING
DISPLAY/LIST HISTORY	SET HELP
DISPLAY/LIST FILES	SET HISTORY
DISPLAY/LIST MEMORY	SET MEMOWIDTH
DISPLAY/LIST STATUS	SET MENUS
DISPLAY/LIST STRUCTURE	SET ORDER
EDIT	SET SAFETY
EXPORT	SET STATUS
HELP	SET STEP
IMPORT	SET TITLE
INSERT	SET TYPEAHEAD
LOAD	SET VIEW
MODIFY COMMAND	SET TALK
MODIFY STRUCTURE	SUSPEND

[a] APPEND FROM and APPEND BLANK are supported.
[b] CREATE *New file* FROM *Old File* is supported.

Table B.2:   dBASE commands not supported by Clipper

Debugging Commands

The dBASE III PLUS debugging commands (such as SET ECHO and SET DEBUG) are not supported by Clipper for two reasons. First, you don't want to compile a program until it is fully tested and debugged. (If it didn't work in dBASE III, it isn't gonna work in Clipper either.) Secondly, Clipper has its own debugger to help you debug compiled programs.

Create/Modify Commands

Generally, you create and modify database files, format files, report formats, and label formats while you are creating your custom system. Rarely do you include a CREATE or MODIFY command in your finished custom system.

Keep in mind that Clipper does support the DO, REPORT FORM, LABEL FORM, SET FORMAT, and USE commands, so that the compiled program can access previously created command, report, mailing label, format, and database files. In addition, Clipper provides utilities that allow you to create the various format files, and therefore you need not even use dBASE III PLUS to create them.

Full-Screen Operations

Commands like APPEND, EDIT, BROWSE, and INSERT are not supported, partly because most systems use custom screens rather than standard dBASE screens. You can use SET FORMAT and READ instead to provide editing capabilities to the user.

Index Files

Clipper creates its own index files with the extension .NTX. After creating your database, you can run a special Clipper utility to create index files directly from the DOS prompt. Also, if a command file contains an INDEX ON command, Clipper creates the .NTX index file rather than the dBASE .NDX index file.

PUBLIC CLIPPER

Now you may be wondering how you go about working with dBASE programs that contain features that are unique to Clipper. A simple and elegant solution to this problem is the PUBLIC Clipper command. You can place the command

PUBLIC Clipper

near the top of any command file. dBASE will create the variable "Clipper", assigning it the value "False" (.F.). (dBASE always initializes public memory variables as false.) Then, you can place Clipper-specific commands inside IF statements. For example, since dBASE uses .NDX for index file names, and Clipper uses .NTX, you could enter a routine as below:

```
PUBLIC Clipper

IF Clipper
    USE MyFile INDEX MyFile.NTX
ELSE
    USE MyFile INDEX MyFile.NDX
ENDIF
```

dBASE III PLUS will use the .NDX file.

Unlike dBASE III PLUS, Clipper always sets the PUBLIC Clipper variable to True (.T.) when it first encounters it. (It does this *only* with the variable specifically named "Clipper".) Therefore, the compiled version of the routine uses the .NTX index file.

⊙THE QUICKSILVER COMPILER

The Quicksilver compiler, manufactured by WordTech systems, was released in the summer of 1986. This latest version, Quicksilver 1.0, of the original dBIII compiler is a true native code compiler that converts dBASE programs into DOS-executable **.EXE** files. Quicksilver offers several unique features to dBASE programmers, the most impressive of which is probably its "windows," which we'll discuss later.

Quicksilver comes with several optional linkers that allow you to be specific about the type of machine the compiled program will run on. You can select among PC-DOS machines (IBM PC and 100-percent compatible), and MS-DOS machines (will run on any MS-DOS machine, including the IBM PC). There is also an option that allows the compiled program to use both dBASE II and dBASE III data.

Full compilation is a three-step process. For example, to compile a program named Test1.PRG, you enter the command

```
dB3C Test1.PRG
```

Then, to link the compiled file into a DOS-executable .EXE file you enter the command

```
dB3L Test1
```

To maximize the performance of the final compiled program and link it, you can use a single command with the flag -f (for fastest exeuction), -l (for link). For example, if linking the Test1 program you would enter

QS -f -l Test1

QUICKSILVER ENHANCEMENTS

Quicksilver offers several general features that are not available in dBASE III PLUS. One is the command SET DEVICE TO ALTERNATE. This allows a program to store text printed with @ SAY commands on a file. (dBASE III PLUS allows @ SAY commands to be displayed only on the screen or printer.) Similarly, the SET FEED command allows the programmer to control page ejects sent to the printer from @ SAY commands.

The SET DBF and SET NDX commands allow you to specify drives and directories for database files and index files. Programs and other files can exist on a separate drive or directory.

For more advanced programmers, the BITSET, IN, OUT, and DOSINT commands provide control over "low-level" functions, such as the speaker or an external port. BITSET returns a "True" if the bit at a specified position is set on. IN returns a single numeric value from a specified port. OUT sends a single value to the specified port. DOSINT allows data to be sent to, and read from, DOS interrupt vectors.

NETWORKING

Quicksilver offers complete networking and file-sharing capabilities. The commands and functions used in Quicksilver networking are summarized below.

FLOCK()	Locks a database file and returns a .T. or .F. value indicating the status of the lock.
RESTORE FROM EXCLUSIVE	Recalls memory variables from disk but prevents other users from changing memory variables until they are placed back on disk with the SAVE command.
RETRY	Returns control to the first line of a program in which an error occurred.

LOCK() (or RLOCK())	Locks a specific record in a database and returns a .T. or .F. about the status of the lock.
SET AUTOLOCK	When AUTOLOCK is set on, file and record locking are handled automatically by the networker.
SET DELAY	Sets a time, from 0 to 21,540 seconds, that specifies how long the automatic networker will wait before attempting to reaccess a locked file.
SET EXCLUSIVE	When EXCLUSIVE is off, all files are opened and shared on a network. With exclusive ON, all files are opened in a locked state.
SET INDEX...SHARED	Activates an index file so that two or more network users can use the index simultaneously.
SET LASTLOCAL	Allows each workstation in a network to define which drive designators are local (physically attached to the workstation), and which reside on the network file server.
SET MULTIUSER	When set to OFF, the MULTIUSER option suspends the operation of the networker and ignores attempts to lock files or records.
SET RETRY	Determines the number of times (from 0 to 65535) that the networker will retry an unsuccessful attempt to lock a record or file.
UNLOCK	Releases the file or record lock in a SELECT area. The ALL option releases all current locks in all work areas.
USE *File* EXCLUSIVE	When EXCLUSIVE is determined in the USE command, the file is opened and access limited to the current user.

USERNO()   Returns the current workstation's number assignment.

WINDOWS

Words can hardly describe the windowing capability that Quicksilver offers. Unlike simple boxes drawn on screens, Quicksilver offers true windows that can display several different activities simultaneously on different parts of the screen.

Windows allow you to develop quick pop-up menus and help screens that can temporarily obscure data to provide information, then instantly disappear to return full view of the data. You can also determine any colors and shapes you want for your windows, and even move the windows very quickly about the screen.

Again, words can hardly describe the visual impact that windows can add to a custom application. The Quicksilver compiler comes with a program named Demonat, which really demonstrates what windows can do. If you should decide to purchase Quicksilver, be sure to run the Demonat program.

QUICKSILVER FUNCTIONS

Quicksilver supports most dBASE III PLUS functions, and also, like Clipper, lets you create your own user-defined functions. QuickSilver offers a few of its own functions as well, as summarized below.

CEIL()   Returns the smallest integer greater than or equal to the entered value.

FLOOR()   Returns the largest integer less than or equal to the entered value.

LOG10()   Returns the logarithm base 10 of the argument.

SINKEY()   Like INKEY(), this function can capture any keypress, but SINKEY returns the character representation, rather than the ASCII code, of the key pressed.

ENVIRONMENTAL VARIABLES

Quicksilver offers several environmental variables, which are arguments passed from the command line used to start a program into the executing program. You can pass up to 30 variables in this fashion, named XARG01 through XARG30.

In addition to the 30 arguments you can define yourself, Quicksilver automatically initializes eight other environmental variables, which are summarized below.

XARGC	Provides count of passed arguments.
XCOMMANDLN	Lists arguments specified on the command line.
XPRINTON	Provides status of printer when compiled program was loaded into RAM.
XPRINTBUSY	Returns .T. if printer was off-line or in use when compiled program was loaded into RAM.
XCOLOR	Returns .T. if a color monitor is in use; otherwise returns .F.
XDRIVE	Contains a character representing the current default drive.
XCURRDRV	Contains both the current default drive and directory when the program was loaded into RAM.
XARG00	Provides name of the command used to load the current program into RAM (actually, the name of the program itself).

COMMANDS NOT SUPPORTED BY QUICKSILVER

Like the Clipper compiler, Quicksilver does not support interactive (dot prompt) commands or debugging aids. (Quicksilver also has its own debugger.) Commands not supported by Quicksilver are listed in Table B.3.

The reasons for the exclusion of all these commands are discussed in the section on Clipper in this appendix.

QUICKSILVER INDEX FILES

Index files created and maintained in dBASE III PLUS are completely compatible with Quicksilver index files, and vice versa.

THE *\ COMMENT

To keep dBASE III PLUS from attempting to execute a Quicksilver-compiler-specific command, simply precede the command line with the

APPEND[a]	ON *Key, Escape, Error*
ASSIST	RELEASE MODULE
BROWSE	RETRY
CHANGE	SET
CREATE[b]	SET CARRY
CLEAR FIELDS	SET DATE
CREATE/MODIFY LABEL	SET DEBUG
CREATE/MODIFY QUERY	SET DOHISTORY
CREATE/MODIFY REPORT	SET ECHO
CREATE/MODIFY SCREEN	SET FIELDS
CREATE/MODIFY VIEW	SET HEADING
DIR	SET HELP
DISPLAY/LIST HISTORY	SET HISTORY
DISPLAY/LIST FILES	SET MEMOWIDTH
DISPLAY/LIST STATUS	SET MENUS
EDIT	SET ORDER
EXPORT	SET SAFETY
HELP	SET STATUS
IMPORT	SET STEP
INSERT	SET TITLE
LOAD	SET TYPEAHEAD
MODIFY COMMAND	SET VIEW
MODIFY STRUCTURE	SET TALK
	SUSPEND

[a] APPEND FROM and APPEND BLANK are supported.
[b] CREATE *New File* FROM *Old File* is supported.

Table B.3:   dBASE commands not supported by Quicksilver

characters *\. dBASE will treat the line as a comment; Quicksilver will ignore the *\ characters and compile the line. For example:

*\ SET DEVICE TO ALTERNATE

SET ALTERNATE TO AltFile

SET ALTERNATE ON

dBASE III PLUS will ignore the "illegal" SET DEVICE TO ALTERNATE command.

MACRO RESTRICTIONS

Macros can be used in place of all file names, and as conditions in DO WHILE loops. Keywords and commands cannot be stored in macros. For example, the sequence

Mac = "ON"

SET FLASH &MAC

is not allowed.

⊙PERFORMANCE COMPARISONS

Compiling a custom system does not guarantee that the entire system is suddenly going to run at the speed of light. Keep in mind that a compiler basically just preinterprets your command files and stores these already interpreted commands in a separate file. It does not make the "physical" attachments to the basic computer move any quicker.

When you compile a program, you can expect major speed improvements in routines that do not access the screen, printer, or disk. (That's because these external devices won't slow down the execution speed.) dBASE III PLUS commands that in themselves manage data already in RAM (like SEEK and FIND) are likely to show no apparent improvement in performance when compiled. (Arguably, 0.8 seconds is 20 percent faster than 1.0 second, but few people are going to notice the 0.2-second difference.)

Processes that are heavily disk bound, such as a LOCATE command, will not likely show a major increase in performance. That's because most of the time spent in a LOCATE command goes to physically searching the disk for data. The compiled program cannot speed up the physical movement of the disk drive.

To demonstrate the effect of the compilers, we compiled and tested four different programs. The first, named Test1.PRG, is shown in Figure B.5. This program simply displays a starting time, repeats a loop 1,000 times, and displays the time when done. Since it does not access the screen or disk, its speed will be most improved when compiled.

```
************************************* Test1.PRG
*---- Program that accesses no external devices.

SET TALK OFF
? TIME( )

Counter = 1
DO WHILE Counter <= 1000
   Counter = Counter + 1
ENDDO

? TIME( )
```

Figure B.5:   The Test1.PRG command file

The second program, Test2.PRG, also repeats a loop 1,000 times, but displays a number on the screen each time through the loop. In this case, the screen slows down the brute-force execution of the compiled program, so the performance improvement is not as dramatic as for Test1.PRG. (Obviously, a printer would slow things down even more.) Test2.PRG is shown in Figure B.6.

```
************************************* Test2.PRG
*-------- Program that accesses only the screen.
SET TALK OFF
StartTime = TIME( )

Counter = 1
DO WHILE Counter <= 1000
   ? Counter
   Counter = Counter + 1
ENDDO

? StartTime
? TIME( )
```

Figure B.6:   The Test2.PRG command file

The third program, Test3.PRG, attempts to LOCATE the last name Smith in an unindexed database named CTest.DBF. (In this example, Smith was stored at the 1,000th record.) Since the primary job of this program is to search the disk for a particular piece of information, we'd expect little speed improvement when compiled. Test3.PRG is shown in Figure B.7.

```
********************************* Test3.PRG
*-------- Program that is heavily disk bound.
SET TALK OFF
? TIME()

*-------- Locate the 1,000th record.
USE CTest
LOCATE FOR LName = "Smith"
? RECNO()

? TIME()
```

Figure B.7:   The Test3.PRG command file

Test4.PRG, shown in Figure B.8, accesses both the screen and disk through a LIST command. The effect of the compiler on the speed of this program is an "averaging" of the Test2 and Test3 programs.

The actual processing times on an IBM AT 339 with an 8 MHz clock, 1.5 megabytes of RAM, and a 30-megabyte hard disk drive are shown in Table B.4. (These processing times will differ on other computers.) Keep in mind that the winter 1985 version of Clipper was used for comparisons because the Autumn 1986 version was not available for testing. Processing times on the later version of Clipper may be slightly different.

```
************************************ Test4.PRG
*-------- Program that is disk and screen bound.
SET TALK OFF
StartTime = TIME()

*-------- Show 1,000 records on the screen.
USE CTest
LIST LName, FName, Company, Address

? StartTime
? TIME()
```

Figure B.8:   The Test4.PRG command file

	Test 1	Test 2	Test 3	Test 4	
dBASE III PLUS	13	34	3	53	Seconds
	256+	256+	256+	256+	Bytes
Clipper	2	16	3	35	Seconds
Compiled	126,944	126,992	127,024	127,056	Bytes
QuickSilver	3	19	3	31	Seconds
Compiled	119,520	119,584	112,096	119,632	Bytes

Table B.4:   Comparison of source and compiled code

The sizes of the files are also shown in Table B.2. For the dBASE III PLUS row, you need to add 440K if dBASE III PLUS is used to run the program.

As would be expected, Test1.PRG shows the most significant improvement when compiled. The 13-second dBASE program was reduced to 3 seconds with Quicksilver, and a slim 2 seconds with Clipper.

The screen accessing (with the ? command) in Test2.PRG slows down all three versions as expected. However both the Clipper- and Quicksilver-compiled versions are definitely faster than the dBASE III PLUS version; more than twice as fast with Clipper.

The Test3.PRG program, which used the LOCATE command to locate the thousandth record on the database, ran at the same speed regardless of whether it was compiled. The strong ties between the physical speed of the disk drive overpowered any improvement in speed the compiler might have offered.

Test4.PRG, which accesses both the disk and screen, was improved when compiled with Clipper (35 seconds vs. 53 seconds), and improved even more by Quicksilver (31 seconds).

⊙ COMPILING THE PROCEDURES IN THIS BOOK

Most of the procedures in this book are readily compilable with both the Quicksilver and Clipper compilers, though some may require minor modifications. Generally speaking, you never actually compile a procedure file. Instead, you just compile the main program that includes the SET PROCEDURE TO command for the appropriate procedure file. The compiler will then be sure to include a copy of the compiled procedure file in the final .EXE file.

To give you an idea of the performance improvements the compilers can offer with some of the larger procedures and programs in this book, I'll list a few examples. These performance times were all measured on on IBM AT 339 with an 8 MHz clock.

The uncompiled EzGraf.PRG command file took about 16 seconds to display a graph with 12 bars on the screen. When compiled, it took 2 seconds to display the same graph. The Debug.PRG command file took about 20 seconds to debug the TestDbug.PRG command file shown in Chapter 10. When compiled, the program did the same job in about 6 seconds.

In Chapter 11, the uncompiled PlusGen program generator required about 98 seconds to generate the Club application shown in that chapter. After compilation, PlusGen was able to generate the same application in about 42 seconds. (On a RAM disk, the compiled PlusGen program created the Club application in about 30 seconds.)

dBASE III PLUS
VOCABULARY

Command	**Definition**
!	Converts character to uppercase in @. . . SAY. . . GET commands (@ 5, 5 GET Answer PICTURE "!").
#	Not equal to. Also used in templates of @. . . SAY. . . GET statements to allow entry of only numbers, blanks, and symbols.
$	Substring function, used for finding a character string embedded within a larger character string (LIST FOR 'Lemon' $ADDRESS). In @. . .SAY statements, $ displays dollar signs in place of leading zeros.
&	Used as a prefix on a name to declare that name as a macro function instead of as a literal.
()	Used for logical and mathematical grouping [?(10 + 10)*5].
*	Multiplies numbers (? 10*10), or acts as a wild card in a DIR command. As a template symbol in @. . .SAY statements, * displays asterisks in place of leading zeros.
**	Exponent symbol. ? 99**2 displays 99 squared. X = 1234**(1/3) stores the cube root of 1234 to memory variable X.
;	Splits long command lines into separate lines.
^	Exponent symbol. ? 34^5 displays 34 raised to the fifth power (45435424.00). In text, the ^ symbol usually means "hold down the Control key."
+	Adds numbers or links character strings.
−	Subtracts numbers or links character strings with trailing blanks removed.
.AND.	Tests whether two things are true simultaneously (LIST FOR 'Oak' $ADDRESS .AND. City = 'San Diego').
.NOT.	Tests whether a condition is not true (DO WHILE .NOT. EOF).

Command	Definition
.OR.	Tests whether one or another of two conditions is true (LIST FOR City = 'San Diego' .OR. City = 'Los Angeles').
/	Divides two numbers (? 10/5).
<	Less than (LIST FOR LName < 'Smith').
< =	Less than or equal to (LIST FOR LName < = 'Smith').
=	Equal to (LIST FOR LName = 'Smith').
>	Greater than (LIST FOR LName > 'Appleby').
> =	Greater than or equal to [LIST FOR Date > = CTOD("03/01/86")].
?	Moves to the beginning of a new line and displays the contents of a field, memory variable, or the results of a mathematical equation (? 1 + 1).
??	Displays the contents of a field, memory variable, or expression at the current cursor position [?? SQRT(X)].
@	Displays information in specified format on screen or printer (@ 5,1 SAY 'Hi').
ABS	Returns the absolute value of a number [? ABS(− 234) displays 234].
ACCEPT	Displays a prompt on the screen and waits for a response. Stores answer in a memory variable as character data (ACCEPT 'Do you want more?' TO Y/N).
ALIAS	Allows a database to be accessed through two different names (USE Mail ALIAS Names).
ALL	Refers to all records in the database (DISPLAY ALL, DELETE ALL, REPLACE ALL).
APPEND	Adds new records of data to the end of the currently open database.
APPEND BLANK	Adds a new record to the bottom of a database, with all fields blank.

Command	Definition
APPEND FROM	Reads the records from another database and adds them to the bottom of the database in use (APPEND FROM Temp). If the source file is not a dBASE III or dBASE III PLUS file, use the SDF or DELIMITED options with APPEND FROM to import the database.
ASC	Displays the ASCII value of a character [? ASC("A") displays 65].
ASSIST	Activates the menu-driven interface to access dBASE III PLUS.
AT	Shows the position at which one character string starts in another [? AT("B","AABBCC") displays 3 because B appears as the third character in "AABBCC"].
AVERAGE	Computes the average of a Numeric field in a database [AVERAGE AMOUNT FOR MONTH (Date) = 12].
B:	Signifies drive B for storing data files (CREATE B:Mail).
B–>	Refers to a field from a database open in work area 2 (or B) with the SELECT command. C–> refers to a field open in work area 3 or C, and so forth (LIST Code, B–>Title,Qty, Amount).
BOF()	Function that determines whether the beginning of the file has been reached. Opposite of EOF() [? BOF()].
BROWSE	Displays a "screenful" of the database and allows you to scan and make changes to the database.
/C	Used with the SORT command to ignore upper-/lowercase in a sort (SORT ON LName/C, FName/C TO Temp).
CALL	Executes an assembly-language program (binary file) that has been placed into memory with the LOAD command.

Command	Definition
CANCEL	Aborts command file execution and returns to the dot prompt.
CDOW()	Displays the day of the week as a character (Sunday, Monday, etc.) for a Date field or memory variable [? CDOW(Date)].
CHANGE	Same as EDIT command.
CHR()	Displays the ASCII character for a number [? CHR(65) displays "A", ? CHR(7) rings the bell].
CLEAR	Clears the screen and repositions the cursor to the upper-left corner.
CLEAR ALL	Closes all database, index, format, and relational databases. Undoes all SELECT commands. Frees all memory used by memory variables.
CLEAR FIELDS	Releases all fields from all work areas originally set with the SET FIELDS command.
CLEAR GETS	Releases GET variables from READ access.
CLEAR MEMORY	Erases all current memory variables.
CLEAR TYPEAHEAD	Empties the typeahead buffer so that old keypresses do not affect current prompts.
CLOSE	Closes open files, of either alternate, database, format, index, or procedure types (CLOSE DATABASES).
CMONTH()	Displays the month for a Date field or memory variable as a Character string (e.g., January) [? CMONTH(Date)].
COL()	Returns the current column position of the cursor [? COL()].
COMMAND	Indicates a command or text file (MODIFY COMMAND Menu).
CONTINUE	Used with the LOCATE command to find the next record with a particular characteristic specified by the LOCATE command.

Command	Definition
COPY	Copies the contents of one database into another database, including any associated Memo fields.
COPY FILE	Copies a file to another file (COPY FILE MyProg.PRG TO MyProg.BAK).
COPY STRUCTURE	Copies the structure of a database to another database without copying the contents (COPY STRUCTURE TO Mail2).
COUNT	Counts how many records in a database meet some criterion [COUNT FOR MONTH(Date) = 12 TO December].
CREATE	Allows you to create a database and define its structure (CREATE Mail).
CREATE LABEL	Creates a format file for mailing labels (same as MODIFY LABEL) (CREATE LABEL B:TwoCol).
CREATE REPORT	Creates a custom report format (same as MODIFY REPORT) (CREATE REPORT ByName).
CREATE QUERY	Creates a query form and allows the user to fill in a query.
CREATE SCREEN	Accesses the screen painter for creating custom forms.
CREATE VIEW	Creates an editable and displayable screen, pulling together data from several linked databases.
CTOD()	Converts a date stored as a character string ("01/01/86") to a Date data type [LIST FOR Date = CTOD("01/01/86")].
/D	Used with SORT to sort in descending order (largest to smallest) (SORT ON Zip/D TO Temp).
DATE()	Displays dBASE internal date [? DATE()].
DAY()	Displays the day of the month for a Date data type as a number [? DAY(Date)].
DBF()	Returns the name of the database file currently in use [? DBF()].

Command	Definition
DELETE	Marks a record for deletion (DELETE RECORD 7).
DELETED()	Evaluates to True if record is marked for deletion [LIST FOR DELETED()].
DELIMITED	Copies dBASE databases to other data file formats (COPY TO MM.TXT. DELIMITED).
DIR	Shows files on disk (DIR B:*.PRG displays command file names on drive B).
DISKSPACE()	Returns the amount of space available, in bytes, on the currently logged disk drive [IF DISKSPACE( ) < 200].
DISPLAY	Shows information about a database or its contents (DISPLAY ALL, DISPLAY STRUCTURE).
DISPLAY HISTORY	Displays the last 20 commands typed in at the dot prompt.
DISPLAY MEMORY	Displays the name, type, size, and status of all current memory variables.
DISPLAY STATUS	Displays the current status of databases and index files in use, SET parameters, and function-key (F1–F10) assignments.
DO	Runs a command file or procedure (DO Mail).
DO CASE	Sets up a clause of mutually exclusive options in a command file. Terminated with the END-CASE command.
DO WHILE	Used with ENDDO to set up a loop in a command file [DO WHILE .NOT. EOF()].
DTOC()	Converts a Date field or memory variable to a character data type [LIST FOR DTOC(Date) = "01/01/86"].
EDIT	Displays existing data in a record and allows you to change its contents (EDIT 17).
EJECT	Advances paper in printer to top of new page.

Command	Definition
ELSE	Performs a set of commands if the criterion in an IF statement is false.
ENDDO	Used with the DO WHILE command to mark the bottom of a loop in a command file.
ENDIF	Marks the end of an IF clause in a command file.
EOF()	Returns True if the end of the database file has been reached and passed. Used primarily in DO WHILE loops in command files [DO WHILE .NOT. EOF()].
ERASE	Deletes a specific file from the directory (ERASE Temp.DBF).
ERROR()	Returns a number indicating the error caught by an ON ERROR command.
EXIT	Escapes from a DO WHILE loop without terminating execution of the command file. Control is transferred to the statement immediately following the ENDDO statement.
EXP()	Returns the natural exponent of a number [? EXP(1)].
EXPORT	Copies data from a dBASE III PLUS database into another file in PFS format.
FIELD()	Returns name of a field in a database file [? FIELD(3) displays the name of field number 3 in the currently open database].
FILE	Refers to a disk file. DISPLAY FILES shows disk files.
FILE()	Returns True if the named file exists on disk, otherwise returns False. [IF FILE("My-Data.DBF")].
FIND	Looks up information rapidly in an indexed database file (FIND "Miller").
FKLABEL()	Displays the names of function keys on a computer. [? FKLABEL(1) would display F2, the

Command	Definition
	name of the key on an IBM keyboard. On another computer, FKLABEL(1) might display another label.]
FKMAX()	Determines the number of programmable function keys on a given terminal [? FK-MAX( ) returns 9 on an IBM keyboard, for programmable function keys F0 through F9].
FOUND()	The FOUND() function is True (.T.) when a FIND, SEEK, LOCATE, or CONTINUE command finds the requested record. Otherwise, FOUND() returns False (.F.).
GET	Used with the READ command to accept field and memory variable data from the screen (@ 5,1 SAY 'Last name' GET LName).
GETENV()	Returns information about the operating system environment [? GETENV("COMSPEC") might display C:Command.COM, indicating that the Command.COM file is on the root directory of drive C].
GO BOTTOM	Goes to the last record in a database.
GO TOP	Starts at the first record in a database.
HELP	Provides help on the screen for a command or function [HELP RECNO()].
IF	Determines whether to perform commands in a command file based on some criteria (IF ZIP = '92122').
IIF()	Abbreviated version of the IF command using the syntax IIF(<this is true>, <do this>, <otherwise do this>). Unlike IF . .ENDIF constructs, you can execute IIF( ) at the dBASE III PLUS prompt. [ROOT = SQRT(IIF-(X>0,X,ABS(X))) takes the square root of the absolute value of X if X<0.]
IMPORT	Reads data from a PFS:FILE database into dBASE III PLUS format.

Command	Definition
INDEX	Creates an index file of sorted data (INDEX ON LName TO Names) or uses an existing index to display data in sorted order (USE Mail INDEX Names).
INKEY()	Scans the keyboard to see whether a key has been pressed and returns the keypress as an ASCII code between 0 and 255. Does not interrupt program execution to scan the keyboard.
INPUT	Displays a prompt on the screen and waits for a response terminated by pressing the Return key. Used with numeric data (INPUT 'How many labels per page' TO PER:PAGE).
INSERT	Puts a new record into the database at the current record location. Also, INSERT BEFORE.
INT()	Returns the integer part of a number, with decimal places truncated (not rounded) [? INT(1.99999) displays 1].
ISALPHA()	Determines whether the first letter of a variable is a letter. Example: ? ISALPHA("123 A St.") returns .F.
ISCOLOR()	Returns .T. if color monitor is in use; otherwise returns .F.
ISLOWER()	Determines whether the first letter of a character string is a lowercase letter [? IS-LOWER("alan") returns .T.].
ISUPPER()	Determines whether the first letter of a character string is uppercase [? ISUPPER("Snowball") returns .T.].
JOIN	Creates a third database based on the contents of two existing databases (JOIN TO NewDB FOR CODE = B->Code).
LABEL	Displays or prints mailing labels in the format specified in a file created with the MODIFY LABEL command (LABEL FORM TwoCol TO PRINT).

Command	Definition
LEFT()	Returns the specified left part of a character string [? LEFT("Snowball",4) returns Snow].
LEN()	Returns the length of a string [? LEN-("Word") would display 4].
LIST	Shows the contents of a database.
LIST FOR	Lists data that have some characteristic in common (LIST FOR LName = 'Smith').
LOAD	Places an assembly-language (binary) file into memory where it can be executed with a CALL command.
LOCATE	Finds a record with a particular characteristic (LOCATE FOR LName = 'Smith').
LOG()	Calculates the natural logarithm of a number [? LOG(2.72)].
LOOP	Skips all commands between itself and the ENDDO command in a DO WHILE loop.
LOWER()	Converts uppercase letters to lowercase [? LOWER(Name)].
LTRIM()	Removes leading blanks from character strings [? LTRIM(" Hello") displays Hello without leading blanks].
LUPDATE()	Returns the date of the last update for the currently open database file [? LUPDATE()].
M->	Specifies a memory variable. Useful when a field and memory variable share the same name (? M->LName).
MAX()	Returns the higher of two numbers [? MAX(20,40) returns 40].
MEMORY	Displays memory variables in RAM (DISPLAY MEMORY or LIST MEMORY).
MIN()	Returns the lower of two numbers [? MIN-(20,40) returns 20].

Command	Definition
MOD()	Returns the modulus (remainder) of two numbers [? MOD(5,3) returns 2].
MODIFY	Used to create or change a command file, database structure, label format, report format, screen, view file, or query file (MODIFY COMMAND, MODIFY STRUCTURE, MODIFY LABEL, and so forth).
MONTH()	Returns the month of a Date field or variable as a number (1–12) [LIST FOR MONTH(ExpDate) = 12].
NDX()	Displays the names of active index files (1–7). To display the name of the master index file, enter the command [? NDX(1)].
OFF	Leaves record numbers out of displays (LIST OFF). Also, turns off parameters (SET PRINT OFF).
ON	Sets dBASE parameters into ON mode (SET PRINT ON).
ON ERROR	Executes a dBASE command when an error occurs.
OS()	Returns the name of the operating system in use [? OS()].
PACK	Permanently deletes records marked for deletion from the database.
PARAMETERS	Command used to define variables passed by a DO. . .WITH command.
PCOL()	Displays the current column position of the printer head [? PCOL()].
PICTURE	Used with the GET command to make templates and define acceptable character types [@ 12,1 SAY 'Phone number' GET PHONE PICTURE'(999)999-9999'].
PRIVATE	Specifies memory variables that are automatically erased when a command file terminates (PRIVATE ALL LIKE M∗).

Command	Definition
PROCEDURE	An advanced programming technique whereby tasks are broken down into flexible routines accessed throughout a system. The PROCEDURE command names a procedure; SET PROCEDURE loads a procedure file into memory for global access.
PROW()	Displays the current row position of the printer head [? PROW()].
PUBLIC	Specifies memory variables that are not to be erased when command file terminates (PUBLIC CHOICE, LP, X, Y, Z).
QUIT	Closes all files and exits dBASE III PLUS back to the operating system's A> prompt.
RANGE	Specifies a range of acceptable values with @. . . SAY. . .GET and READ commands (@ 12,5 SAY "Enter choice" GET CHOICE RANGE 1,5).
READ	Used with @. . .SAY. . .GET statements to read in field and memory variable data from the screen.
READKEY()	Returns the key pressed to exit a full-screen operation like APPEND, BROWSE, CHANGE, CREATE, EDIT, INSERT, MODIFY, or READ. Keypress is stored as an integer in the range of 0 to 255.
RECALL	Brings back a record marked for deletion (RECALL RECORD 14) but not yet permanently deleted with PACK.
RECCOUNT()	Displays the number of records in the open database file [? RECCOUNT()].
RECNO()	Returns the current record number [LIST FOR RECNO() > = 10 .AND. RECNO() < = 20 lists all records in the range of records 10 to 20].
RECORD	Refers to a single record (DELETE RECORD 4).
RECSIZE()	Returns the number of bytes in each record in a database [? RECSIZE()].

Command	Definition
REINDEX	Recreates all active index files.
RELEASE	Erases current memory variables to free memory space for other use (RELEASE ALL).
RENAME	Changes the name of a disk file (RENAME Old.DBF TO New.DBF).
REPLACE	Changes the current contents of a field with new data. Used in global changes (REPLACE ALL LName WITH 'Smith' FOR LName = 'SMITH').
REPLICATE()	Replicates a character in a variable up to 255 times [ULine = REPLICATE("-",80) creates a memory variable named ULine consisting of 80 hyphens].
REPORT	Allows you to either create a report format (MODIFY REPORT) or display data in report format (REPORT FORM ByName).
RESTORE	Recalls memory variables that were saved to disk with the SAVE command back into RAM (RESTORE FROM Thought).
RESUME	Continues running a program that has been temporarily suspended for debugging.
RETRY	Used in networking to retry executing a command that failed because of a locked record or file.
RETURN	Returns control from a command file to the dot prompt or to the calling command file.
RETURN TO MASTER	Returns control from a subprogram back to the first-run program (usually the main-menu program).
RIGHT	Takes characters from the right side of a character string [? RIGHT("Snowball",4) displays ball].
ROUND()	Rounds a number to a specified number of decimal places [? ROUND(Rate*Hours),2].

Command	Definition
ROW()	Returns the current row position of the cursor on the screen [? ROW()].
RTRIM	Same as the TRIM function below.
RUN	Executes a program outside dBASE III PLUS. For example, RUN WS runs the WordStar program. The RUN command can also be represented with an exclamation point (! WS).
SAVE	Stores a copy of a memory variables to a disk file (SAVE TO Thought).
SAY	Used with @ to position output on the screen or printer (@ 5,2 SAY 'Hi').
SDF	Standard data format. Copies dBASE files to other database formats (COPY TO Basic.DAT SDF FOR RECNO() < 100).
SEEK	Looks up the contents of a memory variable n an indexed database file [STORE CTOD ("01/01/86") TO Lookup ↵, SEEK Lookup].
SELECT	Assigns databases in use to any one of ten work areas numbered 1 through 10 or lettered A through J (SELECT 1, SELECT A).
SET	Displays a menu of SET parameters and allows changes to be made via a menu of options.
SET ALTERNATE	Transfers all screen activity (except @. . . SAY commands) to a text file, after the file name is specified and the alternate is on (SET ALTE TO file, SET ALTE ON).
SET BELL	Determines whether the bell sounds when a field is filled on an APPEND, EDIT, or custom screen (SET BELL OFF).
SET CARRY	When the CARRY option is on, a newly appended record automatically receives the contents of the previous record, which can then be edited.
SET CATALOG	Creates catalog files and sets recording of file names either ON or OFF.

SIMPSON'S dBASE TIPS AND TRICKS

Command	Definition
SET CENTURY	ON displays the century in date displays; OFF hides the century.
SET COLOR	Changes the color of the screen foreground, background, and border.
SET CONFIRM	Determines whether pressing the Return key is necessary after filling a screen prompt (SET CONFIRM ON).
SET CONSOLE	When console is off, nothing is displayed on the screen (SET CONSOLE OFF).
SET DATE	Determines the format for displaying Date data. Options are AMERICAN, ANSI, BRITISH, ITALIAN, FRENCH, GERMAN.
SET DEBUG	Determines whether the SET ECHO command directs output to the printer or the screen. With SET DEBUG ON, SET ECHO ON directs debugging output to printer while execution goes to screen.
SET DECIMALS	Sets the minimum number of decimals displayed in the results of mathematical calculations (SET DECIMALS TO 2).
SET DEFAULT	Determines which disk drive dBASE uses when looking for disk files with the USE, DO, INDEX, SELECT, and other commands that access files (SET DEFAULT TO B). Can be overridden by using drive designators in file names.
SET DELETED	Determines whether records marked for deletion are displayed with LIST, DISPLAY, ?, REPORT, and LABEL commands (SET DELETED ON hides deleted records).
SET DELIMITER	Determines how field entries are displayed on the screen with APPEND, EDIT, and custom screens (SET DELIMITER TO "[]" encloses fields in brackets).

Command	Definition
SET DEVICE	Determines whether @. . .SAY commands display data on the screen or on the printer (SET DEVICE TO PRINTER, SET DEVICE TO SCREEN).
SET DOHISTORY	When ON, lines from command files are recorded in the HISTORY file. When OFF, only lines typed in from the dot prompt are recorded.
SET ECHO	A debugging aid that displays each line of a command file as it is being processed (SET ECHO ON).
SET ESCAPE	Determines whether a command file terminates when Esc is pressed (SET ESCAPE OFF aborts the power of the Esc key).
SET EXACT	Determines whether dBASE compares two values with an exact match or with first letters only. With EXACT off, Smith will match Smithsonian.
SET FIELDS	Determines which fields will be displayed.
SET FILTER	Limits display of data to those records that match a criterion (SET FILTER TO LName = "Smith" will limit output of LIST, REPORT, LABEL, etc., to Smiths).
SET FILTER TO FILE	Uses the contents of a query (.QRY) file to set up a filter condition. (SET FILTER TO NotBilld gets filtering information from the NotBilld.QRY file. SET FILTER TO with no file name clears all filter conditions.)
SET FIXED	Sets the number of decimal places that will appear with all numeric displays. Usually used in conjunction with the SET DECIMALS command (SET FIXED ON).
SET FORMAT	Specifies a custom screen display stored in a format (.FMT) file to be used with an EDIT or

Command	Definition
	APPEND command (SET FORMAT TO Add-Names, SET FORMAT TO).
SET FUNCTION	Reprograms the function keys (F1–F10) to perform custom tasks (SET FUNCTION 10 TO 'BROWSE'). DISPLAY STATUS shows current settings.
SET HEADING	Determines whether field names will be displayed above data in DISPLAY, LIST, SUM, and AVERAGE commands (SET HEADING OFF removes field names from displays).
SET HELP	Determines whether the message "Do you want some help? (Y/N)" appears during an error (SET HELP OFF removes the prompt).
SET HISTORY	Specifies the number of commands stored in the HISTORY file or the status of HISTORY. (SET HISTORY TO 50 stores 50 lines in the history file. SET HISTORY OFF stops recording command lines.)
SET INDEX	Specifies index file(s) to make active with a database (SET INDEX TO NAMES, ZIPS).
SET INTENSITY	Determines whether field entries on full-screen EDIT and APPEND operations are displayed on the screen in reverse video (SET INTENSITY OFF removes reverse video).
SET MARGIN	Adjusts the left margin for printer displays (SET MARGIN TO 5).
SET MEMOWIDTH	Determines the width of Memo field displays.
SET MENUS	Determines whether cursor-control commands appear in a menu above APPEND, EDIT, BROWSE, and other displays (SET MENUS ON displays the menus).
SET MESSAGE	Displays a message at the bottom of the screen (SET MESSAGE TO "How are you today?").
SET ORDER	Selects an index file from a list to make primary.

Command	Definition
SET PATH	Specifies directory paths to search for disk files (SET PATH TO \C:DBIII will cause dBASE to search path DBIII on drive C if a file is not found on the current drive).
SET PRINT	Determines whether displays will be echoed to the printer (SET PRINT ON causes all screen displays to be printed; SET PRINT OFF returns to normal mode).
SET PROCEDURE	Advanced programming technique whereby sub-programs are combined into a single file and assigned procedure names (SET PROCEDURE TO Routines).
SET RELATION	Sets up a relationship between two data files in use, based on a field they have in common (SET RELATION TO Code INTO Master).
SET SAFETY	Determines whether the message "*file name* already exists—overwrite it? (Y/N)" appears when a file is about to be overwritten (SET SAFETY OFF disables).
SET SCOREBOARD	Determines whether messages in the top line or status bar appear.
SET STATUS	Turns the status bar at the bottom of the screen on or off.
SET STEP	Debugging aid used to limit command file execution to a single line at a time (SET STEP ON).
SET TALK	Determines whether dBASE displays a response to various commands. Usually, SET TALK OFF is used in command files to eliminate dBASE messages.
SET TITLE	Determines whether prompts for titles appear in active catalogs.
SET TYPEAHEAD	Determines the number of characters to be held in the typeahead buffer. The default is 20; the possible range is 0 to 32000 (SET TYPEAHEAD TO 9999).

Command	Definition
SET UNIQUE	Used with the INDEX command to display an ordered listing of unique field values (SET UNIQUE ON). Can be used to temporarily delete records with duplicate key values.
SET VIEW	Opens a view (.VUE) file (SET VIEW TO AcctRec).
SKIP	Skips to next record in the database. Can also skip more or less than 1 record (SKIP 10, SKIP −3).
SORT	Rearranges records in a database into sorted order. Requires that records be sorted to another database (SORT ON LName TO Temp).
SPACE()	Generates a string of blanks [LName = SPACE(20) creates a memory variable called LName that consists of 20 blank spaces].
SQRT()	Displays the square root of a number [? SQRT(64), STORE SQRT(64) TO X].
STORE	Assigns a value to a memory variable (STORE 1 TO Counter).
STR()	Converts a number to a string. Useful for complex sorting with index files [INDEX ON Code + STR(AMOUNT,12,2) TO Test].
STRUCTURE	Refers to the structure rather than the contents of a database (DISPLAY STRUCTURE).
STUFF()	Allows you to put data into an existing character string without dismantling the original string [? STUFF("HaHoHa",3,2,"Ha") returns HaHaHa—because Ha was stuffed at the third character, replacing two characters].
SUBSTR()	Isolates a part of a string [? SUBSTR("ABCDEFG",3,2) displays CD, a substring starting at the third character, 2 characters long].
SUM	Adds a column of fields and displays the total (SUM AMOUNT).

Command	Definition
SUSPEND	Halts execution of a command file and returns control to the dot prompt. The RESUME command restarts execution.
TEXT	Starts a block of text in a command file, terminated with the command ENDTEXT.
TIME()	Displays the current system time in the form hh:mm:ss [? TIME()].
TOTAL	Summarizes and totals a database to another database. Files must be either presorted or pre-indexed (TOTAL ON Code TO SaleSumm).
TRANSFORM()	Like a PICTURE statement, lets you define formats for data displayed with the LIST, DISPLAY, REPORT, and LABEL commands[LISTTRANSFORM(AMOUNT,"###,###,###.##") displays all amounts in ###,###,###.## format].
TRIM()	Removes trailing blanks from a character string [LIST TRIM(FName),LName].
TYPE	Displays the contents of a DOS ASCII (text) file (TYPE MyReport.TXT).
UPDATE	Revises the file in use by adding or replacing data from another database (UPDATE ON Code FROM Sales REPLACE Price WITH B->Price).
UPPER()	Converts lowercase letters to uppercase [INDEX ON UPPER(LName) TO Names].
USE	Tells dBASE which database to work with (USE Mail).
VAL()	Changes character strings to numerics [? VAL(Address)].
VERSION()	Displays the version number of dBASE III PLUS in use [? VERSION()].
WAIT	Stops execution of a command file and waits for user to press a key. Keypress is stored in a memory variable (WAIT TO Data).

Command	Definition
YEAR()	Displays the year of a Date field or variable in 19XX format [LIST FOR YEAR(Date) = 1986].
ZAP	Permanently removes all records from a database and active index files.

Index

Selections from The SYBEX Library

Software Specific

DATABASE MANAGEMENT SYSTEMS

UNDERSTANDING dBASE III PLUS
by Alan Simpson
415 pp., illustr., Ref. 349-X
Emphasizing the new PLUS features, this extensive volume gives the database terminology, program management, techniques, and applications. There are hints on file-handling, debugging, avoiding syntax errors.

ADVANCED TECHNIQUES IN dBASE III PLUS
by Alan Simpson
500 pp., illustr., Ref. 369-4
The latest version of what *Databased Advisor* called "the best choice for experienced dBASE III programmers." Stressing design and structured programming for quality custom systems, it includes practical examples and full details on PLUS features.

MASTERING dBASE III PLUS: A STRUCTURED APPROACH
by Carl Townsend
350 pp., illustr., Ref. 372-4
This new edition adds the power of PLUS to Townsend's highly successful structured approach to dBASE III programming. Useful examples from business illustrate system design techniques for superior custom applications.

ABC'S OF dBASE III PLUS
by Robert Cowart
225 pp., illustr., Ref. 379-1

Complete introduction to dBASE III PLUS for first-time users who want to get up and running with dBASE fast. With step-by-step exercises covering the essential functions as well as many useful tips and business applications.

UNDERSTANDING dBASE III
by Alan Simpson
250 pp., illustr., Ref. 267-1
The basics and more, for beginners and intermediate users of dBASEIII. This presents mailing label systems, bookkeeping and data management at your fingertips.

ADVANCED TECHNIQUES IN dBASE III
by Alan Simpson
505 pp., illustr., Ref. 282-5
Intermediate to experienced users are given the best database design techniques, the primary focus being the development of user-friendly, customized programs.

MASTERING dBASE III: A STRUCTURED APPROACH
by Carl Townsend
338 pp., illustr., Ref. 301-5

SIMPSON'S dBASE III LIBRARY
by Alan Simpson
362 pp., illustr., Ref. 300-7
Our bestselling dBASE author shares his personal library of custom dBASE III routines for finance, graphics, statistics, expanded databases, housekeeping, screen management and more.

UNDERSTANDING dBASE II
by Alan Simpson
260 pp., illustr., Ref. 147-0
Learn programming techniques for mailing label systems, bookkeeping, and data management, as well as ways to interface dBASE II with other software systems.

ADVANCED TECHNIQUES IN dBASE II
by Alan Simpson
395 pp., illustr. Ref., 228-0
Learn to use dBASE II for accounts receivable, recording business income and expenses, keeping personal records and mailing lists, and much more.

MASTERING Q&A
by Greg Harvey
350 pp., illustr., Ref. 356-2
An experienced consultant gives you straight answers on every aspect of Q&A, with easy-to-follow tutorials on the write, file, and report modules, using the Intelligent Assistant, and hundreds of expert tips.

MASTERING REFLEX
by Robert Ericson and Ann Moskol
336 pp., illustr., Ref. 348-1
The complete resource for users of Borland's Reflex: The Analyst, with extensive examples and templates for practical applications.

POWER USER'S GUIDE TO R:base 5000
by Alan Simpson
350 pp., illustr., Ref. 354-6
For R:base 5000 users who want to go beyond the basics, here is an in-depth look at design and structured programming techniques for R:base 5000—packed with expert tips and practical, usable examples.

UNDERSTANDING R:base 5000
by Alan Simpson
413 pp., illustr., Ref. 302-3
This comprehensive tutorial is for database novices and experienced R:base newcomers alike. Topics range from elementary concepts to managing multiple databases and creating custom applications.

MASTERING 1-2-3
by Carolyn Jorgensen
466 pp., illustr., Ref. 337-6
Here is a thorough, lucid treatment of 1-2-3, including Release 2, with emphasis on intermediate to advanced uses—complex functions, graphics and database power, macro writing, and the latest add-on products.

SIMPSON'S 1-2-3 MACRO LIBRARY
by Alan Simpson
298 pp., illustr., Ref. 314-7
Share this goldmine of ready-made 1-2-3 macros for custom menus, complex plotting and graphics, consolidating worksheets, interfacing with mainframes and more. Plus explanations of Release 2 macro commands.

ADVANCED BUSINESS MODELS WITH 1-2-3
by Stanley R. Trost
250 pp., illustr., Ref. 159-4
If you are a business professional using the 1-2-3 software package, you will find the spreadsheet and graphics models provided in this book easy to use "as is" in everyday business situations.

THE ABC'S OF 1-2-3 (2nd Ed)
by Chris Gilbert and Laurie Williams
245 pp., illustr., Ref. 355-4
A complete introduction to 1-2-3, featuring Release 2—for first-time users who want to master the basics in a hurry. With comprehensive tutorials on spreadsheets, databases, and graphics.
" . . . an easy and comfortable way to get started on the program."
—*Online Today*

MASTERING SYMPHONY (2nd Edition)
by Douglas Cobb
817 pp., illustr., Ref. 341-4
"*Mastering Symphony* is beautifully organized and presented . . . I recommend it," says *Online Today. IPCO Info* calls it "the bible for every Symphony user . . . If you can buy only one book, this is definitely the one to buy." This new edition includes the latest on Version 1.1

ANDERSEN'S SYMPHONY TIPS AND TRICKS
by Dick Andersen
321 pp., illustr. Ref. 342-2

Hundreds of concise, self-contained entries cover everything from software pitfalls to time-saving macros—to make working with Symphony easy, efficient and productive. Includes version 1.1 and new Add-in programs.

FOCUS ON SYMPHONY DATABASES
by Alan Simpson
350 pp., illustr., Ref. 336-8

An expert guide to creating and managing databases in Symphony—including version 1.1—with complete sample systems for mailing lists, inventory and accounts receivable. A wealth of advanced tips and techniques.

FOCUS ON SYMPHONY MACROS
by Alan Simpson
350 pp., illustr., Ref. 351-1

Share Symphony expert Alan Simpson's approach to planning, creating, and using Symphony macros—including advanced techniques, a goldmine of ready-made macros, and complete menu-driven systems. For all versions through 1.1.

BETTER SYMPHONY SPREADSHEETS
by Carl Townsend
287 pp., illustr., Ref. 339-2

For Symphony users who want to gain real expertise in the use of the spreadsheet features, this has hundreds of tips and techniques. There are also instructions on how to implement some of the special features of Excel on Symphony.

MASTERING FRAMEWORK
by Doug Hergert
450 pp., illustr. Ref. 248-5

This tutorial guides the beginning user through all the functions and features of this integrated software package, geared to the business environment.

ADVANCED TECHNIQUES IN FRAMEWORK
by Alan Simpson
250 pp., illustr. Ref. 257-4

In order to begin customizing your own models with Framework, you'll need a thorough knowledge of Fred programming language, and this book provides this information in a complete, well-organized form.

MASTERING THE IBM ASSISTANT SERIES
by Jeff Lea and Ted Leonsis
249 pp., illustr., Ref. 284-1

Each section of this book takes the reader through the features, screens, and capabilities of each module of the series. Special emphasis is placed on how the programs work together.

DATA SHARING WITH 1-2-3 AND SYMPHONY: INCLUDING MAINFRAME LINKS
by Dick Andersen
262 pp., illustr., Ref. 283-3

This book focuses on an area of increasing importance to business users: exchanging data between Lotus software and other micro and mainframe software. Special emphasis is given to dBASE II and III.

MASTERING PARADOX (2nd Edition)
by Alan Simpson
463 pp., illustr., Ref. 375-9

Total training in Paradox from out bestselling database author: everything from basic functions to custom programming in PAL, organized for easy reference and illustrated with useful business-oriented examples.

JAZZ ON THE MACINTOSH
by Joseph Caggiano and Michael McCarthy
431 pp., illustr., Ref. 265-5

Each chapter features as an example a business report which is built on throughout the book in the first section of each chapter. Chapters then go on to detail each application and special effects in depth.

MASTERING EXCEL
by Carl Townsend
454 pp., illustr., Ref. 306-6

This hands-on tutorial covers all basic operations of Excel plus in-depth coverage of special features, including extensive coverage of macros.

MASTERING APPLEWORKS
by Elna Tymes
201 pp., illustr., Ref. 240-X
This bestseller presents business solutions which are used to introduce AppleWorks and then develop mastery of the program. Includes examples of balance sheet, income statement, inventory control system, cash-flow projection, and accounts receivable summary.

PRACTICAL APPLEWORKS USES
by David K. Simerly
313 pp., illustr., Ref. 274-4
This book covers a breadth of home and business uses, including combined-function applications, complicated tasks, and even a large section on interfacing AppleWorks with external hardware and software.

APPLEWORKS: TIPS & TECHNIQUES
by Robert Ericson
373 pp., illustr., Ref. 303-1
Designed to improve AppleWorks skills, this is a great book that gives utility information illustrated with every-day management examples.

SPREADSHEETS

UNDERSTANDING JAVELIN
by John R. Levine, Margaret H. Young, and Jordan M. Young
350 pp., illustr., Ref. 358-9
A complete guide to Javelin, including an introduction to the theory of modeling. Business-minded examples show Javelin at work on budgets, graphs, forecasts, flow charts, and much more.

MASTERING SUPERCALC 3
by Greg Harvey
300 pp., illustr., Ref. 312-0
Featuring Version 2.1, this title offers full coverage of all the sophisticated features

of this third generation spreadsheet, including spreadsheet, graphics, database and advanced techniques.

DOING BUSINESS WITH MULTIPLAN
by Richard Allen King and Stanley R. Trost
250 pp., illustr., Ref. 148-9
This book will show you how using Multiplan can be nearly as easy as learning to use a pocket calculator. It presents a collection of templates for business applications.

MULTIPLAN ON THE COMMODORE 64
by Richard Allen King
250 pp., illustr. Ref. 231-0
This clear, straightforward guide will give you a firm grasp on Multiplan's function, as well as provide a collection of useful template programs.

WORD PROCESSING

INTRODUCTION TO WORDSTAR (3rd Edition)
by Arthur Naiman
208 pp., illustr., Ref. 134-9
A bestselling SYBEX classic. "WordStar is complicated enough to need a book to get you into it comfortably. Naiman's **Introduction to WordStar** is the best."
—*Whole Earth Software Catalog*

" . . . an indespensable fingertip guide, highly recommended for beginners and experienced users."
—*TypeWorld*

PRACTICAL WORDSTAR USES
by Julie Anne Arca
303 pp., illustr. Ref. 107-1
Pick your most time-consuming wordprocessing tasks and this book will show you how to streamline them with WordStar.

MASTERING WORDSTAR ON THE IBM PC
by Arthur Naiman
200 pp., illustr., Ref. 250-7

The classic Introduction to WordStar is now specially presented for the IBM PC, complete with margin-flagged keys and other valuable quick-reference tools.

WORDSTAR TIPS AND TRAPS
by Dick Andersen, Cynthia Cooper, and Janet McBeen
300 pp., illustr., Ref. 261-2
The handbook every WordStar user has been waiting for: a goldmine of expert techniques for speed, efficiency, and easy troubleshooting. Arranged by topic for fast reference.

THE COMPLETE GUIDE TO MULTIMATE
by Carol Holcomb Dreger
250 pp., illustr. Ref. 229-9
A concise introduction to the many applications of this powerful word processing program, arranged in tutorial form.

PRACTICAL MULTIMATE USES
by Chris Gilbert
275 pp., illustr., Ref. 276-0
Includes an overview followed by practical business techniques, this covers documentation, formatting, tables, and Key Procedures.

MASTERING DISPLAYWRITE 3
by Michael McCarthy
447 pp., illustr., Ref. 340-6
A complete introduction to full-featured word processing, from first start-up to advanced applications—designed with the corporate user in mind. Includes complete appendices for quick reference and troubleshooting.

MASTERING WORDPERFECT
by Susan Baake Kelly
397 pp., illustr., Ref. 332-5
Solid training and support for every Word-Perfect user—with concise tutorials, thorough treatment of advanced features and "recipes" for business uses. Covers all versions through 4.1.

WORDPERFECT TIPS AND TRICKS
by Alan R. Neibauer
350pp., illustr., Ref. 360-0
A practical companion for users of Word-Perfect versions through 4.1—packed with clear explanations and "recipes" for creative uses, including outline processing, graphics, spreadsheet and data management.

MASTERING SAMNA
by Ann McFarland Draper
425 pp., illustr., Ref. 376-7
Learn the power of SAMNA Word and the SAMNA spreadsheet from an expert user and teacher. This comprehensive tutorial lets you build on the basics to get the most from the software's unique features.

MASTERING MS WORD
by Mathew Holtz
365 pp., illustr., Ref. 285-X
This clearly-written guide to MS WORD begins by teaching fundamentals quickly and then putting them to use right away. Covers material useful to new and experienced word processors.

PRACTICAL TECHNIQUES IN MS WORD
by Alan R. Neibauer
300 pp., illustr., Ref. 316-3
This book expands into the full power of MS WORD, stressing techniques and procedures to streamline document preparation, including specialized uses such as financial documents and even graphics.

INTRODUCTION TO WORDSTAR 2000
by David Kolodnay and Thomas Blackadar
292 pp., illustr., Ref. 270-1
This book covers all the essential features of WordStar 2000 for both beginners and former WordStar users.

PRACTICAL TECHNIQUES IN WORDSTAR 2000
by John Donovan
250 pp., illustr., Ref. 272-8
Featuring WordStar 2000 Release 2, this book presents task-oriented tutorials that get to the heart of practical business solutions.

dBASE III PLUS TIPS AND TRICKS

Sample Programs
Available on Disk

If you'd like to use the procedures and programs in this book but don't want to type them in yourself, you can send for a disk containing all the procedure files and command files in the book. To obtain this disk, complete the order form and return it along with a check or money order for $40.00. California residents add 6 percent sales tax.

SMS Software
P.O. Box 2802
La Jolla, CA 92038-2802
(619) 943-7715

Name_____

Company_____

Address_____

City/State/ZIP_____

Enclosed is my check or money order.
(Make check payable to *SMS Software.*)
dBASE III PLUS Tips and Tips

SYBEX is not affiliated with SMS Software and assumes no responsibility for any defect in the disk or program.

SYBEX Computer Books are different.

Here is why . . .

At SYBEX, each book is designed with you in mind. Every manuscript is carefully selected and supervised by our editors, who are themselves computer experts. We publish the best authors, whose technical expertise is matched by an ability to write clearly and to communicate effectively. Programs are thoroughly tested for accuracy by our technical staff. Our computerized production department goes to great lengths to make sure that each book is well-designed.

In the pursuit of timeliness, SYBEX has achieved many publishing firsts. SYBEX was among the first to integrate personal computers used by authors and staff into the publishing process. SYBEX was the first to publish books on the CP/M operating system, microprocessor interfacing techniques, word processing, and many more topics.

Expertise in computers and dedication to the highest quality product have made SYBEX a world leader in computer book publishing. Translated into fourteen languages, SYBEX books have helped millions of people around the world to get the most from their computers. We hope we have helped you, too.

For a complete catalog of our publications:

SYBEX, Inc. 2021 Challenger Drive, #100, Alameda, CA 94501
Tel: (415) 523-8233/(800) 227-2346   Telex: 336311